1985

# MASS COMMUNICATION THEORIES AND RESEARCH

# Alexis S. Tan
Texas Tech University

# MASS COMMUNICATION THEORIES AND RESEARCH _____

SECOND EDITION

**John Wiley & Sons**
New York
Chichester
Brisbane
Toronto
Singapore

*Library of Congress Cataloging in Publication Data:*

Tan, Alexis S.
  Mass communication theories and research.

  Includes index.
  1. Mass media.  2. Communication.  I. Title.

P90.T347  1985       302.2′34       84–20817
ISBN 0–471-84135-8

Printed in the United States of America

10  9  8  7  6  5  4  3  2  1

*To Gerdean, Marco
and my parents*

# PREFACE _____

A lot has transpired in mass communication research since I wrote the first edition of this text about four years ago. The field has continued to mature as a scientific discipline. There has been a remarkable growth both in the quantity and quality of research. New terrain is being explored. Research continues at the intrapersonal level of analysis; however, many people are studying communication at the interpersonal and institutional levels. Learning theories continue to be influential, but there is increased attention to information-processing theories of communication. At the social level, structural functionalism continues to direct many mass communication researchers, but Marxist and neo-Marxist theories of social change are gaining a foothold.

The second edition of *Mass Communication Theories and Research* reflects these changes. In the first edition, I emphasized the interpersonal and intrapersonal analyses of communication. This was evident in the dominance (at least in terms of length) of the chapters on persuasion and socialization. In the second edition, I have added two lengthy chapters on communicators and their environment and on mass communication and social change. These new chapters reflect my own renewed interest in the social forces that constrain or limit communication behavior. I have also added sections and a chapter that explain the "new" (or revived) theories and research strategies that have recently been influential in our field—reciprocal determinism, structural functionalism, group dynamics, information processing, conflict theories, and analysis at the macro levels.

The second edition represents change as I see it occurring in our field. However, there is also an emphasis on continuity. The basic format of the book is unchanged. I continue to insist on discussing only the studies that are based on empirical and scientific methods of research. The research sections in all chapters have been updated; studies completed in the last four years, up to late 1983, are discussed. I refuse to get involved in the ongoing debate between the empirical and "critical" or "evaluative" research camps in mass communication, mainly because I think this debate is beside the point. Empiricism and critical research are not mutually exclusive. One can apply scientific methods to test hypotheses based on evaluative or critical analysis. I also do not accept the notion that to be scholarly is to write obtusely. I have tried to maintain a conversational tone in the book, using understandable language with a minimum of "scientific" jargon.

I hope the changes I have introduced in the second edition will make this a stronger, more complete, and more useful text. I believe that it continues to be appropriate for upper-level undergraduate and beginning graduate courses in communication theory. Since the material has been greatly expanded, instructors may wish to emphasize some chapters more than others, depending on their particular interests.

We have been gratified by the kind and sometimes critical reception that the first edition received. The text was successful beyond my most optimistic expectations. I thank the students, instructors, and scholars in mass communication who gave me the opportunity to publish a second edition and for their many suggestions regarding the book. I also thank the editors at Wiley and the many communication scholars whose work constitutes the foundation of this book.

My thanks again to Gerdean, Marco, and my parents. Writing this second edition was even more fun than writing the first one.

**Alexis S. Tan**

*Lubbock, Texas*
*April 1984*

# PREFACE
# TO THE
# FIRST EDITION _____

As communication technology continues to develop at an accelerated rate, new questions are being asked—and answers to old ones are being reexamined—about the role of the mass media in society. There is renewed interest in the power of the mass media over its audiences. Is this power mainly mythical, as was suggested by communication researchers in the late 1950s and early 1960s, or is it pervasive and unavoidable, as some current scholars proclaim? In any case, the renewed focus on mass media effects has helped establish the study of mass communication as a scientific discipline. The coming age of mass communication as a behavioral science is evident in many ways:

1. The increase in the amount and quality of research output from communication scholars. Ten years ago, there were only three or four scholarly journals devoted primarily to mass communication research. Today, there are at least a dozen.
2. The increase in the number and amounts of grants awarded to communication scholars by industry and government for basic and applied research. Over $1 million was awarded by the Surgeon General to researchers to study the relationship of televised violence to aggressive behavior among viewers. The National Science Foundation has recently sponsored substantial research programs to evaluate the feasibility of interactive cable television and to determine effective methods of communicating science information to the public.
3. The infusion of courses on mass communication theory and research methodology into the curricula of many of the top journalism and mass communication schools in the country. Most accredited mass communication programs have at least one course in theory of mass communication and society at the intermediate level. Almost all of the graduate programs require a course in communication theory. The theory courses, unlike the more common Introduction to Mass Communications taught at the freshman or sophomore level, take a behavioral and research approach to the analysis of communication problems. The introductory survey courses generally have a historical and descriptive emphasis.

The increase in research productivity of communication scholars has led to a proliferation of scholarly journals in the field. Unfortunately for the undergraduate and beginning graduate student of mass communication, and for practitioners as well, most of these journals report research findings in highly technical and scientific language—which is, to be sure, brief, concise, and parsimonious—but mostly unintelligible to readers without a background in communication theory, methodology, and statistics. This is unfortunate, since many of the models, theories, and principles derived from such research can be useful to the practitioner and can help students of communication better understand the role of the mass media in today's societies.

This, then, is the main objective of the present volume: to present and integrate results of significant communication research within theoretical frameworks that can be useful to readers with little or no background in communication theory, methodology, or statistics. It is written for the college student interested in communications as a profession or field of study and for the practitioner of communications in business, government, or education.

The book begins with a discussion of scientific method and theory, explaining concepts that will be needed to evaluate and understand mass communication research. Current methods used by communication researchers are also discussed in basic, simple terms. From here, significant research findings in the field of mass communication are discussed in historical order, that is, beginning with early research on persuasion in the 1950s to the current interests in media socialization. When appropriate, general principles are offered and theoretical explanations explored. The tone of the book, although academic, is not technical.

The book can be used as a text for upper-level undergraduate and beginning graduate courses in mass communication theory or mass media and society. I have been teaching these courses for over seven years and have been dismayed at the lack of a comprehensive text on mass communication theory that discusses not only early theories, but recent developments in the field as well. Most available texts are anthologies, and even though some of these are competently edited, there is a need for an integrated, up-to-date discussion of mass communication theory in one volume. Through the years, I have tried to compensate for the lack of an adequate text by assigning readings from several reference books and from research journals. And each year, I hear the same complaints from students early in the semester—lack of integration of the material in the readings and incomprehensible articles in the journals. I have tried to integrate and interpret the articles in my lectures, but it occurred to me that the task could be greatly simplified by a text that would accomplish these objectives. I hope this one will do the job.

As a strategy in writing the book, I have adopted the Aristotelean didactic philosophy of *logos*. Most chapters begin with a discussion of a few general principles, which lead to specific studies providing empirical evidence for the principles. The evidence is then summarized, and the original principles are evaluated on the basis of research findings.

I have emphasized research to a greater extent than authors of other communication theory texts. Recent studies are discussed in detail, particularly those published within the last five years. I believe that students should be taught not only the *what's,* but also the *why's* and *how's* of communication theory. By discussing relevant studies in detail, I hope to help the reader understand how a certain communication principle (or "law") was established, so that he or she can evaluate its validity. I have also tried to explain research findings using a few general principles or theories, so that the reader can gain a total instead of a fragmented view of human communication.

The material in the text can be covered in a one-semester or one-quarter course for juniors and seniors. For graduate classes, the instructor may wish to supplement text material with journal articles. Graduate students may benefit from a more thorough discussion of the original studies. The review questions at the end of each chapter are intended to motivate the student to pursue the material further or to apply theoretical principles to practical problems.

As with any major undertaking, this project would not have been possible without the help of many others. Although I must bear sole responsibility for any failings this book might have, I must share its merits with my colleagues in communication research whose work I have liberally cited. Five people deserve special mention, since my intellectual debt to them is considerable: Albert Bandura, Steve Chaffee, Jack McLeod, Leonard Berkowitz, and William McGuire. Directly and indirectly, they have influenced my own approach to communication theory.

I thank Janice Juneau, Carol Bogle, and Sandy Mitchell for patiently typing the manuscript. My students—past, present, and future—also deserve mention. They provided the stimulus for this undertaking.

Finally, my thanks to Gerdean and Marco. Because of them, writing this book was fun.

**Alexis S. Tan**

*Lubbock, Texas*
*October 1980*

# CONTENTS _____

# PART I

# THE SCIENCE OF MASS COMMUNICATION

Our basic assumption in this textbook is that the study of mass communication is a science. Part I establishes the foundations for this assumption.

In Chapter 1, we define the field of mass communication to include the study of the mass media, the messages they generate, the audiences they attempt to reach, and their effects on these audiences. Chapter 1 also discusses the evolution of mass communication research, including early "powerful effects" models of the 1940s, the "limited effects" research of the late 1950s and 1960s, and the current interest in socialization effects of the mass media.

In Chapter 2, we discuss four ways of "knowing": tenacity, authority, intuition, and scientific method. We examine scientific method in detail—its unique characteristics, its procedural steps, its basis in empiricism and formal logic, and its value to the study of mass communication.

Chapter 3 is a discussion of research methods commonly used by mass communication researchers. It begins with an examination of the criteria often used to evaluate all scientific research—internal and external validity. We then discuss hypothesis testing, experiments, field surveys, and content analysis. An understanding of these basic research principles and methods will help the reader appreciate the research presented in later chapters.

In Chapter 4, we present three communication models that have gained acceptance among communication researchers through the years: Shannon and Weaver's mathematical model, Newcomb's social psychological model, and Westley and MacLean's general model. We then integrate these models into a transactional model, which considers communication to be purposive interaction between two or more individuals. The transactional model identifies variables that can be studied in communication, criteria for evaluating the communicative act, and common causes of failure in communication.

# 1_____

# DEFINING THE FIELD_____

Mass communication involves the scientific study of the mass media, the messages they generate, the audiences they attempt to reach, and their effects on these audiences. Traditionally, the field has included the academic disciplines of journalism, telecommunications, advertising, public relations, and some subdivisions of speech communication. These areas are commonly concerned with mediated messages that reach their audiences indirectly through a medium, most often a mass medium such as television, radio, newspapers, or magazines. However, as we will see in Chapter 4, an understanding of mediated communication will require analysis of the encoding and decoding of messages (intrapersonal communication) and of person-to-person and small group communication (interpersonal communication). Although we will be primarily concerned with the mass media and their effects on large groups of people, we will also discuss research dealing with how individuals communicate directly with each other. The main emphasis of the book will be on the functions of the mass media in modern society and their effects on audience values, cognitions, and behaviors.

A major objective of the book is to integrate research findings into general explanations of mass communication functions, processes, and effects. These explanations, to be considered here, should be based on empirical evidence derived from scientific method, an objective and verifiable way of establishing "truths" about the nature of reality. This qualification eliminates from the scope of the book significant work in historical and legal research. Even though historical and legal analysis can add significantly to our understanding of the functions of the mass media in modern society, our concern with theory limits the discussion to principles that can be objectively verified. A more thorough discussion of scientific method and theory in mass communication is presented in Chapter 2.

## HISTORICAL PERSPECTIVE

Mass communication is a relatively young discipline compared to other social and behavioral sciences such as psychology, sociology, political science, and economics. Even now, many teachers and researchers in the field will argue with the assertion that mass communication is a scientific discipline. We believe it has achieved this status, as indicated by the extensive use in the field today of scientific research methods (laboratory and field experiments, time series and longitudinal designs, systematic and systems-wide content analyses), advanced statistical tools, and mathematical models. We will discuss some of these research methods in Chapter 3. More important, researchers in the field are beginning to integrate research findings into systematic and general explanations (theories) of mass communication processes, many of which are discussed in this book.

Mass communication research has not always been characterized by scientific method and a concern with formulating theory. Many of the important contributions in the 1920s and 1930s were historical analyses of newspapers and magazines or descriptions of media messages.[1] Early issues of *Journalism Quarterly*, the oldest scholarly journal in the field of journalism and mass communication, emphasized historical, legal, and content analysis studies.

During the 1930s and 1940s, researchers from other disciplines—particularly political science and social psychology—formulated a model of the powerful influences of the mass media. According to this model, the mass media could be used to bring about almost any kind of effect on their passive audiences. Much of the basis for the powerful effects model came from analyses of successful propaganda techniques in World Wars I and II.[2] Additional support for the model was provided by Lazarsfeld's and Stanton's analysis of the effects of radio,[3] Merton's study of the successful Kate Smith war bond broadcasts,[4] and Cantril's analysis of panic effects resulting from Orson Welles' broadcast of "War of the Worlds."[5]

Experimental evidence for the powerful effects model of mass communication was provided by Hovland and his colleagues in the late 1940s and through the early 1950s at the Army's Information and Education Division and later at Yale's Attitude Change Center.[6] These studies were originally designed to provide solutions to problems encountered by the U.S. Army in World War II, such as evaluating the effects of persuasive films on soldiers, getting housewives to change the food habits of their families, assessing the attitudes of bomber crews, and improving the morale of new recruits. Through experiments, Hovland and his colleagues identified characteristics of the communicator, messages, and audiences that could lead to attitude change. Hovland's influence on mass communication research has been considerable. Even today, this line of research is being pursued by many in the field.

In 1944, Lazarsfeld, Berelson, and Gaudet published *The People's Choice*, an analysis of the effect of mass media on voting decisions.[7] This work provided the basis for what has proven to be an enduring model of mass communication—the "limited" or "reinforcement" model of mass media effects. Lazarsfeld and his colleagues found that the mass media had very little direct effect on voters during political campaigns. The main effect was reinforcement of existing attitudes, and the small percentage who did change were more likely to be affected by personal communication sources (opinion leaders) than by the mass media. According to the limited effects model, the mass media merely reinforce existing attitudes and behaviors, because audiences are "stubborn" and because they can use a variety of defensive strategies such as selective attention, selective perception, and selective recall to insulate themselves against attacking or contradictory messages. The limited effects model gradually replaced the "powerful effects" model of mass communication and was adopted by many researchers and writers in the field.[8] Even today, the limited effects model has many proponents among mass communication researchers.[9]

The late 1960s saw a revival of the powerful effects model of mass communication. There has been renewed interest in the impact of the mass media on their audiences, except now the interest is no longer confined to attitude or behavioral change. Researchers today are interested in the many other important ways in which audiences are affected by the mass media, such as their knowledge of public and political issues, their structuring of social realities, role expectations of self and others, the acquisition of political attitudes and behaviors, use of leisure time, antisocial behaviors (aggression, violence, prejudice), prosocial behaviors (altruism, cooperativeness), learning of motor and cognitive skills, perceptions of the importance of public issues (agenda setting), satisfaction of individual needs (diversion, entertainment), and others. Thus, the powerful effects model has been expanded to include not only attitude and behavioral change, but other facets of the human experience as well.

At this point you may ask: How can one model be appropriate yesterday and invalid today?

We can answer this question in at least two ways. A historical explanation suggests that the effects of mass communication on society can best be understood by analyzing the prevailing social and political climate of the time.[10] The early powerful effects model found its greatest acceptance during war and economic depression, when there were ample opportunities and the conditions were conducive for the media to be powerful. During these times, there is some degree of insecurity in audiences (or "imbalance," using the terminology of cognitive consistency psychologists), which can make them more receptive to persuasive communications. This is particularly true if the audience perceives that following the messages' recommendations will help restore security or balance. Thus, the purchase of bonds for a war that is generally supported may remove guilt feelings or may convince the individual that this action will help achieve a desired goal—victory and an end to the war. During the relative calm and economic prosperity of the 1950s and early 1960s, media audiences were relatively satisfied with their lives. There was less reason to be discontented; thus there was a preference for the status quo. The cognitive consistency psychologists predict that when consistency is present in people, they will be resistant to suggestions for change. So we find that during this time, the limited effects model was the prevailing model of mass media effects.

The expanded powerful effects model became a significant influence on researchers as political and social turmoil enveloped the country in the late 1960s and early 1970s. The unpopular Vietnam war and issues raised by the civil rights movement were sources of insecurity (cognitive inconsistency) for many people, making them more receptive to media influence. The mass media became a source of reassurance to some, of escape to many. And, as the media become more pervasive, this model continues to exert considerable influence on mass communication researchers up to this time.

A second explanation for the shift from a powerful to limited and again to powerful view of mass media effects is methodological. We are often able to observe communication effects in the laboratory (an artificial research setting where the researcher has almost complete control over the procedures), but not in a real-life setting. Thus, it is easier to change attitudes in the laboratory, where effects are often short term, as Hovland and his colleagues did, than in the community. However, with advanced techniques of measurement, research design, and analysis and with the help of computers, we are now able to track down these effects in the real world, effects that often build up over time and that early researchers found difficult to isolate, given the limited procedures available to them.

The contents of this book reflect a preference for the expanded powerful effects model. Although communication and persuasion following the social psychological tradition of Hovland is treated in the early chapters, the greater part of the book is devoted to a discussion of how the mass media are affecting societies today.

## CURRENT CONCERNS

Communication scholars today are interested in how the mass media are affecting societies and also in how social institutions are affecting the mass media. Communicators do not perform their work in a vacuum. They encode and decode messages as members of small social groups, mass media organizations, communities, and nation states. Communication behaviors of individuals are influenced by the groups and institutions to which they belong. These groups and institutions often impose rules or constraints on their members. We are taking a closer look at these constraints on individual communication behaviors. Parts V and VI of this text, for example, discuss how mass communication organizations and social institutions affect the individual communicator.

Another concern of today's communication scholars has been the level of analysis at which communication is studied. Traditional communication research analyzes the individual communication behaviors at the intrapersonal level. Most studies of persuasion, for example, look at attitude and behavior change in the individual as *the* measure of communication effectiveness. More researchers today are looking at communication from the larger perspectives of social groups and institutions. We are still interested in the individual's communication behavior. However, we are now also looking at how groups and social institutions are affected by communication and at how communication is affected by groups and social institutions. The different levels of analysis in mass communication are discussed in Chapter 5. Beginning with Part II, we have organized this book according to level of analysis, from the intrapersonal analysis of communication (Part II, "Communication and Persuasion," and Chapter 14, "Mass Media Uses and Audience Needs"), analysis at the interpersonal level (Chapter 13, "Coorientation," and most chapters in Part IV, "Mass Communication and Socialization"), and through analysis at the organizational and institutional levels (Part V, "Communicators and Their Environment," and Part VI, "Mass Communication and Society"). Our journey through the mass communications field will take us from the smallest level of analysis (the individual) to the largest levels (organizations and social institutions.)

## SUMMARY

Mass communication involves the scientific study of the mass media, the messages they generate, the audiences they attempt to reach, and their effects on these audiences. A major objective of this book is to integrate research findings into general explanations or theories of mass communication functions, processes, and effects.

Mass communication is a relatively young discipline. Early research in the 1920s and 1930s consisted mostly of historical, legal, and content analysis studies of the mass media. Researchers formulated a "powerful effects" model of mass communication during the 1930s and 1940s. According to this model, the main effect of the mass media is persuasion. Laboratory studies of attitude and behavioral change by Hovland at Yale provided much of the evidence for this model, which continued to be popular through the 1950s.

Lazarsfeld and his colleagues completed a series of field surveys in the 1940s and 1950s to determine how voters were affected by the mass media. Their studies led to still another view of mass communication effects—the "limited effects" model. According to this model, the main effect of mass communication is reinforcement. Audiences protect themselves from information they do not like by selective attention, selective perception, and selective reception. The limited effects model gradually replaced the powerful effects model and was adopted by many researchers in the field.

The late 1960s saw a revival of the powerful effects model. There is renewed interest in the impact of the mass media on audiences, except now the interest is not confined to attitude or behavioral change. Most researchers today are interested in how audiences are socialized by the media: how we develop values, patterns of behavior, and perceptions of social reality from the information and images presented by the media.

We are interested in how the mass media are affecting societies and in how social institutions are affecting the mass media. We are giving more attention to individual communicators and their groups, organizations, and communities. Communication is being analyzed more today at the social and organizational levels.

## REVIEW QUESTIONS

1. Look through past issues of *Journalism Quarterly*. Pick two examples of each of the following types of mass communication studies: (*a*) early historical and content analysis studies (1920s and 1930s); (*b*) "powerful effects" studies of persuasion; (*c*) "limited effects" studies exploring audience resistance to persuasion; (*d*) "social effects" studies investigating the influence of the mass media on life-styles, formation of values, and social perceptions of audiences. Summarize the results of each study and discuss why the author or authors considered the research problem to be important.

2. Which of two media effects models—powerful effects or limited effects— best describes the influence of the mass media on *today's* audiences? Support your answer with examples and research evidence from published studies.

## ENDNOTES

1. Wilbur Schramm, "The Challenge to Communication Research," in R. O. Nafziger and D. White (eds.), *Introduction to Mass Communications Research* (Baton Rouge: Louisiana State University Press, 1958), pp. 3–28.

2. See, for example, George Bruntz, *Allied Propaganda and the Collapse of the German Empire in 1918* (Stanford, Calif.: Stanford University Press, 1938); Harold Lasswell, *Propaganda Technique in the World War* (New York: Knopf, 1927); Daniel Lerner, *Sykewar: Psychological Warfare Against Germany, D-Day to VE-Day* (New York: Stewart, 1949); Louis Lochner (ed.), *The Goebbels Diaries* (Garden City, N.Y.: Doubleday, 1948).

3. Paul Lazarsfeld and Frank Stanton (eds.), *Radio Research 1941* New York: Duell, Sloan and Pearce, 1941); Paul Lazarsfeld and Frank Stanton (eds.), *Radio Research, 1942–43* (New York: Duell, Sloan and Pearce, 1944).

4. Robert Merton, *Mass Persuasion* (New York: Harper, 1946).

5. Hadley Cantril, *The Invasion From Mars* (Princeton, N.J.: Princeton University Press, 1940).

6. Carl Hovland, A. Lumsdaine, and Fred Sheffield, *Experiments on Mass Communication* (Princeton, N.J.: Princeton University Press, 1949); Carl Hovland, Irving Janis, and Harold Kelley, *Communication and Persuasion* (New Haven, Conn.: Yale University Press, 1953).

7. Paul Lazarsfeld, Bernard Berelson, and Hazel Gaudet, *The People's Choice* (New York: Columbia University Press, 1944).

8. Joseph Klapper, *The Effects of Mass Communication* (Glencoe, Ill.: Free Press, 1960).

9. Walter Weiss, "Effects of the Mass Media on Communication," in G. Lindzey and E. Aronson (eds.), *The Handbook of Social Psychology*, 2nd ed., Vol. 5 (Reading, Mass.: Addison-Wesley, 1969).

10. James Carey, "The Ambiguity of Policy Research," *Journal of Communication*, Spring 1978, pp. 114–119.

# 2

# SCIENTIFIC METHOD AND THEORY IN MASS COMMUNICATION

Mark is seven years old. He has always been good natured and played well with his classmates. However, his parents have noticed a drastic change in him these past several weeks. He has become irritable and destructive. His teacher reports that he has initiated several fights in school. This change bothers his parents, and they attempt to come up with an explanation. In fact, they come up with several possible explanations.

1. The change in temperament is a normal stage in Mark's development.
2. He has contracted an illness that is affecting his disposition.
3. Something has gone wrong with his home life. They (his parents) are quarreling more often, which is causing him to be irritable and more aggressive.
4. Television is causing his recent aggression. He has been watching more television than usual—mostly the crime and police shows. Several weeks ago, he began to spend Saturday mornings watching TV cartoons.

All of these explanations seem possible, but Mark's parents decide that the fourth explanation is nearest to the truth. They argue that the change is too drastic to be a normal stage in his development, so they drop explanation 1. Similarly, they reject explanations 2 and 3 because they know that Mark is not sick and that they have a good family life. So they are stuck with the TV explanation. How can they prove that it is true?

First, Mark's parents can convince themselves that the TV explanation is true because they had *always* believed that television was a bad influence on children. *All* their friends (and most of them are students at a nearby university) believe this, and it was obvious that Mark's watching of violent television shows made him more aggressive.

But then suppose Mark's parents run across a magazine article claiming that some violent television shows may actually make viewers less aggressive and that the evidence for their previous explanation is not conclusive. Then they are no longer sure of their original "proof," so they use a second method.

They can quote a professor in mass communication, who had lectured last week on the subject and had concluded that exposure to TV violence led to aggression among viewers. To reinforce this "evidence," they also remember that their minister in church last Sunday had said the same thing.

But again, suppose Mark's parents are reminded by a friend that a professor in psychology wrote in a journal article that exposure to TV violence does *not* lead to aggression among viewers. Finally, they throw up their hands in exasperation and say, "But can't you see? It is *so* obvious."

## METHODS OF PROOF

It would indeed be unfortunate if Mark's parents stopped at this point. For what we have described are the three methods of establishing truth most subject to bias and error. These methods, as discussed by the philosopher Peirce[1] and later by Cohen and Nagel in their classic text on logic and scientific method[2] are, respectively, the methods of tenacity, authority, and intuition. Let us take a closer look at each of these methods and see why they often lead to conclusions that have no basis in reality.

### The Method of Tenacity

Many of our beliefs are held simply because we have always considered them to be true. Frequent repetition enhances our beliefs. So does reinforcement from those around us.

The method of tenacity depends to large extent on the influence of family, community, and peers. Many of the beliefs handed down to us are seldom challenged because there seems to be (to the believer) common agreement about them. Thus, the mass communication student "knows" that the press should be free, that the inverted pyramid form is the best way of writing a news story, and that advertising sells. In a more general context, beliefs about our political and economic systems and our race, religion, and family are subject to the method of tenacity. In our previous example, Mark's parents had always believed, and so did their friends, that television was a bad influence on children, probably because they lived in a university community where it was socially desirable to have such a belief.

What if these beliefs were suddenly challenged? What if there occurs some serious dissent among those around us (our community)? Then we have to reinforce those beliefs using another method.

### The Method of Authority

When there is no longer agreement about our beliefs, the method of authority is often used to support them. There are two kinds of authority that we can appeal to. First, we can appeal to experts—or "credible" and "competent" sources. These are sources that we consider to have far greater knowledge on the topic than ourselves or anybody else. Thus, we consult a physician on matters of health, a lawyer on legal problems, and a mass communication professor on the issue of television violence and aggression. Also, researchers cite, as evidence or justification for their hypotheses, previous studies by others working on the same problem whom they consider to be competent. This is not necessarily an invalid way of establishing evidence, particularly if, as Cohen and Nagel put it, "we reserve the right to others (also competent to judge), or to ourselves (finding the time to acquire competence), to modify the findings of the expert."[3]

Another form of authority is not based on expertise, necessarily, but on an "external force" that invests the source's decisions with infallibility and finality. We often use these sources on questions of religion, morals, and politics. These sources become authoritative not necessarily because they are perceived as experts on the issue, but because they occupy a position that invests them with the power to make the "correct" decisions. Examples are ministers and priests on matters of morality, television newscasters on the nation's economy, and a college professor on the marital problems of his or her students. We sometimes consult these sources for advice not because we consider them to be experts on the problem, but because we respect the positions or roles that they occupy.

### The Method of Intuition

When sources we consider to be competent or authoritative disagree, the method of authority may have to be reinforced by citing the "self-evident" truth of our beliefs. This is the method of intuition. It is often based on common sense, values, or early socialization. It is related to the method of tenacity in that many of the beliefs we have always held to be true are often based on intuition. Thus many of us may claim that it is self-evident that women are weaker than men, that children are more persuasible than adults, that watching television news increases our knowledge of world events, and that television violence leads to aggression.

The methods of tenacity, authority, and intuition are clearly not satisfactory for confirming our beliefs, since none of them leads to conclusions that can be *objectively verified*. Repetition and community agreement can just as easily perpetuate a false belief as they can a true belief. Authorities often disagree, and very often we have no way of knowing the basis for their own positions. And, self-evident truth, like proverbial beauty, is in the eye of the beholder. We therefore need a more objective method of establishing truth—one that we will call "scientific method."

## SCIENTIFIC METHOD

There is no one scientific method. Any method of inquiry or of establishing the truth of our beliefs that has the following characteristics can be called "scientific."[4]

## Objectivity

Scientific method is not subject to the whims or capriciousness of the researcher. It seeks evidence by analyzing information from the "real world," that is, the world outside of the scientist. Evidence is selected not because it supports the wishes of the scientist or the idiosyncracies of a few selected authorities, but because it can be tested or verified repeatedly by other researchers.

Objectivity can be achieved in at least two ways: empiricism and formal logic. Empiricism requires that a belief or proposition should be tested in the real world—that is, a world we can touch, smell, taste, and see, or that can be "experienced."[5] Formal logic studies the conditions under which a belief (or proposition) necessarily follows and therefore may be deduced from other propositions. We will discuss empiricism and logic in greater detail in succeeding sections.

## Problem-Oriented

Scientific method can be initiated only when the researcher recognizes a practical or theoretical *problem* in need of a *solution*. The problem is often put in the form of the question, "Why . . . ?" It may arise out of simple curiosity or out of a desire by researchers to find some *order* among facts and observations so that they can better understand their environment. Finding a solution to the problem is a major objective of scientific method.

## Hypothesis-Guided

Scientific method is guided by hypotheses. A hypothesis is a suggested explanation or solution to the problem that initiated the inquiry. It is usually formulated in an "If . . . then" statement suggesting connections between facts or observations. If one observation is found to be true, then the following observation must also be true.

Hypotheses guide the researcher in the search for a solution to the problem. Because of hypotheses, this search is not random. A scientist first studies previous knowledge bearing on the present problem before testing possible solutions. There are, of course, an infinite number of facts that may be related to the problem, but the scientist identifies those that might have the greatest probability of providing a solution and states them in hypothesis form. An important characteristic of scientific method is that hypotheses are stated *before* the investigation begins.

Now that we know what a hypothesis is, the next question might be: What is a "good" hypothesis? We can identify several characteristics of a good hypothesis.

### Relational

A hypothesis specifies a *relationship* between conditions or observations. This relationship, as stated, should provide an answer or explanation to the problem being investigated. It is often expressed in causal form (If *this*, then *that*). We refer to the cause as the independent variable, and the effect, which is usually an observation we are attempting to explain, as the dependent variable.

### Based on Previous Knowledge

A hypothesis is more than a guess or a hunch. It is based on previous knowledge of the problem, on a sifting and selection of facts bearing on the problem. Prior to verifying a hypothesis, the researcher should be able to point out instances that would verify it. Thus, a solution (or several solutions) are offered before the investigation. This is important for two reasons. First, it narrows the scope of the problem by defining what it is that we are trying to verify. Second, it provides some guarantee of objectivity. We will not deliberately select a hypothesis so that it will, in fact, be confirmed by a particular set of instances without providing for a test of its confirmation by *other* instances. Cohen and Nagel call this the "fallacy of selection." It is, of course, possible for a problem to have more than one solution. It is also possible for a researcher to formulate the hypothesis so generally that instances verifying it can easily be observed.

### Objective Verification

The researcher should be able to verify the hypothesis objectively. Objective verification can be accomplished through direct empirical measurement and observation in the real world. Many hypotheses in the social sciences, however, cannot be put to direct empirical test because the facts they include cannot be directly observed. Hypotheses dealing with how people think, for example, cannot be tested directly, since we cannot see or measure "thoughts" or "cognitions" directly. (We can ask a person what he or she thinks, but this is an indirect measure.) These hypotheses can be tested indirectly by first deriving, through formal techniques of logic and mathematical models, their consequences if they were true and subjecting those implications to empirical test. In either case, a hypothesis is never proved beyond any or every doubt. It is simply verified in terms of the most *probable* relationships or occurrences.

For a hypothesis to be verified objectively we should clearly define its variables *conceptually* and *operationally*. Conceptual definitions are what we usually refer to as dictionary definitions. This is defining a concept using other concepts—adjectives, adverbs, or nouns. A conceptual definition of television violence might be "any act perpetrated by a human or humanized character on another in which a character is physically hurt or killed." Operational definitions explain in some detail *how* the variables will be measured or observed. An operational definition of TV violence might be the number of acts per thirty-minute segment in which a human or humanized character is physically hurt or killed by another character. Conceptual and operational definitions make clear to other researchers how you are defining and measuring your variables. This minimizes confusion, especially when many definitions are used for the same concepts.

### Theory-Directed

The immediate goal of scientific method, as we have seen, is to discover objectively facts that can provide a solution to the problem. The long-range goals are theory and science.

A theory is a set of interrelated laws or general principles (hypotheses that have been repeatedly verified) about some aspect of reality. The function of theory is to explain, predict, and discover systematic relationships between facts. The layperson, using common sense, may be content with a fragmented view of reality. That is, he or she picks up information here and there when it is useful without necessarily attempting to draw logical or empirical connections between facts. The scientist, on the other hand, is interested not in bits of information but in the total picture that the facts present to him or her. How are these facts related to each other? How does a change in one fact affect another? If these questions can be answered, then a theory can be formulated. And, by taking a systematic view of reality, prediction is possible. That is, propositions can be deduced from a few general principles that have been verified. Theory can give us a simple (although *not simplified*), ordered view of reality. It is the scientist's abstract representation of reality.

"Theory" is sometimes used synonymously with "science." Cohen and Nagel define science as "knowledge which is general and systematic, that is, in which specific propositions are all deduced from a few general principles." This definition is very much like our definition of theory. There is at least one difference, however. Whereas we can speak of a *science* of mass communication, it would not be appropriate to refer to a *theory* of mass communication. There is no *one* theory of mass communication (neither is there *one* theory in any field of study). Often there are competing theories in a field, offering alternative explanations to the same phenomenon. These various theories, taken together and representing accumulated knowledge, can be referred to as the *science* of that field.

### Self-Corrective

Science places value on *doubt,* on questioning existing principles and laws. Since principles are established only through repeated testing, many principles have to be modified as new evidence is discovered. As a result, scientists believe that theories are dynamic and are in a constant state of flux. No laws are final or beyond question.

The self-corrective nature of science makes it necessary for the scientist to submit his or her work to close scrutiny by others working in the field. This is done not only to disseminate new knowledge on which other investigations might be based (to build theory), but also to make it possible for the procedures to be replicated in different situations. Thus some value is placed on the publication and dissemination of the objectives, methods, and results of scientific investigations.

## THE EMPIRICAL BASIS OF SCIENCE

Objectivity, as we have seen, can be achieved by the scientist through repeated empirical testing of hypotheses. The philosophical position that scientists cannot know their hypotheses to be true without depending at some stage during the investigation on experience is known as *epistemic empiricism*. If we are to know anything about our world, we must first be able to experience it, that is, to sense it. What cannot be experienced cannot be known. An extension of epistemic empiricism suggests that not only knowledge but also meaning depend on experience. This view is often called semantic empiricism, of which there are three forms.[6]

### Logical Positivism

Logical positivism, sometimes called "verifiability theory," holds that a proposition can be meaningful only if it can be verified empirically and that its meaning is the method or mode of verification. The emphasis then is on whether the proposition can be verified in the real world by "experiencing" or sensing the hypothetical relationships. If so, then its meaning *is* this verification.

Logical positivism is limited in its utility for theory building by its singular emphasis on verification or, in statistical terminology, by the value it places on "significant effect." Often, a proposition that is *not* verified can also be meaningful because, as the philosopher Kaplan argues, if a proposition is meaningful then so also is its negation.[7] Furthermore, a universal law, which is the ideal of science, can be falsified by a single instance of nonsupport. The dependence on verification can limit the pursuit of knowledge.

In spite of these limitations logical positivism has served a useful function in the development of science. It was originally used to draw distinctions between scientific and unscientific statements. The concern was to weed out metaphysical or "unscientific" explanations in science and to focus attention on propositions that could be verified in the real world. The proposition, for example, that "life exists after death" cannot be studied scientifically. However, we can verify empirically that *rigor mortis* sets in on a body several hours after death.

### Operationism

Like logical positivism, operationism stresses the importance of experience in assigning meaning to scientific propositions. However, the stress is not on if and how the proposition can be verified through experience, but on how the concepts in the proposition are *operationalized,* or *measured.* If the concepts are to be experienced (or sensed), then certain physical operations must be performed on them so that they can be recognized and manipulated in the real world. Thus the concept "intelligence" is recognized by scores on a test, attitudes are identified by scores on attitudinal scales or questionnaires, and TV violence is measured by coders who use an agreed-on criterion for violence.

The operationist principle is, first, that the meaning of a concept in a scientific proposition is its operationalization (how it is measured) and, second, that different operations define different concepts. Thus, the operationist will claim that intelligence is what intelligence tests measure, or that racial prejudice *is* the score on a prejudice questionnaire. Furthermore, the operationist will argue that once a different operation or measure is used on a concept, the meaning of the concept changes. A concept cannot be defined or used in the same way if different operations are performed on it. The radical operationist may even claim that if the same racial prejudice test were administered to the same people at different times during the day, the test is not measuring the same concept.

The operationist principle is useful in science because it forces the scientist to specify very clearly how his or her concepts are to be measured in the real world. However, there are some difficulties with it. First, many scientific concepts cannot be experienced *directly,* or cannot be directly observed. Whereas the physicist can measure "mass" and "length" directly, the behavioral scientist working with concepts such as "fear," "cognitive dissonance," or "empathy" will have to depend on "symbolic operations" to observe these concepts. Symbolic operations are measures of a concept by observation of other concepts that theory suggests are related to the original concept. Thus cognitive dissonance is concluded to be present in individuals if they avoid information contradicting an important belief. Avoidance of information can be directly observed, whereas dissonance, which presumably occurs in the minds of people, cannot. There is nothing wrong with this procedure *if* the symbolic operations indeed have a theoretical connection with the original concept. But this is not always easy to establish, particularly when a science such as mass communication is in its early stages of development.

Another difficulty with the operationist position is the contention that different operations define different concepts. It is, of course, possible for *different* measures to measure the same thing. Often, such multioperationism can be useful in validating the scientist's observations and in increasing the generalizability of derived principles. Take, for example, the concept of aggression as an effect of TV violence. There are many ways we can measure aggression: a questionnaire in which respondents are presented with a hypothetical problem and asked to pick which of several solutions they would most likely use (the solutions indicate varying degress of aggressive behavior), ratings by teachers, ratings by parents, and by direct observation in the classroom or some other natural environment. Suppose each of these measures results in identical aggression ratings of five children. Are we to say that the measures *meant* different concepts? The operationist would probably say so, but there clearly is the possibility, and one that is more valuable in theory building, that they were all measuring aggression.

## Pragmatism

In analyzing the meaning of a proposition the logical positivist asks, "What would the world be like if it were true?" The operationist asks, "What would we have had to do to come to believe it?" The pragmatist asks, "What would we do if we did believe it?"[8]

Pragmatism was first formulated by the philosopher Charles Peirce in 1878. Its main concern is on how the principle to be established by scientific method can be used or applied in everyday life. Pragmatists ask, "What difference would it make to me if the proposition were true?" They would want to know what could be done with the proposition if it were believed. How could it be used and would it matter? The main contribution of pragmatism to the methodology of science is that it puts to test scientific propositions in our everyday world of action and goes beyond the artificial confines of the laboratory. According to the pragmatist, scientific propositions, to be meaningful and useful, must make a *difference* in everyday life.

Logical positivism, operationism, and pragmatism, despite differences in philosophy about what gives meaning to a proposition, all adhere to the principle of empiricism—that is, the ultimate verification of a proposition is to be found in experience. It will be clear in the chapters to follow that each of these positions has been influential in the development of mass communication theories. There is in our field an emphasis on verification of hypotheses and on concise measurement of variables. And a growing number of researchers are investigating theoretical problems that are *real* problems in everyday life. The concern with mass media effects can be interpreted as a manifestation of the pragmatist view.

## LOGIC AND SCIENTIFIC METHOD

As we had discussed in a previous section, the ultimate goal of scientific investigations is the formulation of theory, then science. Science is knowledge that is general and systematic and ideally provides for the deduction of specific propositions from a few general principles. It is this deductive nature of science that makes logic indispensable to its formulation.

Logic is traditionally concerned with the study of what constitutes proof and asks the questions, "How are the conclusions related to the evidence?" "Do they necessarily follow from the evidence?" "Can they be deduced from the evidence?" Deduction is the process by which an inference of truth is made from the premise (evidence, or antecedent condition) to the conclusion (the consequent condition). Let us examine some of the ways in which deduction can be useful to the scientist.

## Formulation of Hypotheses

Many hypotheses are developed deductively. By deduction, the investigator can conclude which hypotheses are *more* or *less* probable.

As an illustration, let us return to the problem regarding the irritability and aggressiveness of Mark. Mark's parents had rejected, on an intuitive basis, the first three explanations of the boy's aggression. They intuitively knew that Mark's condition was not a normal stage in his development, that he was not physically ill, and that his home life was not the cause of his aggression. Similarly, and more reliably, deductive reasoning could have been used to reject each of these hypotheses. Let us see how deduction might have worked with the home life explanation.

> If parents quarrel, their children will be aggressive (general rule, or hypothesis to be tested).
>
> Mark's parents have been quarreling more than usual these past few months (observed fact).
>
> Mark has been more aggressive these past few months (observed fact or inferred event).
>
> If parental quarreling produces aggression in children, other children with quarreling parents should be as aggressive as Mark is (elaborated rule).
>
> David, Mark's eight-year-old brother, has not shown any increase in aggression (observed fact).
>
> Parental quarreling does not invariably produce aggression in children.

This final inference, of course, cannot be taken as conclusive proof that the hypothesis is *not* true. However, this analysis, sometimes called the "deductive elaboration" of hypotheses, can be used to determine which hypotheses are the most probable and which are the least probable explanations of the problem. We could then test empirically and more elaborately those that we consider to be the most probable explanations.

## Indirect Testing of Hypotheses

In science we are concerned with establishing the truth of propositions. Very often, however, there is no practical way to test these propositions *directly*. Take, for example, the proposition: "Cognitive dissonance is an uncomfortable drive state that will motivate the individual to remove it." We cannot test this proposition directly, since we cannot get into a person's mind and measure whether dissonance is present or not. We can, however, formulate another proposition that can be tested directly and that can be objectively related to the original proposition to establish its truth. In our example we could formulate a second proposition: "A person will be in a dissonant cognitive state when an important belief is contradicted by a valued source; when this happens, that person will avoid such contradictory information." This second proposition can be tested directly. We can operationalize and, therefore, we can observe valued sources, contradictory information, and avoidance of information. Thus we can conclude that if the second proposition were true, and given our definition of cognitive dissonance, then the first proposition *can* also be true. It is through a process of deduction that many of our more abstract propositions can be tested empirically.

### Theory Building

Logic helps the scientist build theory. Theory, as previously defined, is a set of interrelated principles and observations. Logic allows us to establish the connection between these principles and discover whether any principles are incompatible with each other. By using logic we can examine the connections between diverse propositions that might lead to theory. Again, take the cognitive dissonance researcher. He or she observes that voters avoid speeches by candidates they oppose and that new car owners like to read magazine advertisements for the car that they had bought. Through deduction, and given a theory of cognitive dissonance, the researcher concludes that both sets of observations can be explained by the motivation to avoid dissonance.

## USING SCIENTIFIC METHOD

So far we have discussed the philosophy and principles of scientific method. But how do you use it? The steps are outlined in Figure 2-1. We begin with a problem in need of a solution. This problem can be derived from our real-world experiences (practical or professional concerns) or deductively from existing theory. We then analyze what we know about the problem—studying the literature, talking to authorities, preliminary observation—and select the most probable explanation. This we state as a proposition (If . . . then. . . . ). We then define concepts included in the proposition conceptually and operationally and subject the resulting hypothesis to empirical and logical tests. Empirical testing can be done using any of the research methods discussed in the next chapter—experimentation, field surveys, content analysis. If the hypothesis is verified, then we have a tentative law. If the hypothesis is not confirmed, then we look for another possible explanation (or hypothesis). In either case we relate our results back to theory and determine how they can connect with other known principles dealing with the same problem. We may be able to relate our hypothesis to some other hypothesis undergoing testing at the same time or with some previously confirmed law. The process is circular—from theory to hypothesis to empirical and logical test and back to theory. When you have several theories (or even one general theory), then science develops.

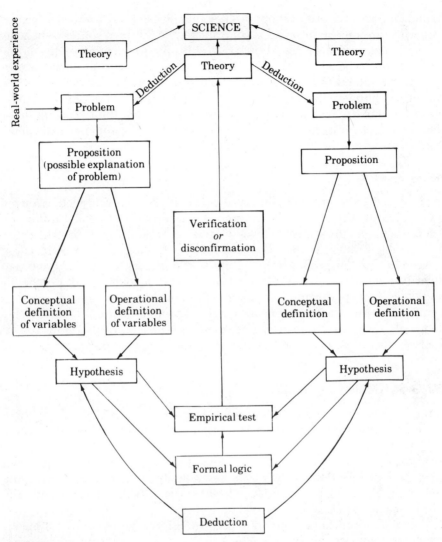

**FIGURE 2.1.** Scientific method

Let us now return to our problem with Mark's aggression and see how scientific method can be used to explain it.

**Step 1.** We observe a problem—Mark's aggression. This is important to us practically (his parents are friends of ours) and theoretically (we are interested in the general problem of children's learning from the mass media).

**Step 2.** We propose several solutions (or explanations) to the problem—normal development, illness, parental quarreling, TV violence. Through deduction we eliminate the first three (as illustrated earlier in this chapter) and decide that the TV explanation is most probable. Here is how deduction can be used to select the TV explanation as probable.

If children watch TV violence they will be more aggressive.

Mark has been watching violent shows these past two months.

Mark has been more aggressive these past two months.

If TV violence leads to aggression in Mark, it should have the same effect on other children.

David, Mark's eight-year-old brother, has watched TV with Mark these past two months and has watched the same shows.

David has also been acting more aggressively.

On the basis of this reasoning, we decide to select the TV explanation as our hypothesis to be subjected to more rigorous testing. The hypothesis, formally stated, is: "If a child watches violent shows on television, he or she will be more aggressive." The implication, of course, is that children who watch violent TV shows will be more aggressive than children who do not watch such shows.

**Step 3.** We define TV violence and aggression more rigorously, TV violence as "the overt expression of force against human or humanized characters in which somebody is physically hurt or killed," and aggression as the "willful infliction of pain on another person." These are our conceptual definitions. TV violence is defined operationally as the number of such acts per thirty minutes of TV watched, and aggression as ratings by teachers.

**Step 4.** We subject our hypothesis to empirical test. We decide that experimentation is the best way to do this. (Experiments are discussed in more detail in the next chapter.) We solicit the cooperation of a nearby school, divide sixty of their children randomly into two groups, show one group TV shows previously coded to be violent, and another group similar shows but without violence. We expose the children to these shows continuously for three months. During this time, at one-week intervals we get aggression ratings for each child from their teachers. We then compare aggression ratings for each week at the end of three months. If the group exposed to violence shows a statistically greater aggression rating score than the other group, then we accept our hypothesis as a probable explanation of Mark's aggression. If there are no differences, then we look around for another possible explanation.

**Step 5.** Assuming that our hypothesis is verified by the data, we look for other principles relating to children's aggression and see how our findings can be related. Another researcher has shown that new acts of violence can be learned by children from simple observation of those acts performed on TV. We see a connection and decide that the primary mechanism by which children are affected by TV violence is learning. We then tentatively call our theory of children's aggression and TV violence a "social learning theory of aggression."

## THE VALUE OF SCIENTIFIC METHOD TO MASS COMMUNICATION

After this brief introduction to scientific method, you may ask: Why is it important to study scientific method and theory in the fields of mass communication? This is an important question, since many readers will probably agree that communication is first and foremost an art. The most effective communicators through the ages, from Aristotle to Shakespeare to modern-day advertising strategists, were or are creative individuals who infused their messages with unique qualities that appealed to their audiences. What can scientific method and theory contribute to the creative process that is communication?

### Order Among Facts

The development of theory makes it possible for us to sort out what we know about communication, to make connections between disparate observations, and to form an integrated view of communication processes. We will therefore be in a better position to see a total picture instead of only a portion of it. The search for order among facts presupposes there is some regularity (or laws) that can explain communication behaviors of humans. Although these laws may change with time, their *discoveries* make it possible for us to *predict* future occurrences of similar phenomena. Prediction can be useful both to the practitioner (as in the prediction of consumer behavior) and to the theoretician who may wish to test the generalizability of specific laws.

### Explanation

Scientific method and theory can provide us with explanations of communication processes. The search for answers to problems and the emphasis on relationships between facts make it possible for us to understand the underlying processes in communication. We are able to determine not only that a certain communication strategy works, but why.

### Objective Verification of Facts

The most important contribution of science is that it gives us some assurance that the principles we believe to be true are *indeed true* and are not based on our own biases or the biases of others. We demand, in scientific inquiry, that hypotheses be tested in the real world. Verification comes only when this test is repeatedly passed.

## Pursuit of Knowledge

Scientific method places a value on doubt. Facts and laws are constantly challenged. There is no final law. This attitude encourages the pursuit of new knowledge in the field and prevents both practitioners and researchers from being too complacent with the state of their art.

## SUMMARY

According to the philosopher Charles Peirce, there are four ways of "knowing": tenacity, authority, intuition, and science. Tenacity, authority, and intuition often lead to conclusions based on a person's values, past experiences, and interests. Only scientific method leads to beliefs that have been objectively verified. Besides being objective, scientific method is problem oriented, hypothesis guided, theory directed, and self-corrective.

Scientific method is guided by hypotheses. A hypothesis is a suggested explanation or solution to the problem that initiated the inquiry. It is relational, based on previous knowledge, and can be tested empirically.

Scientific method is based on empiricism and formal logic. The philosophical position that a scientist cannot know his or her hypothesis to be true without depending at some stage during the investigation on experience is epistemic empiricism. An extension of epistemic empiricism suggests that not only knowledge, but also meaning, depends on experience. This view is often called semantic empiricism, of which there are three forms: logical positivism, operationism, and pragmatism.

Logic is traditionally concerned with the study of what constitutes proof and asks the questions: "How are the conclusions related to the evidence?" "Do they necessarily follow from the evidence?" "Can they be deduced from the evidence?" Logic helps the scientist formulate hypotheses, test hypotheses indirectly, and build theory.

Scientific method is important to mass communication for the following reasons: (1) it helps us form an integrated view of communication processes, by ordering facts; (2) it provides explanations of communication processes; (3) it provides for the objective verification of facts; and (4) it is a useful tool in the pursuit of knowledge.

## REVIEW QUESTIONS

**1.** Discuss how the following concepts are interrelated: science, theory, scientific method. What must be accomplished in the mass communication disciplines before they can be considered "sciences?" Why is it important for these disciplines to achieve the status of "science?" How does one "build" theory?

**2.** List some of your beliefs. Analyze the reasons why you hold each belief, categorizing them when possible according to Peirce's ways of "knowing."

**3.** From articles in *Journalism Quarterly* or other communication journals, pick out three hypotheses you consider to be "poor" and three hypotheses you consider to be "good." Why is the second set better than the first? Rewrite the poor hypotheses.

**4.** Take a practical or professional communication problem that is of particular concern to you. Apply scientific method to the analysis or solution of the problem. Outline the steps and discuss how logic or empiricism was used in each step.

## ENDNOTES

1. Charles Sanders Peirce, *Collected Papers of Charles Sanders Peirce*, Vol. 2 (Cambridge, Mass.: Bellknap Press of Harvard University, 1932); J. Buchler (ed.), *The Philosophy of Peirce* (New York: Harcourt, Brace, 1940).
2. Morris Cohen and Ernest Nagel, *An Introduction to Logic and Scientific Method* (New York: Harcourt, Brace, 1934).
3. *Ibid.*, p. 194.
4. *Ibid.*, pp. 391–403
5. Abraham Kaplan, *The Conduct of Inquiry* (San Francisco: Chandler, 1964), pp. 34–36.
6. *Ibid.*, pp. 36–46.
7. *Ibid.*, p.37.
8. *Ibid.*, p. 42.

# 3

# RESEARCH METHODS IN MASS COMMUNICATION

In the previous chapter we discussed some general principles and characteristics of scientific method. The objective verification of hypotheses in the real world, we stressed, is what distinguishes scientific method from other ways of "knowing." In this chapter we will discuss several methods of objective verification commonly used in mass communication. This discussion is not intended to be a comprehensive treatment of methodology. Instead, it is an overview to give you a basic understanding of research design and analysis and to acquaint you with some of the research concepts that will come up later in our discussions of theory. Since theory and research are interdependent, an understanding of concepts in this chapter will help you evaluate the mass communication studies discussed in succeeding chapters.

## EVALUATING RESEARCH METHODS

By research method, we mean the design and procedures used by the investigator to gather information for hypothesis testing. Research methods can be evaluated using two general criteria—internal validity and external validity.[1]

### Internal Validity

If a study has internal validity, then we can be reasonably sure, within specified limits of error (usually 5 percent), that we are discovering *true* relations between the variables investigated. The question is: Did $X$, our presumed cause or explanatory variable, really affect $Y$, the presumed effect?

The internal validity of a research design is usually determined by the amount of *control* that the investigator has over all the factors that may affect the relationship between the variables being studied. Our purpose in scientific investigation is to discover relations between explanatory or causal variables and dependent variables or effects. Ideally, we should be looking for *causal* relationships. A study with maximum internal validity is one that establishes cause-and-effect relationships. We can conclude that one variable ($X,$), such as viewing of television violence, causes another variable ($Y$), such as aggression in children, when the following conditions are present.

### Concomitant Variation

If two variables are causally related, then a change in one variable should always be accompanied by a change in the other variable. The two variables may change in the same direction, that is, as one variable increases in value so should the other, or they may change in opposite directions, with an increase in one variable accompanied by a decrease in the other. Thus, if TV violence were causally related to aggression we should be able to show that increased viewing of TV violence is always accompanied by either an increase or a decrease in aggression of viewers.

### Time Order

If $X$ causes $Y$, then $X$ should precede $Y$ in time. This may sound like a simple enough requirement, but it causes quite a bit of controversy among mass communication researchers. For example, the question of time order has been raised in TV violence and aggression studies (which comes first—viewing of TV violence or a child's tendency to be aggressive?), and in investigations of mass media use and the development of political attitudes (does extensive use of the mass media for public affairs information precede the development of supportive political attitudes, or do people who have strong supportive attitudes use the mass media more?). The time order of many of the variables in mass communication research is difficult to establish, since these variables often can be observed only in the natural environment, such as in the community, where they cannot be directly manipulated.

### Control of Other Possible Causes

The effects or observations of interest to the mass communication researcher often have many possible causes. Aggression in a child can be caused by brain damage, family life, economic deprivation, *and/or* TV violence. Active political campaigning for a candidate can be caused by education, political party affiliation, economic class, family influence, peer influence, *and/or* mass media use. If we are to conclude that $X$ (the variable we have isolated for the study) causes $Y$, then we should be able to control for, or to account for, the influence of all other possible causes.

The observed relationship between $X$ and $Y$ can often be caused by their mutual dependence on another variable. For example, we may observe that increased use of the mass media is accompanied by increased campaign activity. We then conclude that media use leads to campaign activity. This conclusion could be in error, since another variable, such as education, could be causing both increased media use and active campaigning. Unless education were controlled or accounted for, the original conclusion should not be made.

### Control of Error Variance

Individuals may differ on the variable being measured not only because of differences in the independent variable being studied, or other possible independent variables, but also because of error. Error has many causes—transient personal characteristics of respondents or subjects (such as mood, fatigue, mental state), situational factors (such as time that the interview is taken or physical characteristics of the room in which testing is taking place), and deficiencies in the measuring instrument (the questions are not understood or they are understood in a manner not intended by the investigator). These sources of differences in our observations are causes of error and are often referred to as error variance. They can lead us to "false" conclusions about the relationships between the variables studied. Their influence on our observations should therefore be minimized.

A research design has internal validity if the investigator can show that each of these four conditions has been met primarily through control of the variables and their observation. Concomitant variation can be shown by the systematic (that is, guided by hypotheses) and objective observation of the variables under study. This observation often occurs in the natural environment, in which we do not interfere with their functioning. Studies of this type are called *field surveys*. In a field survey, we measure the variables as they occur in their natural state (as attitudes toward the mass media in a community). We do not attempt to control or change any of the variables.

Observation to establish concomitant variation can also be accomplished in an artificial, rigidly controlled situation in which we create the conditions that will elicit the occurrence of the variables. Here, we do not wait for the behaviors to occur in the natural environment; we make these behaviors "happen." We may, for example, try to elicit aggressive behavior in children by showing them a violent TV film. This type of study is called an experiment. Field studies and experiments are discussed in greater detail in succeeding sections.

Time order of the variables, the second condition for causality, can be established by controlling for the occurrence of the variables observed. This is, of course, more easily done in an experiment, where we manipulate $X$ (the presumed cause) and *then* observe $Y$ (presumed effect). Time order is more difficult to establish in field studies, where we often do not have enough reliable information to determine which variable occurred first in the natural environment.

We can control the effects of other causes more easily in experiments than in field studies. One way of doing this is by randomization. In an experiment we assign subjects randomly by giving each person to be studied an equal chance of being assigned to a specific experimental condition. We can also build other possible causes into the study by actual manipulation of those causes. In a field survey other possible causes of the effect in question can be accounted for by *asking* the respondents about those causes (building them into the questionnaire). Control of other causes in experiments and field surveys are discussed in greater detail in succeeding sections.

We control error variance in an experiment by randomization and by testing the groups under identical conditions (except, of course, for the condition being manipulated). Control of error variance in field surveys is accomplished by careful training of interviewers, so that their asking of the questions will not bias responses, and by pretesting the questionnaire to insure that the questions are understood by the respondents. Again, error variance is more easily controlled in the experiment than in the field survey.

## External Validity

External validity refers to the representativeness or generalizability of the study. There are many questions that the researchers must ask with regard to the external validity of the study, some of which follow.

To what other populations can we generalize our results? If we find that TV violence causes increased aggression in an eighth-grade sample or subject group, are these results true for *all* eighth graders in the school system? For all eighth graders in the state? All eighth graders in the country? All schoolchildren? These questions pertain to the *population validity* of the study.

If we find that TV violence leads to aggression in a low-income school, will the same relationship hold in a middle- or high-income school? In a country school? A large city school? Questions pertaining to the generalizability of our findings to different environments are often referred to as *ecological validity*.

Are our treatments, observations, and measurements concrete representations of broader classes of behaviors that we are really interested in? We are interested in aggression in real life, not in check marks on a questionnaire or in the number of times a child hits a plastic doll. We are also interested in *all* violent TV shows, not only in the thirty-minute segment from a violent film that we show our subjects. If our operations in a particular study can be *generalized* to a larger class of behaviors and observations (that we are really interested in, but that would be impractical to study), then our study will have *conceptual* or *content validity*.

To what extent can our results be used to predict other operationally different but conceptually similar behaviors? If we find that the amount of viewing TV violence (X) predicts aggression in the classroom (as rated by teachers), will X also predict aggression at home, or on the playground? Aggression, whether it occurs at home, on the playground, or in the classroom, is anchored on the same underlying concept—the excessive use of force in social relationships. A study that can predict from its specific results to other conceptually similar situations is said to have *predictive validity*.

A good research design, then, is one that has both external and internal validity. In addition to these two characteristics, the design should be able to provide the answers to the questions initiating the investigation. Can the hypotheses be adequately tested using the design and procedures of our study? This question leads us to another important topic in research methodology—hypothesis testing.

## HYPOTHESIS TESTING

As discussed in Chapter 2, hypotheses guide our investigation of the problem. We put forth in our hypotheses possible answers to the scientific question and test those that seem to be most probable. There are at least two types of hypotheses in mass communication research—correlational and causal hypotheses. In a correlational hypothesis we predict that there will either be a positive or negative linear relationship between $X$ and $Y$ or that there will be concomitant variation between the variables. Thus, we may predict that amount of television viewing and grade point average (GPA) of high school students will be positively related; that is, as TV viewing goes up, so will GPA. Or, we may predict the opposite; as TV viewing goes up, GPA will decrease (a negative relationship). These are examples of correlational hypotheses. We often use them when we cannot be sure of the time order of the variables and are therefore unable to say that one variable is causing the other. (We may have some idea regarding which variable is the cause and which is the effect, but we may be unwilling to say so definitely on the basis of our research design.) Correlational hypotheses are used in field surveys when we do not have enough knowledge about the causal ordering of our variables. They are often used to formulate causal hypotheses in subsequent studies.

Causal hypotheses state that there is a causal relationship between $X$ and $Y$, and they also state the *nature* of this relationship. If we had enough information on the time order in which TV viewing and the ability to do well in school (GPA) occur, then we could predict that TV viewing causes high (or low) GPAs. Causal hypotheses are often formulated in terms of differences between groups. We could say that students viewing three hours or more of TV per day will have lower GPAs than those who view less (implying that high TV viewing causes low GPAs), or that children who watched a violent TV show will be more aggressive immediately after viewing than children who watched a neutral show (implying that TV violence causes aggression). Causal hypotheses can be stated if all four conditions for determining causality are met by the study design.

### Research and Null Hypotheses

In any one study the researcher will be dealing with two specific types of hypothesis—the *null* hypothesis (symbolized as $H_0$) and the research hypothesis $(H_1)$. The null hypothesis often, but not always, states that there is no relationship between variables or that there is no difference between groups (and, therefore, no causal relationship between variables). The research hypothesis is set up as an alternative to the null hypothesis. It predicts either a negative or positive correlational or causal relationship. Often we set up a null hypothesis that we would really like to reject but must proceed as if it were true because the hypothesis actually tested in the study is the null.[2] Statistical tests provide us with some criterion—usually called *significance*—for accepting or rejecting the null hypothesis.

## Significance

Significance in hypothesis testing refers to the probability of accepting $H_1$ (concluding that there is a relationship between variables, or that $X$ causes $Y$) when $H_0$ is true (there is no relationship). It therefore indicates the probability of being wrong in rejecting the null (when it indeed is true). Significance is sometimes referred to as the probability of making a Type I error, or as an alpha error.[3]

Significance is often set arbitrarily in the social sciences (including mass communication) at $p \leq .05$. This notation means that the probability, or $p$, of committing an alpha or Type I error is 5 percent, or that only 5 times out of 100 will we be in error in saying that there was an effect (or there were significant differences) when, in fact, there were no effects. There are times, of course, when the researcher may select a smaller probability for significance such as $p \leq .01$ (1 percent) or $p \leq .001$ (.1 percent). Generally, researchers should be conservative—that is, they should lean over backward to prove themselves wrong. This, as we had discussed earlier, is one of the characteristics of scientific method. The researchers set the significance level *before* the study is done. The decision is often based on how the results are to be used, the size of the sample or number of observations (it is easy to get "significant" effects with large samples, so with samples of several hundred or more, the level is often set at $p \leq .01$ or $p \leq .001$), and on the state of knowledge regarding the problem (the more previous justification we have for rejecting the null, the more we can afford to gamble, by setting $p$ at .05, the *maximum* allowable error, in the present study).

Let us use an example to clarify how significance levels are used in hypothesis testing. Suppose we set up our null hypothesis as follows.

**$H_0$.** There will be no differences in subsequent play aggression between children who viewed a violent TV cartoon and children who viewed a similar nonviolent cartoon.

The alternative hypothesis, or $H_1$, is set up as indicated.

**$H_1$.** Children who watched a violent TV cartoon will be more aggressive in subsequent play situations than children who watched a similar nonviolent cartoon.

We decide to set the significance level at $p \leq .05$, since previous studies support the rejection of $H_0$ and the acceptance of $H_1$ and since we will be using only thirty subjects in each group of children, the minimum often prescribed for laboratory experiments.

After testing $H_0$ in a laboratory experiment and using the appropriate statistical tests, we decide to reject $H_0$ at $p \leq .05$ and accept $H_1$. We can conclude that TV violence caused aggression (within the confines of our experiment), and our conclusion would be "wrong" only 5 times out of 100. Or, put another way, the differences we found would occur by chance alone only 5 times out of 100. Therefore, we can be reasonably sure that there was an effect of TV violence on aggression.

## EXPERIMENTS

As a science develops, more attention is given to the testing of causal hypotheses. As seen in a previous section, four conditions should be established before we can conclude that variable $X$ causes variable $Y$—concomitant variation, time order, control of error variance, and control of other possible influences on $Y$. The experiment is the most efficient and reliable method of meeting all four conditions. What exactly is an experiment?

Experiments are research designs in which the investigators have complete control over the presumed cause (the independent variables) and where they attempt to control *other* possible variables that might affect the dependent variable. The researchers control the independent variable by *manipulating* or *producing* it. Other possible influences on the dependent variable are controlled primarily through *random* assignment of subjects to the different conditions being studied. Most experiments are done in an artificial environment such as a classroom or a TV lounge in a university building. These are called *laboratory experiments*. Some experiments can be carried out in the "real world" (such as in a small city) if the researchers are able to control the independent variable in its natural environment. These studies are called *field experiments*. In either case the procedures are the same. In general, these are the steps involved in carrying out experiments.

### Formulation of Hypotheses

As with any study, experiments begin with hypotheses. Experimental hypotheses specify a cause-and-effect relationship between variables. We identify the effects or responses that we are interested in and then determine what variables (or stimuli) might best elicit these responses. Our choice of variables will depend on practical and theoretical interests. In mass communications we are often interested in the effects of media use on opinions and behaviors of audiences.

Causal hypotheses in experiments are often stated as differences between experimental groups. If there are differences between groups in the dependent variable after the causal variable is introduced, then we can conclude that a causal relationship exists. Our previous hypothesis on TV violence and aggression is an example of a causal hypothesis: "Children who watched a violent TV cartoon will be more aggressive in subsequent play situations than children who watched a similar nonviolent cartoon." In this hypothesis, we are predicting that exposure to the violent cartoon will *cause* subsequent aggressive behavior.

## Selection of Subjects

The next step is to decide on the subjects to be studied. What group is of interest to the researcher? Children, adolescents, or adults? From which economic classes? Which ethnic groups? These are some of the decisions on subjects that the researcher will have to make.

Most experiments use homogeneous groups of subjects, that is, subjects who are alike. This is one way of controlling for the effects of outside influences on the dependent variables. Very often, experiments use relatively small groups of subjects; about thirty subjects per experimental condition are usually adequate.[4] The decision on which group to study will depend primarily on the theoretical and practical interests of the researcher. We may be interested in studying the effects of TV violence on children, since previous studies and theory suggest that children are most likely to be influenced by the media or because we are practically concerned about possible harmful effects of TV on our own children. Another consideration in selection of subjects is their availability. It is not always easy to recruit "ordinary people" (the "average" middle-aged woman or man, for example) for experiments. Often we have to use fixed groups, or groups already in existence. Because of their availability to researchers, many experiments in mass communication (as well as the other social sciences) use college students as subjects. This has led some critics to ask, "Are college students people?" The translation, of course, is "Are college students representative of any other group, besides themselves?" This raises the issue of *external validity* of experiments, which was discussed earlier in this chapter.

## Selection of Experimental Design

The appropriate experimental design will depend on the hypotheses of the study. Generally, the design will be either an "after-only" or a "before-after" design. These are the most common and simplest of experimental designs.[5] To simplify our discussion, the following symbols will be used:

$X$—This is the independent variable, or the presumed cause in the study. It is produced or manipulated by the researcher. Subjects in the experiment are exposed to it.

$X_1$—one level of $X$
$X_2$—another level of $X$
$X_n$—the $n$th level of $X$

$Y$—This is the dependent variable, or the presumed effect that the researcher observes and measures in the subjects. It is the *response* to $X$ that the researcher wishes to isolate.

$Y_b$—the measurement or observation of $Y$ *before* the subjects are exposed to $X$
$Y_a$—the measurement of $Y$ *after* subjects are exposed to $X$
$Y_1$—the measurement of $Y$ for Group 1
$Y_2$—the measurement of $Y$ for Group 2
$Y_n$—the measurement of $Y$ for Group $n$

$R$—random assignment of subjects to experimental conditions. (Procedures for random assignment are discussed in a later section.)

## After-Only Design

In its simplest form, the after-only design may be diagrammed as follows:

Group 1 (experimental group): $RXY_{a1}$
Group 2 (control group): $\quad R \;\; Y_{a2}$

In this design we assign subjects randomly to two groups, an experimental or treatment group that is exposed to the stimulus or independent variable (sometimes called the "treatment"), and a control group that is *not* exposed to the independent variable ($X$). The dependent variable, $Y$, is then measured or observed in both groups after the experimental group is exposed to $X$. We compare $Y_{a1}$ and $Y_{a2}$. If there is a significant difference (as determined by the appropriate statistical test), then we can conclude that $X$ caused this change. With this design all the conditions for establishing causality are met: $X$ occurs *before* $Y$, concomitant variation is observed, since introducing $X$ changed $Y$, and other possible causes of $Y$ were controlled through random assignment of subjects to the conditions.

As an example, let us return to our problem regarding television violence and aggression in children. Using the after-only design, we randomly assign sixty children to two groups, thirty children in each group. We then randomly assign conditions to these two groups. We show one group a violent animated cartoon and the other group no cartoon at all. We keep the groups of children in separate but similar rooms. After the experimental group has finished watching the cartoon, we give an aggression test to all the children. This can be a paper-and-pencil test (such as a questionnaire) or direct observation of aggression (such as play behavior toward a plastic doll). We then compare aggression scores of the two groups. If aggression scores are significantly higher in the experimental group than in the control group, we reject the null hypothesis and accept our research hypothesis. We can conclude that viewing the violent cartoon led to, or caused, the increased aggression in our subjects.

Another form of the after only design can be diagrammed as follows:

Group 1 (experimental group 1): $RX_1Y_{a1}$
Group 2 (experimental group 2): $RX_2Y_{a2}$
Group 3 (control group): $\quad R \;\; Y_{a3}$

In this design more than one level of the independent variable $X$ is administered in the experiment. Often we may be interested in different levels of the independent variable instead of simply comparing a group exposed to $X$ and another group not exposed to $X$, as in the previous design. Researchers investigating the effects of varying levels of fear appeals in a persuasive message may, for example, wish to compare which of three levels—high, medium, or low—causes the most attitude change. Comparisons can then be made between the experimental groups and the control group (the group *not* administered the treatment).

In our previous example we can add a second experimental group, which will be shown a TV cartoon similar in quality and substance to the violent cartoon shown the first experimental group, except *without* the violence. We would add this group to make sure that whatever increase in aggression observed in the first experimental group over the control group will be caused by exposure to TV *violence* and not to *any* TV program (in this case, a neutral cartoon). We can then compare aggression scores for Groups 1 $(Y_{a1})$, 2 $(Y_{a2})$, and 3 $(Y_{a3})$. (Remember that Group 1 is shown the violent cartoon, Group 2 the nonviolent cartoon, and Group 3, no cartoon.) If only exposure to violence causes increased aggression, then $Y_{a1}$ should be significantly greater than $Y_{a2}$ and $Y_{a3}$, and there should be no difference between $Y_{a2}$ and $Y_{a3}$.

### Before-After Design

The basic before-after design can be diagrammed as follows:

Group 1 (experimental group): $RY_{b1}XY_{a1}$
Group 2 (control group): $RY_{b2} \ Y_{a2}$

In this design, we assign subjects randomly to two groups. We then measure $Y$ for both groups before $X$ is introduced to the experimental group. The first measure of $Y$ should be identical or equivalent to the second, or "after," measure. This allows us to compare the extent of change in the experimental group $(Y_{a1} - Y_{b1})$ with change in the control group $(Y_{a2} - Y_{b2})$. If $X$ had an effect on $Y$, then $Y_{a1} - Y_{b1}$ should be significantly greater or less than $Y_{a2} - Y_{b2}$. We can make this conclusion because of the assumption that random assignment of subjects to both groups will make then equal on before measures of $Y$, and that outside influences on $Y$, occurring between the before and after measures, will also be equal. Thus any difference between the after measures should be caused by $X$.

When and why should we use a before-after design instead of an after-only design? The most common use of the before-after design is to give the researchers some prior knowledge about how their subjects measure on the dependent variable. This prior knowledge is necessary in several situations. First, the major hypothesis of the study may specify that the independent variable $X$ will have different effects on subjects whose initial positions on the dependent variable were different. As an example, suppose we wanted to determine the effects of an antiprejudice film on attitudes of our adult subjects toward blacks. We might hypothesize that the film will be most effective in changing attitudes toward blacks in a favorable direction among those who did not have a feeling for blacks one way or the other (the "neutrals") and among those who were only slightly prejudiced. We could predict that the film would not be effective among those who were highly prejudiced against blacks, since these subjects would be more likely to use perceptual defenses against the message. We could also expect little change among those who were already favorable toward blacks, since the message would simply reinforce existing beliefs. To be able to test these hypotheses, we would need to know how our subjects initially felt toward blacks, information that can be given by our before measures (sometimes called a "pretest"). After taking an initial assessment of $Y$ in both randomized groups, we could then compare the after measures of $Y$ for individuals in experimental and control groups who started out with the same or similar initial positions on $Y$. For the before-after design to be effective in this situation larger pools of subjects are needed, since the original groups will be subdivided into smaller groups based on how they measure initially on $Y$.

To illustrate this use of the before-after design, let us return to our research problem regarding TV violence and aggression in children. We may suspect that TV violence will have a greater effect (that is, elicit the most subsequent aggression) among children who are *already* predisposed to aggression. We would therefore need to assess the initial aggressiveness of our subjects to test this hypothesis. This could be done by administering the aggression test to our subjects before the film is shown to the experimental group and then comparing after measures of aggression for those who scored high in the test and those who scored low. If our hypothesis were correct, then there should be more subsequent aggression among those who were initially high in aggression in the experimental group compared to those who were initially low in aggression, also in the experimental group. The mean aggression should be greater in the experimental than in control groups.

### Factorial Designs

Factorial designs are used when we have two or more different sets of independent variables (also called treatments) that we would like to study in one experiment for their effects on a dependent variable. For example, if we wanted to determine the effects of the subject's sex and the level of fear in a persuasive message to which the subject is exposed on his or her intention to stop smoking, we could use the factorial design shown in Table 3.1. This is a factorial design, since we are "crossing" two different sets of treatments—subject sex and fear in message. We have six distinct subject groups; each group is given or assigned a unique combination of the two factors or treatments. With this design, we can ask three questions.

1. Are there systematic effects on intention to quit smoking due to subject sex alone, regardless of fear level in the message?

**TABLE 3.1. An Example of Interaction Effects**

| Subject Sex | Fear in Message | | | Row Means |
|---|---|---|---|---|
| | *Low* | *Medium* | *High* | |
| Male | 5 | 7 | 6 | 6 |
| Female | 6 | 8 | 10 | 8 |
| Column means | 5.5 | 7.5 | 8 | |

2. Are there systematic effects due to fear level in the message, regardless of subject sex?
3. Are there systematic effects due neither to sex alone nor to fear alone, but which we could attribute only to a combination of a particular level of fear with a particular sex?

The first two questions deal with main effects; the third question deals with an interaction effect. Factorial designs allow us to study main effects and interaction effects. You can cross more than two factors or treatments. However, it is best to limit factorial designs to two factors. Interaction effects are difficult to interpret when you have more than two factors.

Let us illustrate what we mean by an interaction effect. Look at Table 3.1. The scores shown are means or averages; the higher the score, the greater the subject's intent to quit smoking.

The row means in Table 3.1 show that females were more likely to say that they would quit smoking after exposure to a persuasive message (their mean score of 8 is greater than the males' mean of 6). The column means show that high fear levels in the persuasive message were generally the most effective (disregarding subject sex), since the mean score of 8 for high fear is greater than the mean scores for low and medium fear. These conclusions, if supported by the appropriate statistical test (in this case it would be an analysis of variance), deal with main effects.

Now, look at the scores inside the table. We can see that the effect of fear level in the message is not the same for males and females. For males, the medium fear appeal was most effective (a mean score of 7, which is the highest among males). For females, the high fear appeal, with a mean score of 10, was most effective. This is an effect that is not due to sex or fear appeal alone, but that can only be attributed to a combination of fear level (high) with a particular sex (female). This effect is called an interaction effect. It can be detected only when a factorial design is used.

## Operationalization of Independent and Dependent Variables

Once we have decided on the experimental design, the next step is to operationalize our variables. How will we introduce the independent variable to our subjects, and in what form? How will we observe or measure the dependent variable?

First, we should make experimental conditions as different from each other as possible.[6] By doing so we increase the chances of finding significant differences between groups and of increasing internal validity of the study. Of course, we also have to consider whether our experimental manipulations are representative of the conditions as they exist in the real world. It would not be very useful to find significant differences in $Y$ arising from extreme conditions of $X$ if those conditions did not exist, or very rarely exist, in the natural environment. Let us illustrate with an example, using the TV violence and aggression hypothesis. To test this hypothesis, we would have to operationalize TV violence. We could select a film clip from a horrifyingly and unusually violent movie and expose our experimental group to it. One control group would not be exposed to any film at all, and another group could be exposed to a "neutral" film, such as a travelogue. The violent film would represent an extreme example of violence. By operationalizing our independent variable (TV violence) in this way, we are increasing our chances of finding differences in aggression between our experimental and control groups, if indeed, TV or film violence causes an increase in aggression. But of what practical use would these results be if significant differences were found? Children would very rarely be exposed to such violence in television or in movies. Our manipulation of $X$ does not correspond to what our subjects would experience in the real world. We would be better off by producing (or taping) a film clip that shows the type of violence children are likely to see on television. We should select an extreme but common example of TV violence and a neutral film that contains no violence at all. By doing, so we may be decreasing our chances of getting a significant effect, but we are improving the external validity of the design.

If we are introducing two or more levels of the independent variable to our subjects, then we would have to make sure that the different treatments are equal in all respects, except for the characteristic being studied. This is necessary if we are to isolate the effects of that characteristic operationalized as the cause. In our previous example, then, we would pick two films that were of the same length and of the same quality. If possible, the only difference between the two films should be that one is violent and the other is not. If one film were longer than the other, then length would be a possible influence on the effect we are studying. If one film were in color and the other in black and white, this might be a source of contamination on our $Y$. It is not always possible to have the different treatments identical in every other way except for $X$ (the topics of the films may vary, for example), but the researcher should try to do so.

In operationalizing our dependent variable ($Y$, the presumed effect of $X$ on our subjects), we should be concerned with the *reliability* and *validity* of our measures. Reliability is the extent to which our measures give consistent results. If we measure our subjects on $Y$ today and again tomorrow, using the same measure and assuming that there has been no change during that time in $Y$, then a reliable measure should give us the same results and should order our subjects on $Y$ in the same way at both times. A reliable measure gives some assurance that our subjects understand the questions consistently from time to time. This helps minimize error variance.

Validity of our dependent measures refers to the extent to which our measures are giving us the "true" position of our subjects on the effect being measured and whether the hypothesized effect is actually measured. Some of the validity questions we might ask regarding our TV violence and aggression experiment are the following: Is my questionnaire actually measuring aggression and not another characteristic of my subjects such as frustration, anger, or their desire to give us a socially desirable response? Are my measures giving me an accurate assessment of how much aggression there is in each subject (or are they "lying" to us)? The problem of validity is not easily resolved, especially in mass communication and other behavioral sciences where we often have to depend on self-reports from our subjects (that is, we depend on them to tell us how they "measure" on the dependent variable). Current texts on research methodology stress the importance of using several measures of $Y$ as a means of establishing the validity of those measures.[7] If these measures give similar results, then we can have some assurance that our measures were valid. We could, for example, measure aggression using a questionnaire, ratings from teachers, and ratings from parents. If these measures give similar results, then we can say that we were indeed measuring aggression.

## Random Assignment of Subjects to Conditions

After the independent and dependent variables have been operationalized, the next step is to assign subjects randomly to the different conditions. Ideally, we should have at least thirty subjects per condition to be able to detect true differences between conditions.[8]

If we are to isolate the effects of our manipulated independent variable on our subjects, then we should see to it that our groups are equivalent, or close to equivalent, in all respects before $X$ is introduced in the experimrnt. We would not like to have more girls in the experimental group than in the control group, for example, because subject sex might affect how they respond to $X$. The best way of equalizing our groups before $X$ is through *randomization*. Subjects should be assigned randomly to each of the different conditions. Random assignment is giving each subject the same chance as any other subject of being assigned to any given condition. There are many ways of doing this. If we had only two groups, then we could toss a coin (assuming we had an honest coin, where the probability of heads or tails coming up is 50 percent) and assign a person to an experimental group if it comes up heads and to the control group if it comes up tails. If we had more than two groups then a lottery might be set up. We could write down numbers on slips of paper corresponding to our groups (1, 2, and 3, if we had three groups) and ask each person to draw a slip of paper. The number that a subject draws is his or her assigned group. There should, of course, be an equal number of slips for each group, corresponding to the number of subjects per condition.

After subjects have been assigned randomly to groups, *conditions* can be randomly assigned to the groups. Suppose we had three random groups and three conditions—violent film, neutral film, and control (no film). We could match conditions with groups randomly, again by using a lottery. Random assignment of groups to conditions further assures us that our groups are equivalent before the independent variable is introduced.

### Introduction of X, Measurement of Y

After assigning the subjects randomly to the experimental groups, we can introduce the treatments and then measure the effects. We should make testing conditions identical or similar for all conditions. Rooms in which the groups are to be tested should be identical (or similar), and subjects should be tested at the same time of the day. Also, we should use the same experimenter (the person giving instructions to the subjects) if possible. These conditions cannot always be met, but the researcher should try to minimize or eliminate any other influence on $Y$ except for the $X$ that is being studied.

### Analysis and Interpretation of Results

The last step in conducting experiments is to analyze and interpret the results. We analyze our hypothesis using the appropriate statistical tests. We can then decide to accept or reject the null hypothesis at a previously specified significance level (usually $p \leq .05$). We should also discuss the implications of the findings for both theory and practical application.

## EVALUATING EXPERIMENTS

Now that we have some idea of how and why experiments are done, let us discuss some of the general criteria used for evaluating experiments.[9] We should ask the following questions whenever we read reports of experiments or their results in journals, papers, or textbooks like this one.

### Problem Formulation

What is the general problem area being studied? Why are the researchers studying this problem? What is its practical and theoretical justification? Are there contradictory results from previous studies? Will the answer help solve a practical problem? We ask these questions to help us determine, after reading results of the study, whether or not the experiment met its initial objectives.

## Hypotheses

What are the hypotheses of the study? Are they clearly stated? Do they relate to the general problem area? Do they fulfill the criteria of a "good hypothesis," as discussed in Chapter 2?

## Subjects

Who were the subjects? What are their characteristics—age, sex, income level? Why were they chosen for the study? Is there a theoretical justification for using subjects with these characteristics? (For example, why were children studied and not adolescents or adults?) How many subjects were used? How were the subjects selected?

## Operationalization of Variables

How were the independent and dependent variables operationalized? Do their operationalizations correspond to their conceptual definitions? (For example, is the violence in the film representative of violence in television, as defined?) Was the independent variable pretested to make sure that subjects would perceive it according to the researcher's conceptualization of the variable? (Will the children used as subjects consider the the film to be violent?) Is evidence presented regarding the reliability and validity of the dependent measures?

## Procedure

How were the subjects assigned to experimental conditions? Was randomization used? Was there subject attrition? (For example, did the researcher have to drop subjects from any of the conditions because of unforeseen factors—illness, refusal to cooperate, incomplete questionnaires?) Were experimental conditions randomly assigned to the groups?

Were there adequate control groups? Do the control groups relate to the hypothesis?

## Results

Are the hypotheses tested, and do results relate back to the hypotheses? Are there any unexpected findings? Are these unexpected findings adequately explained? Are the conclusions justified by the results?

These are some of the questions that we might ask in evaluating experiments. The major question is whether the experiment had internal and external validity.

# FIELD SURVEYS

In mass communication research, we often cannot manipulate our variables in the laboratory because to do so would be impractical or unethical. Some of the independent variables that mass communication researchers have been interested in but that cannot be manipulated in the laboratory are parental control of a child's television watching, family communication patterns, prolonged use of a mass medium, feelings of support for the political system, and various personality characteristics such as self-esteem, neurotic anxiety, and need for social support. Some dependent variables that are difficult to observe or measure in the laboratory are overt aggression toward other people, sexual behavior, voting in an election, and political campaigning. When faced with such a situation, we need to find a substitute to the experiment as our method of collecting data. A commonly used alternative is the field survey.

A field survey is a method of getting information about a large number of people or objects (often called a *population*) by studying a small proportion of them (a sample). In a field survey we observe the variables as they exist naturally. We attempt to make systematic, objective observations of things "as they are." We do not attempt to interfere with the functioning of the variables or to change or directly control any variable.

Field surveys are often used in descriptive studies when the researchers wish to identify the existence of certain characteristics in a population. Examples of this type of a survey are the public opinion polls—Roper, Gallup, Harris, and others. These polls utilize surveys to describe the opinions of various populations on issues such as international affairs, government, the economy, race relations, and others. Other examples of descriptive use of field surveys are media viewership and readership studies. The Nielsen surveys, for example, tell us how many in the population (and who) are watching which television shows.

Field surveys are also used in more theoretical studies to discover *relationships* between variables in populations. In these studies we test correlational hypotheses, or hypotheses that predict concomitant variation between variables. With more advanced methods and statistical analyses, we can also sometimes test causal hypotheses. Examples of theoretical uses of surveys in mass communication include studies of mass media use and political behavior, studies of prolonged use of television and viewers' perceptions of social realities, and studies of family interaction variables and mass media use of children.

Since field studies are done in a naturalistic environment, their external validity is usually better than experiments. However, internal validity is weaker because the researchers do not directly control any of the variables.

The following steps are often followed in survey research.

## Problem Formulation

The major purpose of most surveys is to describe attitudes, characteristics, or behaviors or to analyze concomitant variation between these variables in a group of people or objects. As a first step, we should identify the group and the characteristics to be studied. We may, for example, be interested in describing television viewing behavior of all children in the United States between the ages of four and six and measure number of hours spent watching TV per day and types of shows watched. Additionally, we may be interested in determining whether there is a relationship between a child's scores on various "intelligence" tests and the number of hours spent watching TV. Intelligence and daily TV viewing are variables that we cannot manipulate or control in the laboratory; thus we choose to study the problem using a survey. Since we cannot be sure which comes first, "intelligence" at a certain age or TV viewing, we state our hypothesis in correlational form,[10] provided there is some previous evidence to back it up: "TV viewing and intelligence in this age group will be negatively related—as TV viewing goes up, intelligence scores will go down." If we do not have any theoretical basis for specifying the nature of the relationship, then we can forego the hypothesis and state an objective instead, as follows: "A major objective of this study is to determine whether there is *any* relationship between TV viewing and intelligence scores in the population studied." A survey should always state objectives or hypotheses and present some justification—theoretical, practical, or both—for the choice of groups and characteristics to be studied.

## Sampling

The group of people or objects that is studied in a survey is called a *population*. This group will have at least one characteristic in common, designated by the researchers and of theoretical or practical interest to them. This characteristic may be age, place of residence, ethnic background, sex, or any combination of these. Very often, members of a specified population may number in the thousands, tens of thousands, or even millions. It could be very expensive in time and money to study, measure, or talk to all of them. What we can do, then, is to draw a smaller subgroup from the population, study this subgroup, and hope that it will be representative of the larger group. This process is called *sampling*, and the smaller subgroup is called the *sample*.

Sampling is a very important step in survey research because validity and usefulness of the results will depend on how it is done. Our major concern is that the *number* and *kinds* of people or objects in our sample should be representative of the population so that we can generalize sample results to the population. Very rarely will we be interested in the sample in itself; the study will usually be about a population.

The only reliable way that we can get a sample representative of a population is through *probability* sampling. With a probability sample we can specify the chances that the sample results will not differ by more than a certain amount from the population values. The simplest, and most representative, type of probability sampling is the simple random sample. In simple random sampling each and every member of the population has an equal chance of being selected in the sample. There are several ways of drawing a simple random sample. A common method is by using a table of random numbers, which is a listing of numbers in no particular order (in *random* order), usually generated by a computer, and found in the appendices of most statistics books. To use a table of random numbers, we first have to secure a list of the members of the population to be studied and then number all members from the first to the last. We enter the table at some random starting point (close our eyes, point at the table, and start with that number). The members whose numbers come up in the table are taken into the sample until we have the desired number in the sample. There are other ways of drawing a simple random sample, but most of them use a table of random numbers in one way or another.[11]

Other types of probability samples are stratified samples and cluster samples. In stratified random sampling we first divide the population into two or more strata (groups) that may be based on one or more characteristics as, for example, sex, or sex and age (males under eighteen, males over eighteen, females under eighteen, females over eighteen). Simple random samples are then taken from each group, and the subsamples are added together to form the total sample. We use stratified samples when we have reason to believe that members within classes will be alike on the dependent variable and that the classes will be different from each other.

Cluster sampling is often the only practical method of sampling a large population that is geographically dispersed. If we wanted a random sample of all children ages four to six in the United States, then the children selected by simple random sampling could be scattered all over the country. It would be very expensive to locate all of them. Besides, we may not be able to secure a list of the children, a prerequisite for simple random sampling. In cluster sampling we arrive at our final sample by first sampling, randomly, larger groupings in which the members of the population are found. We sample clusters or groups instead of individual members of the population. For example, if we wanted to sample all first graders in a particular state, we could first prepare a list of all school districts, from which we then select a simple random sample of school districts. Then, from each school district included in this sample, we list the schools and select a simple random sample of them. Finally, if some or all the schools selected in this sample have more first-grade classes than can be studied, we may take a sample of classes from these schools. We would include all children in the selected classes as our sample. This method is more practical than simple random sampling since we will be able to locate our sample in large groups (classes) and not individually. Of course, it will not be as representative as a simple random sample, but the savings in time and money usually justify the loss in accuracy.

Another important decision in sampling is how large a sample should be drawn. It is true that the larger the sample, the more representative it will be. However, it is not true that the sample size will depend on the size of the population. The size of our sample will depend on the *margin of error,* the *confidence level,* and the *variability* of the characteristics being measured in the population.

Projections from the sample to the population will always involve some error, since the sample is only an approximation of the population. The error in making an estimate of the population characteristics (or values) from the characteristics in the sample is called the margin of sampling error. Before the sample is drawn, we decide what error margin can be tolerated. This decision will be based on how the data are going to be used. If we were attempting to measure voter preferences in a close election, we might want to set error at 1 percent. This means that the actual candidate preferences in the population will vary from the sample percentage by plus or minus one. If, for example, we find that 60 percent of the sample favored candidate A, then the actual percentage in the population that favors candidate A would be between 59 and 61 percent (60 plus or minus 1 percent). Smaller margins of error require larger sample sizes. For most descriptive and correlational research in mass communication, error margins of plus or minus 5 percent are often considered satisfactory.

Also to be considered in determining sample size is confidence level, which is the probability of making the correct population estimate from our sample values, given the margin of error. Confidence level is often set at either 90, 95, or 99 percent. A 90-percent confidence level, with a 1-percent margin of error, would mean that we can expect our population value to be within plus or minus 1 percent of the sample value 99 percent of the time. The higher the confidence level, the larger the sample size that would be required. In most mass communication research, a confidence level of 95 percent is considered satisfactory. Like margin of error, confidence level is set by the researchers before beginning the survey.

The last factor determining sample size is variability in the population of the characteristic being measured. Often we will have some idea about this variability from pretests or previous studies. If we have reason to believe that variability will be large in the population, then we would need a larger sample. An election in which there seems to be a fifty-fifty split (which is maximum variability in a two-choice situation) would require a larger sample than an election where there might be a seventy-thirty split. The reason for this is that we would need more people to represent the population, the greater the distribution among them of the characteristic being measured. If everybody agreed on which candidate to vote for (no variability), then a sample of one could represent the entire population.

Formulas are often used by researchers to arrive at the ideal and practical sample size for a particular problem.[12] A survey should specify the confidence limits and margin of error of the sample drawn and should also explain how the sample was drawn. A sample size of 400 is often considered satisfactory in social science research. This sample size generally gives us 6-percent error at a 95-percent confidence level.

## Constructing the Questionnaire

In surveys we are often interested in measuring facts, opinions, behaviors, and perceptions of our sample. We rely heavily on verbal reports from our survey respondents. We *ask* them to give us the information. There are, of course, many limitations to this method of collecting data. Our respondents may not be willing to tell us the "truth" about themselves for many reasons, one of which might be their motivation to give a socially desirable response or a response that will enhance their social image. Or, our respondents may not be capable of giving a response because they may not be aware of their feelings on the issue that they are asked about. In spite of these limitations, self-reports are often used in surveys because it is often impossible or impractical to observe directly the variables we are interested in.[13]

Validity of self-reports can be increased by using standardized questionnaires in which both the questions and alternative responses allowed the respondents are predetermined by the researchers. Also standardized are the wording of questions, their order, and instructions to respondents. We refer to this type of questionnaire as *structured* questionnaires. They make it easier for the researcher to quantify, code, and analyze responses and to compare responses among sample members. They also improve uniformity from one measurement situation to another.

In contrast to structured questionnaires, the questions and their possible answers in *unstructured* interviews are not predetermined by the researchers. Questions are asked as the need to ask them arises, which is determined by the interviewer. Also, respondents can answer the questions any way they wish, since the list of possible answers is not provided them by the interviewer. Unstructured interviews are more difficult to analyze than structured questionnaires, particularly when we have large samples. Also, comparisons between sample members are more difficult. However, they are useful in preliminary surveys, where the main objective might be to get information for structuring a questionnaire for later use. They are also useful in in-depth surveys, such as studies of consumer motivations where we may wish to get a lot of information from a small group of respondents.

Because most mass communication field studies deal with large samples and because we are usually interested in comparing subgroups within samples, structured questionnaires are used more often than unstructured interviews. Here are some examples of structured questions:

### Questions about Facts

An important objective of survey research in mass communication is to describe media use of various populations and to relate media use to personal characteristics of the audience. We often are interested in getting facts about our respondents—information that we would expect them to *know*, either from direct experience or observations. Examples are questions about age, sex, education, marital status, ethnic origin, income, occupation, amount of television watched per day, time spent reading newspapers daily, number of magazines read per week, and so on. To make analysis easier, we often predetermine both the questions and their possible answers. An example of a structured fact question is the following.

About how many days a week do you read a newspaper? Do you read a paper:
_____ every day _____ almost every day _____ a few days a week
_____ less than a few days a week _____ never

## Questions about Attitudes

Mass communication research is also concerned with how people feel about issues, or their attitudes. For example, we may be interested in describing the attitudes of parents toward television advertising. To measure attitudes, we often use a Likert scale. This scale consists of a series of opinion statements, usually from five to ten, about a specific issue. Each statement expresses either a pro or con attitude regarding the issue. The possible responses are presented in a five-point scale, from strongly agree to strongly disagree. A person's attitude is the summation of his or her scores for all statements.

An example of a single-item Likert scale is the following:

Most television advertising is misleading.
_____ strongly agree _____ agree _____ undecided
_____ disagree _____ strongly disagree

If we decide beforehand that a favorable attitude toward television advertising would be represented by a high score, then we score a response of strongly disagree as five and a response of strongly agree as one. A person's attitude is represented by the total score for all such statements measuring attitudes towards TV advertising.[14]

## Questions about Images

We may be interested in measuring the "meanings" that our respondents give to a concept or a word. Meanings are important because they can tell us how people will act toward the related objects. Also, many of the meanings that people assign to everyday objects are determined by how these objects are presented in the mass media. Studies of social stereotyping, for example, suggest that the meaning of the concept "woman" has been heavily influenced by traditional and stereotyped portrayals of women in the media.[15]

To measure meanings, Charles Osgood devised a scale known as the *semantic differential*. The scale consists of several bipolar (opposite) adjectives, with seven points in between. The respondents are given a concept and are then asked to check the point on each biopolar scale that best describes the object to them. An example of a semantic differential scale is the following:

Check the point between each pair of adjectives below that best describes television to you.
good _____ _____ _____ _____ _____ _____ _____ bad
strong _____ _____ _____ _____ _____ _____ _____ weak
fast _____ _____ _____ _____ _____ _____ _____ slow
active _____ _____ _____ _____ _____ _____ _____ passive

After the ratings are made, a profile of the concept can be drawn that would indicate that concept's image to the respondents. According to Osgood, there are three dominant, independent dimensions that people use to describe concepts. These dimensions are the evaluative factor (whether a concept is good or bad), the potency factor (the strength of the concept), and the activity factor (whether the concept is active or passive).[16]

## Data Collection

After the questionnaire has been constructed, the next step is to collect the data from the sample. There are several ways of administering the questionnaire (or asking our respondents the questions). Some of these follow.

### Personal Interviews

The most direct way of getting information from our respondents is by personally interviewing them, using the questionnaire as a guide. Interviewers are sent to each person identified in the sample, and each person is asked the question on the questionnaire. An advantage of the personal interview is that we are usually able to get a better sample than by other methods. If only persons on the sample list are interviewed and if we interview all of them, then random samples are better secured. Another advantage of personal interviews is that trained interviewers can elicit responses to questions that respondents may not understand or may not be willing to answer. Most people respond favorably to polite, professional interviewers. We are thus better able to secure *completed* questionnaires by using personal interviews.

A major disadvantage of personal interviews is that they are expensive in both time and money. Also, there are some respondents who may react to the interviewer instead of the questionnaire. If the interviewer is liked, then the respondent may give the response that he or she thinks is expected. Finally, respondents are more likely to doubt the anonymity of their responses in personal interviews. Very often the only way that some respondents may be willing to answer controversial questions is by assuring them that their answers will be kept confidential. This is more difficult to do in personal interviews than in mailed or self-administered questionnaires.

### Telephone Interviews

Some interviews are done over the phone instead of in person. An advantage of this method is that information can be acquired in a short period of time. It is often possible to conduct and complete a survey using phone interviews within a few hours of an event, such as a political broadcast. In addition, phone interviews are less costly than personal interviews.

A major criticism of phone interviews is that the people listed in a phone directory are not representative of the general population. Low-income groups and the elderly are less likely to have phones than the general population. Also, people with unlisted numbers will not be represented in the sample. However, recent data indicate that phones today are available to 93 percent of U.S. households. Also, new techniques of drawing random phone samples (such as random digit dialing) give better samples and can include unlisted numbers in the population.[17]

### Self-administered Questionnaires

We can secure data by leaving the questionnaires with the respondents and collecting them after they have been completed. Instructions are given in the questionnaire, and the respondents answer the questions on their own. The researcher may be present in the room when the questionnaire is answered, but he or she does not read out the questions to the respondent and simply collects completed questionnaires.

There are several advantages to this method of collecting sample data. It is less expensive than personal interviews, since the questionnaires can be administered to large numbers of individuals simultaneously. Respondents generally have greater confidence in the anonymity of self-administered questionnaires than personal interviews. They are less likely to give socially desirable responses, since they can be assured that the responses will not be identified as coming from particular individuals.

However, self-administered questionnaires have some disadvantages. The sample resulting from self-administered questionnaires is usually less representative than in personal interviews, since there is more of a possibility that respondents will not answer the questionnaire or will only answer portions of it. Also, some respondents may not be capable of answering the questionnaire without help from an interviewer. This group includes the elderly, children, and people with little formal education.

### Mailed Questionnaires

Questionnaires are sometimes mailed to respondents. The advantage of this type of data collection is that we can reach special groups difficult to reach by phone or personal interviews, such as business executives, politicians, and physicians. The main drawback of mailed questionnaires is that returns are low, usually from 10 to 50 percent. The resulting sample is often less representative of the population than in other data collection methods. People who do return questionnaires are often more interested in the topic of the survey, those with more education, and those who feel strongly about the issues.[18]

### Coding, Analysis, and Interpretation of Data

The last steps in survey research are coding the data for computer analysis, testing the hypotheses using appropriate statistical tests, and interpreting the results. Responses to the questionnaire are assigned numerical values and punched on IBM cards to facilitate data analysis. We can then write computer programs to analyze the data or use packaged (prewritten) programs. Survey results are usually analyzed using descriptive statistics (such as averages and percentages), cross tabulations, and correlations. To interpret the data, we should answer the questions that were asked in the objectives of the study or test our hypotheses.[19]

In evaluating surveys, we ask the following questions: Are the objectives or hypotheses clearly stated? Do they have a basis in theory or practical concerns of the investigator? Can the selection of the population be theoretically justi-fied? Is the sample adequate for the study's purposes? Did the investigator specify sampling error and confidence level of the sample? Was the sample drawn randomly? Were there validity and reliability tests of the question-naire? Do the questions and analyses of responses relate directly to the objec-tives or hypotheses of the study? Were data collection methods adequate? Were the conclusions justified by the data?

## CONTENT ANALYSIS

The last mass communication research method we will discuss is content analysis. According to Berelson, a pioneer in content analysis research, con-tent analysis is "a research technique for the objective, systematic and quan-titative description of the manifest content of communication."[20] By commu-nication content,Berelson meant "that body of meanings through symbols (verbal, musical, gestural), which makes up the communication itself." Thus, we can apply the techniques of content analysis to the study of any book, magazine, newspaper, individual story or article, motion picture, news broad-cast, or television program.

We can use content analysis simply to describe the contents of a message. Or we can compare media, such as television with newspapers. We can also study trends or changes in content of a medium over time. Finally, we can analyze international differences in communication content. As with any other research method, the problem in content analysis should be stated in hypothesis or objective form.

The first decision in content analysis is to select the unit of analysis, or portions of the message, that are to be analyzed. The most commonly used unit is the item itself, or the whole natural unit used by the producers of the material. Examples of items are newspaper stories, magazine articles, radio newscasts, and television programs. The entire item may be analyzed, such as a news story, or only portions of it, such as television program segments.

After deciding on the unit of analysis, we must decide whether we are to sample from all units to be studied (the population) or to study the entire population. When we are studying in depth the contents of messages that may be affected by outside events occurring over short periods of time, it is best to study the entire population. For example, a study of news coverage of the events in Iran in 1979 by the *New York Times* would require analysis of all issues of the newspaper in 1979. As the purpose of our study becomes more general and broader in scope and as the time period and number of messages increase, sampling may be useful. For example, if we wished to describe the types of news items (news categories) reported in the *New York Times* over the last five years, we would sample issues from each year instead of analyzing all issues. As with surveys, sample size will depend on margin of error, confi-dence level, and variability of the contents being studied.

The next step in content analysis is to define the categories of analysis, or the categories that will be used to describe the contents. Some categories often used are subject matter (what is said as, for example, news categories of crime, economics, weather), direction (whether a particular item is pro, con, or neutral, as in analysis of news coverage of a political candidate), values (whether certain values are found in the contents, such as achievement motivation, fatalism, materialism), and theme (whether certain themes are found in the communication content, such as prejudice, violence, and stereotypes). Categories should be clearly defined before the study. They should fit the needs of the study, be exhaustive (describe all of the material being considered), and be mutually exclusive (a coded item should be placed in only *one* category). We usually pretest categories to determine whether they fulfill all these requirements.

After categories have been defined, we can begin the analysis. We will need at least three coders working independently. We cannot be sure that ratings by only one coder were objective—that they were not affected by his or her values, experiences, and needs. With three coders, we can check on the objectivity of the ratings by computing a coefficient of agreement. This is the degree to which coders agree on assignment of items to categories, or on their ratings of the items. Generally, we require 80 percent or more agreement. If there is high agreement, then we can say that our procedures and the categories were valid.

As with any research method, the last step in content analysis is data reduction and analysis of results. We often present results using descriptive statistics such as means and percentages and cross tabulations. We should always relate our results back to the study's original hypotheses or objectives.

The main criteria in evaluating content analysis studies are the adequacy and clarity of the cateogires and the degree of agreement among coders. As in any study, we should also be concerned with internal and external validity and whether the objectives were met.

## SUMMARY

Research methods are the design and procedures used by the investigator to gather information for hypothesis testing. Research methods can be evaluated using two general criteria—internal validity and external validity.

If a study has internal validity, then we can be reasonably sure that $X$ is related to $Y$ or that $X$ causes $Y$. Three conditions are necessary to show causal relationships: concomitant variation, time order of the variables, and control of extraneous variance.

External validity refers to the representativeness or generalizability of the study. Examples of external validity are population validity, ecological validity, content validity, and predictive validity.

Significance in hypothesis testing refers to the probability of accepting the research hypothesis when the null hypothesis is true. An acceptable significance level is set arbitrarily in the social sciences at 5 percent.

Three research methods are often used by communication researchers: experiments, field surveys, and content analysis.

Experiments are research designs in which the investigator has complete control over the independent variable and where dependent variables are measured after introduction of the presumed cause, usually in an artificial setting. Experiments have high internal validity but low external validity. Steps in experimentation include hypothesis formulation, selection of subjects, selection of design, operationalization of variables, random assignment of subjects, introduction and measurement of variables, and analysis and interpretation of results.

In field surveys, we get information about a large number of people or objects by studying a small proportion of them. Surveys often have high external validity but low internal validity. The following steps are followed in survey research: problem formulation, sampling, questionnaire construction, data collection, and coding, analysis, and interpretation of data.

In content analysis we attempt to code and describe objectively the content of communication. Content analysis involves selecting a unit of analysis, defining categories, sampling, and coding.

## REVIEW QUESTIONS

**1.** Look through recent issues of *Journalism Quarterly, Journal of Communication, Public Opinion Quarterly, Journal of Broadcasting, Communication Research,* or any other communication journal. Pick out one example each of an experiment, a survey, and a content analysis. For each study outline the steps taken by the author or authors from problem formulation to conclusion. Evaluate the external and internal validity of each study.

**2.** Given the research question, Does reading violent comic books lead to greater aggression among children? design a laboratory experiment *and* a field survey to investigate this problem.

## ENDNOTES

1. D. T. Campbell and J.C. Stanley, *Experimental and Quasi-Experimental Designs for Research* (Chicago: Rand McNally, 1966).
2. Hubert Blalock, Jr., *Social Statistics* (New York: McGraw-Hill, 1972), pp. 151–175.
3. *Ibid.,* p. 157.
4. William Hays, *Statistics* (New York: Holt, Rinehart and Winston, 1963), pp. 329–335.
5. Campbell and Stanley, *op. cit.*
6. Fred Kerlinger, *Foundations of Behavioral Research* (New York: Holt, Rinehart and Winston, 1973), pp. 395–409.

7. *Ibid.;* also Clair Seltiz, Lawrence Wrightsman, and Stuart Cook, *Research Methods in Social Relations* (New York: Holt, Rinehart and Winston, 1976).
8. Hays, *op. cit.*
9. Philip Zimbardo and Ebbe Ebbesen, *Influencing Attitudes and Changing Behavior* (Reading, Mass.: Addison-Wesley, 1969), pp. 129–135.
10. The notion of correlation, or concomitant variation, will often be used in this book. The linear variation between two observations, or two measured characteristics, can be summarized using a statistic called the Pearsonian correlation coefficient (or Pearsonian correlation), symbolized by $r$. The Pearsonian $r$ has a range of $+1$ to $-1$. An $r$ of $+1$ indicates perfect linear variation between the variables in a *common* direction—that is, as values of one variable increase, so do values of the other variable. An $r$ of $-1$ indicates perfect linear variation in opposite directions; as values of one variable increase, values of the other variable decrease. An $r$ of $0$ indicates that there is no linear relationship. An additional interpretation of $r$ is its square, which is the proportion of one variable *explained or accounted for by the other variable.* An $r$ of 1, interpreted this way, means that one variable is totally accounted for by the other variable ($1^2 = 1$, or 100 percent).

   The influence of other variables on the two variables being analyzed can be statistically controlled for in correlational analysis by computation of partial correlations. A partial correlation is the $r$ between two variables, say $X$ and $Y$, controlling for other variables included in the analysis. For example, a partial $r$ of $-.6$ between education and TV viewing controlling for income means that the linear relationship between education and TV viewing is $-.6$ after the influence of income on both education and TV viewing has been acounted for.

   The significance of correlation coefficients can also be computed. Significance here indicates the probability of making an error in saying that there is a linear relationship between the variables analyzed when, in reality, there is none.

   For a more detailed discussion of correlational analysis, see Hubert Blalock, *Social Statistics* (New York: McGraw-Hill, 1972), pp. 361–464.
11. W. G. Cochran, *Sampling Techniques,* 2nd ed. (New York: Wiley, 1963); also L. Kish, *Survey Sampling* (New York: Wiley, 1965).
12. Cochran, *op. cit.*
13. Selltiz, Wrightsman, and Cook, *op cit,* pp. 291–330.
14. For a more detailed discussion of Likert scales, see R. A. Likert, "A Technique for the Measurement of Attitudes," *Archives of Psychology,* no. 140, 1932.
15. Effects of media stereotypes on our social stereotypes are discussed in Chapter 19 of this text.
16. For a more detailed discussion of the semantic differential, see C. Osgood, C. Suci, and P. Tannenbaum, *The Measurement of Meaning* (Urbana: University of Illinois Press, 1957).
17. For a recent discussion of random digit dialing, see K. Michael Cummings, "Random Digit Dialing: A Sampling Technique for Telephone Surveys," *Public Opinion Quarterly,* Summer 1979, pp. 233–234.
18. Selltiz, Wrightsman and Cook, *op. cit.,* pp. 291–330.
19. A popular packaged computer program in the social sciences is Norman Nie, C. Hull, Jean Jenkins, Karen Steinbrenner, and Dale Bent, *Statistical Package for the Social Sciences,* 2nd ed. (New York: McGraw-Hill, 1975).
20. Bernard Berelson, *Content Analysis in Communication Research* (Glencoe, Ill.: Free Press, 1952).

# 4

# COMMUNICATION AND MASS COMMUNICATION_____

In Chapter 1 we defined the *discipline* of mass communication as the scientific study of the mass media, the messages they generate, the audiences they attempt to reach, and their effects on these audiences. In this chapter we will take a closer look at communication and mass communication as research concepts. Although communication is not unique to humans (some animals are able to communicate to each other), we will limit our discussion to human communication, since mass communication is a distinctively human activity. To understand mass communication, we should first be able to define communication.

Communication as a subject of scientific inquiry is not unique to the field of mass communication. Psychologists, political scientists, anthropologists, mathematicians, engineers, sociologists, and speech communicators all study communication. This is not surprising, since communication is the fundamental social process of humans. It is needed to build up any form of social or group structure. Thus, disciplines concerned in any way with human societies, groups, and behavior include the study of communication. This has led to many definitions and uses of the concept. Let us examine typical definitions from various fields.

Charles Cooley in 1909 gave this sociological definition:

> By communication is here meant the mechanism through which human relations exist and develop—all the symbols of the mind, together with the means of conveying them through space and preserving them in time. It includes the expression of the face, attitude and gesture, the tones of the voice, words, writing, printing, railways, telegraphs, telephones, and whatever else may be the latest achievement in the conquest of space and time.[1]

Two engineers, Claude Shannon and Warren Weaver, defined communication in this way.

> The word communication will be used here in a very broad sense to include all the procedures by which one mind may affect another. This, of course, involves not only written and oral speech, but also music, the pictorial arts, the theatre, the ballet, and in fact all human behavior.[2]

Another engineering-based definition is given by E. Colin Cherry.

Communication . . . is that which links any organism together. Here "organism" may mean two friends in converstaion, newspapers and their reading public, a country and its postal service and telephone system. At another level it may refer to the nervous system of an animal, while at another it may relate to a civilization and its culture. When communication ceases, the organism breaks up.[3]

S. S. Stevens, a behavioral psychologist, defines communication as follows.

. . . the discriminatory response of an organism to a stimulus. This definition says that communication occurs when some environmental disturbance (the stimulus) impinges on an organism and the organism does something about it (makes a discriminatry response). If the stimulus is ignored by the organism, there has been no communication. The test is differential reaction of some sort. The message that gets no response is not a communication.[4]

A simple definition is given by Harold Lasswell.

A convenient way to describe an act of communication is to answer the following questions: Who Says What In Which Channel To Whom With What Effect.[5]

Wilbur Schramm, a pioneer in mass communication research, offered this definition.

When we communicate we are trying to share information, an idea, or an attitude. Communication always requires at least three elements—the source, the message, and the destination.[6]

This list is by no means complete, since there are countless other definitions. However, it is a representative sampling of definitions from the very broad to the specific. The definitions by Cooley and by Shannon and Weaver include in the study of communication all forms of human interaction or behaviors that can affect another person, intentially or unintentionally. These include not only communication using a verbal language, but also gestures, facial expressions, paintings, pictures, the arts, and technology. Stevens offers still a broader definition. To him, communication occurs whenever an organism reacts or responds to some object or stimulus in the environment, which may not even be from another person. Thus, a person taking shelter from a thunderstorm, or blinking the eyes in response to a flash of lightning, is communicating. To Cherry, communication binds two persons (or organisms) *together* in a relationship that can exist only so long as communication continues. Schramm specifies the nature of this relationship—it is *sharing* of information. He defines information, as Shannon and Weaver did, as "any content that reduces uncertainty." Lasswell identifies the necessary components in communication as source, message, channel, receiver, and effect, a model that has been accepted by many students of mass communication. Although these definitions vary in the number and kinds of behaviors that would be included in the study of communication, they all share a concern with effect or response: communication occurs only if the organism reacts to the message or stimulus in some way.

We will now turn our attention to three specific models of communication that have influenced the work of many mass communication researchers. The first model, by Shannon and Weaver, is often referred to as the "mathematical model" of communication. It is primarily concerned with the mechanical transmission of messages from one point to another and expresses relationships between communication components in mathematical form. The second model, by Theodore Newcomb, is known as a "social psychological" model of communication. It specifies the relationships between two people or groups that must be present if communication is to occur and the effects on the communicative act if any of these relationships is changed. The third model is by Westley and MacLean, two researchers whose primary field is mass communication. Their model clearly identifies the source, message, channel, and receiver components in communication and illustrates how messages are encoded and decoded by sources and receivers.

## SHANNON AND WEAVER'S MATHEMATICAL MODEL

In 1949, two electronic engineers, Claude E. Shannon and Warren Weaver, published *The Mathematical Theory of Communication* in which they discussed a model of communication that has since had considerable influence on communication researchers. Their model provided a precise and quantified measure of information. This enables researchers to measure the accuracy of transmission of information from sender to receiver and to identify the conditions that could increase, or decrease accuracy.[7]

Shannon and Weaver were primarily interested in technical problems of electronic communication, such as the relation between the speed of transmission of a message and the fidelity of its transmission, and in improving the quality of transmission of the human voice over the telephone. The model they formulated, however, can be applied to most forms of human communication. This model is shown in Figure 4.1.

In Shannon and Weaver's model an information source selects a message from a set of messages available to him or her. This message is changed by the transmitter into a signal, which is then sent over the channel to the receiver, which changes the transmitted signal back into the message and then sends it on to the destination. When I talk to you in the classroom, for example, my brain is the information source, my vocal system is the transmitter, varying sound pressure is the signal, air is the channel, your ear nerve is the receiver, and your brain is the destination. In the process of transmission the message may be unintentionally distorted or changed. These distortions are called noise. Distortions often occur in the channel, such as static in a radio set, a fuzzy picture in a television set, or a garbled voice over the telephone. Noise could also occur as the information source encodes the message for transmis-

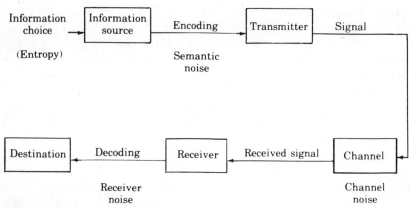

**FIGURE 4.1.** A mathematical model of communication. Adapted from Shannon and Weaver, 1949.

sion. This is called semantic noise. Examples are distortions of meaning unintentionally produced by the information source by misleading use of language or other symbols. A third source of noise is in the receiver. Receiver noise is message distortion arising from decoding of the message. Subjective language or symbol interpretations are a major cause of receiver noise.

The Shannon and Weaver model measures the accuracy of message transmission in a given communication system. To do this, Shannon and Weaver introduced the concept of entropy, which is a quantitative measure of information.

Shannon and Weaver define information as the amount of choice or freedom that the source has in constructing messages. Sources can transmit more information in a message if they had many, instead of only few, messages to choose from, or if there was a greater "randomness of choice." Shannon and Weaver refer to the degree of randomness as *entropy*. When there is high entropy, the receiver will find it difficult to guess correctly what the message of the source will be, since many messages can be sent. Thus, high entropy leads to greater uncertainty in the receiver. This uncertainty can be reduced by a message from the source. The amount of information in a message is the amount of uncertainty it reduces. The greater the uncertainty or entropy, the more information a message can transmit. Let us illustrate with an example.

If all I could say was yes or no, and if each word were *equally* probable to be used in a message, then you would already have a 50 percent chance of guessing what my message will be at any given time. In this situation there is not a great deal of uncertainty or randomness in what I could communicate to you, since my choices are limited to two words. Entropy is low, and any message I sent to you would be "low" in information content (you would have been able to guess the correct message five times out of ten). Suppose, however, that instead of only two words I could say ten words. If my message consisted of only one word at a time, and if all of the words were equally likely to be used in the message, then your chance of selecting the correct word (message) at any given time would only be one-tenth, or one in ten times. There is greater randomness in my choice of messages. Any message I send you will contain more information, since greater uncertainty is reduced by it.

Shannon and Weaver use this notion of uncertainty or entropy to measure information in probabilistic terms. In the simplest communication situation, where all messages are in code and consist only of combinations of two signals (for example, "1" or "0," or the "dit" and "dah" in the Morse code), then for a message $n$ signals long the total number of distinct signals that can be sent is $2^n$. For example, if we wanted a message of only two signals, and each message would be a combination of two signals ("1" and "0"), then the total number of distinct messages would be $2^2$, or 4. These messages would be 10, 01, 11, and 00. If we knew that there were $2^n$ different messages possible, our chance of correctly guessing the contents of any one message correctly would be one in $2^n$. We could take the number $2^n$ as a measure of the amount of uncertainty, entropy, or information. However, to facilitate comparisons between different messages, Shannon and Weaver suggest that instead of taking $2^n$ as our measure of information, we use the logarithm of that number.[8] Using this procedure, it becomes possible to compute the amount of information per signal or message from any source in which the occurrence of one signal does not influence the occurrence of another. This allows us to calculate source, channel, and receiver information capacities and to determine the accuracy of information transmission from source to destination. Perfect communication, according to this model, is when amount of information transmitted by the source is equal to amount of information received at the destination. When these amounts are not equal, the channel may not be capable of transmitting the information or there may be sources of noise (distortion).

As we have seen, Shannon and Weaver's mathematical model provides us with a system that measures communication effectiveness in purely objective, quantified terms. However, we should not forget that their model deals only with the technical aspects of communication and with the amount, not the contents or substance, of information transmitted. Meanings of messages are not treated directly in the model at all. Also, the communication process in their model is linear; it has a starting point and an end. This model has been useful in providing mass communication researchers with a purely objective approach to measuring effectiveness but, in itself, it has not been sufficient to describe or analyze the various subjective processes in human communication.

## NEWCOMB'S SOCIAL PSYCHOLOGICAL MODEL

While Shannon and Weaver's model is a purely mechanistic, technical representation of communication, Newcomb's social psychological model (often referred to as the A-B-X model) looks at relationships between the participants and the *object* of communication and how these relationships affect and

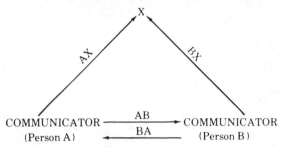

OBJECT
(Topic of Communication)

X

AX    BX

COMMUNICATOR  ——— AB ———▸  COMMUNICATOR
(Person A)      ◂——— BA ———      (Person B)

**FIGURE 4.2.** A social-psychological model of communication. Adapted from Newcomb, 1953.

are affected by communication. Newcomb is not so much concerned with *how* communication takes place as he is with *when* it will occur and its *effects* on the participants.[9]

Newcomb assumes that in any communication situation, at least two persons will be communicating about a common object or topic. A major function of communication is to enable them to maintain simultaneous orientation toward one another and toward the object of communication. Orientation is how we feel about objects or persons and our cognitive awareness of them. Feelings are often described by positive (+) or negative (−) attitudes. A positive attitude is characterized by liking and attraction, a negative attitude by disliking and avoidance. Cognitive awareness refers to our perceived knowledge of the objects or persons—how much we think we know about them. Communication enables the participants to determine what their orientations are toward each other and to the object of communication. These relationships are illustrated in Figure 4.2.

In this model, persons A and B are communicating about a common object in their environment, X. Assuming that both A and B "know" about X and about each other (that is, some previous knowledge is assumed), the relationships or orientations between A and B, A and X, and B and X can be summarized as positive or negative attitudes. These attitudes are indicated in the model by AB (A's attitude toward B), BA (B's attitude toward A), AX (A's attitude toward X), and BX (B's attitude toward X). At any given point in time, the orientations in this communication system may either be *symmetrical* or *asymmetrical*. There is symmetry when A's and B's orientation toward X are similar. To illustrate, let us say that you are person A and I am person B. We are engaged in a conversation about the good and bad effects on viewers of television. Television, then, is the X in the model. In this situation, I will have an orientation toward you (BA) that could be one of either liking or disliking, and you will have an orientation toward me (AB). Also, I will have an orientation or attitude toward television, and so will you. When our orientations are similar toward television (as for example, when we both agree on what the good and bad points of TV are and agree that TV is a bad influence on viewers), then there is symmetry in the system. Symmetry is both a common understanding of what we are communicating about (cognitive orientation) and an agreement on how we feel about it (affective orientation). When there is disagreement, there is no symmetry.

Symmetry is a central concept in Newcomb's model. He suggests that in a communication situation there is a "persistent strain" toward symmetry, or that the communicators will be motivated to arrive at similar evaluations and understanding of X. There are several reasons for this desire to achieve symmetry. First, symmetry allows each person to calculate readily the other's behavior. That is, interaction between A and B will be more predictable and will require less effort. It is easier to interact with another person when there is agreement than when there is disagreement. Second, symmetry reinforces one's orientations toward X. Person A can convince himself that his under-standing of and feelings towards X are "correct" because B agrees with him. This is a comfortable feeling for most people. Thus, symmetry is reassuring and comfortable. It also facilitates continued interaction between A and B, since people who agree with each other are generally attracted to each other.

The strength of the strain toward symmetry, according to Newcomb, varies with attraction or liking between the communicators (A and B) and with intensity of their attitudes toward X. The greater the attraction between A and B, the more each person will be motivated to achieve symmetry with regard to X. If I liked you a lot and we disagreed on X (television), I would be motivated to arrive at an evaluation of TV similar to yours. Similarly, the more strongly I feel about X, the more I will be motivated to arrive at symme-try. Symmetry, according to Newcomb, is primarily reached through commu-nication between A and B. Thus, his predictions regarding symmetry also hold for the probability of communication between A and B. Assuming an initial lack of symmetry, the greater the attraction between A and B, and the stronger the intensity of their attitudes toward X, the more likely it is that communication will occur between them. The effects on the system (rela-tionships between A, B, and X) of increased communication could be one of the following (let us assume that *you* are A in the model).

1. Arrive at an agreement with B regarding X (to achieve symmetry):
    (a) By changing B's orientation to agree with yours.
    (b) By changing your orientation to agree with B's.
    (c) By convincing yourself that B really agrees with you on X (this is usually referred to as cognitive distortion).
2. Changing your orientation toward B.
    (a) Change your attraction (or liking) for B.
    (b) Change your judgment of your liking for B.
3. Tolerate the disagreement (asymmetry) without change.

In our previous example, if you and I disagree on our orientations toward TV (mine is negative, yours is positive) and if you liked me, then this would be an asymmetrical state. Since you liked me and since the topic is important to both of us, there would be a strain toward symmetry and we would communicate (talk) about it. The results of our communication could be one of the following: (1) you could convince me that TV was a positive influence on viewers; (2) I could convince you that TV was a negative influence; (3) you could convince yourself that I agreed with you regardless of whether I *really* did or not; (4) you could hold on to your initial orientation toward television but change your orientation toward me from liking to disliking; (5) you could convince yourself that you really did not like me in the first place and maintain your original orientation toward TV; (6) we both could "agree to disagree" and tolerate the asymmetry.

Newcomb's model is useful because it tells us when communication is likely to take place and the possible effects of communication. Although it was formulated primarily to explain the interaction between persons involved in face-to-face communication, many of its principles (for example, "strain toward symmetry") have been applied to persuasion studies involving mass communication. A major weakness, though, is that it does not explain how communication works. It takes communication as a "given" variable—it simply happens. The next model we will discuss—Westley and MacLean's—combines both the mechanistic and interactional elements in the first two models and gives us some idea about how messages are sent from source to receiver and from receiver to source.

## WESTLEY AND MACLEAN'S GENERAL MODEL

Westley and MacLean's model shown in Figure 4.3, explains both face-to-face and mass communication.[10] Communication begins when B, which may be either a person, group, or social system, feels a need to orient itself with certain objects in its environment ($O_1$ to $O_\alpha$ in the model) at a certain point in time. Westley and MacLean adapt Newcomb's definition of orientation as including both affective (feeling) and cognitive (knowing) relationships with the objects. People or social systems orient themselves with environmental objects to satisfy needs or to solve problems. There are, of course, an infinite number of objects ($O_\alpha$) that B can orient to at any point in time. Because of sensory limitations, our capabilities for ordering and digesting information are limited. B must orient toward Os selectively and pick those that are most likely to give him or her maximum satisfaction. It sometimes happens that B can directly observe the Os and react directly to them ($O_{3B}$ in the model). In this case, no second person or group is needed for B to get its information. B will simply react or respond to O. Communication could be said to have taken place if B *reacts* to an O. Let us illustrate with an example. I am reading a book at home late at night. I hear a loud bang from outside. I immediately feel a need (to satisfy my curiosity) and perceive a possible problem (the noise may be the source of a problem). I go outside to the front of the house. (I select this alternative, since the sound seemed to come from that direction.) I notice that

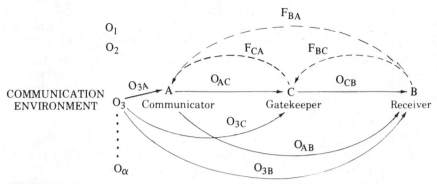

**FIGURE 4.3.** A general model of communication. Adapted from Westley and MacLean, 1957.

it is raining. I look up at the sky. I hear another bang and see a flash of lightning. I decide that thunder was the cause of the sound and go back to reading my book.

It often happens that B will not be able to observe directly some of the objects in his or her environment. (The objects may be beyond their sensory fields.) In this case, B will need to depend on another person or source to orient himself to those objects. In our previous illustration, suppose I heard the bang, went outside, and could see or hear nothing. I stand outside for a few minutes and then see my neighbor standing by his front porch. I walk over to him and he tells me that the house next to him on the other side is on fire and the bang came from it. He also tells me that the noise was probably caused by a gas tank exploding. This information is $O_{AB}$ in the model. My neighbor is the source (A in the model), and I am the receiver (B). We are communicating about the cause of the explosion, (the house on fire, or O).

But what if I went out after hearing the sound and saw the fire *and* my neighbor standing by his house. We very likely would communicate about the fire. We could agree (or disagree) on what was happening and on what to do about it. This is the situation described by Newcomb's A-B-X model. My neighbor (A) and I (B) would be orienting toward a common object (X), the fire.

Now for the final possibility allowed for in the Westley and MacLean model. Suppose I was out of town the night of the fire and arrived home late the next day. I see that the house down the street is damaged. There is no one around to ask about what had happened. I am curious, so I turn on the TV set to watch the late news. The newcaster tells me all about the fire ($O_{CB}$).

In this situation, both my neighbor (A) and the object (the fire) were beyond my sensory field. The information, therefore, is communicated to me by a television newscaster (C in the model). C becomes a gatekeeper of information, a relayer of messages. C may depend heavily on As who were able to observe the event (O) directly. Most mass media perform this gatekeeper function. They decide what information is important or not and relay important information to large audiences.

This, then, is how communication works in the Westley and MacLean model. It explains communication at the one person (a person reacting to objects in the environment), two persons (A and B orienting toward O), and the mass communication levels. Additionally, it provides for feedback from B to A ($F_{BA}$ in the model), B to C ($F_{BC}$), and C to A ($F_{CA}$). Feedback is communication from the receiver to the source to ask a question, evaluate the message, agree, disagree, or offer more information.

Some examples of feedback in the Westley and MacLean model are the following: letters by readers to the editor of a newspaper ($F_{BC}$ in the model); responses of a television viewer to a Nielson survey ($F_{BC}$); a newspaper reader calling a reporter to find out why his or her story was "biased" ($F_{BA}$); a newspaper editor telling a news writer to revise a story because it is poorly written ($F_{CA}$). Feedback helps sources or gatekeepers correct themselves.

## A TRANSACTIONAL MODEL OF COMMUNICATION

We have discussed three models of communication, each with its own strengths and weaknesses. In Figure 4.4, we present a model that combines elements from these three. Let us take a closer look at this model and see how it explains communication.

Communication begins when a person or a social organization such as a mass medium ($C_1$ in the model) reacts to a stimulus (S) in the environment. The stimulus could be any object in $C_1$'s immediate sensory field (objects that can be sensed directly) or it could be an object from $C_1$'s past experience. $C_1$ could react to an infinite number of stimuli at any given moment. This selection is purposive and is guided by $C_1$'s objectives in initiating the communication act. The objective may simply be to reduce uncertainty in another person's sensory field (as a weather report informing us that there is a 60-percent chance of rain tomorrow). Or, it may be for self-gratification (satisfaction of $C_1$'s needs), such as an advertiser, motivated to increase sales, telling us that their brand of toothpaste "cleans teeth the whitest." In any case, communication in our model is always purposive. The selection of objects that $C_1$ communicates about to the receiver is not random. $C_1$ initiates communication to achieve some objective.

$C_1$'s selection of objects for communication also depends on its perception of that object. Perception refers to mental activity involved in knowing and understanding.[11] Before we can communicate about any object, we must first be aware that the object exists. Our perception of objects is influenced by culture. A person's culture is the system of shared beliefs, values, symbols, language, and patterns of behavior that he or she shares with a group, community, or society. Perception and culture are important elements in our model because they determine what messages will be sent, why, and how.[12]

Once the stimulus has been perceived and selected for communication, $C_1$ must transform it into symbols shared by the intended receiver. This process

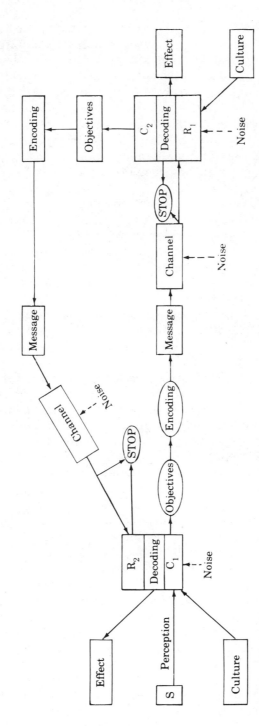

**FIGURE 4.4.** A transactional model of communication.

is called encoding. It often involves, but is not limited to, the use of language. Stimuli can also be encoded in pictures, paintings, sculpture, body movements, and architecture. What is important is that the symbols used should be shared by the intended receiver. Communication would obviously not be possible if the symbols used by $C_1$ could not be understood by the receiver.

We have described the mental and perceptual processes that occur *within* $C_1$ when $C_1$ encodes messages. When $C_1$ is a person, these processes are referred to as *intrapersonal* communication. Intrapersonal communication is usually studied by perceptual and cognitive psychologists interested in information processing by people.

What happens after the stimuli are encoded? The result is a message, which has a form and existence separate from the communicator. The message may be a news story, a television show, or a lecture. It is $C_1$'s translation of the stimulus in a form that can be transmitted to the receiver, using some medium or channel. In face-to-face communication the channel is air. In mass communication the message is sent by a television or radio set, a newspaper, a book, or some other mass medium.

The destination of the original message can be a person, group, or social organization $(R_1)$. If the message does not *physically* reach $R_1$, then the process STOPs. Communication has not occurred. If the message reaches $R_1$, then $R_1$ will decode it. Decoding refers to those perceptual and cognitive processes leading to awareness, understanding, and interpretation of the message. As with the source $(C_1)$, $R_1$'s culture will influence its decoding of the message.

After decoding the message, $R_1$ has at least three alternatives. First, it can ignore the message and not react to it. (An example of this is when an editor of a magazine reads your manuscript and then throws it in the wastebasket). When this happens the process STOPs. As in the first STOP, communication has not occurred. $R_1$, however, may respond to the message. If $R_1$ is *changed* in any way at all by the message, then we say that it has responded, and its response is the message's *effect*. $R_1$'s response may be voluntary or involuntary, conscious, or unconscious. The key element is *change*. We ask: Has there been a change in the receiver after decoding the message? This change can be a reduction of uncertainty brought about by new knowledge, arousal of an emotion (joy, sadness, anger, fear), motivations to action (as the desire to buy a new automobile), or a change in attitudes and behavior. Quite often, $R_1$'s response may be involuntary. A child, for example, may not want to learn about eating habits from TV commercials, but she may learn anyway. Also, $R_1$ may not be conscious that it has responded (been changed) by the message. (A child may not even be aware that he or she is learning about eating habits from TV commercials.) As long as a change in $R_1$ can be objectively measured, we say that *communication has occurred*. In the absence of a response we conclude that the attempt at communication by $C_1$ has failed. From the viewpoint of $C_1$, communication is *successful* to the extent that the observed response in $R_1$ corresponds to $C_1$'s objectives in initiating the communication act.

A third alternative for $R_1$ at this point (after decoding the message) is to encode and send a message to the original source. This is usually called feedback in other models. Thus $R_1$ becomes, in this second stage of the process, a communicator ($C_2$). As with $C_1$, $C_2$ will have an objective in sending a message back to the original source. It may be to report on $C_2$'s response to the original message ("I agree" or "I disagree"), to ask for clarification ("What did you say?") or for more information ("What other attributes does your toothpaste have?"), to offer more information or to correct the original message. Thus, the process begins all over again, with $C_2$ sending its message through a channel to $R_2$ (the original source now acting as receiver). If the message does not reach $R_2$, then communication stops. After decoding the message, $R_2$ may choose not to react to it (in which case communication stops), or it may respond to the message. As with $R_1$, any change in $R_2$ that can be attributed to decoding of $C_2$'s message is the *effect* of that message. Very often, this response may be to correct the original message (a common function of feedback) and send the corrected message back to the original destination. (A magazine article, resubmitted after the editor suggests revisions, is an example of this.) Theoretically, communication between two persons (or social organizations) could go on forever.

An important element in the model is *noise*. Shannon and Weaver, in their mathematical model, defined noise as any cause of message distortion within the system. Perfect communication in their model is when information in the message transmitted by the source equals information in the message received at the destination. Shannon and Weaver were concerned only with the *amount* of information delivered and received. In our model we are not only interested in the quantity of information but in its meaning as well. Perfect communication is when the quantity of information delivered is the quantity received and when meanings sent are the meanings received. Because of cultural influences on perception, perfect communication is rarely achieved. Noise in our model is therefore defined as any source of distortion in the quantity and meaning of the message. There are several sources of noise. Within the communicator two common sources are the use (or misuse) of language and selective perception due to cultural factors. A textbook such as this, when written in technical, esoteric jargon, is an example of language noise. An American reporter deeply devoted to the capitalist system who can only see the evils of the Soviet economic system is an example of cultural noise. Source noise is often discernible (if you look for it hard enough) in the messages encoded by the communicator. Some examples are value-laden statements, cultural biases, and the misuse of language.

Another source of noise is the channel. Here we refer to physical distortions of the message—static in the radio, a fuzzy television picture, typographical errors in the newspaper. These sources of noise are more easily recognized than source noise, since the distortions in the message are more apparent.

A third source of noise, and the most difficult to control, is the receiver. Receiver noise can be classified as selective attention, selective perception, and selective retention. For a message to have some effect it must first reach the intended receiver. Various communication principles suggest that this is not easily accomplished. The selective exposure hypothesis from cognitive dissonance theory, for example, predicts that people will avoid information contradicting existing attitudes, choices, and behaviors and will seek out supportive information.[13] Schramm suggest that attention to a particular message is determined by its perceived reward value, perceived punishment value, and effort required.[14] Rewards could be either delayed (learning of a new skill that may be useful in the future) or immediate (arousal of a positive emotion such as joy or excitement). The "punishment value" of a message is the extent to which it can arouse negative emotions such as fear or guilt. According to Schramm, receivers will be receptive to a message if it has high reward value, low punishment value, and if little effort is required to decode it.

Selective perception and selective retention are other types of audience noise. Perception is determined to a large extent by cultural factors. The way we perceive or understand objects in our environment, including communication messages, is influenced by previous experiences, values, and the groups to which we belong.[15] Studies of the television show "All in the Family," for example, indicate that perceptions of Archie and his son-in-law Mike depended on audience bigotry scores. Similarly, selective retention sometimes *reinforces* existing attitudes and behaviors. Thus, even if the message reaches our audience, receiver noise can distort its meaning.

In summary, let us point out the important characteristics of our communication model.

1. Our model looks at communication as a *system* made up of various components (source, message, channel) and behaviors (encoding, decoding, formulating objectives). These components are interdependent. Any change in one component will affect the whole system. A change in source objectives, for example, could affect encoding of the message, choice of a channel, and effects observed in the receiver.

2. Communication is purposive. Communication is initiated deliberately by a source to achieve some effect (response) in the receiver. Observation of different forms of mass communication can show us that mass communication is certainly purposive. Businesses advertise to increase sales. Newspapers publish to inform. Television networks produce shows to entertain and to make money. Editorials are written to change opinions. By limiting our discussion to purposive communication, we are able to measure *effective* communication, thus increasing the practical and theoretical value of the model.

3. Communication is a transaction. It is not what someone does to another person. The distinction between source and receiver is arbitrary, since both are actively involved in the transaction. The original source may affect the receiver, but receivers also often affect sources. Consider, for example, the influence of audience ratings on television producers.

4. Communication is subjective. Perceptions of the objects in our environment and encoding and decoding of messages are all influenced by culture.

## MASS COMMUNICATION

Our discussion of communication has so far focused on intrapersonal and interpersonal communication. Intrapersonal communication deals with the cognitive and perceptual processes involved in encoding and decoding of messages. Interpersonal communication is face-to-face communicaton between two or more persons. In this section we will discuss mass communication.

Mass communication is basically the same process as shown in Figure 4.4. Two interacting components ("source" and "receiver") are involved; messages are encoded, sent through a channel, and decoded; responses in the receiver are observed; feedback allows interaction to continue between source and receiver. However, there are some special characteristics of mass communication that distinguish it from interpersonal communication.

First of these is the nature of the receiver in mass communication. Early definitions of mass communication as a field of study focused on "mass society" as the audience of communication. The concept of mass society was used by sociologists to describe people and their institutions in highly industrialized countries. Kimball Young suggested that, with industrialization,

> there has emerged a vast mass of segregated, isolated individuals, interdependent in all sorts of specialized ways, yet lacking in any central unifying value or purpose.[16]

Leonard Broom and Philip Selznick add:

> The weakening of traditional bonds, the growth of rationality, and the division of labor, have created societies made up of individuals who are only loosely bound together. In this sense the word "mass" suggests something closer to an aggregate than to a tightly knit social group.[17]

Mass society, then, is the milieu within which mass communication functions. Herbert Blumer,[18] using concepts derived from theories of mass society, characterized mass audiences as (1) heterogeneous in composition, its members coming from different groups in society; (2) composed of individuals who do not know each other, who are spatially separated from one another, and who cannot interact with one another; and (3) having no leadership or formal organization.

This early concept of the "mass audience" led to studies that considered the audience to be made up of isolated individuals who did not interact with each other and who did not share common expectations of the media derived from social interaction. The audience was an aggregate of individuals, which could best be classified not on the basis of group memberships, but according to demographic characteristics such as age, sex, socioeconomic status, and education. The important questions for research were how members of the mass selected their communication (what demographic characteristics explained selections of particular media and media contents) and how the "mass" was affected by the media. The prevailing idea was that the mass audience was passive, unstable, and easily influenced.[19]

More recently researchers have discarded the view of "mass audience" as a passive aggregate of disconnected individuals and instead have emphasized social structures or group affiliations among members of the audience, the social nature of most of our contact with the mass media, and the reciprocal nature of media-audience relationships.[20] Freidson, for example, suggests that mass audiences should be studied as social groups "composed of individuals who have absorbed mass communications into their relatively settled ways of behaving and who, in the real or vicarious company of their fellows, behave towards mass communications in an organized, social manner."[21] Using Freidson's definition of a mass audience, the appropriate research questions are: (1) how does a person's ongoing social relationships (interactions with other people) affect that person's use of the mass media?, and (2) How is the mass media used by audiences to achieve social goals or other gratifications?

Freidson's view of the mass audience is closer to the process described in Figure 4.4 than the earlier "aggregate" view. As in person-to-person communication, the interaction in mass communication is goal directed, transactional, and influenced by the participant's ongoing culture. The main difference is that in mass communication we are considering as the receiver "a vast number of people receiving simultaneously but independently the communications of a very few."[22] This definition of a mass audience, however, is not without its problems. What is "a vast number?" Is the audience in a convention hall a mass audience in the same way that the audience of the six o'clock news on television is one? It would seem that defining mass communication solely on the basis of a "mass audience" is inadequate.

A more useful approach is to consider also the original communicator ($C_1$ in Figure 4.4), and the method by which the message is transmitted to the receiver. In mass communication the communicator is a social organization *capable* of reproducing the message and sending it simultaneously to large numbers of people who are spatially separated. With this definition the actual number of people reached is of secondary importance; what is significant is the communicator's capability to reproduce the message and send it simultaneously to scattered individuals. The communicator in mass communications is often a mass medium—a newspaper, television station or network, magazine or book publisher. It is a social organization because it is made up of many individual communicators with well-defined role responsibilities. (For example, the newspaper reporter gathers facts, and the editor edits copy.) Gerbner offers a definition that focuses on the communicator instead of the audience.

Mass communication is the technologically and institutionally based production and distribution of the most broadly shared continuous flow of messages in industrial societies.[23]

Another characteristic of mass communication that distinguishes it from interpersonal communication is that the messages are sent to the receivers *indirectly*, using some form of mechanical device. In mass communication the source and receiver are not physically in the same place; thus face-to-face or direct interaction is not possible. Also, the message is sent through mechanical devices (such as a radio transmitter) that allow it to be reproduced and distributed to many receivers at the same time.

## WHY COMMUNICATE?

An important characteristic of communication is that it is purposive, or goal directed, both from the viewpoint of the sender of the message and the receiver. The sender has definite objectives in initiating the communicative act. The receiver participates in the communicative act by being receptive to the message to the extent that doing so will fulfill certain goals. Thus, communication is transactional. Both parties (sender and receiver) participate in the transaction, expecting a return for their efforts.

Why do people and social institutions communicate? What do they expect out of the transaction?

To answer these questions, we go back to one of the classic papers on mass communication written by Harold Lasswell in 1948.[24] In "The Structure and Function of Communication in Society," Lasswell discussed three functions or objectives of communication in a community, broadly defined by him as "society." The first function is surveillance. Communication informs the community about threats and opportunities by scanning the immediate and faraway environment. Members of the community are therefore able to extend their knowledge beyond what they can directly experience to places, events, and persons in the distant environment. Successful *control* of the environment requires knowledge of its components. This surveillance function is often attributed today to the mass media.

The second function of communication is "correlation of the components of society in making a response to the environment." The continued existence of the community depends on how effectively it can adapt to its environment. Adaptation requires some form of response to the environment, such as a tribal community building a dam to prevent flooding of its farmlands or a modern nation negotiating a peace treaty with a hostile neighbor. In either case the response, to be effective, must be a concerted effort from members of the community. That is, there must be some agreement or consensus on what the response should be and then some cooperation in carrying it out. Communication, according to Lasswell, accomplishes this in a community. Only through communication can the environmental problem be understood and consensus regarding the appropriate response reached. The mass media in many modern societies attempt to fulfill this correlation function by providing their publics with "a free marketplace of ideas" or with a discussion of the day's issues.

The third function of communication, according to Lasswell, is transmission of the social inheritance. For a community to survive, its members must share common values and must agree on what behaviors and roles are appropriate. The United States survives in its present form today because Americans generally agree on values such as freedom, participation in government, the work ethic, capitalism, and so on. The process by which members of a community are taught appropriate values, behaviors, and roles is called socialization. Communication is necessary for socialization as, for example, from parent to child, school to its students, the mass media to the public, and the government to its polity.

Lasswell analyzed the functions of communication at the *societal* level. The question he asked was, "What does communication do for a community?" His analysis can be adapted to other levels of communication. Figure 4.5 shows the possible communicator and receiver goals in any given communicative act. The communicator in this analysis can be a person, a group of persons, or a mass medium. The receiver also can be a person, a group of persons (a "mass" audience), or a mass medium. Since communication is transactional, our distinction between communicator and receiver is based only on who initiated the communicative act. The communicator initiates and the receiver subsequently can decide whether to participate in the transaction.

In Figure 4.5 the major objective of the communicator is preservation of its system. This system could be an interpersonal relationship between communicator and receiver (as, for example, the relationship between husband and wife) or a relationship between a social group or institution and its members (a

| Communicator's Goals (Preservation of system) | Receiver's Goals (Adaptation to the system; satisfaction of needs) |
| --- | --- |
| 1. To inform | 1. To learn of threats and opportunities; to understand the environment; to test reality; to reach decisions |
| 2. To teach | 2. To acquire skills and knowledge necessary to function effectively in the community; to learn appropriate values, behaviors, and roles for acceptance in the community |
| 3. To persuade | 3. To reach decisions; to adopt appropriate values, behaviors, and roles for acceptance in the community |
| 4. To please; to satisfy receiver needs | 4. To enjoy, relax, be entertained, be distracted from problems |

**FIGURE 4.5.** Functions of communication.

school and its student body, a mass medium and its audience, a government and its polity). From the veiwpoint of the receiver the major objective is adaptation to the system and to "maximize rewards and minimize punishments." The receiver, whether it is a person, social group, or social institution, will belong to an ongoing social system (a marriage partnership, a business, social, or political organization). Continued participation in that system (assuming there is a desire for such) will depend on how well the receiver can adapt to its requirements. Continued participation in the system is not, however, the only reward possible from a communicative relationship. People (and social institutions) have other needs, such as the need to relax and be entertained (in a person) or to make money (in a business organization). This analysis is similar to Schramm's prediction that the message most likely to be attended to by the receiver is one that has high "perceived reward value" and "low punishment value." To maintain ongoing social relationships, the communicator *informs,* which is the transfer of information to the receiver so that the message can be recalled (as, for example, a newspaper story informing readers of an increase in oil prices); *teaches,* which is transmitting information so that it can be used in the subsequent performance of motor or cognitive tasks (a TV program on gardening can teach us how to transplant tomato seedlings); *persuades,* which is convincing the receiver to accept new attitudes or behaviors; and *pleases,* which involves satisfaction of receiver needs.

The corresponding receiver goals are shown in Figure 4-5. They involve the acquisition of information for effective adaptation to the system, to reach decisions, to accept demands from the system, and for enjoyment, entertainment, and distraction from problems.

We presented several models of communication in this chapter. We discussed in detail a model that is transactional and goal directed. The rest of the book will be devoted to an analysis of research dealing with the interaction between communicator and receiver goals. The main question is: To what extent are these goals obtained, and how?

## SUMMARY

Communication as a subject of scientific inquiry is not unique to the field of mass communication. Three models, in particular, have influenced the work of many mass communication researchers—Shannon and Weaver's mathematical model, Newcomb's social psychological model, and Westley and MacLean's general model. These models can be combined into a transactional model, which has been discussed in detail in this chapter.

Although mass and interpersonal communication differ in many ways, both forms are purposive, or goal directed. Communication is effective to the extent that specific goals are attained.

## REVIEW QUESTIONS

1. Using the transactional model, analyze a communication experience in which you were either source or receiver and that you consider to have *failed*. Identify components in this experience and discuss reasons why it failed.

2. Apply the same analysis to a communication experience that you consider to have *succeeded*.

## ENDNOTES

1. Charles Cooley, "The Significance of Communication," in B. Berelson and M. Janowitz (eds.), *Reader in Public Opinion and Communication* (New York: Free Press, 1966), pp. 147–155.

2. Claude Shannon and Warren Weaver, *The Mathematical Theory of Communication* (Urbana: University of Illinois Press, 1949).

3. E. Colin Cherry, *On Human Communication* (New York: Wiley, 1957).

4. As quoted in John Newman, "A Rationale for a Definition of Communication," in Alfred Smith (ed.), *Communication and Culture* (New York: Holt, Rinehart and Winston, 1966), pp. 55–63.

5. Harold Lasswell, "The Structure and Function of Communication in Society," in L. Bryson (ed.), *The Communication of Ideas* (New York: Harper and Row, 1948), pp. 37–51.

6. Wilbur Schramm, "How Communication Works," in W. Schramm (ed.), *The Process and Effects of Mass Communication* (Urbana: University of Illinois Press, 1954), pp. 3–26.

7. Shannon and Weaver, *op. cit.*

8. *Ibid.*

9. Theodore Newcomb, "An Approach to the Study of Communicative Acts," *Psychological Review, 60*, 1953, pp. 193–404.

10. Bruce Westley and Malcolm MacLean, Jr., "A Conceptual Model for Communications Research," *Journalism Quarterly, 34*, 1957, pp. 31–38.

11. Edward Jones and Harold Gerard, *Foundations of Social Psychology* (New York: Wiley, 1967), pp. 131–142.

12. *Ibid.*

13. Leon Festinger, *A Theory of Cognitive Dissonance* (Stanford, Calif.: Stanford University Press, 1957.)

14. Wilbur Schramm, "The Nature of Communication between Humans," in W. Schramm and D. Roberts (eds.), *The Process and Effects of Mass Communication*, 2nd ed. (Urbana: University of Illinois Press, 1974), pp. 3–53.

15. For a discussion of perceptual processes, see David Krech and Richard Crutchfield, "Perceiving the World," in W. Schramm and D. Roberts (eds.), *The Process and Effects of Mass Communication*, 2nd ed. (Urbana: University of Illinois Press, 1971), pp. 233–264.

16. Kimball Young, *Sociology* (New York: American Book, 1949), p. 24.

17. Leonard Broom and Philip Selznick, *Sociology*, 2nd ed. (Evanston, Ill.: Row, Peterson, 1958), p. 38.
18. Herbert Blumer, "Elementary Collective Behavior," in A. McClung Lee (ed.), *New Outline of the Principles of Sociology* (New York: Barnes and Noble, 1939), pp. 185–189.
19. *Ibid.*
20. See, for example, John Corner, "Mass in Communication Research," *Journal of Communication*, Winter 1979, pp. 26–32.
21. Eliot Freidson, "Communications Research and the Concept of the Mass," *American Sociological Review, 18,* 1953, pp. 313–317.
22. Schramm, "The Nature of Communication Between Humans," pp. 49–53.
23. George Gerbner, "Mass Media and Human Communication Theory," in F. E. X. Dance (ed.), *Human Communication Theory* (New York: Holt, Rinehart and Winston, 1967), pp. 40–57.
24. Lasswell, *op. cit.*

# 5

# LEVELS OF ANALYSIS AND THEORIES OF HUMAN BEHAVIOR

Mass communication is a complex phenomenon that can be studied at many levels using different theoretical approaches and methodological tools. Scientific method and empiricism—the methodology emphasized in this book—can be used to analyze mass communication at various levels. In this chapter, we will study these different levels of analysis and then discuss three general theories of human behavior that have influenced mass communication researchers.

## LEVELS OF ANALYSIS

Human behavior, including communication behavior, can be studied at four levels: the individual level, the interpersonal or small-group level, the social-system level, and the cultural-system level.[1]

### The Individual Level

At the individual level (which is also called the intrapersonal or microlevel), human behavior is generally considered to originate and reside primarily in the individual person. Freudian and behavioral psychologists often analyze the actions of people at this level. Freud, for example, traced social actions to infant sexuality and the individual's natural instinct to preserve his or her ego.[2] He explained most human actions as being based on the individual's need to be loved by others and on the individual's suppression of erotic desires.

Behavioral psychologists also study the individual. They are interested in explaining how individuals react to objects (usually called stimuli) in their external environments. They study the relationships between basic psychological processes (such as cognitions, emotions, and motivations) and the physical properties of the individual's external environment. The most common re-search method of the behavioral psychologist is the laboratory experiment, in which stimuli from the social world are controlled. Here is how Proshansky and Seidenberg, two behavioral psychologists, explain the use of the laboratory experiment in studying individual-level variables.

> In the laboratory the effects of social factors are minimized or held constant, and . . . essentially the properties of the basic psychological processes in relation to the physical world are revealed.[3]

Mass communication is often studied at the individual level. Some scholars say that most studies of communication have, indeed, been at this level and that there has been an overemphasis on studying individual communication processes, resulting in a very limited view of communication. At the individual level, we are interested in how the source encodes messages and how the receiver decodes them. Thus, we study communication variables that can help the source become more effective in communication, such as source cred-ibility or believability, message appeals and structure, and media charac-teristics. We are interested in the relationships of these external stimuli to responses in the receiver. The responses most commonly studied at the intra-personal level are attention to the source and to the message, understanding the message, yielding to the source's recommendations (attitude change), re-tention of the message and the source, and overt or behavioral compliance with the source's recommendations. The emphasis is on how the receiver reacts to external communication stimuli. Early mass communication research almost exclusively used the intrapersonal approach. Even today, many re-searchers study communication processes at the intrapersonal level because communication effects can be more easily isolated at this level. For example, it is easier to trace the response of a receiver to a communication stimulus (such as physical attractiveness of the source) if that stimulus were manipulated in the laboratory and if the response were measured at the individual level (such as attention.) Of course, exclusive reliance on analysis at the intrapersonal level in the laboratory to explain communication processes limits the gener-alizability of the findings. However, individual analysis continues to be a pop-ular approach, considering the practical importance of effects analysis in the communication fields. We are interested in educating communication stu-dents to understand basic communication processes and to be better or more effective communicators—whether they are in advertising, journalism, tele-communications, or public relations. Effects analysis at the intrapersonal level provides the raw materials for this component of education in the commu-nication sciences. Part II of this book discusses communication and persua-sion. For the most part, the material in Part II is based on studies of commu-nication processes at the individual level.

## The Interpersonal Level

The second level of analysis is the interpersonal or small-group level. At this level, the researcher is interested not only in the individual but also in the social context in which the individual responds to external stimuli. Social psychologists who study group dynamics are interested in how an individual's social setting constrains, controls, or otherwise influences behavior. Mead explains the influence of interpersonal relationships on individual behavior in this way.

> The self is something which has a development; it is not initially there at birth but arises in the process of social experience and activity, that is, develops in the given individual as a result of his relations to that process as a whole and to other individuals within that process.[4]

The analysis of communication behavior in social settings cannot be over-emphasized; after all, communication almost always takes place in the presence of others. Unfortunately, research at this level in mass communications is lacking. Organizational communications (the study of communication behavior within groups and organizations) is a growing field of research. However, this research usually is undertaken by scholars whose interest in mass communication is only secondary and who have primary interests in organizational and industrial psychology. There is little empirical research on how interpersonal relationships affect the behavior of mass communicators such as news reporters and editors. In this book, the interpersonal level of analysis is represented by our discussion of coorientation in Chapter 13 and by some sections of Chapter 21, "Communication, Mass Communication Organizations, and Social Institutions."

## The Social-System Level

The third level of analysis is the social system. At this level, the unit of analysis is *not* the individual but groups of individuals and characteristics or properties of these groups. The group is considered to be a social system, with physical properties or structures that influence individual behavior. A social group can be a small unit of co-workers, a social class, or a nation-state. The major requirement for an aggregation or collection of persons to be considered a social group is that it should be able to constrain or control the individual. Also, the group should have an existence "outside" of the individual members. The sociologist Durkheim defines groups in this way.

> Whenever . . . elements combine and thereby produce, by the fact of their combination, new phenomena, it is plain that these new phenomena reside not in the original elements but in the totality formed by their union. . . . If, as we may say, this synthesis constituting every society yields new phenomena, differing from those which take place in individual consciousness, we must, indeed, admit that these facts reside exclusively in the very society itself which produces them, and not in its parts, i.e., its members. They are, then, in this sense external to the individual consciousness. Here, then, are ways of acting, thinking, and feeling that present the note-worthy property of existing outside the individual consciousness.
> These types of conduct or thought are not only external to the individual but are, moreover, endowed with coercive power, by virtue of which they impose themselves upon him, independent of his individual will.[5]

Research on human behavior at the social-system level studies how the characteristics of the social structure (sometimes referred to as the *macrostructure*) constrain or influence individual behavior. According to Hernes, another sociologist, social structures have two sets of characteristics: an institutional or collective set and a distributive or aggregate set.[6] The institutional or collective set consists of structural constraints on behavioral alternatives of the individual. They are structural because they can be found in the *physical* or tangible properties of the system. Examples are the reward structure (such as laws), social stratification system, language system, transportation system, political system, and economic system. These properties of the system determine what an individual can and cannot do. They are therefore *constraints* on individual behaviors.

The other set of characteristics of a social structure—the distributive or aggregate set—is made up of the collective outcomes of individual behaviors within the system that, although they originate from individual behaviors, are properties of the system and not of the individuals. Examples are marriage rates, prices, sex ratios, suicide rates, and age structures. In mass communication, examples of distributive characteristics are the distributions of television sets, newspaper copies, and radio receivers within a population (or group), the cost of advertising, various aggregate (averaged or summed) measures of public opinion on current issues, the knowledge gap between individuals with low and high educational levels, and the averaged ratings by people in a community of the importance of public issues (such as in agenda-setting research). These are characteristics of groups or collections of individuals and not of any one individual within the group. It does not make sense, for example, to refer to an individual's suicide rate or knowledge gap. These are characteristics of groups or social structures to which the individual belongs.

There has been a rejuvenation of research at the social-system level in mass communications. Recent interest in structural constraints on the communication behaviors of individuals is evident in studies of communication organizations.[6] In this book, analysis of mass communication at the social-system level is represented by Chapter 21, "Communication, Mass Communication Organizations, and Social Institutions," and Chapter 22, "Mass Communication and Social Change."

## The Cultural-System Level

The fourth level of analysis—the cultural system—shares many of the characteristics of social-system analysis. A cultural system is also a social system. However cultural-system analysis focuses on *one* process in social systems—*the transmission of culture.*[7] Cultural-system analysis could therefore be considered as a special case of social-system analysis.

What do we mean by "the transmission of culture?" First, let us define culture. According to the sociologist Parsons:

... human action is "cultural" in that meanings and intentions concerning acts are formed in symbolic systems (including the codes through which they operate in patterns) that focus most generally about the universal of human society, language.[8]

Another definition is given by Hoebel (1960).

Culture is the integrated sum total of learned behavior traits which are manifest and shared by the members of a society.[9]

Culture includes the values, beliefs, and behaviors that are shared and accepted by members of a social system. The social system could be a small group, a community, a nation-state, or any other aggregate of persons that can control or constrain the behaviors of the individual members, directly or indirectly. For any social system to continue existing, it is important that its culture—the "rules" that guide individual behaviors and beliefs—be transmitted from generation to generation. The analysis of human behavior at the cultural-system level studies how culture is transmitted over time, with major emphasis on the transmission of values and symbols.

Cultural-system analysis is important in mass communication research. The mass media are major transmitters of culture, mainly because they are a major source of information and entertainment in most societies. Cultural-system analysis is represented in this text by the chapters on mass communication and socialization. In these chapters, we discuss how we learn behaviors, values, and ways of perceiving the world from the mass media. The major characteristic of cultural-system analysis is its topic of analysis, which is the transmission of culture. Analysis is often done at the social level. However, we can also learn about the transmission of culture by studying individuals and small groups.

We have discussed four levels of analysis that are often used to study human behavior. To show how these different levels of analysis are interrelated, let us summarize the four levels into two. Let us call analysis at the individual level *micro-analysis* and analysis at the small-group and social-system levels *macroanalysis*. Interpersonal or small-group analysis has more in common with social-system analysis than individual-level analysis. In small-group analysis, as in social-system analysis, the emphasis is on how group, organizational, and social-system properties influence individual behavior. The analysis of cultural systems includes analysis at the individual, interpersonal, and social-system levels. It is, therefore, a category in itself and will not be treated in the following discussion.

How can we relate analysis of human behavior at the micro- and macrolevels? The sociologist Hernes provides us with a model that shows this relationship.[10] This model is shown in Figure 5.1.

In Figure 5.1, we see that analysis at the microlevel begins with the identification of the individual's preferences, capacities, and expectations, which are determined primarily by that person's "history" or past experiences. Individuals make certain *assumptions* about their behaviors. First, behavior should be "optimizing"—that is, a person's actions should result in an optimal reward in relation to the costs (such as effort) required. Second, behavior is "result controlled." Behaviors will be repeated depending on their results. Rewarded actions will be repeated, while actions that are punished or not rewarded will not be repeated. In this model, individual volition or choice is an important determinant of action. The combined actions of individuals in a social system make up *aggregations,* which are properties of the social system and not of any individual. Aggregations are usually expressed as frequencies (for example, percent of the population preferring newspapers over television as a source of public affairs information), average or means (such as the average number of hours that members of the population watch television), and other descriptive statistics (such as variances, modes, and ranges). These aggregations of individual actions are then used to describe the social system.

Although we assume that individuals have some choice regarding their actions, this choice is not absolute. Properties of the social system to which the individual belongs can influence individual behavior by providing incentives, constraints, and alternatives. These social-system properties can either be *material conditions,* such as the physical infrastructure (roads, distribution of television stations, and newspapers) or *collective conditions,* such as institutional rules (for example, laws) and norms. Material and collective properties of the social system affect individual action by providing incentives, alternatives, and other constraints. The process is circular; the social system influences individual behavior, but individual behaviors also affect the institution. Let us illustrate Hernes' model with an example from mass communications.

Let us analyze the acquisition of public affairs knowledge by individuals in a social system, say a rural community of 100,000 in the South. We begin by identifying individual preferences (what are their preferences in media con-

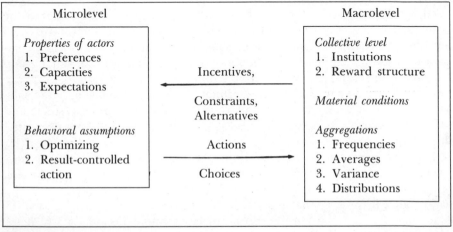

**FIGURE 5.1.** The micro- and macrolevels of analysis. From Hernes, 1976. Reprinted by permission.

tents—entertainment or news?), capacities (do their educational levels allow them to understand and be interested in public affairs news?), and expectations (how will they be rewarded by reading or watching public affairs news?). Then we analyze behavioral assumptions. Did previous exposure to public affairs information lead to rewards?

The next step is to take all the individuals in the social system and average their "knowledge of public affairs," which we could summarize as "low," "medium," or "high," depending on the descriptive statistics (such as mean knowledge score). We then look at how properties of the social system might explain these aggregates. Are sources of public affairs information available? How much space and time are devoted to public affairs news? Does the community reward citizens who are knowledgeable about public affairs (that is, is this a politically conscious community or is it apathetic?)? These social-system properties (and others) will help explain why the public affairs knowledge of individuals is low, moderate, or high. Individual actions can also affect the system. If individuals are motivated to learn about public affairs, the system (for example the city government or the media structure) may make more sources of news available, such as by increasing support for a PBS television station.

For the most part, mass communication researchers in the past decade have focused on either the individual or the social-system levels. Scholars with an orientation in behavioral and social psychology have analyzed communications processes at the individual level, focusing on how receivers respond to various communication stimuli such as source, message, and channel characteristics. Researchers with a sociological orientation have looked at communication processes at the social-system level, emphasizing how structural constraints in society—such as political, economic, and organizational structures—have influenced individual behaviors of mass communicators. The ideal strategy is to analyze mass communication at both the micro- and macrolevels so that we get an idea of individual and social-system influences on communication behaviors. Although this is often not feasible for practical reasons (macro- and microanalysis of a phenomenon will be more expensive and time consuming), individual and social-system variables should be accounted for whenever possible.

## GENERAL THEORIES OF HUMAN BEHAVIOR

Mass communication researchers have been influenced over the years by various theories of human behavior. These theories, many of them borrowed from the field of social psychology, explain how people act in their social worlds (around other people). Each theory makes certain basic assumptions about human nature, and these assumptions determine which variables and processes are studied and which ones are ignored. By studying these different theories of human behavior, we will be able to understand more fully the development of mass communication research and the important philosophical influences on mass communication researchers.

## Behaviorism

The oldest theoretical tradition in mass communication research is behaviorism. Behaviorism is a general theory of human behavior that is most closely associated with the work of B. F. Skinner.[11] According to behaviorism, the most important conditions determining human behavior are a person's external environment (objects and events that exist outside of the person) and the reinforcing characteristics of external objects or events. We respond to external objects and events and engage in behavior primarily to gain rewards or to avoid punishments. We learn which objects and events lead to rewards and which result in punishment. Rewards can be material (monetary compensation) or nonmaterial (social approval). We seek out the objects and events that are rewarding and avoid those that result in punishment. The major focus of behaviorism is on a person's external environment (often referred to as "stimuli") and whether particular objects and events are rewarding or punishing. Some behaviorists claim that they can explain almost all human behavior using these principles.

In mass communication research, the behaviorism tradition is represented by early persuasion research. In most of the early persuasion studies, researchers studied how audiences responded to external communication variables such as source credibility, message structure, message appeals, and channel characteristics. The response usually studied was attitude change. Researchers predicted—and often found in laboratory studies—that audiences could be persuaded to change their attitudes when they were rewarded for accepting the recommendation of the source or message. In this book, behaviorism is represented by the early persuasion research of Hovland and others (Chapters 8 to 11.) Although behaviorism has been an important influence in mass communication research, very few researchers today use this theoretical approach as the *only* basis for their studies.

## Gestalt Theory and Phenomenology

*Gestalt* is a German word meaning "good form" or "wholeness." In psychology, Gestalt theory explains how people organize their perceptions of the world in general (including themselves), their place in the world, and their attitudes and values.[12] The term phenomenology was used by the Gestalt psychologists to refer to an individual's perception of the world—his or her *subjective* experience of the world, which was based not on objective characteristics but on how he or she perceived it. This perception is subjective because it can change from individual to individual.

Two Gestalt psychologists who were important influences on communication researchers were Kurt Lewin and Fritz Heider. Lewin maintained that human behavior could not be adequately explained by a person's responses to objective environmental conditions.[13] It is more important to study a person's perceptions of the environment, because these perceptions do not necessarily correspond to the objective features of the environment. Lewin and his students were also concerned with how people organized their perceptions of the world in order to maintain "consistency" and to avoid "dissonance" among their different attitudes and behaviors. Like Lewin, Heider was interested in how people organized their perceptions of the world.[14] He said that we organize these perceptions to maintain harmony or balance among the attitudes and objects in our external environment.

The influence of Lewin and Heider in psychology is evident in the many "balance" theories that were popular during the 1950s and early 1960s. The major difference between behaviorism and the Gestalt psychology of Lewin and Heider is that behaviorists focus on the objective properties of the external environment, while Gestalt psychologists are primarily concerned with internal variables or how people perceive the objective environment.

In mass communication research, the Gestalt influence is represented by the use of the many balance theories (including the theory of cognitive dissonance) to explain communication behavior. The major assumption is that people communicate to reduce imbalance or dissonance. This influence was most apparent in the 1960s. In this text, the Gestalt influence is represented by our discussion of Newcomb's social psychological model of communication (Chapter 4), and Festinger's theory of cognitive dissonance (Chapter 11). Few researchers in mass communications today rely exclusively or even primarily on Gestalt psychology to explain communication behavior.

### Reciprocal Determinism

The general theory of human behavior that is the most accepted today in psychology and communications is what Albert Bandura calls "reciprocal determinism."[15] Reciprocal determinism says that human behavior is best explained by taking into account both internal and external factors, and that these factors often interact. Internal factors include the processes in which the Gestalt and motivational psychologists are interested—the individual's perceptual, cognitive, and motivational processes. The external factors are the factors emphasized by the behaviorists, including the objective characteristics of external events, and the consequences of actions in the environment (such as whether they are rewarded or punished). Thus, reciprocal determinism says that human behavior is determined by both external and internal events and that these processes are interrelated. It assumes that individuals are in control of their actions through processes such as goal setting and self-monitoring (observing the results of their actions) and by providing self-incentives (generating internal rewards).[16] However, this "self-directed" behavior is also constrained or limited by objects and events in the external environment. To understand human behavior, we must account for both internal and external processes.

Most contemporary theories of human behavior in social psychology are based on principles of reciprocal determinism.[17] In mass communications, the influence of reciprocal determinism is perhaps not as pervasive as in psychology. We still have researchers concentrating only on either internal processes (such as cognitive processing of messages) or external processes (such as the rewarding qualities of a source or message.)

Reciprocal determinism is the major influence in this book. It is represented in many ways—by the transactional model of communication discussed in Chapter 4, by our choice of Bandura's social learning theory to explain the socialization effects of the mass media, and by our emphasis on cognitive and perceptual processes *and* on objective characteristics of the external communication environment to explain persuasion and other communication effects.

## SUMMARY

Mass communication can be studied at the individual, interpersonal, social-system, and cultural-system levels. Analysis at the individual level is often called microanalysis. Analysis at the interpersonal, social-, and cultural-system levels is called macroanalysis.

Three general theories of human behavior that have influenced mass communication research are behaviorism, Gestalt theory, and reciprocal determinism. The most influential theory today is reciprocal determinism, which says that human behavior is best explained by both internal and external forces.

## REVIEW QUESTIONS

1. Discuss how the different levels of analysis are related to each other. Give examples of studies that analyze communciation at each level.
2. Why is reciprocal determinism the most influential theory of human behavior in many of the social sciences today? Give an example of a communication study that was influenced by reciprocal determinism.

## ENDNOTES

1. Richard Appelbaum, *Theories of Social Change* (Chicago: Markham Publishing, 1970).
2. Sigmund Freud, *On Creativity and the Unconscious* (New York: Harper & Brothers, 1958).
3. Harold Proshansky and Bernard Seidenberg, *Basic Studies in Social Psychology* (New York: Holt, Rinehart and Winston, 1965).
4. George Herbert Mead, *On Social Psychology* (Chicago: University of Chicago Press, 1964).

5. Emile Durkheim, *The Rules of Sociological Method* (New York: Free Press, 1964).
6. James Ettema and D. Charles Whitney, *Individuals in Mass Media Organizations* (Beverly Hills, Calif.: Sage Publications, 1982).
7. Appelbaum, *op. cit.*
8. Talcott Parsons, *Societies: Evolutionary and Comparative Perspectives* (Englewood Cliffs, N.J.: Prentice Hall, 1966).
9. Adamson E. Hoebel, "The Nature of Culture," in H. L. Shapiro (ed.), *Man, Culture and Society* (New York: Oxford University Press, 1960).
10. Gudmund Hernes, "Structural Change in Social Processes," *American Journal of Sociology, 82,* 1976, pp. 513–47.
11. B. F. Skinner, *The Behavior of Organisms: An Experimental Analysis* (New York: Appleton-Century-Crofts, 1938).
12. Drury Sherrod, *Social Psychology* (New York: Random House, 1982).
13. Kurt Lewin, *Dynamic Theory of Personality* (New York: McGraw-Hill, 1935).
14. F. Heider, *The Psychology of Interpersonal Relations* (New York: Wiley, 1958).
15. Albert Bandura, "Model of Causality in Social Learning Theory," in S. Sukemune (ed.), *Advances in Social Learning Theory* (Tokyo: Kaneko-Shoho, 1983).
16. *Ibid.*
17. Sherrod, *op. cit.*

# PART II

# COMMUNICATION AND PERSUASION

In the late 1940s and the 1950s persuasion research *was* communication research. Scholars were primarily interested in analyzing how communication changed people's attitudes and behaviors. Researchers today are studying other communication effects; however, the interest in persuasion lingers.

In Part II we discuss recent developments in persuasion research and theory. Many of the earlier theories and principles are being reevaluated by current research. For example, recent evidence provides little support for the "selective retention" principle of message reception. Selective retention has been accepted by communication scholars for decades, and even today communication theory textbooks discuss it uncritically. Conversely, most current texts have dismissed the "selective exposure" hypothesis. However, current research indicates that in ongoing communication situations we do pay more attention to supportive than to contradictory messages.

Our main objective in Part II, therefore, is to update the research and theoretical literature in persuasion. Most of the studies we discuss were done in the late 1970s and early 1980s. When possible, we relate this research to the earlier "classical" studies.

In Chapter 6 we discuss the traditional attitude change model of Hovland and the more recent learning and belief models of McGuire and Fishbein. Chapter 7 explains what happens in persuasion and why, using Hovland's instrumental learning theory Kelman's functional theory, and information-processing theories.

What communicator characteristics determine effectiveness in persuasion? How should messages be structured to achieve maximum effect? What message appeals should be used and in what medium? These questions are discussed in Chapters 8, 9, and 10.

In Chapter 11, we present new evidence on the selective attention, selective perception, and selective retention hypotheses. We also discuss the effects of personality on persuasibility and how audiences can affect communicators. Chapter 12 analyzes the enduring problem of predicting behavior from attitudes.

# 6

---

# ATTITUDES, BEHAVIOR AND COMMUNICATION

As we discussed in the previous chapter, one of the primary objectives of communication is to persuade. A mother tells her son to turn off the television set; an editorial asks its readers to vote for a particular candidate; an advertisement proclaims that Brand A is better than Brand B. These are examples of persuasion, and they have two things in common. First, they are attempts at *social influence;* that is, they involve an attempt by a person or group to modify or bring about some change in another person or group. Second, the major strategy for inducing change is *communication.* There are, of course, many ways in which a person can be influenced by another person. McGuire[1] mentions other strategies such as intensive indoctrination (child rearing, psychotherapy, and brainwashing); group discussion, wherein both sides of the issue are actively discussed by the influencing agent and the receiver; suggestion, where the major change mechanism is simple repetition of statements suggesting the desired change, without presenting arguments supporting the change (as in hypnosis); and conformity, in which the influence induction consists of communicating to the receiver the fact that peer groups or authority figures desire the change without presenting other arguments supporting the change. Persuasion is a special instance of social influence in which a person or group attempts to change another person or group by communicating *information* supporting the desired change. The main difference between persuasion and other social influence situations is that in persuasion, the key induction for change is a message that contains arguments why the receiver should adopt a certain conclusion on some issue.

## PERSUASION MODELS

A major problem in persuasion research is to define the nature of *change* in the target person or group that the persuasive message is to accomplish. Early persuasion research, such as the work of Hovland and his colleagues at Yale[2] focused on *attitude change* as the major dependent variable or effect; more recent models have broken down change into subprocesses of attention to the message, understanding of the message, yielding to or acceptance of the message, retention and, finally, action.[3] More recently also, researchers have distinguished between attitudes, beliefs, behavioral intentions, and overt behavior as targets of persuasion.[4] Let us first consider the traditional model, in which attitude change is the major effect of persuasion, and then discuss more recent models.

### The Traditional Model: Attitude Change

Over forty years ago, Gordon Allport said that "attitude is probably the most distinctive and indispensable concept in contemporary American social psychology. No other term appears more frequently in experimental and theoretical literature."[5] In 1975 Fishbein and Ajzen reiterated this view, claiming that "Allport's words are as true today as they were in 1935. The centrality of the attitude concept remains unchallenged and, if anything, its importance has increased."[6] Although these statements were directed at the field of social psychology, many mass communication researchers could make the same assertions regarding the importance of attitudes to their field. Until recently, attitude change has been the major dependent variable in mass communication research.[7] What are attitudes and why are we concerned about them?

Unfortunately, there has been little agreement among researchers on what attitudes are. Attitudes are generally considered to be an intervening variable—that is, a variable that cannot be measured directly since it occurs in our minds, but that can be used to predict related overt (or observable) responses. Most definitions of attitude include one or more of the following characteristics: a *cognitive* component, which is information or knowledge that a person has about the attitude object; an *affective* component, which is how one *feels* about the attitude object, usually summarized as liking or disliking; and a *conative* or *behavioral* component, which is how a person will overtly act toward the attitude object. Early researchers included all three components in their definitions of attitude.

Allport, in 1935, gave this definition. An attitude is a "mental and neural state, of readiness to respond, organized through experience, and exerting a directive influence upon the individual's response to all objects and situations with which it is related."[8]

Krech and Crutchfield, in 1948, defined attitude as "an enduring organization of motivational, emotional, perceptual, and cognitive processes with respect to some aspect of the individual's world."[9]

The early definitions implied that attitudes are based on what we know about the attitude object, that they are our feelings (liking or disliking) toward the object, and that they will motivate us to act toward the object in a manner consistent with how we feel. For example, let us take a college student's attitude toward the legalization of marijuana use. If the student believed that marijuana use is not deterimental to a person's health (cognitive component), he or she would probably favor the legalization of marijuana use (affective component) and would probably sign a petition supporting the legalization of marijuana (behavioral component). These early definitions assumed that by knowing a person's attitude we could predict how that person would behave toward the attitude object in a given situation. Attitudes became a popular research concept, since an attitude is easier to measure than actual behavior. Although researchers may be interested in behavioral change as a result of communication, they instead measure attitudes using "paper-and-pencil tests" (questionnaires) and assume that the attitude will predict behavior. It is, for example, easier to measure a voter's attitudes regarding the issues and the candidates than it is actually to observe how he or she will vote.

One of the problems with these three component definitions of attitudes, however, is that attitudes are often inconsistent with behavior. Researchers have observed, for example, that racial attitudes often do not predict how a person will react toward a member of the target race.[10] The attitude-behavior inconsistency is one of the most debated issues in the social sciences.[11] (We will discuss this issue in greater detail in Chapter 12). Most current attitude researchers are content to define attitudes as the "amount of affect for or against some object."[12] Thus, current usage looks at attitude as having only one major component—the affective or "feeling" dimension, which can be summarized as liking or disliking for the attitude object.

One last characteristic of attitudes should be mentioned, since it has direct bearing on theories of persuasion and communication that will be discussed in the next chapter. *Attitudes are learned.* Predispositions to respond in consistently favorable or unfavorable ways toward the attitude object are based on previous knowledge about that object. This knowledge may be the result of direct experience with the object or it may be the result of communication from another person or group about the object. Most researchers are in agreement that attitudes are learned and that they are not genetically inherited by offspring from parents.

## McGuire's Persuasion Model

McGuire presents a general framework for analyzing the effects of communication on persuasion.[13] His model is shown in Figure 6.1. McGuire first identifies the different components in the communication process. These components are the source, message, channel, and the receiver. He then breaks down the persuasion process into five steps, including attention to the message, comprehension, yielding, retention, and action. According to McGuire, the receiver generally should go through all of these steps in succession if the communication is to have any effect on him or her at all. Thus, the first step is for the receiver to attend to the message. The message cannot be effective unless it first reaches the intended audience. After attention, the next step is message comprehension. The arguments and the conclusion in the message must be understood. Attention and comprehension are referred to by McGuire as message "receptivity" factors. The next step is yielding, or

| Steps in Persuasion | Communication Factors | | | |
|---|---|---|---|---|
| | Source | Message | Channel | Receiver |
| Attention (reception) | | | | |
| Comprehension (reception) | | | | |
| Yielding | | | | |
| Retention | | | | |
| Action | | | | |

**FIGURE 6.1.** McGuire's matrix of persuasive communication. Adapted from McGuire, 1968.

acceptance of the message's conclusions and recommendations. This is what is usually referred to as attitude change. Most laboratory studies of persuasion stop at this point, assuming that yielding to the message (or attitude change) will predict related behaviors. Very often, however, the receiver will not be able to act immediately on the message's recommendations. (I may be convinced by a television commercial to buy a particular make of automobile but will not be able to do so until I am able to sell my old car and arrange for a bank loan.) Thus the next step, retention of the message, becomes necessary. The last step is what most researchers (and users of research) are really interested in, and that is action or overt behavior. The advertiser is not interested in brand preference but in actual purchase of the product. The political campaigner is not interested in voter attitudes toward his or her candidate but in how they will vote. Very often, action resulting from a persuasive message is not actually measured but is inferred from the yielding variable.

McGuire's model avoids the oversimplification common in many early studies of persuasion that measured attitude change or yielding as the primary effect of communication. If forces us to look at the five different steps separately and consider how each step will be affected by a communication variable. His model can also explain some contradictory findings, which are not uncommon in persuasion research. Let us consider how the model does this.

Many of the communication variables we study, according to McGuire, can have *opposite effects* on the receptivity (attention and comprehension) and the yielding steps in persuasion. This is particularly true for personality factors in receivers. Self-esteem, for example, has a positive effect on reception but a negative effect on yielding. That is, we can expect receivers with high self-esteem to be receptive to persuasive messages, since they will have confidence in their initial positions. They will therefore not be easily threatened by the contradictory information in the persuasive message. However, we can also expect high self-esteem receivers to be more resistant to yielding (or change), since they will be more satisfied with existing attitudes and behaviors. A similar prediction can be made for "intelligence" of receivers. Receivers with high intelligence will be receptive to the message, since they may have longer attention spans and will be better able to comprehend the arguments. At the same time, we can also expect them to be more resistant to change (the yielding factor), since they will be more confident in their existing attitudes or behaviors.

A similar analysis is possible for some message factors. High fear appeals in a message can "turn off" the audience, since the inductions usually involve gruesome pictures depicting consequences of not accepting message recommendations. However, high fear appeals can be more convincing if we can get our audience to attend to the message.

A common result of opposite effects of communication variables on the receptivity and yielding steps, according to McGuire, is a nonmonotonic or curvilinear relationship between the variables. The most common form of this curvilinear relationship is an inverted U curve. Thus we find that a persuasive message often will have the most effect on receivers with moderate levels of self-esteem and intelligence. And medium levels of fear in a message (as opposed to high and low fear appeals) are often the most effective in bringing about acceptance of the recommendations. Failure to consider interactions between communication variables and the different steps in persuasion, according to McGuire, often leads to results that are contradictory and difficult to interpret.

The model, however, is not without its weaknesses (many of which are pointed out by McGuire himself). First, it assumes a completely *rational* receiver, one who will take a new course of action or adapt a new attitude only when he or she is convinced of the arguments supporting the change. Is it not possible for a person to skip the comprehension step and go from attention to yielding, retention, and action? Some of the research we will review in succeeding chapters indicates that receivers sometimes accept message recommendations on the basis of the source (whether the source was liked or not) without paying too much attention to the message. Another situation that the model does not provide for is when the sequence of the steps is reversed. Again, as we will see in the chapters to come, there are times when yielding to the message comes *before* attention to the message. The selective exposure hypothesis, for example, predicts that receivers will first determine whether they have yielded to the message's conclusion before deciding whether to attend to it or not. Also, research in compliance indicates that action sometimes precedes yielding. People forced to do things they do not believe in can eventually end up accepting the forced behavior. Finally, is retention of the message always necessary for action? Krugman's model of advertising effects suggests that some buyers do not necessarily remember the advertising message but are able to make the connection between advertisement and brand once they see the product on the supermarket shelf.[14] Despite these short-comings, McGuire's model provides a framework that enables us to order and evaluate research on communication and persuasion.

## Fishbein and Ajzen's Belief Model

Fishbein and Ajzen have proposed a model that considers a person's beliefs to be the building blocks of persuasion.[15] In their model persuasion begins when a person's beliefs regarding the object of persuasion are changed. Belief change is followed by attitude change, then by the creation of appropriate belief intentions and, finally, by behavioral change. Like McGuire, Fishbein and Ajzen consider people as "rational animals who systematically utilize or process the information available to them."[16] The key to persuasion is to provide the receiver with convincing information supporting the desired change.

Beliefs, according to Fishbein and Ajzen, represent the information that a person has about the object. A belief links an object to some attribute. The object of a belief could be a person, group of people, institution, behavior, policy, or event. The associated attribute could be any object, quality, characteristic, outcome, or event. For example, the belief that "marijuana use is not detrimental to the user's health" links the object "marijuana use" to the attribute "not detrimental. . . ." Quite often a person's belief will have little or no basis in reality—that is, the belief will not have been objectively verified. We acquire beliefs not only from direct experience with the object but also from other people, groups, institutions, and the mass media. Belief strength is the perceived likelihood that the object has been or is associated with the attribute in question. The stronger a person's belief strength, the more resistant it will be to change.

An attitude is defined by Fishbein and Ajzen as the amount of affect or liking that a person has for an object. The only component of an attitude in their model is the evaluative component, which can be summarized as a feeling of favorableness or unfavorableness toward the object. While a belief represents a person's perceived knowledge about an object, an attitude summarizes his or her feelings toward that object. Thus, a person who believes that "marijuana use is not determintal to the user's health" would probably have the attitude, "I am in favor of the legalization of marijuana use."

Behavioral intentions refer to a person's motivations to perform various behaviors associated with his or her attitudes and opinions regarding the object. The strength of an intention is the probability that a person will perform an associated behavior. There are many different behaviors that a person can perform in relation to any given belief or attitude. In our previous example a person who supported the legalization of marijuana use could, among other behaviors: (1) sign a petition for the legalization of marijuana use; (2) attend a "pot rally" to protest existing laws; and (3) smoke marijuana whenever he or she pleases. According to Fishbein and Ajzen, the probability that a behavioral intention will be performed (its strength) depends on that person's beliefs that performing the behavior will lead to certain consequences and his or her evaluation of those consequences, and on normative pressures from that person's reference groups (social groups to which one belongs or aspires for membership). The greater the probability that performance of the behavior will lead to rewards and avoidance of punishments, the more likely it is that the behavior will be performed. Also, the stronger the pressure from reference groups for behavioral performance, the more likely it is that the behavior will be performed. In our example, participation in a rally is likely to lead to punishment (arrest), so most people would stay away from it even if they had a positive attitude toward marijuana legalization. On the other hand, signing a petition is less likely to lead to punishment, so it will be a more probable response.

The final effect of persuasion in the Fishbein and Ajzen model is behavior, or observable acts of the receiver. A person's behavior is first determined by relevant beliefs which, in turn, determine attitudes, which affect behavioral intentions. The causal chain linking these variables is shown in Figure 6.2.

In this model a person may have several beliefs about an object. Many of these beliefs will be supportive of each other, but some may be contradictory. These beliefs will also vary in strength; the person will be more convinced that the object is associated with certain attributes than with others. The totality of these beliefs—that is, the total impression that they give of the object—will be the informational base on which related attitudes, behavioral intentions, and behaviors are based.

The model suggests that a person's attitude will be based on his or her salient beliefs about that object. If those beliefs associate the object with positive attributes, then the attitude will be positive. If the associated attributes are negative, the attitude will be negative. The attitude leads to behavioral intentions that in their totality, will follow the direction of the attitude. Positive attitudes lead to behavioral intentions that support the object, and negative attitudes lead to avoidance of the object. Like beliefs, intentions will vary in strength (probability that they will be performed). Each intention will be associated with the corresponding behavior. Attitudes and beliefs about an

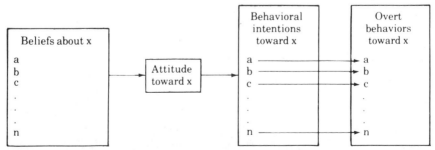

**FIGURE 6.2.** Fishbein and Ajzen's belief model of persuasion. Adapted from Fishbein and Ajzen, 1975.

object will be related to the *total* behavioral pattern and not to any specific behavior. Attitudes and opinions, according to this model, cannot predict specific behaviors by themselves, since other factors (normative pressure and beliefs regarding the consequences of the behavior) will affect the performance of any specific behavior. However, an attitude will be related to the overall behavioral pattern of the person. If the attitude is positive, then the behaviors that *are* performed will be favorable.

Let us illustrate the Fishbein and Ajzen model with an example. Take a person with several beliefs regarding marijuana use:

**Belief 1.** Marijuana use is not detrimental to the user's health.

**Belief 2.** Marijuana use is not addictive.

**Belief 3.** Marijuana is a psychological crutch.

The first two beliefs are favorable toward marijuana use, while the third belief is negative. The total effect of these three beliefs would probably be a moderately favorable attitude toward the legalization of marijuana use. This attitude would give rise to several behavioral intentions, such as signing a petition supporting legalization, attending a rally, writing to legislators in support of legalization, writing a letter to the editor of the local paper, and so on. These intentions will have varying strengths, depending on perceived consequences of the act and on normative pressure. Our person may sign a petition but may not perform any of the remaining behaviors. His total behavioral pattern will correspond to his moderately positive attitude toward marijuana.

This model is useful to communication researchers because of the central role it assigns to information in the persuasion process. To change behavior according to this model, one starts by changing a person's beliefs. Communication is the usual way in which information can be transmitted to other people. Also, this model helps explain why attitudes do not always predict behavior, an issue that is discussed in greater detail in Chapter 12. Finally, the distinction made between beliefs, attitudes, behavioral intentions, and behavior provides a framework by which the effects of communication can be better analyzed.

## SUMMARY

One of the primary objectives of communication is to persuade. Early persuasion research focused on attitude change as the major effect of persuasion. More recent models, such as those suggested by McGuire and by Fishbein and Ajzen, have broken down persuasion into subprocesses of attention to the message, understanding of the message, yielding to the message, retention and, finally, action. Also, recent models have distinguished between attitudes, beliefs, behavioral intentions, and overt behavior as goals of persuasion.

## REVIEW QUESTION

**1.** List three of your attitudes pertaining to any object, person, or issue. Using Fishbein and Ajzen's model, analyze each attitude according to its affective, cognitive, and behavioral components. Discuss your reasons for holding each attitude.

## ENDNOTES

1. William McGuire, "The Nature of Attitudes and Attitude Change," in G. Lindzey and E. Aronson (eds.), *The Handbook of Social Psychology*, 2nd ed., Vol. 3 (Reading, Mass.: Addison-Wesley, 1969), pp. 136–314.
2. Carl Hovland, A. Lumsdaine, and Fred Sheffield, *Experiments in Mass Communication* (Princeton, N.J.: Princeton University Press, 1949); Carl Hovland, Irving Janis, and Harold Kelley, *Communication and Persuasion* (New Haven, Conn.: Yale University Press, 1953).
3. McGuire, *op. cit.*
4. See, for example, Martin Fishbein and Icek Ajzen, *Belief, Attitude, Intention and Behavior: An Introduction to Theory and Research* (Reading, Mass.: Addison-Wesley, 1975).
5. G. W. Allport, "Attitudes," in C. Murchison (ed.), *Handbook of Social Psychology* (Worcester, Mass.: Clark University Press, 1935), pp. 798–884.
6. Fishbein and Ajzen, *op. cit.*, p. v.
7. Donald Roberts, "The Nature of Communication Effects," in W. Schramm and D. Roberts, *The Process and Effects of Mass Communication*, 2nd ed. (Urbana: University of Illinois Press, 1971), pp. 346–388.
8. Allport, *op. cit.*
9. D. Krech and R. S. Crutchfield, *Theory and Problems in Social Psychology* (New York: McGraw-Hill, 1948).
10. M. L. DeFleur and F. R. Westie, "Verbal Attitudes and Overt Acts: An Experiment on the Salience of Attitudes," *American Sociological Review, 23,* 1958, pp. 667–673.
11. See, for example, M. Fishbein and I. Ajzen, "Attitudes toward Objects as Predictors of Single and Multiple Behavioral Criteria," *Psychological Review, 81,* 1974, pp. 59–74.
12. Fishbein and Ajzen, 1975, *op. cit.*
13. McGuire, *op. cit.*
14. H. E. Krugman, "The Impact of Television Advertising: Learning without Involvement," *Public Opinion Quarterly, 29,* 1965, pp. 349–356.
15. Fishbein and Ajzen, 1975, *op. cit.*
16. *Ibid.*, p. 14.

# 7

# THEORIES OF COMMUNICATION AND PERSUASION

In the previous chapter we discussed several models that identified the steps and variables in persuasion. In this chapter we will consider theories of communication and persuasion that explain what happens in persuasion and why.

The social behavioral sciences do not suffer from a lack of attitude change theories. Ostrom, in 1968, estimated that there were thirty-four different theories of attitude change.[1] Our concern in this book, however, is communication and persuasion. Our review of the attitude change literature turned up two general theories in which communication is the *major* independent or causal variable in the persuasion process. These are learning theories of persuasion and Kelman's functional theory of social influence.

## LEARNING THEORY

Learning theories in psychology, also often referred to as stimulus-response and behavioristic theories, explain how a given response by an organism becomes associated with a given stimulus in its environment. The process by which an organism repeatedly associates a given response to a given stimulus is called *conditioning* or *learning*. There are two major learning models: classical conditioning and instrumental conditioning. These models are derived from the theories of Hull, Spence, Tolman, and Miller.[2]

### Classical Conditioning

The basic elements in the classical conditioning model are an unconditioned stimulus (UCS), an unconditioned response (UCR), and a conditioned stimulus (CS). The UCS is any object in the organism's environment that automatically elicits, without previous learning, an overt or observable response (the UCR). For example, a dog salivates (UCR) at the sight of a T-bone steak

(UCS); a child cries (UCR) when he sees a gorilla (UCS); a child laughs (UCR) when she sees a clown (UCS). The UCR is performed automatically by the organism when confronted with the UCS and is, therefore, a "natural" response. Classical conditioning occurs when a previously neutral stimulus (the CS) is able to elicit, by itself, the UCR. This is accomplished through repeated pairing of the UCS with the CS; that is, the CS is presented to the organism at the same time that the UCS is presented. Each pairing will elicit the UCR, since the UCR is a natural response to the UCS. Classical conditioning is accomplished when, in the absence of the UCS, the CS is able to elicit the UCR from the organism.

As an example, take a child who always laughs when she sees a clown. Suppose the clown (the UCS) is repeatedly associated in a television commercial with a breakfast cereal (the CS). The child laughs at these pairings because of the clown. Classical conditioning occurs when the breakfast cereal (or its package) is able to make the child laugh even when the clown is not present. Thus, the child will associate a pleasurable feeling with the cereal, even without the clown. This technique, of course, is often used by advertisers. Repeated associations of stimuli result in the transfer of response-eliciting characteristics of one stimuli (the UCS) to the other (CS).

Research has shown that a number of factors influence classical conditioning. One of these is the frequency with which the UCS and the CS are paired. The more frequent the pairings, the stronger the conditioning effect. Also, maximal learning occurs when the CS precedes the UCS by short time intervals, such as by half a second.[3]

### Instrumental Learning

Instrumental learning, also known as operant conditioning, involves a situation in which an organism already responds in many different ways to a stimulus in its environment. One of the responses is reinforced by providing rewards or by withholding punishments. This particular response therefore becomes instrumental in obtaining rewards or avoiding punishments. The reinforced response is increasingly performed by the organism with each reinforcement. The response is learned when it occurs with high probability.[4]

As an example, take a child who finds a desirable toy each time he opens a box of cereal A but not when he opens boxes of cereals B, C, or D. The reinforcer (toy) will strengthen a particular response (opening a box of cereal A). The child will learn to prefer opening cereal A boxes to boxes from other manufacturers.

Many factors influence instrumental conditioning. Some of these are the frequency of reinforcement or the number of times that the response is followed by a reward, the time differential between the response and the reinforcement, how much reinforcement is given, and schedules of reinforcement.[5]

## Hovland, Janis, and Kelly's Instrumental Theory of Persuasion

In 1953, Hovland, Janis, and Kelly published *Communication and Persuasion,* in which they outlined a program of attitude research that was based on the instrumental model of learning.[6] They defined persuasive communication as "the process by which an individual (the communicator) transmits stimuli (usually verbal) to modify the behavior of other individuals (the audience)." One of the main ways in which persuasive communication leads to attitude change is through changing related opinions. Opinions are "verbal answers that an individual gives in response to stimulus situations in which some general question is raised." Attitudes are "those implicit responses which are oriented toward approaching or avoiding a given object, person, group or symbol." These definitions are similar to the distinction that Fishbein and Ajzen make between beliefs and attitudes.[7] Beliefs, or opinions, represent the "information" that a person has about an object. Hovland, Janis, and Kelly add that opinions are "verbalized." Attitudes are affective reactions of a person toward the object.

According to Hovland, Janis, and Kelly, attitudes can be changed by changing related opinions (or information) that a person has about the object. Opinions are like other "habits" in that they tend to persist unless the person undergoes some new learning experience. One way in which a new opinion can be learned is by exposure to persuasive communication that contains arguments why the new opinion should be accepted. The learning of new opinions is governed by principles that apply equally to the learning of various other verbal and motor skills. Equally important to the learning of new opinions, for example, are mental rehearsal or practice of the new opinion and incentive motivation for accepting the new opinion.

### Mental Rehearsal of New Opinions

Hovland, Janis, and Kelly regard a persuasive communication as a stimulus that raises a question and suggests an answer. A persuasive message arguing that television violence leads to aggression among viewers, for example, implicitly asks the question, "Does TV violence lead to aggression among viewers?" and suggests that the answer is yes. Reasons are then given to support the answer.

A person presented with such a persuasive message initially reacts by first thinking of his or her own answer to the question and then the answer suggested by the communicator. Thus, the major initial effect of the communication is to stimulate the individual to think both of his or her own opinion and the new opinion recommended in the message. The new opinion is "rehearsed," memorized, and learned. For learning to occur, the individual must first *attend* to the message and then *comprehend* it. Learning of the new opinion, however, is not sufficient for opinion change. The individual must also be provided with some motivation for accepting instead of rejecting the opinion.

### Incentives for Acceptance of New Opinions

Acceptance of the new opinion, according to Hovland, Janis, and Kelly, depends on incentives or reinforcements in the message. Among these incentives are the expectation of being right or wrong. We have often been rewarded in the past for taking "right" stands on issues. We will therefore be motivated to accept a stand on the issue in question if we can be convinced that it is the correct stand. One way of doing this is by attributing the message to an expert source, one who has an objectively verifiable correct stand on the issue. A second incentive that can influence the individual to accept a new opinion is lack of bias or manipulative intent in the source. In the past we may have met with unpleasant experiences (punishment) when influenced by someone who had something to gain from the manipulation. We will therefore be more likely to accept a message from a trustworthy source (one who has nothing to gain from the influence) than from an untrustworthy source. A third incentive is social approval. Social approval has been rewarding in the past. Thus new opinions leading to social approval will likely be accepted. These are some of the incentives possible in a communication for acceptance of new opinions. Hovland, Janis, and Kelly do not attempt to list all of them, but their main point is that a person should be *rewarded* in some way for accepting the new opinion.

### Stimulus Characteristics of the Communication Situation

Hovland, Janis, and Kelly's interest in effects of communication stimuli on acceptance of new opinions (the response) led them to vary systematically in their research characteristics of the source, message, and receivers and to observe resulting attitude change. Their research model is shown in Figure 7.1.

The major independent variables studied were source characteristics, message factors, and audience characteristics. The effects on attitude change of these variables were assumed to be mediated by attention to the message, comprehension of the arguments, and acceptance of the new opinions. Although attitude change was the major effect studied, opinion change, perception change, and behavioral change were also sometimes studied. The major objective was to determine communication situation characteristics that could facilitate *learning* of the message and *acceptance* of opinions. Research following the Hovland, Janis, and Kelly research model is discussed in the next four chapters.

### Evaluation of Hovland, Janis, and Kelly's Instrumental Theory

The major weakness of Hovland, Janis, and Kelly's theoretical approach to persuasion, as Insko[8] has pointed out, is that it does not adequately explain how a persuasive communication provides the reinforcement for acceptance of the new opinion. Although some of the possible reinforcing characteristics of communication sources and other elements in the communication situation are given, none of these are empirically tested. Hovland assumes, for exam-

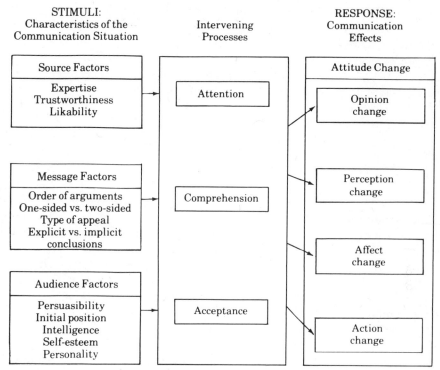

**FIGURE 7.1.** Hovland, Janis, and Kelly's instrumental model of persuasion. Adapted from Fishbein and Ajzen, 1975.

ple, that "being right" on an issue is reinforcing; therefore an expert source will be effective in changing opinions, since correct stands are often associated with expert sources. This all sounds very logical, but no direct evidence from their experiments supports that being right and expert sources are indeed reinforcing. In the original formulations of learning theory, reinforcers were conceptualized and operationalized as drive reducers.[9] The drive reduced could be a primary drive (such as hunger or thirst) or a secondary drive (such as need for social approval). A more adequate specification of the drives that a persuasive communication can reduce is needed before Hovland, Janis, and Kelly's theoretical approach to persuasion can be completely linked with more general theories of learning.

Another weakness of the model is the failure to specify relations between the three steps considered necessary for persuasion: attention to the message, comprehension, and acceptance. Are all these steps necessary for persuasion? Should they happen in sequence? Is comprehension needed for acceptance? As we will see in the next four chapters, the evidence is inconclusive. We cannot make the generalization that, for persuasion to occur, the individual must follow through these three steps in sequence.

In spite of these weaknesses, Hovland, Janis, and Kelly's instrumental theory is a significant and influential contribution to communication and persuasion research. Their research program was one of the first to vary stimulus characteristics systematically and quantitatively in the communication situation and to observe the effects of these variations on attitude change. The influence of their approach can be seen in the next four chapters, where specific research dealing with communication sources, messages, channels, and receivers is discussed. Many of the studies we will review are based on Hovland, Janis, and Kelly's theoretical approach.

## KELMAN'S FUNCTIONAL THEORY

Kelman's theory of social influence is one of many functional theories of attitude change. According to the functional approach, the key to changing and understanding attitudes is to know the reasons why people hold the attitudes they do. By knowing the motivations that people have for holding certain attitudes, we can predict when and how these attitudes will change.[10]

Kelman's theory differs from other functional theories in several respects.[11] First, it is the only one that focuses on communicator characteristics as determinants of attitude change. Second, it specifies the antecedent conditions as well as motives leading to attitude change. Third, it is the only one that has been subjected to direct empirical test.[12]

Kelman defines three processes of social influence—compliance, identification, and internalization. For each process he identifies a specific set of antecedents (conditions leading to a process) and consequents. His theoretical model is outlined in Figure 7.2.

### Social Influence

According to Kelman, there are three processes of social influence, and each type leads to a different opinion, attitude, or behavior.

Compliance is public acceptance of an opinion, attitude, or behavior without private commitment to it. It occurs when we accept the influence or change because we expect to gain some reward or to avoid punishment by doing so. The new response is accepted not because we actually believe in it (or accept supporting arguments), but because acceptance is instrumental in achieving some satisfying social effect. An example of compliance is a young executive who abides by the company's dress code even if he or she thinks it is ridiculous or an infringement on individual rights. However, the executive will dress as the company pleases because such compliance may be necessary for promotion or continued employment in the firm.

Identification is public and private acceptance of an opinion, attitude, or behavior because such acceptance is necessary to maintain a desirable role relationship with the influence agent. This role relationship can take the form of classical identification, in which the individual attempts to be like or actu-

|  | Compliance | Identification | Internalization |
|---|---|---|---|
| **Antecedents** | | | |
| 1. Basis for the importance of the induction | Concern with social effect of behavior | Concern with social anchorage of behavior | Concern with value congruence of behavior |
| 2. Source of power of the influencing agent | Means control | Attractiveness | Credibility |
| 3. Manner of achieving prepotency of the induced response | Limitation of choice behavior | Delineation of role requirements | Reorganization of means-end framework |
| **Consequents** | | | |
| 1. Conditions of performance of induced response | Surveillance by influencing agent | Salience of relationship to agent | Relevance of values to issue |
| 2. Conditions of change and extinction of induced response | Changed perception of conditions for social rewards | Changed perception of conditions for satisfying self-defining relationships | Changed perception of conditions for value maximization |
| 3. Type of behavior system in which induced response is embedded | External demands of a specific setting | Expectations defining a specific role | Person's value system |

*Source:* Kelman, 1961, p. 67.

**FIGURE 7.2.** Kelman's functional model of persuasion. Adapted from Kelman, 1961.

ally to be the influence agent. Or it could be a reciprocal relationship, in which the individual and the influence agent interact in a mutually satisfying way. In either case, the individual accepts influence to maintain the role relationship. An example of classical identification is copying by a child of his or her parents' behaviors. A reciprocal role relationship is illustrated by husband and wife accepting influence from each other to maintain their relationship.

Identification differs from compliance in that the individual actually believes in the new attitude, opinion, or behavior. It is similar to compliance in that the individual does not accept influence on the basis of its contents but because of an external source.

Internalization, the third type of social influence, occurs when we accept a new opinion, attitude, or behavior because we actually believe in its content, which is intrinsically rewarding. Internalization often involves the integration of the new response into the individual's value system. The new response is accepted because it is congruent with the individual's value system. An example of internalization is when we accept influence because we are convinced of the *reasons* for the recommended change. A physician may stop smoking, for example, because he or she is convinced that smoking leads to lung cancer. Internalization, unlike compliance and identification, does not depend on an external source, since the content of the behavior in itself is rewarding, and external incentives are not important.

## Antecedents

For each of the three social influence processes Kelman identifies a set of antecedent conditions: the motivational basis for change, the characteristics of the influencing agent, and the conditions when influence can occur.

Compliance occurs when we are concerned with the social effects of behavior; that is, when we are concerned with attaining rewards or avoiding punishment, goals that can be achieved by accepting influence. The main characteristic of the influence source is power, which is the extent to which the source can control the means whereby rewards are attained and punishments avoided. Power also depends on the source's interest in compliance and on ability to scrutinize whether or not the receiver complies. Compliance occurs when a powerful source limits "choice behavior" of the receiver—that is, when the receiver is given an alternative to comply "or else".

As an example, take the young executive who complies with the dress code of the company even though he or she does not agree with it. He or she obviously is concerned with attaining certain rewards (promotion) and avoiding punishment (loss of the job). The company (or its executive officer) is a powerful source that controls the means by which such rewards and punishments can be delivered to the executive. We can logically assume that the company is interested in compliance with its dress code and can observe whether employees comply or not. Compliance occurs when the company makes clear to the executive that compliance is desired. In so doing it limits choice behavior of the executive.

Identification occurs when we are motivated to maintain a satisfying role relationship with the influence agent, which may be classical identification or a reciprocal relationship. In either case the role relationship is rewarding to us and we would like to continue it. The important source characteristic in identification is attractiveness. According to Kelman, an influence agent (or communication source) is attractive if it occupies a role that the receiver would like to occupy or if it occupies a role reciprocal to or supportive of the role that the individual wishes to maintain. A source is attractive to the receiver not necessarily because it possesses "likable" characteristics but because it has qualities that make a continued relationship desirable. Identification occurs when role requirements in a relationship are specified or made clear. One of these requirements may be the acceptance of influence from the source.

As an example, take the relationship between husband and wife. Assuming that both partners would like to continue the relationship and assuming that role requirements of each are made clear for such continuance, identification will often occur. Each partner is attractive to the other because each possesses qualities that make the marital relationship desirable. These qualities often, but not necessarily, lead to mutual liking.

Internalization, the third type of social influence, occurs when we are concerned with how new opinions, attitudes, and behaviors will fit into our value systems, or the sum total of what we already believe in. The major source characteristic in internalization is credibility, or the extent to which we think the source knows the "right anwer" (expertise), and the source's lack of bias or intent to manipulate (trustworthiness). In internalization we are likely to be influenced by credible sources because arguments from such sources are likely to be the "truth." Internalization occurs when the individual perceives that acceptance of the influence will be instrumental in reinforcing his or her important values.

An example of internalization is a physician who stops smoking because he or she believes information from a scientific journal regarding the causal link between smoking and lung cancer. The new behavior fits into the doctor's value system, since it implies a concern for health and a respect for science. Its acceptance, therefore, reinforces what he or she already believes in. The scientific journal is credible because, to the doctor, it is an expert and trustworthy source.

## Consequents

After social influence occurs, there are three types of consequents: the conditions in which the opinion, attitude, or behavior will be expressed; conditions for change; and the type of behavior system in which the new attitude, belief, or behavior exists.

A response brought about through compliance will be expressed only under conditions of surveillance by the influence agent. Thus the individual will tend to perform the response only when the agent is physically present or if he or she is likely to find out about the receiver's actions. A response based on compliance will be abandoned when the receiver no longer sees it as the best method of attaining social rewards. Compliance is therefore anchored in the external demands of the situation or the rules of conduct required in specific situations.

Responses adopted through identification will be expressed when the role relationship between receiver and source is made salient, or made important, in a given situation. A relationship between husband and wife, for example, may be more salient in the home than at work. These responses can be changed when they are no longer perceived as the best path toward maintaining or establishing the role relationship or when the role relationship itself ends. Thus husband and wife may agree that it is not necessary for each to accept influence from the other for the maintenance of the marriage. And if the marriage is terminated, identification will no longer occur. The behavioral system in which internalization is embedded is a person's expectations and definitions of specific roles and role relationships. For example, our expectations of a marriage role relationship will determine whether identification occurs or not.

Internalization responses tend to be performed whenever the values to which the responses are attached are relevant or made important. Thus these responses will occur whenever the issues under consideration are mentioned, regardless of surveillance or salience of the influence agent. A response based on internalization will be abandoned if it is no longer perceived by the individual as the best way to "maximize values," that is, if it no longer supports the existing value system. Internalized responses become integrated into a person's value system and should, therefore, be more difficult to change than responses based on identification or compliance.

## Evaluation

Kelman's theory was regarded as the "most promising" of the functional theories by Insko in 1968 and again by Suedfield in 1971. Unlike other functional theories, it is amenable to both field and laboratory testing, since antecedent and consequent conditions are specified.

Unfortunately, there has been little empirical testing of hypotheses derived from Kelman's theory. Even in this regard, however, Kelman's theory is an improvement over other functional theories, none of which has been put to empirical test.[13]

Another weakness of Kelman's theory is a weakness of all functional theories, and that is in the enumeration of functions that attitudes perform. How are attitudes to be classified, and why? Is it possible to identify all the major attitudinal functions, and how? Are these functions mutually exclusive? These are some of the questions that have been raised regarding the functional approach to attitude change.

## CURRENT THEORETICAL PERSPECTIVES

Most persuasion research today is guided by information-processing and functional theories. Persuasion researchers begin with the assumption that persuasion, like other human behaviors, is influenced by external and internal conditions. Information-processing theories consider new information (an external variable) as the most important influence on persuasion. Functional theories focus on individual motivations, or how needs can be met (internal variables) as bases for persuasion. These two theoretical approaches are not mutually exclusive. Individual needs are also important in information-processing theories, and external communication variables such as information are important in functional theories.

## Information-Processing Theories

Information-processing theories make two basic assumptions about persuasion. First, persuasion results when new information is processed by an individual. Second, people are sophisticated problem solvers who evaluate available information carefully.[14] The major question in information processing theories is, "How does a communication receiver evaluate and process new information?" Norman Anderson's information integration theory provides us with an answer to this question.[15]

According to Anderson, we adapt a new opinion, attitude, or behavioral intention by forming a general impression which, in turn, is based on many pieces of information. Some of this information may support a change in opinion, attitude, or behavioral intention; other information may argue against a change. Also, information will be available from sources that vary in expertise and objectivity. We assign weights to each piece of information based on the expertise and objectivity of the source and on other communication factors; we then average the weights of all the information and use this average to form a general impression. Persuasion occurs depending on whether the general impression supports a change in opinions, attitudes, or behavioral intentions.

Let us illustrate information integration theory with an example. Suppose you were exposed to the following new information about the proposed withdrawal of the United States from the United Nations Educational, Scientific and Cultural Organization (UNESCO).

Information 1. UNESCO has provided many developing countries with educational and health services that would otherwise not have been available to them.

Information 2. UNESCO has become increasingly politicized, and often sides with the Soviet bloc on issues of international politics.

Let us say that Information 1 was attributed to the U.S. ambassador to the United Nations and that Information 2 was attributed to a minor official at the U.S. State Department. You are now ready to assign weights to the information. Weights could be assigned depending on how convincingly each piece of information supports or opposes the proposition that the United States should withdraw from UNESCO. We could use a 5-point scale with the scale points −2 (strongly opposed), −1 (opposed), 0 (neither opposed nor supportive), +1 (supportive) and +2 (strongly supportive). Suppose you assign a score of −2 to Information 1 and a score of +2 to Information 2. Having done this, you still would not be able to make up your mind, since the average for the two statements is 0 (−2 plus +2 = 0). You then assign weights to the sources of each piece of information, depending on how believable they are. You can rate the sources on a similar 5-point scale (as in rating the information), with the scale points $-2$ (not believable at all) to $+2$ (very believable). You assign a score of $+2$ to the United Nations ambassador and a score of $-1$ to the U.S. State Department official. You could then multiply these source weights by the respective information weights to get an overall evaluation of each piece of information. Doing this, you get a $-4$ for Information 1 and a $-2$ for Information 2. The last step is to take the average of these two overall scores, which is $-3$. A score of $-3$ indicates opposition to the U.S. plan to withdraw from UNESCO. This, therefore, would be the opinion that you would adapt. Of course, we do not ordinarily go through all these computations in our everyday activities, but Anderson and his colleagues have shown in laboratory experiments that people use a similar, generalized procedure (without actually assigning the numerical weights) when they process many pieces of contradictory information.

Another information-processing theory is based on Fishbein and Ajzen's belief model of persuasion, which we discussed in Chapter 6. The Fishbein and Ajzen theory is similar to Anderson's, except that it uses the perceived probability of an attribute being associated with an attitude object as a weight to determine the validity of information instead of weights based on source characteristics. For example, suppose you received the following information.

Information 1. The increased production of nuclear arms stimulates the national economy.

Information 2. There are already enough nuclear arms in the world to blow us all up ten times over.

Information 3. The increased production of nuclear arms would increase the danger of a final world war.

On a 5-point scale (from $+2$, a positive quality, to $-2$, a negative quality), you assign Information 1 a weight of $+2$, Information 2 a weight of $-2$, and Information 3 a weight of $-2$. These weights are assigned on the basis of whether the prescribed outcome is positive or negative, as you see it. You could also assign another weight to each piece of information, depending on how probable the prescribed outcome is. Suppose you are quite certain about nuclear arms stimulating the economy (a respected economist said so) and also about there being enough nuclear arms to blow up the world ten times over (a respected senator said so). However, you are not so certain about more nuclear arms leading to a world war (you do not remember where you got this information). You then assign subjective probabilities of .9 to Information 1, .9 to Information 2, and .5 to Information 3. (A subjective probability of 1 means that you are 100 percent certain that the prescribed outcome will occur.) Finally, you average the weights of the three pieces of information by multiplying the evaluation of each information piece by its subjective probability, adding the three products together, and dividing by 3. Doing this, you get an average score of $-.33$, meaning that you have a moderately negative attitude toward the increased production of nuclear arms.

Information-processing theories consider the receiver to be an intelligent, problem-solving individual who accepts or rejects information based on situational factors such as source believability and subjective probabilities of occurrences of the prescribed outcomes.

## Functional Theories

There has been a resurgence of interest in functional theories of persuasion such as Kelman's, which we discussed in the preceding section. The basic assumption of functional theories is that people use information to fulfill needs and to achieve goals. Consequently, persuasion, from the viewpoint of the receiver, is also functional. People change attitudes, opinions, and behaviors because change performs a function or fulfills a need for them. The functional approach is evident in "mass media uses and gratifications research" (which is discussed in Chapter 14) and in what speech communication researchers call "rules-based theories of persuasion."[16] These theoretical approaches support our view of the audience as being active and of communications as being a transaction.

## SUMMARY

In this chapter, we discussed two general theories of communication and persuasion that explain what happens in persuasion and why. Hovland, Janis, and Kelly's instrumental theory suggests that attitudes are changed by changing related opinions. Acceptance of new opinions is based on information and incentives or rewards in the message.

Kelman's functional theory of persuasion suggests that the key to changing attitudes is to know the reasons why people hold the attitudes they do. By knowing these motivations, we can predict when and how attitudes will change.

Current theoretical approaches emphasize how receivers process and evaluate information and how their needs are met by information.

## REVIEW QUESTION

**1.** What are some of your attitudes that have *changed* recently? Using instrumental or functional theories of persuasion, analyze *why* these attitudes changed.

## ENDNOTES

1. T. M. Ostrom, "The Emergence of Attitude Theory," in A. G. Greenwald, T. C. Brock, and T. M. Ostrom (eds.), *Psychological Foundations of Attitudes* (New York: Academic Press, 1968), pp. 1–32.

2. See, for example C. L. Hull, *The Principles of Behavior* (New York: Appleton-Century-Crofts, 1943); K. W. Spence, *Behavior Theory and Conditioning* (New Haven, Conn.: Yale University Press, 1956).

3. G. A. Kimble, *Hilgard and Marquis' Conditioning and Learning* (New York: Appleton-Century-Crofts, 1961).

4. M. Fishbein and I. Ajzen, *Belief, Attitude, Intention and Behavior* (Reading, Mass.: Addison-Wesley, 1975), pp. 22–26.

5. Kimble, *op. cit.*

6. Carl Hovland, Irving Janis, and Harold Kelly, *Communication and Persuasion* (New Haven, Conn.: Yale University Press, 1953).

7. Fishbein and Ajzen, *op. cit.*

8. Chester Insko, *Theories of Attitude Change* (New York: Appleton-Century-Crofts, 1967), pp. 12–63.

9. Hull, *op. cit.*

10. See, for example, H. Kelman,"Compliance, Identification and Internalization: Three Processes of Attitude Change," *Journal of Conflict Resolution, 2,* 1958, pp. 51–60; for a good review of functional theories, see Insko, *op. cit.,* pp. 330–344.

11. Kelman, *op. cit.*

12. Insko, *op. cit.*

13. *Ibid.*

14. Drury Sherrod, *Social Psychology* (New York: Random House, 1982).

15. N. H. Anderson, "Integration Theory Applied to Cognitive Responses and Attitudes," in R. E. Petty, T. M. Ostrom, and T. C. Brock (eds.), *Cognitive Responses in Persuasion* (New York: Erlbaum, 1980).

16. For example, Mary John Smith, *Persuasion and Human Action* (Belmont, Calif.: Wadsworth, 1982).

# 8

# COMMUNICATION SOURCES

In this chapter we will discuss how communication sources can affect their audiences. The main question is: What characteristics of a communication source will make him or her more effective in persuasion?" Following the models of McGuire and Hovland, we will break down persuasion into reception of the message, yielding or attitude change, and action or behavioral change.

The interest in communication source characteristics in persuasion is not new. Aristotle referred to persuasion attempts that focused on the source's character instead of on the message, as "ethos" appeals. He suggested that an effective communicator must have good sense, good will, and good moral character.[1]

To Machiavelli, an effective communicator is an authority in his or her field, disguises the intent to persuade, and is prestigious. The following excerpts from *Discourses* illustrate Machiavelli's idea of the effective communicator.

> Nothing is so apt to restrain an excited multitude as the reverence inspired by some *grave and dignified man of authority* who opposes them. Therefore whoever is at the head of an army, or whoever happens to be a magistrate in a city where sedition lies broken out, should present himself before the multitude with all possible grace and dignity, and attired with all the insignia of his rank, so as to inspire more respect.[2]

> For he who for a time has seemed good, and for purposes of his own wants to become bad, *should do it gradually,* and should seem to be brought to it by the force of circumstances.[3]

> In truth, there never was any remarkable lawgiver amongst any people who did not resort to *divine authority,* as otherwise his laws would not have been accepted by the people.[4]

To Goebbels, Hitler's minister of propaganda, an effective communicator was both credible and prestigious. Credibility to him was whether the message from the source could be proved or could *not* be disproved. Leaders were useful in propaganda campaigns only when they had prestige—when they were perceived to be competent and were admired by the public.[5]

More recently, the public relations men behind Richard Nixon's 1968 campaign for the presidency saw "source image" as a problem with their candidate. Joe McGinnis, in his book *The Selling of the President,* 1968, quotes one of Nixon's campaign strategists.

> Our advertising between Labor Day and the election will have two objectives—to present Nixon the Man in ways that will dispel existing negative feelings about his personality and sincerity—that will show him as a knowledgeable, experienced, and likeable candidate.[6]

Today's persuasion researchers have concentrated on three characteristics of communication sources—credibility, attractiveness, and power. Other characteristics such as dynamism, sociability, authoritative manner, and reliability also affect source effectiveness,[7] but most of the research has dealt with either credibility, attractiveness, or power.

## SOURCE CHARACTERISTICS

### Credibility

Source credibility consists of two components—expertise and trustworthiness. Expertise is the extent to which the source is perceived by the audience to know the "right answer" to the question or the "correct" stand on the issue.[8] Expertise depends on training, experience, ability, intelligence, professional attainment, and social status. An expert source is one who has valid and reliable knowledge about the issue. Very often expertise is topic bound. We would not expect very many sources to be experts on more than a few topics.

Receivers who are influenced by an expert source often are rational, problem-solving individuals who are trying to adjust their attitudes as closely as possible with external reality, or with the "real world." If influenced by the source's expertise, these individuals usually internalize the new attitude, which becomes part of their existing value systems. Theoretically, the new attitude will be resistant to change.

Examples of expert sources are the physician on problems of health, the lawyer on legal matters, the automobile mechanic on car repairs, and the communication professor on persuasion. Communication audiences will perceive these sources as knowledgeable on topics dealing with their specialized fields because of experience, training, or education.

Learning theory predicts that expert sources will be effective in persuasion because receivers have been rewarded in the past for taking "correct" stands on issues and because they have learned that knowledgeable sources are likely to advocate correct stands. We are likely to believe a physician's diagnosis of an illness because he has been right before and following his recommendations has led to better health.

Functional theory predicts that expert sources will be effective with receivers who are concerned with value congruence. These individuals would like to fit new attitudes and opinions with what they already believe in. Since they consider themselves as being primarily "rational," a source that is likely to be right on the issue in question will be influential.

A credible source is not only perceived to be an expert on the issue in question; he or she is also perceived to be trustworthy. Trustworthiness is the extent to which a source is perceived as being motivated to communicate his or her stand without bias. A trustworthy source, therefore, is an objective source. Also, a trustworthy source is perceived by the audience to have no intention to manipulate and to have nothing to gain if the audience accepts the recommendations of the message. For example, a used-car salesperson is rarely perceived by prospective automobile buyers to be a trustworthy source. We know that he or she is likely to be biased, out to convince us to buy a car from him or her, and has something to gain from the manipulation.

Learning theory predicts that trustworthy sources are more likely than untrustworthy sources to change attitudes and behaviors because of our previous experiences with them. In the past, being manipulated by biased sources who had something to gain from the influence led to unpleasant feelings or consequences, such as the loss of self-esteem or loss of valued possessions (as when we are convinced to buy a "lemon" by a dishonest car salesperson). In addition, most adults have a natural tendency to resist persuasion. We do not like to be manipulated because this is usually an unpleasant experience and because accepting influence is admission that the replaced behavior or attitude was not adequate.

According to functional theory, trustworthy sources are likely to be effective with communication receivers who, as in the case of expert sources, are seeking value congruence. Trustworthy sources are more likely to give objective information that can be verified in the real world. Recommendations based on this information are therefore more likely to be believed.

A credible source is both knowledgeable and trustworthy. Such sources are, of course, quite rare in the real world. The more common source is one that is an expert but is not trustworthy. The used-car salesperson, for example, might be an expert source of information about the value and condition of his or her cars, but most of us would consider him or her to be untrustworthy.

## Attractiveness

Another characteristic of the communication source determining effectiveness in persuasion is attractiveness. Most of us would define attractiveness as physical attractiveness, or charisma. However, communication researchers have generally refrained from using physical attributes of the source as criteria of attractiveness because of the difficulty in quantifying and measuring these characteristics objectively. Instead, they have focused on similarity, familiarity, and liking as determinants of source attractiveness. The general hypothesis is that attractive sources will be more effective than neutral or unattractive sources in persuasion. The following source characteristics determine attractiveness.

### Similarity

In general, we are attracted to people who are similar to us.[9] The same principle holds for communication sources.[10] We find communication sources that are like ourselves to be attractive, and we are more likely to be influenced by them than by sources that are different. There are two major components of communication source similarity: demographic similarity and ideological similarity.

Audiences are attracted to communication sources that share common demographic characteristics with them—such as age, education, occupation, income level, religion, race, and place of residence.[11] These sources are attractive because the audience is able to identify with them. Since many diverse characteristics are shared, receivers perceive the source to be "one of us" and that they have common needs and goals. If the source can show the audience that their interests and needs are mutual because of similarities in characteristics, the audience will perceive that what the source is recommending is good for "our kind of people."

Another component of similarity is ideological similarity. We are attracted to communication sources that have similar attitudes and opinions. The greater the number of common attitudes and the more important these attitudes are to the receiver, the more attractive the source will be. In general, research has shown that ideological similarity is a more powerful determinant of attractiveness than demographic similarity. Americans, for example, have been found to be influenced more by ideological similarity than by racial differences in persuasion situations.[12] That is, we can be attracted to and influenced by communicators of a different racial background provided we perceive some similarity in attitudes and opinions with them.

Learning theory predicts that sources similar to us will be effective in persuasion because we have been rewarded in the past for interacting with and for listening to communicators who were "one of us." Similar communicators are likely to recommend attitudes or behaviors that lead to psychological or material rewards. Also, interaction with others who are similar is in itself a rewarding experience. Behaviors are predictable and participants are likely to reinforce each other.

Functional theory predicts that similar communicators will be effective in persuasion because of the motivation of receivers to identify with them. Identification helps the receiver maintain a rewarding role relationship with the source. We are more likely to engage in relationships with similar than different sources. To maintain such relationships, we often accept influence from the other participants in the relationship.

### Familiarity

An old proverb proclaims "Absence makes the heart grow fonder." Another says about the good man "to know him is to love him." In communication and persuasion, not only do we love *good* communicators by knowing them; we learn to like *all* communicators by knowing them.

There is considerable evidence that as interaction between persons increases, so also does their liking and attraction for each other. In addition, familiarity in itself has been found to enhance liking.[13]

We seem therefore to be attracted to sources that are familiar to us, sources we have read or heard or seen before. Consider how easily we become "addicted" to a particular newspaper, magazine, or television newscaster. Also consider how difficult it is to accept *new* communication sources in our daily routines.

The general prediction is that familiar sources will be attractive and will therefore be more effective in persuasion than unfamiliar sources. According to learning theory, interaction with familiar sources will be more predictable, effortless, and rewarding than interaction with unfamiliar sources. Functional theory predicts that we are more likely to engage in continuing role relationships with persons already familiar to us.

### Liking

We are attracted to communicators we like; the more we like a communicator, the more we will be persuaded by him or her.[14] But what determines liking? Research indicates that similarity and familiarity lead to liking. Liking, in turn, enhances the perceived similarity of the source. We tend to exaggerate real similarities between ourselves and communicators (or other people) we like.

Reinforcement is another key to liking other people.[15] We like communicators who reward us, and we dislike those who punish us. Communicators who provide rewards that are scarce are more likely to be attractive and liked than those who provide rewards that are relatively common. The probability of liking is also increased when the amount of the reward is considerably greater than the cost of interaction (such as effort required). These principles are derived from the learning theories we discussed in the previous chapter.

How can communicators reward us? According to Berscheid and Walster,[16] communicators (and other persons, in general) can provide us with the following rewards.

**1. Reduction of anxiety, stress, loneliness, or insecurity.** When we feel anxious, afraid, lonely, or unsure of ourselves, the sheer presence of others can be rewarding. According to Schachter, anxious people have this special desire to affiliate or interact with others, especially those in similar situations, because other people can offer comfort and reassurance.[17] Also, interaction with others can provide diversion from the source of anxiety, as in "getting one's mind off one's troubles." We often use other people as a guide or source of information about our own feelings. We look at how others are reacting to the same situation and label and identify our own feelings accordingly. Schachter's analysis can explain why we often like communicators who are comforting, who can divert our attention from our own feelings of anxiety, and who can provide us with guidance on how to cope with our feelings.

Television, the medium used most by the public for entertainment and news, provides diversion. Soap operas, popular with many men and women, provide diversion and information on how to cope with stressful feelings. In times of crisis, as during the days immediately after John F. Kennedy's assassination, many people are attracted to the mass media for information and comfort.

**2. Social approval.** According to motivational psychologists, the desire for the esteem of others is a very strong and pervasive human motivation. Thus, we are extremely responsive to social approval or esteem.[18] We like others who like us or who can help us win the admiration and affection of others. We are therefore responsive to communicators who like us or who can show us how to be liked by others. Social approval is valuable not only because it reinforces our self-esteem but also because it facilitates the satisfaction of many of our needs, particularly those requiring the cooperation of others.

**3. Proximity.** Other things being equal, individuals who are physically close to each other will be attracted more to each other than individuals who are far from each other. Studies have shown, for example, that students develop stronger friendships with other students who share the same classes, or their dormitory or apartment building, or who sit near them, than those who are physically located only slightly farther away.[19] Also, white persons who experience increased contact with blacks because of physical proximity become less prejudiced subsequent to that contact.[20] However, some research suggests that close proximity can also lead to increased hostility between individuals.[21] The key to whether liking or disliking is fostered seems to be in the nature of information exchanged and interaction between the individuals. Close proximity allows for the exchange of information and for increased interaction. If the information is positive and if the interaction leads to rewards, then liking will result. Otherwise hostility is the more likely effect.

A common finding in persuasion research is that face-to-face communications are generally more effective than indirect or mediated communications.[22] This finding can be explained by the proximity principle. It is easier to like (or be attracted to) communicators that are physically close because proximity allows for more interaction and for the exchange of information. The proximity principle is also supported by research on familiarity and liking. We like familiar sources; a most effective way of fostering familiarity is by establishing physical proximity.

**4. Cooperation.** Research has shown that we like others who cooperate with us in our attempts to obtain rewards for ourselves. Also, we dislike those who frustrate our attempts to obtain a reward because of maliciousness or because they are competing for the same rewards.[23]

To summarize this section on liking, the general hypothesis is that liked sources are more effective in persuasion than disliked sources. Communicators we like tend to be demographically and ideologically similar to ourselves, familiar, and rewarding. Some common rewards are the reduction of anxiety, stress, loneliness, or insecurity; giving or making possible social approval; proximity; and cooperation. A communicator who delivers one or more of these rewards will be liked and will therefore be effective in persuasion.

### Physical Attractiveness

Most of us would like to believe that physical beauty is only "skin deep" and that we are able to judge other people on factors other than physical appearance. However, research on interpersonal attraction tells us otherwise: physical attractiveness often determines how we evaluate other persons.

The first question in physical attractiveness research is, "Who is physically attractive?" Darwin once said, "It is certainly not true that there is in the mind of man any universal standard of beauty with respect to the human body." The lack of a standard has, however, not hindered research on physical attractiveness. Most researchers have used a "truth by consensus" method to determine the physical attractiveness of the stimulus person. If a significant number of "judges" designates a person as physically attractive, then that person is defined as physically attractive.[24]

There is an increasing amount of evidence that physical attractiveness is an important determinant of a wide variety of interpersonal processes: heterosexual liking, peer popularity in young children, attributions of personal characteristics and future success, adults' judgments of children's transgressions, and employers' evaluations of prospective employees. In many of these studies, subjects attribute more positive characteristics to and expect better performance from physically attractive people compared to unattractive people. Dion, for example, found that college students of both sexes expected physically attractive men and women to possess more socially desirable traits (such as sensitivity, strength, and modesty) than unattractive people. Attractive people were also expected to have more prestigious occupations and happier marriages in the future than unattractive people.[25] In another study Dion and Berscheid found that adults judged attractive nursery school children to be more popular with their peers and to manifest less socially undesirable interpersonal behavior than unattractive children.[26]

Physical attractiveness affects our evaluations about actual task performances of people. In an experiment by Landy and Sigall, subjects evaluated a writer and her work (an essay) most favorably when she was attractive, least when she was unattractive, and intermediately when her appearance was unknown.[27] Physical attractiveness had greater impact when the quality of her work was poor instead of good. A poor essay by an attractive source was rated considerably "better" than the same essay attributed to an unattractive source.

There seems to be adequate evidence, then, that physical attractiveness affects our evaluations of how other people perform and interact in a wide variety of interpersonal relationships. On the basis of this evidence, we can predict that physical attractiveness is also a significant factor in persuasion.

Unfortunately, communication researchers have not adequately investigated the relationship of physical attractiveness to persuasive impact. One study by Mills and Aronson in 1965 did show that a physically attractive source was more influential in changing receiver opinions than an unattractive source, but only when both sources announced their intention to persuade.[28] Mills and Aronson manipulated physical attractiveness by presenting a female communicator in two conditions. In the attractive condition, she (the communicator) "wore chic, tight-fitting clothing; her hair was modishly coiffured; she wore becoming makeup." In the unattractive condition, the same communicator "wore loose, ugly, ill-fitting clothing; her hair was messy; her make-up was conspicuously absent; the trace of a mustache was etched on her upper lip; her complexion was oily and unwholesome looking." Although validity checks indicated that subjects did perceive the first communicator to be more attractive than the second, it is obviously difficult to generalize results of this study, since such extremes in physical attractiveness are not common in the real world. Recent studies have studied communicator physical attractiveness in more realistic settings and have attempted to explain why physically attractive communicators are more effective. Many of these explanations are based on theories of impression formation in social psychology. People need to form impressions of their environment in a way that makes sense to them. Quite often, we attempt to form these impressions too hastily, using the first pieces of information that become available. Since physical attractiveness is a characteristic of people that we can "see" right away, we use this information to form impressions of other people. We often associate pleasant personality characteristics with physical attractiveness. Therefore, we are influenced by sources that we consider to be physically attractive. Initial impressions of sources based on physical attractiveness can be modified as more information about them becomes available. The effects of physical attractiveness on persuasion are often short term and are most likely when the receiver does not have the opportunity to learn more about the source.

## Power

Some communication sources have neither credibility nor attractiveness but are nevertheless effective in changing other people's attitudes and behaviors. These sources have power, the third component determining source effectiveness.

Powerful sources have three characteristics: perceived control, perceived concern, and perceived scrutiny.[29] Perceived control is the extent to which the audience perceives the source to be able to administer rewards and punishments to them. Research has shown that punishing power and rewarding power are equally effective in producing compliance.[30] The more important the rewards and the more costly the punishments to the receivers, the more powerful the source will be. Perceived concern is the audience's estimate of how much the source cares whether the audience conforms or not. Perceived scrutiny is the extent to which the source will be able to observe whether the audience conforms or not. A powerful source will therefore be able to administer rewards and punishments, will be interested in conformity, and will be able to observe whether the audience conforms or not.

The process by which a powerful source is able to effect change in attitudes and behaviors is compliance. Compliance involves public acceptance of the source's recommendations without private commitment. According to learning theory, powerful sources can change attitudes and behaviors because they are able to reinforce such changes. Functional theory explains compliance in terms of the receiver's motivation to attain rewards or avoid punishments that the powerful source can administer.

## RESEARCH

In this section we will review some of the major studies dealing with source effectiveness in persuasion. Almost all of these studies have used experimental designs. Typically, an identical message is attributed to sources varying in credibility, attractiveness, or power and is then presented to randomized groups of subjects. Thus one group might receive the message from a source low in credibility while another group receives the same message from a source high in credibility. Attitude change is measured by taking the difference between before measures (attitudes of the subjects before receiving the message) and after measures (attitudes after receiving the message). Some studies measure attitude change by comparing attitudes of the experimental groups (those groups receiving the message) with a control group (which does not receive the message). Source effectiveness is analyzed by comparing attitude change between the different experimental groups as, for example, between low and high-credibility groups. Subjects in these studies are often college students, and testing is usually done in the classroom.

### Source Credibility

Intuitively, we might guess that credible sources, or sources that we perceive to be knowledgeable and trustworthy, are more effective in persuasion than sources that are not credible. However, we can still ask how *much more* effective are high-credibility than low-credibility sources and whether or not low-credibility sources produce attitude change in the opposite direction from the message.

#### Hovland and Weiss's 1951 Study

The first systematic study of source credibility was done at Yale by Hovland and Weiss in 1951.[31] Their study was quite simple. Subjects were undergraduate college students who were first asked to fill out an opinion questionnaire a week before receiving the persuasive messages. Four messages were then administered to each of two random groups. Except for source attribution, the messages were identical. Some subjects received the message from high-credibility sources, while others received the same message from low-credibility sources. The messages dealt with the following topics: the advisability of selling antihistamines without a prescription, the practicality of building atomic submarines, whether or not there will be a decrease in movie theaters because of television, and whether or not the steel industry was to blame for the steel shortage. The messages were attributed to high- or low-credibility sources for different groups of subjects. For the antihistamine issue, the credible source was the *New England Journal of Biology and Medicine* and the low-credibility source was a mass circulation, monthly pictorial magazine. The high-credibility source for the atomic submarine issue was Robert J. Oppenheimer, while the low-credibility source was *Pravda*. On the steel shortage the credible source was the *Bulletin of National Resources Planning Board,* and the low-credibility source was an anti-Labor, rightist newspaper columnist. High- and low-credibility sources for the movie theater message were, respectively, *Fortune* magazine and a female movie gossip columnist.

After the subjects had read the messages, they were asked to fill out a second opinion questionnaire that differed in format from the first one but that dealt with the same issues. Subjects were also given a multiple-choice fact quiz on the contents of the messages they had just read. A final questionnaire identical to the second one was given four weeks later to measure delayed effect.

Hovland and Weiss predicted that high-credibility sources would be more effective than low-credibility sources in changing opinions. Their prediction was based on learning theory: subjects would associate rewards (such as taking the "correct" stand on an issue) with the credible sources and would therefore be more receptive to them.

Hovland and Weiss found general support for their hypothesis, but only immediately after the message was presented to the subjects. Analysis of the first questionnaire indicated that their source credibility manipulations worked. The four high-credibility sources were judged by the students to be more trustworthy than the four low-credibility sources. These ratings were made before the students read the messages and were intended to check on the validity of the source credibility manipulations. Analysis of the difference in opinion scores between the before and immediately after questionnaires for all four topics showed that significantly more subjects were influenced by the high-credibility than by the low-credibility sources. For all topics the net change (percentage of subjects changing in the direction of the message minus the percentage changing in the opposite direction) for the high-credibility sources was 22.5 percent, while the net change for low-credibility sources was 8.4 percent. The difference in net change of 16.4 percent is significant at the 0.03 level, which means that it would occur by chance only three times in one hundred. Four weeks later, however, the number of subjects agreeing with the high-credibility sources had decreased, while the number of subjects agreeing with low-credibility sources had increased. The difference in change over four weeks between high-credibility and low-credibility groups was significant; that is, there was more change (a decrease in agreement) in the high-credibility group than in the low-credibility group (an increase in agreement). This phenomenon has been called the "sleeper effect." According to Hovland and Weiss, low-credibility sources have greater persuasive impact after some time delay than on original exposure because communication receivers tend to dissociate the source and content over time. This does not mean that we forget sources or messages. What happens is that we forget which messages came from which sources. The result is that the effectiveness of a credible source is diminished, while the effectiveness of a low-credibility source is increased.

Hovland and Weiss also found that source credibility did not affect recall of message contents either immediately after the message was presented or four weeks later. There were no significant differences in message recall between groups receiving the message from high- and low-credibility sources.

What can we conclude from the Hovland and Weiss experiment? First, the study shows that high-credibility sources produce more attitude change than low-credibility sources immediately after presentation of the message. Second, agreement with a credible source decreases over time (four weeks). This change is greater than the change in low-credibility subjects, which is in the direction of agreement with the low-credibility source. Third, credibility of the source does not affect message recall.

### Kelman and Hovland's 1953 Study

Kelman and Hovland tested the hypothesis that high-credibility sources will continue to be more effective in persuasion than low-credibility sources over a period of time if the subjects are reminded of the sources prior to the measurement of attitudes.[32] Thus they predicted that reinstatement of the source would erase the sleeper effect.

An identical message arguing for more lenient treatment of juvenile delinquents was presented to two random groups of college students. One group received a message that was attributed to a high-credibility source (a judge in a juvenile court who had authored several authoritative books on juvenile delinquency); the other group received the message from a low-credibility source (a dope peddler out on bail). The message was taped and presented to the students in the context of an educational program. Attitudes were measured immediately after the communication. Three weeks later the attitude measure and a test of message recall were administered. At this time, half of the subjects filled out the questionnaire after hearing part of the message that introduced the source (a "reinstatement" of the source), and half completed the questionnaire without the reinstatment.

Their results show that immediately after the communication more subjects agreed with the high-credibility than with the low-credibility source. Three weeks later reinstatement of the high-credibility source increased agreement with the message (compared to the subjects in the nonreinstatement condition), while reinstatement of the low-credibility source decreased agreement. According to Kelman and Hovland, these findings support the conclusions that the sleeper effect is due to a tendency to dissociate message sources and contents and that the effectiveness of credible sources can be maintained by reinstatement of the sources.

### Gillig and Greenwald's 1974 Study

Gillig and Greenwald conducted a series of seven experiments to determine whether audiences reject persuasive messages on the basis of contents or sources.[33] Tests of their hypotheses would have been possible only if the sleeper effect could be replicated. None of the seven experiments showed a sleeper effect. This led them to examine previous studies on the sleeper effect and to compare previous results with their own.

As originally defined by Hovland and Weiss, the sleeper effect occurs when a message from a low-credibility source has a greater persuasive impact after some delay than on original exposure. Gillig and Greenwald report, however, that the original sleeper effect was found only for a subset of the opinions that Hovland used; agreement with the low-credibility source increased for some items but not for others. Also, there was no logical reason why the sleeper effect was observed for some items and not for others.

Subsequent studies of the sleeper effect, according to Gillig and Greenwald, have never reported a statistically significant increase in attitude change, over time, for a group receiving the message from a low-credibility source. What is typically reported is a decrease in agreement with a high-credibility source. The change in high-credibility groups (which is toward less agreement) is then compared with change in the low-credibility groups. This comparison often results in statistical significance but, according to Gillig and Greenwald, it should not be taken as evidence of the sleeper effect, since significance can be attained even if there was no change within the low-credibility group. The sleeper effect can be shown only if there is an increase, over time, in the persuasive impact of a message from a low-credibility source.

Gillig and Greenwald used three different messages in their experiments. One message argued against the widespread use of penicillin, another argued against routine annual medical checkups, and the third argued in favor of massive daily doses of vitamin C. Subjects were randomly assigned to a high-credibility or low-credibility condition. In some of the experiments the high-credibility source was described as a "leading medical researcher" whose research was on the topic of the communication. The low-credibility source was introduced as a "nature therapist" who was generally antagonistic to therapeutic use of drugs and to other modern medical techniques. In other experiments subjects in the low-credibility condition were simply informed that the content of the message was not necessarily drawn from factual material, while subjects in the high-credibility conditions were told that the communication consisted only of factually accurate material. All messages were presented to the subjects by videotape.

Two dependent measures were used for message effects: opinion measures and cognitive responses. Opinions were measured with fifteen-point response scales. Cognitive responses were measured by presenting subjects with twelve short paragraph segments from the message immediately after exposure to the communication. They were then asked to recall and report in writing, after each segment, the thoughts that had occurred to them upon the original presentation of that segment of the communication. These written reactions were then sorted into four categories by judges: (1) agreement, (2) discounting of the source, (3) counterargument of the message, or (4) neutral. Opinions were measured immediately after presentation of the message and ten to fourteen days later. Cognitive responses were measured only immediately after exposure to the communication.

Analysis of cognitive responses indicates that high-credibility sources produced about twice as many agreement responses as did low-credibility sources ($p<.01$) and fewer disagreeing responses. Subjects in the low-credibility conditions also indicated more discounting responses and counterarguments than subjects in the high-credibility conditions.

Analysis of the opinion measures shows that immediately after exposure to the communication, agreement was higher with the high-credibility than with the low-credibility sources. There was a slight, but nonsignificant, increase in agreement with the low-credibility source between the immediate and delayed (ten to fourteen days later) opinion tests. For subjects receiving the message from the credible source, the decrease in agreement between the immediate and delayed opinion tests was significant ($p<.01$). The interaction between source credibility and time of opinion measure was also significant ($p<.01$), indicating that agreement with the source decreases over time, but only for subjects in the high-credibility condition.

What conclusions can we draw from Gillig and Greenwald's experiments? (1) High-credibility sources are more effective than low-credibility sources in producing immediate opinion change. (2) Agreement with a high-credibility source diminishes with time. (3) Agreement with a low-credibility source does not increase over time.

As in the Hovland and Weiss study, highly credible sources produced more opinion change in the audience immediately after the message was delivered. However, Gillig and Greenwald's experiments provide no evidence for the sleeper effect.

### Fishbein and Ajzen's 1975 Study

Fishbein and Ajzen reanalyzed the data from the 1951 Hovland and Weiss experiment and concluded that the study provides only limited support for the hypothesis that high-credibility sources produce more opinion change or that the effect of credibility is due to increased yielding (change in at-

TABLE 8.1. Effects of Communicator Credibility

| | Dependent Variables | | | |
| | Net Opinion Change, % | | Number of Correct Items on Fact Quiz | |
| Topic | High Credibility | Low Credibility | High Credibility | Low Credibility |
|---|---|---|---|---|
| Antihistimines | 22.6 | 13.3 | 3.42 | 3.17 |
| Atomic submarines | 36.0[a] | 0.0 | 3.48 | 3.72 |
| Steel shortage | 22.9[a] | −3.8 | 3.34 | 2.73 |
| Future of movies | 12.9 | 16.7 | 3.23 | 3.27 |
| Mean | 23.0[a] | 6.6 | 3.36 | 3.26 |

[a]Significant difference between high- and low-credibility scores.
*Source:* Adapted from Hovland and Weiss, 1951, and Fishbein and Ajzen, 1975.

titudes).[34] Fishbein and Ajzen argue that a clear distinction should be made between opinion change (change in information about an issue) and attitude change (change in feelings about an issue) as effects of source credibility. We may change opinions without necessarily changing attitudes, particularly if the opinions are not related to the attitude.

Fishbein and Ajzen's analysis of the Hovland and Weiss data is shown in Table 8.1. As you can see from the net opinion change columns for high- and low-credibility sources, the effect of communicator credibility is not the same for the four different topics. The high-credibility communicator produced greater opinion change than the low-credibility source in three topics, but only two of the differences are statistically significant. For the message dealing with the future of movie theaters, the low-credibility source produced more attitude change than the high-credibility source; this difference, however, is not significant. Although the overall difference in net opinion change between the high-credibility (23.0 percent) and low-credibility (6.6 percent) groups is significant, we cannot conclude that source credibility had an effect on attitude change for all topics. Following Fishbein and Ajzen's model, the information in some of the persuasive messages was probably directly related to attitudes on the issue and thus changed them, while for others, it was not.

### McCroskey's 1970 Study

McCroskey tested the hypothesis that a message from a low-credibility source can change opinions if the message contains highly convincing supportive arguments.[35] His message dealt with attitudes toward federal control of education. Source credibility and strength of arguments supporting the conclusion were manipulated. Subjects received the message either from a high-credibility or low-credibility source; the message had either strong supportive evidence supporting the conclusion or minimal supportive evidence. His results indicate that high-credibility sources produced more attitude change only when the message had minimal supportive evidence. There was no difference in attitude change between high-credibility and low-credibility groups when strong supportive evidence was presented. One explanation of this finding is that subjects in the strong supportive evidence conditions changed their attitudes on the basis of the evidence and irrespective of the source's credibility. We can conclude from this study that both message contents and source credibility affect persuasion and that the effects of source credibility are more pronounced when little or weak evidence is given in the message supporting the conclusion.

### Birnbaum and Stegner's 1979 Study

Most of the studies we have reviewed so far used communication sources that were either high in both expertise and objectivity (trustworthiness) or low in both expertise and objectivity. Some did not distinguish between expertise and objectivity and instead used a summary judgment from subjects as to the source's overall credibility. What happens when you have a source that is expert and biased, or a source that is not an expert, but objective? How effective will they be in persuasion? Which is more important, expertise or trustworthiness? How do expertise and bias interact with the receiver's initial position on the issue in determining source effectiveness? These are some of the questions that Birnbaum and Stegner investigated in a series of experiments in 1979.[36]

Previous research on the effects of a source's trustworthiness or bias on attitude change has produced contradictory evidence.[37] Common sense leads us to predict that the more biased a source, the less effective he or she would be in changing attitudes. Research, however, has not been able to provide unequivocal support for this prediction. Warning of a source's persuasive intent (and therefore of his or her bias) sometimes decreases the source's persuasive impact, but only when the warning precedes the message by a long (about ten minutes) rather than a short (two minutes) time.[38] When the source is simply introduced as being biased (or objective), perceived trustworthiness does not affect persuasive impact, particularly when both sources were perceived by the receivers to be experts on the issue.[39] Other studies have shown that perceived bias actually enhances persuasive impact when the communicator is also powerful or attractive.[40] It seems then that the effects of source trustworthiness on attitude change depend on other factors in the communication environment. Birnbaum and Stegner studied two of these factors: source expertise and receiver bias.

According to Birnbaum and Stegner, the effect of source credibility on opinion change depends on three components: source expertise, source bias, and the receiver's point of view (or receiver bias). We can predict the persuasive impact of a communicator only when these three components are taken into account. Birnbaum and Stegner conducted several experiments to test various mathematical models depicting the relationships between these three components and receiver opinions. Students were asked to judge the values of hypothetical used cars based on blue book value and/or estimates of value provided by sources who varied in bias and expertise. The low-expertise source was described as "a competent person who drives a car regularly and has purchased cars for himself." The medium-expertise source had "taken some classes in auto shop and can make repairs himself." The high-expertise source was "an expert mechanic whose hobby is the repair and modification of sports cars." Source bias was manipulated by introducing each source as a friend of the buyer, a friend of the seller, or an independent, neutral observer. Thus, the independent variables were source expertise and bias and the dependent variables were estimates by subjects of the value of the car. Birnbaum and Stegner were interested in finding out how subjects' estimates would be affected by the blue book value (an objective standard) and by manipulations of source expertise and bias.

Among their many findings, the following are directly relevant to source credibility and persuasion:

1. Sources of high expertise influenced the subjects' estimates of the value of the car more than sources of medium or low expertise.
2. Source bias affected subject estimates of car values in the expected directions. For example, judged values of the car were greater when the source was a friend of the buyer than when he was a friend of the seller. It was as if subjects were expecting a friend of the buyer to undervalue the car, so they increased their own estimates. Conversely, subjects probably expected a friend of the seller to overestimate the car's value, so they gave lower estimates.
3. Expertise magnifies the effects of bias. Expert sources were not judged to be more biased, but the effects of bias were greater for sources of greater expertise. In general, biased sources were less likely to be believed if they were also perceived to be experts. Subjects gave higher estimates of the car when the source was the buyer's friend (biased) *and* high in expertise, compared to when the source was the buyer's friend but low in expertise. Also, lower estimates of the car's value were given by subjects when the source was the seller's friend and an expert, compared to when he was the seller's friend but not an expert.
4. A source may be more influential if he or she makes an estimate (or communicates a recommendation) that would not be expected on the basis of his or her bias. For example, a seller's friend who gives a low estimate of the car's value (when he or she would be expected to give a high estimate) would be believed more and therefore would be more influential than an unbiased source who gave the same estimate.
5. Biased sources are likely to be believed if their recommendations support existing beliefs of the receiver. Although biased sources may not be effective in changing opinions, they are effective in reinforcing them.

In summary, Birnbaum and Stegner provide evidence that expert sources are more influential than nonexpert sources, that biased sources are generally less effective than unbiased sources, that expertise magnifies the effects of source bias, that sources recommending the unexpected (on the basis of their biases) are more effective than neutral sources, and that biased sources can be effective in reinforcing opinions.

### Birnbaum and Mellers' 1983 Study

This study tested predictions from a "scale-adjustment averaging model" that Birnbaum and Stegner had proposed in 1979. The scale-adjustment model is one of many information-processing models that explain how communication receivers evaluate information. According to this model, we sum up or aggregate the average strength of evidence before making decisions. We evaluate the different pieces of evidence by evaluating the source's bias, expertise, and whatever "base rate information" is available. Base rate information is "average" information. For example, in judging the value of used cars, blue book values are base rate information. We assign weights to different pieces of information depending on the expertise and bias of the source and on their discrepancies with any base rate information that we may have. The effect of information is directly proportional to its weight and inversely related to the number and weights of opposing information.

Birnbaum and Mellers used an experimental procedure similar to that in the 1979 study by Birnbaum and Stegner except this time, they asked their subjects to judge the probability that a used car would "stay in working condition for 3 years" instead of judging their dollar values.[41] Information was provided from sources that varied in expertise (very low, low, high, and very high) and bias (friend of seller, friend of buyer, and independent). Base rate information (blue book values of the car) was also provided. Subjects were told that the probability that a used car would last was directly proportional to its blue book value. They were told, for example, that of 100 cars with blue book values of $300, 30 are expected to last three years and the remaining 70 are expected to fail.

Some of the results of the Birnbaum and Mellers study are the following.

1. Subjects were more influenced by sources high in expertise than by sources low in expertise.
2. Source bias influenced the subjects to give recommendations in the opposite direction. Subjects who received information from a friend of the buyer gave more favorable evaluations to the cars, while subjects who received the information from a friend of the seller gave less favorable evaluations. A friend of the buyer is presumably biased and will say that the cars are in bad shape; a friend of the seller will tend to say that the cars are in good shape. When a source is biased, we adjust the recommendation to make up for the bias before combining it with other information.

3. A source's opinion was more influential when no base rate information was given.

4. The greater the expertise of a source, the greater the effect of the source's bias. Subjects gave judgments that were opposite to the source's recommendations most often when the source was high in expertise *and* biased.

5. Independent sources were more effective than biased sources.

6. Subjects were influenced more by base rate information when the sources were biased. They were least influenced by base rate information when the source was independent or unbiased.

Birnbaum and Mellers showed that communication receivers are sensitive to base rate information, the source's opinion, and the bias and expertise of the source. Many of the results of the 1979 Birnbaum and Stegner study were replicated in this study. We can conclude that communication receivers actively evaluate information and are quite careful in assigning values to information.

### Kelman's 1958 and 1961 Studies

The studies we have reviewed so far derive their predictions from learning theory. Now we will examine two studies by Kelman that are based on functional theory. If you will recall, functional theory assumes that to understand the processes of opinion change, we must first know *why* the individual holds the opinion in question. Different motivations lead to different opinions, and the appropriate change procedure depends on those motivations.

Kelman in 1958 conducted an experiment to study how communicator characteristics could determine the conditions under which the newly acquired opinions would be expressed.[42] He had three predictions: (1) a source with power would produce opinion change through compliance, and the new opinions would be expressed only under conditions of high source surveillance and high issue salience (when the source and issue are important); (2) an attractive source would change opinions through identification, and the new opinions would be expressed only under conditions of high source salience (the source-receiver relationship is important); and (3) a credible source will change attitudes through internalization, and the new opinions will be expressed whenever the issue is brought up, as in an opinion questionnaire, and regardless of source salience or surveillance.

Kelman's subjects were freshman students in an all-black college just before the announcement of the Supreme Court decision on desegregation. The communication was a taped interview presented as part of a transcribed radio program. The interview featured a guest speaker who argued that it would be desirable to keep some of the black colleges segregated in order to preserve black culture and tradition. The same message was delivered in all conditions, but communicator characteristics were varied in four ways. The powerful communicator was introduced as the president of the National Foundation of

Negro Colleges, who was primarily responsible for the allocation of the foundation's funds to the subjects' college (perceived control). The interview revealed that he would not hesitate to withdraw the funds if the students at the college expressed opinions contrary to his on the issue in question (perceived concern). The attractive communicator was introduced as a senior and the president of the student council in a leading black university. He was also the chairman of his university's "student poll" and was presenting not only his own opinions but also the opinions of a large majority of black college seniors recently polled. The highly credible source was introduced as a professor of history in a leading university who was a highly respected authority on the history and problems of minority groups, who had great concern for the black community, and whose position was based on research and historical evidence. A fourth communicator was an "ordinary citizen," a white man from Mississippi with a Southern acent. This was the low-power condition.

Salience was manipulated by administering three identical questionnaires. The first two questionnaires were administered immediately after the communication (high salience), and the third was administered one to two weeks later in a different context (low salience). Surveillance was manipulated by asking the subjects to sign the first questionnaire and by telling them that their signed questionnaires would be turned in to the communicator. The first questionnaire was therefore high in salience and surveillance, the second questionnaire was high in salience but low in surveillance, and the third questionnaire was low in both salience and surveillance. Kelman predicted that agreement with the powerful source would be expressed in the first questionnaire (high salience and high surveillance), agreement with the attractive source would be expressed in the first and second questionnaires (high in salience), and agreement with the credible source would be expressed in all three questionnaires (issue relevancy).

Results support these predictions to a high degree. Agreement with the powerful source was highest in the first questionnaire. In the attractive communicator condition, agreement was higher on the first and second questionnaires than on the third. In the high-credibility condition, there were no significant differences in opinion change between questionnaires. There were no other significant differences in agreement with the source within each source condition. Unfortunately, Kelman did not report any significance tests between experimental groups, so we do not know whether communicator characteristics affected the amount of opinion change. Also, repeated testing of the subjects may have sensitized the subjects, but Kelman does not discuss this potential problem. In spite of these shortcomings, Kelman's study provides some support that agreement with a credible source is more permanent and is expressed under more conditions than opinion change from either an attractive or powerful source. Also, agreement with a powerful source is expressed only under conditions of high surveillance and high salience, while agreement with an attractive source is expressed under conditions of high salience.

In a later experiment, Kelman studied how the motivational bases for identification and internalization determine the conditions under which the new opinion is expressed.[43]

The communication was a taped radio broadcast that advocated a novel program in science education that involved having science students study ethics, political science, and international relations to help them make practical decisions in modern society. Two versions of the communication were presented to random groups of college students. The versions varied only in the manipulation of the motivational basis for opinion change. In the role-orientation or identification condition three different speakers were used. One was presented as a physics professor who reported that the faculty and students at his university, as well as important science educators, were very much in favor of the program. With this speaker Kelman intended to produce both a concern for the social anchorage of the opinion and a specification that agreement with the source on the education issue was necessary for identification with the positive reference groups (faculty, students, and science educators). The second speaker was introduced as the president of a super-patriotic women's organization who denounced the education program as a Communist plot. The third speaker was a local school board member who argued that the program was an attempt by college professors to control educational policy. The second and third sources were clearly not attractive to the students and should therefore have no effect on opinion change.

In the value-orientation or internalization condition, the physics professor argued that the new opinion (support for the program) was necessary for maintaining an important value—personal responsibility for the consequences of one's actions. The professor also argued that scientists should be better educated in political science, international relations, and ethics if they are going to maintain personal responsibility for the consequences of their actions. With these arguments Kelman intended to make an important value, which he assumed his subjects already held, salient. The communication then showed how the new opinion (support for the educational program) was congruent with the existing value.

Half of the subjects in each group filled out the opinion questionnaire immediately after the communication and half a few weeks later. Thus, the first questionnaire was high in salience and second questionnaire was low in salience. Kelman predicted that subjects who were motivated to agree with the attractive source because of role-orientation (identification) should show more agreement when salience is high (first questionnaire) than when salience is low (second questionnaire). He also predicted the subjects who were motivated to change opinions because of value congruence (internalization) should show the same amount of agreement in the first and second questionnaires. The results support these predictions significantly.

These two studies provide empirical support for Kelman's functional model of opinion change. More recently, Kelman has extended this analysis to the integration of the individual into the national system,[44] influence processes in psychotherapy,[45] and the linkage of the influence recipient to the broader social system.[46]

## Source Attractiveness

There is considerable evidence that we are influenced more by attractive than by unattractive sources. The general finding is that liking, similarity, and familiarity are positively related to opinion change.[47] The researchers are not always sure whether attraction causes opinion change or whether the holding of similar opinions leads to attraction. However, there seems to be little doubt that attraction is one of the keys to effective persuasion. This finding, in itself, would not be too remarkable. Common sense leads us to predict it, and you could argue that research is not needed to confirm it. What makes research on source attractiveness and persuasion interesting is the investigation of unexpected relationships between the two variables. For example, when can an unattractive source be effective? When will an attractive source *not* be effective? How can an attractive source be even more effective? These are some of the questions that recent research has investigated.

### Eagley and Chaiken's 1975 Study

According to Eagley and Chaiken, the less expected a communicator's position, given his or her personal characteristics and situational pressures, the stronger the communication receiver's inference that the message corresponds to external reality.[48] Attributing a position to external reality instead of to particular characteristics of the communicator (which may lead to bias) or to pressures from the situation should enhance persuasiveness. A communicator advocating an unexpected position, therefore, should be more effective than a communicator advocating a position expected of him or her.

This general hypothesis had been confirmed prior to Eagley and Chaiken's study, when the source characteristic manipulated was credibility. Walster, Aronson, and Abrahams found that a low-credibility source (a criminal) was more persuasive than a high-credibility source (a prosecutor) when recommending more powerful courts.[49] The prosecutor was more persuasive when recommending less powerful courts. The explanation of this finding is that receivers expected a criminal to advocate less powerful courts and the prosecutor to recommend more powerful courts. These recommendations are to be expected because of the sources' personal characteristics and their situations. Since the receivers could not attribute the unexpected recommendations to biases of the sources, they presumably attributed the positions to external reality (or the "objective" truth). Similar findings are reported by Koeske and Crane.[50] They found that subjects agreed more with a statement attributed to an author whose ideological position was thought to be contrary to the statement than with the same statement attributed to an author whose ideology was consistent.

Eagley and Chaiken studied how receiver expectancies of source position affected persuasive impact of sources that were high or low in attractiveness. Their main hypothesis was that attractive sources would be more effective when they advocated unexpected positions on an issue than when they advocated expected positions, and that effectiveness of unattractive sources would improve when they advocated unexpected positions, compared to when they advocated expected positions. In addition, Eagley and Chaiken also predicted that attractive sources would *generally* be more effective in changing opinions than unattractive sources but that unattractive communicators would be more effective than attractive ones when the subjects choose to receive the message (compared to when they were "forced" to receive the message).

Subjects were 358 undergraduate psychology students, who were assigned to one of the 16 conditions in a 2 (choice versus no choice) × 2 (attractive sources versus unattractive source) × 2 (expected versus unexpected issue position advocated by source) × 2 (venereal disease versus unemployment topic) experimental design. The last condition (topic) was added to provide for internal replication—that is, to determine whether the results would depend on specific topics of the messages. In addition to these conditions, 88 other subjects were used to check on expectancy manipulations. They were asked to determine which positions on each of the issues would more likely come from attractive and unattractive sources. Finally, 39 subjects were used in a control condition. They responded only to the opinion questionnaire. Responses of the control subjects served as a baseline with which opinions of the experimental subjects were compared after exposure to the persuasive messages.

Subjects read a transcript of an interview that had been tape-recorded as part of an opinion survey that was supposedly conducted on campus. Choice subjects were allowed to refuse participation in the experiment, an option that was not available to the no-choice subjects. Some of the subjects read an interview about venereal disease, while others read about unemployment. The communication source was introduced as a counselor who had worked for the past eight years at either the university infirmary (in the venereal disease messages) or the university job placement center (in the unemployment messages). Attractiveness was manipulated by having the counselor either praise or insult college students. In the attractive source condition the communicator praised college students. He said that undergraduates were "extremely responsible and mature people who are concerned, in general, with their role in society." In the unattractive source condition the communicator insulted college students by saying that undergraduates are "extremely irresponsible and immature people who are unconcerned, in general, with their role in society." Message expectancy was manipulated by having the communicator advocate either a desirable or undesirable position on one of the topics. Eagly and Chaiken reasoned that, in general, "attractive people say pleasant things, and unattractive people say unpleasant things." We should therefore expect an attractive source to advocate desirable positions and the unattractive one to advocate undesirable positions. The desirable position for the venereal disease message was, "Venereal disease will be controlled so successfully during the next five years that the current epidemic will be completely curtailed." The undesirable position was, "Venereal disease will spread at such an astounding rate that it will soon become America's number one health problem." The desirable position for the unemployment message was, "During the next three years, unemployment among recent college graduates will drop sharply," while the undesirable position was, "During the next three years, unemployment among recent college graduates will surpass even the devastating level which occurred during the Great Depression of the 1930s." Thus, subjects read one of the following messages: a desirable position advocated by an attractive source, an undesirable position advocated by an attractive source, a desirable position from an unattractive source, or an undesirable position advocated by an unattractive source.

The communicator then presented arguments supporting his position. After reading the transcripts subjects were asked to fill out an opinion questionnaire.

To verify their manipulations, Eagly and Chaiken presented the following results. Subjects in choice conditions perceived that they had more choice about reading the interview than did no-choice subjects ($p < .001$); expectancy subjects rated desirable positions on venereal disease and unemployment more desirable than undesirable ones ($p < .001$); expectancy subjects judged attractive communicators more likely than unattractive ones to advocate desirable positions, while unattractive communicators were judged more likely than attractive ones to advocate undesirable positions ($p < .001$); experimental subjects rated the attractive communicators more favorably than unattractive communicators on twelve adjective scales ($p < .001$). Thus, all of the experimental manipulations worked.

All of Eagly and Chaiken's hypotheses, except one, were supported. Attractive sources were generally more effective than unattractive sources, regardless of message topic, choice condition, and desirability of position advocated. When undesirable positions were advocated, the attractive source was much more persuasive than the unattractive source ($p < .001$). However, when desirable positions were advocated, the unattractive source was just as persuasive as the attractive source. There was no support for the hypothesis that unattractive sources would be more effective than attractive ones when subjects choose to receive the message.

Eagly and Chaiken also found that desirable positions were more persuasive than undesirable ones and that subjects recalled more of the arguments of desirable positions when the source was unattractive as opposed to attractive. However, for undesirable positions, subjects remembered more of the arguments from attractive sources than from unattractive sources. The subjects apparently paid closer examination to the message and remembered more of it if the position advocated was *not* expected of the source.

In summary, Eagly and Chaiken provide support for the general hypothesis that attractive sources are more persuasive than unattractive ones. Also, they found that attractive and unattractive communicators were equally persuasive when advocating desirable positions but that attractive communicators were considerably more effective than unattractive ones when advocating undesirable positions. These results are explained by Eagly and Chaiken in terms of what subjects expect of communication sources. Communicators, in general, increase effectiveness by advocating unexpected positions. Thus, the attractive communicator enhanced persuasive impact (compared to unattractive sources) by advocating an undesirable (and unexpected) position, while the unattractive source was not totally ineffective when advocating a desirable (and unexpected) position.

### Chaiken's 1979 Study

Few researchers have studied the effects of communicator physical attractiveness on persuasion. Results of these studies, for the most part, have been contradictory. Some have shown that physical attractiveness enhances a male communicator's persuasiveness with both male and female receivers.[51] Others have shown that physically attractive communicators are more effective only under certain conditions, such as when he or she explicitly expresses a desire to manipulate the receivers.[52] Still others have shown no significant effect on physical attractiveness on persuasion.[53]

Chaiken argues that physical attractiveness may influence receivers more when studied outside the laboratory.[54] All previous studies manipulated communicator physical attractiveness in highly artificial, contrived situations. Laboratory settings, according to Chaiken, are not the best environments to study communicator physical attractiveness, for two reasons. First, experiments may inflate the importance of physical attractiveness in persuasion, since extremes in communicator attractiveness are typically used. Second, the laboratory setting may sensitize the college students who are often used as subjects to giving the socially desirable response in persuasion experiments. This would be to give answers based on highly logical and rational thinking, a response that would negate the influence of communicator physical attractiveness. In either case, the effects of physical attractiveness on persuasion would not be accurately measured.

In 1979, Chaiken studied the effects of communicator physical attractiveness on persuasion in a field setting.[55] She used live, physically attractive and unattractive communicators who delivered a persuasive message to receivers in a college campus. She predicted that attractive communicators would be more persuasive than unattractive ones.

Chaiken recruited 110 male and female communicators from an undergraduate psychology class at the University of Massachusetts. These communicators were trained to deliver a persuasive message that argued that "the University should stop serving meat at breakfast and lunch at all dining commons." Their final practice sessions were videotaped. They also filled out a battery of personality tests. Finally, the communicators were photographed.

To evaluate physical attractiveness of the communicators, Chaiken asked an independent group of fifty-six judges to rate the photographs on physical attractiveness. A 15-point scale was used. These ratings were used to rank order the 110 communicators on the basis of mean physical attractiveness ratings. Those ranking in the top third and bottom third of their sex were then chosen to participate in the field experiment. Sixty-eight communicators were selected, 34 males and 34 females. The mean attractiveness scores on a 15-point scale were 8.80 for the attractive males, 9.09 for the attractive females, 6.10 for the unattractive males, and 6.34 for the unattractive females.

The communicators were then taken to five campus locations by the experimenter. Communicators were instructed to approach every passerby until he or she had secured the cooperation of two university students (receivers) of each sex. Only persons walking alone were approached. The communicator introduced himself or herself to the receiver and requested that the receiver complete an opinion survey. If the receiver agreed, the communicator said that he or she was in a campus group favoring the proposition that "the University should stop serving meat at breakfast and lunch at all dining commons." The communicator then supported this position with two brief arguments. He or she gave the receiver a confidential questionnaire to complete that measured the receiver's agreement with the communicator's position. The communicator also asked the receiver to sign a petition supporting the message.

What were the results of Chaiken's field experiment? First, the attractive communicators were clearly perceived by the judges to be more physically attractive than their unattractive counterparts ($p < .0001$). The receivers also rated the physically attractive communicators to be more attractive ($p < .05$). With regard to persuasive impact, attractive communicators elicited greater agreement from the receivers than did unattractive communicators ($p < .05$). Also, a greater proportion of receivers signed the petition when the communicator was attractive than when he or she was not ($p < .06$).

Chaiken's study clearly shows that physically attractive communicators can be more effective than those who are not attractive. To determine why this might be so, Chaiken analyzed individual personality differences between the attractive and unattractive communicators in her study. She found that the judges did not rate the two sets of communicators to differ in their knowledge of the subject matter. However, attractive communicators were judged to be somewhat friendlier than unattractive ones and to be faster and more fluent speakers. They did not differ with regard to vocal confidence, gaze, or smiling. Physically attractive (compared to unattractive) communicators reported higher SAT scores and regarded themselves to be more persuasive and interesting. These results, according to Chaiken, indicate that attractive and unattractive individuals do differ on characteristics other than physical appearance. Chaiken suggests that attractive individuals may be more persuasive than unattractive persons because they possess characteristics or skills that facilitate persuasion.

## Source Power

How effective are powerful sources in eliciting compliance? Kelman showed that subjects complied with a powerful source as long as the source was salient and could scrutinize whether subjects followed the recommendations or not. Compared to influence by attractive and credible sources, compliance with a powerful source was the most restrictive and, presumably, the least permanent.

Powerful sources often use threats (to withhold rewards or deliver punishments) to gain compliance. This is probably why powerful sources seem to be less effective, in the long run, than either attractive or credible sources. Receivers are generally better convinced to engage in nonpreferred behaviors when they are promised rewards than when they are threatened with punishments.[56] Although *mild* threats sometimes lead to long-range, internalized compliance,[57] strong threats often boomerang, producing defiance instead of compliance. Recent research on powerful sources has investigated why threats are often not successful in persuasion and how threats can be used more effectively.

### Heilman and Garner's 1975 Study

According to Heilman and Garner, threats, as compared to promises, may be more likely to elicit defiance because of the receiver's desire to preserve his or her integrity and freedom of action.[58] When threatened by a powerful source, the receiver is left with a choice between two evils: engage in the nonpreferred activity (the source's "recommendation") or bear the punishment (which may be in the form of lost rewards or actual costs to the receiver, such as loss of a job). Unless defying the threat results in severe punishment, it is likely to fail, since compliance would be damaging to the receiver's self-concept. Also, the receiver may feel that compliance would make him or her seem weak and foolish before others. Thus, maintaining one's self-concept and social image often becomes more important than avoiding the punishment for noncompliance with a powerful source.

The main reason threats fail, according to Heilman and Garner, is because of the receiver's perceived loss of freedom. Threats can be as effective as promises of rewards when the receivers are allowed some freedom as, for example, when they are given several alternatives for compliance and when they are then allowed to choose from among these alternatives. Heilman and Garner tested this general hypothesis in an experiment. Their specific hypotheses were: (1) threats would produce more compliance when subjects were allowed to select the method of compliance than when they were not allowed to do so, and (2) promises would be considerably more effective than threats when subjects were *not* given a choice of compliance methods than when they were given a choice. In addition, Heilman and Garner also predicted that prescriptive threats (those that say "do this, or else"), would be more effective than proscriptive threats (those that say "don't do this, or else"). This last hypothesis is based on the assumption that being forbidden to act (proscriptive threats) is more likely to remind subjects of their loss of freedom than prescriptive threats.

Subjects were ninety-six female high school students who were told at the time of recruitment that they could earn $2 to $3 for participating in the experiment. The study was presented as a consumer taste-testing session. Subjects were told that they would be working in pairs with an unseen peer in another room. The peer would be the "tabulator," while the subject would be the taster. (Actually, the peers were fictitious communicators used by the experimenters to manipulate power.) As tasters, subjects would be tasting a number of samples of either orange juice or *one* of several types of concentrated vinegar concentrate. Presumably, tasting the vinegar concentrate would be the nonpreferred or undesirable activity for the subjects. Subjects were then told that their base pay rate would be $2.50. Their pairmates' pay, however, would depend on what the subject tasted. Pairmates would be paid more if subjects tasted vinegar instead of orange juice.

Source power was manipulated by telling the subjects that their pairmates could fine them or give them a bonus if they wished to do so. All pairmates would have this power to either reward (a promise) or fine (a threat).

Subjects were then told that there was only one type of orange juice to be tasted, but there were four kinds of vinegar: red, white, thyme, and rice concentrates. In the prescriptive threat condition, the communicator sent a written message to the subjects that said: "Taste vinegar concentrate or I'll make sure you are fined fifty cents. Otherwise, nothing will happen." The promise, in the prescriptive message, read: "Taste vinegar concentrate and I'll make sure you are bonused fifty cents. Otherwise, nothing will happen." In the proscriptive threat condition, subjects were told: "Don't taste orange juice or I'll make sure you are fined fifty cents. Otherwise nothing will happen." And, in the proscriptive promise condition, the message read: "Don't taste orange juice and I'll make sure you are bonused fifty cents. Otherwise nothing will happen."

Subjects in the no-choice condition were told, by a written message, that the pairmate (the communicator) would choose the kind of vinegar to be tasted if the subject did choose to taste vinegar. In the high-choice conditions, subjects were told that *they* could choose which vinegar (only one type) to taste if they were to taste vinegar.

The experimental design was a 2 (threat or promise) × 2 (prescriptive or proscriptive message) × 2 (choice or no-choice in compliance) factorial. The main dependent measure was the number of subjects choosing the nonpreferred activity (tasting vinegar).

Validity checks showed that the experimental manipulations were successful. Subjects interpreted the influence notes to be threats or promises of rewards, and almost all of them believed that their pairmates would carry out their threats or promises. Also, all subjects understood the choice manipulations.

Results support two of the three hypotheses. Subjects were more likely to comply with the threats when given a choice than when not given a choice of how to comply ($p < .05$), while perceived choice did not affect compliance in the promise conditions. In no-choice conditions promises were significantly more effective than threats; however, in choice conditions threats and promises were equally effective. There was no support for the hypothesis that prescriptive messages would be more effective than proscriptive messages. These results are explained by the researchers in terms of psychological theories of reactance and interpersonal dynamics.

In summary, Heilman and Garner's study supports previous findings that promises of rewards are more effective in persuasion than threats of punishment. Also, they showed that the effectiveness of threats can be improved by allowing the receiver some freedom in choosing the method of compliance. When choice is available, threats can be just as effective as promises.

### Attention, Comprehension, and Yielding

Learning theory breaks persuasion down into three steps: attention to the message, comprehension of the arguments in the message, and yielding to the source's recommendations. In this section we will consider how source characteristics affect each of these steps.

Intuitively, we would guess that source attractiveness should have the greatest impact on attention. The more attractive the source, the more attracted we should be to the message. Advertisers obviously believe in this principle. Consider the sources used in advertising testimonials. Most of them are attractive either physically or because they are similar, familiar, and likable. Unfortunately, as McGuire points out, there has been very little systematic research on source attractiveness and attention to the message.[59] Dissonance theorists do provide some evidence that we tend to be more attentive to messages and sources that agree with us, compared to those that disagree.[60] However, more research is needed to determine whether source attractiveness leads to message attention and whether attractiveness enhances message comprehension.

Learning theory predicts that for a message to be effective its arguments should be comprehended by the receivers. Surprisingly, research has shown that source credibility, the characteristic we would expect to have the greatest influence on comprehension, does not affect recall of message arguments at all.[61] Although messages from credible sources are judged to be fairer, more factual, more throughly documented, more valid, and more grammatical than messages from low-credibility sources, receivers recall just as much of the message from each source. High-credibility sources seem to be more effective than low-credibility sources not because their arguments are learned better but because their arguments are evaluated more favorably. Messages that present reasonable arguments in favor of the conclusions can be effective, regardless of source credibility. Agreement with the low-credibility source is less than with high-credibility sources, but only when the message does not present adequate arguments do receivers actually move in the opposite direction from that recommended by a low-credibility source.[62] Thus, it seems that comprehension is not affected by source credibility. We do learn equally well from high- and low-credibility sources. The key to agreement with the source is how we evaluate the arguments we have learned.

Yielding, the effect most often measured in studies of communication and persuasion, is affected by source credibility, attractiveness, and power. We yield more to high- than to low-credibility sources, to attractive than to unattractive sources, and to high- than to low-power sources. Also, Kelman's experiments indicate that source credibility leads to more permanent change, followed respectively by attractiveness and power. Another common finding in experimental studies is that source credibility has greater persuasive impact than attractiveness. Receivers are influenced more to the extent that the source is an expert and not their peer.[63]

## SUMMARY

To conclude this chapter, let us again consider what makes a communication source effective in persuasion. We identified three general characteristics—credibility, attractiveness, and power. Credibility is the extent to which the source is perceived to know the "right" answer (expertise) and the extent to which the source is judged to communicate his or her stand without bias (trustworthiness). Our perceptions of a source's expertise depend on factors such as training, experience, ability, intelligence, professional attainment, and social status. Trustworthy sources are not only objective; we perceive them also to have no or little persuasive intent. Attractive sources are demographically and ideologically similar to us. They are also familiar and likable. The key to liking sources is reinforcement. We like communicators who can reward us—by reducing anxiety, stress, loneliness, or insecurity, by helping us gain social approval, and by helping us obtain rewards for ourselves. Powerful sources can reward or punish us, are interested in compliance with their messages, and are able to scrutinize whether we comply or not. Source credibility leads to internalization of the new opinions, attractiveness to identification, and power to compliance.

What do we know about the effects of these source characteristics on persuasion? Research has suggested the following general principles.

1. High-credibility sources produce more immediate opinion change than low-credibility sources. Their persuasive impact, however, diminishes with time unless receivers are reminded of the message and the source prior to the delayed measurement of opinions.
2. Credibility of the source does not affect message recall. However, messages from high-credibility sources are evaluated more favorably than messages from low-credibility sources.

3. Contrary to the "sleeper effect" hypothesis, agreement with a low-credibility source does *not* increase over time.

4. Both message content and source credibility affect persuasion. The difference in persuasive impact between high- and low-credibility sources is more pronounced when little evidence is given in the message supporting the conclusion.

5. Biased sources are generally less effective than unbiased sources. However, biased sources can be more effective than unbiased sources in reinforcing opinions and when the source is also powerful or attractive.

6. Expertise magnifies the effects of bias. Expert sources are *not* judged to be more biased, but biased sources are less likely to be believed if they are also perceived to be experts. Expertise adds more to persuasive impact than trustworthiness.

7. Opinions changed through internalization seem to be the most permanent, followed respectively by identification and compliance.

8. Attractive sources are generally more effective than unattractive sources. Liking, similarity, familiarity, and physical attractiveness are positively related to opinion change.

9. Persuasive impact of expert and attractive communicators is more pronounced when they advocate unexpected positions instead of expected ones. Unattractive sources are more effective when they advocate unexpected positions than when they recommend expected ones.

10. Receivers pay closer attention to the message and remember more of it if the position advocated is *not* expected of the source.

11. Communicators are generally more effective in persuasion when they promise receivers rewards compared to when they threaten receivers with punishment.

12. Mild threats sometimes lead to long-range, internalized compliance. However, strong threats often boomerang, producing defiance instead of compliance.

13. Threats can be more effective when the receiver is allowed some freedom in choosing the method of compliance. When such a choice is available, threats can be just as effective as promises of rewards.

14. Messages that present reasonable arguments in favor of the conclusions can be effective regardless of source credibility.

15. Source credibility has greater impact than attractiveness. We are influenced more when the source is an expert instead of when he or she is a peer.

## REVIEW QUESTIONS

**1.** Give two examples each of communication sources that are credible, attractive, and powerful. Discuss characteristics that are unique to each source.

**2.** Using learning theory as a framework, discuss how source credibility, attractiveness, and power affect persuasion.

**3.** Take two studies discussed in the research section of this chapter. Evaluate the internal and external validity of each study as well as its practical and theoretical value. You may consult the original journal articles for a complete discussion of the studies.

## ENDNOTES

1. See William McGuire, "The Nature of Attitudes and Attitude Change," in G. Lindzey and E. Aronson (eds.), *The Handbook of Social Psychology*, 2nd ed., Vol. 3 (Reading, Mass.: Addison-Wesley, 1969), pp. 177–199.
2. Niccolo Machiavelli, *Discourses*, Vol. 1 (London: Routledge and Kegan Paul, 1950), p. 332.
3. *Ibid.*, p. 329.
4. *Ibid.*, p. 241.
5. As discussed in Leonard Doob, "Goebbels' Principles of Propaganda," in D. Katz *et al.*, *Public Opinion and Propaganda* (New York: Holt, Rinehart and Winston, 1954), pp. 508–522.
6. Joe McGinniss, *The Selling of the President, 1968* (New York: Trident Press, 1969), p. 257.
7. See, for example, K. Griffin, "The Contribution of Studies of Source Credibility to a Theory of Interpersonal Trust in the Communication Process," *Psychological Bulletin, 68*, 1967, pp. 104–120.
8. Michael Birnbaum and Steven Stegner, "Source Credibility in Social Judgement: Bias, Expertise, and the Judge's Point of View," *Journal of Personality and Social Psychology, 37*, 1979, pp. 48–74.
9. Ellen Berscheid and Elaine Walster, *Interpersonal Attraction* (Reading, Mass.: Addison-Wesley, 1969).
10. McGuire, *op. cit.*
11. *Ibid.*
12. *Ibid.*
13. *Ibid.*
14. *Ibid.*
15. Berscheid and Walster, *op. cit.*
16. *Ibid.*
17. S. Schachter, *The Psychology of Affiliation* (Stanford, Calif.: Stanford University Press, 1959).
18. G. Homans, *Social Behavior: Its Elementary Forms* (New York: Harcourt, Brace and World, 1961).
19. L. Festinger, S. Schachter, and K. Back, *Social Pressures in Informal Groups: A Study of Human Factors in Housing* (New York: Harper, 1950).
20. M. Deutsch and M. E. Collins, "The Effect of Public Policy in Housing Projects upon Interracial Attitudes," in E. Maccoby, T. M. Newcomb, and E. L. Hartley (eds.), *Readings in Social Psychology*, 3rd ed. (New York: Holt, 1958), pp. 612–623.
21. Berscheid and Walster, *op. cit.*, p. 48.
22. Norman Miller, G. Maruyama, R. Beaber, and K. Valone, "Speed of Speech and Persuasion," *Journal of Personality and Social Psychology, 3*, 1966, pp. 227–232.

23. R. E. Goranson and L. Berkowitz, "Reciprocity and Responsibility Reactions to Prior Help," *Journal of Personality and Social Psychology 3,* 1966, pp. 227–232.

24. E. Berscheid and E. Walster, "Physical Attractiveness," in L. Berkowitz (ed.), *Advances in Experimental Social Psychology,* Vol. 7 (New York: Academic Press, 1974).

25. K. Dion, "Physical Attractiveness and Evaluation of Children's Transgressions," *Journal of Personality and Social Psychology, 24,* 1972, pp. 207–213.

26. K. Dion and E. Berscheid, "Physical Attractiveness and Social Perception of Peers in Pre-School Children," unpublished manuscript, University of Minnesota, 1972.

27. David Landy and Harold Sigall, "Beauty Is Talent: Task Evaluation as a Function of the Performer's Physical Attractiveness," *Journal of Personality and Social Psychology, 29,* 1974, pp. 299–304.

28. J. Mills and E. Aronson, "Opinion Change as a Function of the Communicator's Attractiveness and Desire to Influence," *Journal of Personality and Social Psychology, 1,* 1965, p. 173–177.

29. H. Kelman, "Compliance, Identification and Internalization," *Journal of Conflict Resolution, 2,* 1958, pp. 51–60.

30. See McGuire, *op. cit.,* pp. 194–195.

31. C. I. Hovland and W. Weiss, "The Influence of Source Credibility on Communication Effectiveness," *Public Opinion Quarterly, 15,* 1951, pp. 635–650.

32. H. C. Kelman and C. I. Hovland, "'Reinstatement' of the Communicator in Delayed Measurement of Opinion Change," *Journal of Abnormal and Social Psychology, 48,* 1953, pp. 327–335.

33. Paulett Gillig and Anthony Greenwald, "Is It Time to Lay the Sleeper Effect to Rest?," *Journal of Personality and Social Psychology, 29,* 1974, pp. 132–139.

34. Martin Fishbein and Icek Ajzen, *Belief, Attitude, Intention and Behavior* (Reading, Mass.: Addison-Wesley, 1975), pp. 489–495.

35. J. C. McCroskey, "The Effects of Evidence as an Inhibitor of Counter Persuasion," *Speech Monographs, 37,* 1976, pp. 188–194.

36. Birnbaum and Stegner, *op. cit.*

37. McGuire, *op. cit.*

38. J. Freedman and D. Sears, "Selective Exposure," in L. Berkowitz (ed.), *Advances in Experimental Social Psychology,* Vol. 2 (New York: Academic Press, 1965), pp. 57–97.

39. C. Hovland and W. Mandell, "An Experimental Comparison of Conclusion-Drawing by the Communicator and by the Audience," *Journal of Abnormal and Social Psychology, 47,* 1952, pp. 581–588.

40. McGuire, *op. cit.*

41. Michael Birnbaum and Barbara Mellers, "Bayesian Inference: Combining Base Rates with Opinions of Sources Who Vary in Credibility," *Journal of Personality and Social Psychology, 45*(4), 1983, pp. 792–804.

42. Kelman, *op. cit.*

43. H. Kelman, "Processes of Opinion Change," *Public Opinion Quarterly, 25,* 1961, pp. 57–58.

44. See Ben Reich and Christine Adcock, *Values, Attitudes and Behavior Change* (London: Methuen, 1976), pp. 126–128.

45. *Ibid.*

46. *Ibid.*

47. McGuire, *op. cit.*

48. Alice Eagly and Shelly Chaiken, "An Attribution Analysis of the Effect of Communicator Characteristics on Opinion Change: The Case of Communicator Attractiveness," *Journal of Personality and Social Psychology, 32,* 1975, pp. 137–144.

49. E. Walster, E. Aronson, and D. Abrahams, "On Increasing the Persuasiveness of a Low Prestige Communication," *Journal of Experimental Social Psychology, 2,* 1966, pp. 325–342.
50. G. F. Koeske and W. D. Crane, "The Effect of Congruous and Incongruous Source-Statement Combinations upon the Judged Credibility of a Communication," *Journal of Experimental Social Psychology, 4,* 1968, pp. 384–399.
51. J. Horai, N. Naccari, and E. Fatoullah, "The Effects of Expertise and Physical Attractiveness upon Opinion Agreement and Liking," *Sociometry, 37,* 1974, pp. 601–606.
52. Mills and Aronson, *op. cit.*
53. Shelly Chaiken, "Communicator Physical Attractiveness and Persuasion," *Journal of Personality and Social Psychology, 37,* 1979, pp. 1387–1397.
54. *Ibid.*
55. *Ibid.*
56. Madeline Heilman and Katherine Garner, "Counteracting the Boomerang: The Effects of Choice on Compliance to Threats and Promises," *Journal of Personality and Social Psychology, 31,* 1975, pp. 911–917.
57. McGuire, *op. cit.,* pp. 187–191.
58. Heilman and Garner, *op. cit.*
59. McGuire, *op. cit.,* pp. 187–191.
60. L. Festinger, *Conflict, Decision and Dissonance* (Stanford, Calif.: Stanford University Press, 1964).
61. McGuire, *op. cit.,* p. 198.
62. *Ibid.,* p. 199.
63. *Ibid.,* p. 197.

# 9

# MESSAGES

In this chapter we will discuss message characteristics that affect persuasive impact. How should you structure the message to achieve maximum learning and agreement? What stylistic variables affect persuasion? What appeals should you use? These are some of the questions we will attempt to answer.

Much of the research on message characteristics is based on learning theories of persuasion. The basic premise is that receivers will accept the message's recommendations to the extent that they are rewarded for, or are able to avoid, punishments by complying. Another general assumption is that learning of the message facilitates persuasion. Let us now discuss some of the questions often asked in message research. Later in this chapter, we will review studies that provide some answers to these questions.

## Message Structure

Research on message structure has focused on three topics: explicit versus implicit conclusion drawing, ordering of arguments within the message, and refuting versus ignoring opposition arguments.

### Conclusion Drawing

Should you draw the conclusion explicitly for the receivers, or should you allow them to draw the conclusion for themselves? Initially, researchers predicted that implicit conclusions would produce more opinion change than explicit conclusions. The basis for this prediction was that explicitly stated conclusions communicate a source's intention to persuade and therefore may lower his or her trustworthiness. Also, it was assumed that receivers would be more likely to accept the validity of the conclusion if they drew it themselves than if the communicator pointed it out to them. However, there is also some theoretical justification for the opposite prediction—that explicit conclusions are more effective than implicit ones. Explicit conclusions, when stated early in the message, can facilitate the learning of arguments by focusing attention on important points. Thus, persuasion can be facilitated both by explicit and implicit conclusions. Research has attempted to determine which strategy has a greater overall impact on opinion change.

### Ordering of Arguments

Suppose we had a communication situation in which a source would have to argue for agreeable positions on some issues and disagreeable ones on others. Which issues should be discussed first? Learning theory principles suggest that communication sources should discuss agreeable positions first and disagreeable ones last.[1] By covering agreeable positions in the early parts of the message, the source is reinforcing the receiver for attention to the message. The receiver will then be more likely to pay attention to the remainder of the message. Conversely, if the first part of the message is disagreeable, the receiver learns to avoid paying attention to the message and may not be fully exposed to the agreeable parts when they do come. The selective exposure hypothesis derived from cognitive dissonance theory similarly suggests that agreeable positions should be discussed early in the message.[2] According to the selective exposure hypothesis, we avoid information we do not agree with and seek out information we agree with. Although the avoidance part of the hypothesis is questionable, research has supported the notion that we are more receptive to agreeable information. Thus, receptivity can be improved by placing agreeable information at the beginning instead of at the end of the message. This principle applies not only to information that the receiver already agrees with but to *any* material that the receiver may find pleasant.[3] Pleasant material helps increase likability of the source, and it is important that this positive bond be established at the beginning of communication.

### One-Sided and Two-Sided Messages

Which is the more effective persuasion strategy—ignoring the opposition arguments (one-sided messages) or refuting them (two-sided messages)? By refuting opposition arguments, the source can add to his or her trustworthiness. Receivers are likely to perceive a two-sided message as more objective than a one-sided message, provided the refutation is competently done. There is, of course, the danger that receivers will not be convinced by the refutation or that introducing opposition arguments may lead the receiver to some reservations about the message's conclusions. Most research in this area has found no main effects. The appropriate strategy depends on audience characteristics and message topic.

Research on one-sided and two-sided messages has recently been applied to comparative advertisements. Comparative advertisements have three characteristics: (1) two or more specifically named or recognizably demonstrated brands of a product or service category are compared; (2) the comparison is based on one or more attributes of the good or service; and (3) it is either stated, implied, or demonstrated that factual information has been gathered as a basis for the comparative claims.[4]

Comparative advertisements that demonstrate that factual information is the basis for the superiority of the advertised product's claims over those of the competition closely resemble our definition of two-sided persuasive messages. The main questions in comparative advertising research are: (1) Is it helpful to consumers? and (2) Does it work?

## Message Style

DeVito defines message style as "the selection and arrangement of those linguistic features which are open to choice."[5] Stylistic variables include all possible linguistic variations in a message not restricted by the rules of grammar or by other norms (such as norms prohibiting the use of profane language).

Recent research on style has focused on variables that affect comprehensibility of the message and subsequent yielding.[6] Some of these variables are number of arguments supporting the message's conclusion, repetition of the message, order of arguments in the message, and readability of the message. The emphasis on comprehensibility is largely derived from learning theories of persuasion. Again, the general assumption is that by increasing message comprehensibility, persuasive impact is improved.

Some recent research has also investigated whether stylistic variables are related to source evaluation.[7] Variables studied here include readability or listenability, human interest, vocabulary diversity, realism, and verifiability.

## Message Appeals

Considerable research attention has been given to fear appeals in the past two decades. The main question is: Which are more effective in changing opinions and behaviors—low or high fear appeals? According to McGuire, high fear appeals can elicit competing tendencies in receivers.[8] As a drive, increases in the level of fear can be expected to increase the likelihood of response tendencies (action) or opinion change. This principle assumes that fear is an uncomfortable drive state (like hunger) that can motivate the individual to do something to minimize or remove it. Thus, a person in fear will be more likely to accept the message's recommendations as a way of reducing fear than a person who is not so aroused. Fear, however, also has "cue" properties. Fear appeals can make the individual aware of undesirable states (such as death, injury, or sickness) that are used to arouse fear. This awareness might then elicit reactions in the individual such as avoidance of the message, hostility toward the source, and aggression toward the source. These reactions can interfere with opinion or behavioral change. Because high fear appeals can elicit these competing tendencies, research has attempted to specify the conditions when high or low fear might be more effective.

Some research attention has also been devoted to the relative effectiveness of emotional and rational appeals in persuasion. McGuire defines rational or logical appeals as those that argue for the truth of a given belief by presenting evidence in favor of the probable truth of premises or antecedents from which the given belief follows.[9] Emotional appeals argue for a given belief by pointing out the desirability of consequents that would follow from holding the given belief. Rational appeals in advertising, for example, would present evidence supporting a product's claims of superiority on a given attribute or attributes over the competition. Emotional appeals would emphasize the desirable consequences of buying the advertised product—such as an increase in social desirability or self-esteem.

## RESEARCH

Research on message characteristics has generally used experimental designs in which subjects are exposed to messages varying in structure, style, or appeal. Opinion or behavioral change is then measured as the dependent variable. In this section we will summarize early research and discuss in some detail a few recent studies.

### Message Structure

#### Conclusion Drawing

The initial hypothesis was that implicit conclusions would be more effective than explicit ones. There is considerable evidence, however, that explicit conclusion drawing makes the message more effective than if conclusions were left up to the receiver. Hovland and Mandell, for example, presented subjects with a message containing the major and minor premises of an argument, each supported by data.[10] In the explicit conclusion form, the message ended with a conclusion to which the premises led. This final statement was left out in the implicit conclusion message. Results indicate that the explicit conclusion message was more effective in changing receiver opinions than the implicit conclusion form.

McGuire offers an interesting explanation of this finding.

> It may well be that if a person draws the conclusion for himself he is more persuaded than if the source draws it for him; the problem is that in the usual communication situation the subject is either insufficiently intelligent or insufficiently motivated to draw the conclusion for himself, and therefore misses the point of the message to a serious extent unless the source draws the moral for him. In communication, it appears it is not sufficient to lead the horse to water; one must push his head underneath to drink.[11]

#### Ordering of Arguments

Research on ordering of arguments within the message has generally shown that more opinion change results when agreeable and not disagreeable positions are discussed first. McGuire found that the agreeable-disagreeable order produced more opinion change and learning of the message than the disagreeable-agreeable order.[12] According to Tannenbaum and his colleagues,[13] the agreeable-disagreeable order is superior because it improves likability of the source. Receivers learn to like the source more by associating early agreeable positions with him or her.

Research on serial-position effects in learning has shown that material in the beginning of the message is learned best, followed by material at the end, while material at the middle or just after the middle is learned least.[14] This suggests that a communicator should place strong and pleasant arguments where they would be learned best, which is at the beginning. The worst place for these arguments is the middle of the message, where material is learned least.

### One-Sided and Two-Sided Messages

Research on the relative effectiveness of one-sided and two-sided messages has shown that the appropriate strategy depends on audience, source, and other message characteristics. For example, Hovland and his colleagues[15] found that ignoring the opposition was better for receivers initially in favor of the source's conclusion, while refuting the opposition was more effective with receivers who were initially opposed. Also, refuting the opposition was better for receivers with higher "intelligence" or with more formal education, while ignoring the opposition was more effective for those with lower intelligence or with less education. According to McGuire, refuting the opposition is more effective when the subjects are familiar with the issue, when there is a high probability that they would be exposed later on to the opposition arguments from other communicators, and when the topic is controversial.[16] On the other hand, ignoring the opposition is more effective when subjects are not familiar with the issue, when they will not likely be exposed in the future to opposition arguments, and when the topic is not controversial.

Research on comparative advertising has attempted to determine whether consumers perceive comparative advertisements to be useful to them and whether comparative advertisements are more effective than noncomparative ads.[17] Critics argue that the risk of consumer deception and confusion is great in comparative advertising, particularly when test methods are biased and not representative. However, supporters of comparative ads say that comparative ads make the consumer more conscious of his or her responsibility to compare before buying and provide more information by contrasting the products side by side.[18] Recent national surveys indicate that most consumers do not see any difference in benefits from comparative and noncomparative ads. A 1977 nationwide random sample of 2005 adults were asked:[19] "Which ads are more useful—comparative, noncomparative, or is there no difference?" Thirty-four percent of the sample said comparative ads, 22 percent replied noncomparative ads, and 43 percent indicated that there was no difference. In answer to the question, "Which ads are more believable" 25 percent said comparative ads are more believable, and 55 percent said that they were about the same. This survey shows that although most respondents did not think that comparative ads made a difference, more consumers had a favorable reaction to comparative ads than to noncomparative ones.

Are comparative ads more effective than noncomparative ones? The answer seems to be, "under certain conditions," but generally, there is no difference. Boddewyn and Marton, in a recent review of comparative advertising research, concluded that there is no clear advantage to using comparative advertising.[20] In some of the studies negative results from comparative ads were observed. Credibility of the advertiser, for example, often was rated lower in comparative ads than in noncomparative ones.

As in most persuasion research, the relative effectiveness of comparative over noncomparative ads depends on other characteristics of the communication situation. According to Boddewyn and Marton, comparative ads can be more effective when:

1. The advertised brand has a small market share or is a newcomer. Then, comparison can "upgrade" the image of the advertised brand by association with the more established brands.

2. The advertised brand has a built-in advantage and the claimed superiority is meaningful, demonstrable, and verifiable by the consumer. If this is true the consumer can be convinced of the claims in the ad, and advertiser credibility will increase.

3. The target audience does not have well-established preferences. We can expect those who are undecided to be more receptive to new, comparative information.

4. A comparative advertisement is a novelty in a particular product category. Comparative ads draw more attention when they are new or unusual compared to ads for other brands in the same product category.

5. Comparative ads are more effective when used in television. It is easier to demonstrate products side by side when both video and audio are used.

On the other hand, Boddewyn and Marton suggest that comparative ads should *not* be used when:

1. A good product can be advertised on its own merit without comparison to others.

2. Products cannot be convincingly compared because product differences cannot be objectively measured.

3. The advertised product has no significant comparative advantage.

4. The competition has valid counterclaims.

5. The appeals are emotional, not rational. Comparative ads cannot be effective when objective evidence for the advertised brand's superiority cannot be established.

## Message Style

To what extent does repetition of the message affect comprehension and agreement? Does message comprehension lead to agreement? What message characteristics affect evaluation of the source? These are some of the questions we will attempt to answer in this section.

### Repetition of the Persuasive Message

Researchers in recent years have devoted increasing attention to the relationship between frequency of exposure to a stimulus and subsequent changes in the evaluation of that stimulus. Often referred to as "mere exposure" effects, the general finding is that repeated exposure to a stimulus is sufficient to increase liking of the stimulus. Zajonc, for example, provides evidence that repeated exposure to words, musical compositions, works of art, and portraits results in increased liking for the objects.[21] Chaffee similarly found that repeated use of nonsense words in the solution of simple word puzzles led to favorable evaluations of the words. In 1983, Gordon and Holyoak found that the liking or positive effect produced by repeated viewing of a set of stimuli generalized to previously unseen stimuli that were similar in structure to the exposed stimuli.[22] Their study shows that we learn to like not only objects that we see repeatedly but also other objects that we had not previously seen but that are similar in form and structure to the objects that we had seen. This explains to some extent why people who learn to like some forms of classical music or modern art also like most forms of classical music and modern art. One explanation of the mere exposure phenomenon is that repeated exposure leads to familiarity and that familiarity in itself is sufficient to produce liking for an object.

The practical implications of the mere exposure finding are considerable. If repeated exposure is sufficient to produce liking for an object, then constant repetition of advertisements would be an effective strategy not only for producing brand awareness but also for brand preference. However, the relationship between repeated exposure and object evaluation is not as simple as early research would lead us to believe. More recent research by Zajonc and others has indicated that the relationship may be nonmonotonic or curvilinear and is best represented by an inverted U curve.[23] This means that liking for the object would be low with lower levels of exposure, then would increase as exposure increased to intermediate levels, but would decrease as exposure levels were increased to even higher levels. Repeated exposure first leads to increased liking because it enables the receiver to become familiar with the object. With continued repetition boredom or satiation develops, which results in disliking for the object. The problem then is to determine the optimum level of exposure and to identify ways of neutralizing the boomerang effect if it occurs. Nonmonotonic relationships between exposure and object evaluation have been reported for political advertising by Becker and Doolittle[24] and for consumer advertising by Greenberg and Suttoni.[25]

Miller in 1976 studied whether disliking of an object from too much exposure is permanent and how the negative effect from repeated exposure can be neutralized.[26] Subjects in his study were 115 undergraduate college students residing in a nine-story dormitory building. They were randomly assigned to one of four conditions: no exposure (pretest), moderate exposure, overexposure, and exposure removal (delayed posttest). The stimulus object was a one-by-two-foot poster that read in four-inch high letters: REDUCE FOREIGN AID. This message was reinforced in smaller print by the words, "Help Stop the Outflow of U.S. Dollars—Equalize our Balance of Payments." Attached to the bottom of the poster were postcards that the students could send in to volunteer in a protest campaign aimed at U.S. congressmen. The dependent measures were the number of postcards sent in (a behavioral measure) and responses to a questionnaire measuring, among other things, opinions regarding foreign aid.

The experiment was done within a one-week period. On the day before the posters were placed on the dormitory walls, subjects randomly assigned to the nonexposure or pretest condition were asked to fill out the opinion questionnaire. On the second day 30 posters were placed in common areas of the dormitory. This was the moderate-exposure condition. These posters were left for the third and fourth days. On the evening of the fourth day subjects randomly assigned to the moderate-exposure condition were asked to complete the opinion questionnaire. On the fifth day 170 additional posters were placed in the common areas of the dormitory. These posters were left for the sixth and seventh days. On the evening of the seventh day subjects randomly assigned to the high-exposure condition were administered the opinion questionnaire. The posters were then removed on the eighth day. On the twelfth day subjects assigned to the delayed posttest condition filled out the opinion questionnaire.

Results support the inverted U prediction. Agreement with the poster (recommending a reduction of foreign aid) was highest in the moderate-exposure condition followed, respectively, by the overexposure and the no-exposure conditions. Thus, maximum effect was attained with moderate exposure. However, agreement was still higher in the high-exposure condition than in the pretest group. Agreement in the delayed posttest condition was not significantly different from agreement in the moderate- and high-exposure conditions but was significantly greater than in the no-exposure group. The behavioral response (number of postcards sent in) did not allow Miller to draw any meaningful conclusions, since the number of students volunteering was small ($n = 22$). However, there was a tendency for greater exposure to be followed by more volunteering.

Miller draws the following conclusions from his study: (1) mere exposure to a persuasive message was sufficient to enhance agreement with the message; (2) overexposure produced less agreement than moderate exposure but was still more effective than no exposure; and (3) the decrease in message agreement following overexposure is temporary, since message evaluations were again significantly positive four days after all posters had been taken down. Miller suggests that a period of nonexposure can neutralize any boomerang effects resulting from overexposure.

Cacioppo and Petty in 1979 studied the effects of message repetition on agreement and recall of message arguments.[27] Like Miller, they predicted that agreement with the message would first increase and then decrease as exposure frequency increased. They also measured counterargumentation and topic-irrelevant thinking by subjects during the message presentation, as well as recall of the arguments after the message had been presented, to determine whether these cognitive processes are related to agreement.

In their first experiment, Cacioppo and Petty used a 2 × 4 factorial design in which the position advocated by the message (agreeable versus disagreeable conclusions) and the number of exposures (zero, one, three, or five) were varied. The agreeable or proattitudinal message argued that university expenditures for students be increased and that the increase be financed by instituting a 25-percent service tax on visitor luxuries. The disagreeable or counterattitudinal message argued that university expenditures be increased but that they be financed by increasing tuition for students by $70 per quarter. Subjects in the no-exposure condition did not hear any message, while subjects in the other exposure conditions heard a taped message through headphones either one, three, or five consecutive times. All subjects heard the same eight arguments in favor of increasing university expenditures. Dependent measures were recall of the arguments and extent of agreement with the advocated position.

As Cacioppo and Petty predicted, repetition led to increasing and then decreasing agreement with the message. The most agreement, combining proattitudinal and counterattitudinal groups, resulted when the message was repeated three times (9.83 on a 13-point scale), followed respectively by one repetition (8.23), and then by five repetitions (7.74). The least agreement was observed in the no-exposure group (5.58). These results support the inverted U hypothesis. Cacioppo and Petty also found that subjects agreed more with the pro- than with the counterattitudinal message, but that type of message did not affect the inverted U relationship between exposure and agreement.

Learning increased with repetition. The average number of arguments recalled by the subjects at one, three, and five repetitions, respectively, was 4.08, 4.67, and 6.00 (p < .001). More message arguments were recalled when the position advocated was counterattitudinal than when the position was proattitudinal, indicating that subjects paid closer attention to the message when the conclusion was disagreeable to them.

In their second experiment, Cacioppo and Petty utilized a 2 × 3 factorial design in which the position advocated (pro- versus counterattitudinal) and the number of exposures (one, three, or five) were manipulated. Subjects were 193 introductory psychology students. Procedures and messages were identical to those in the first experiment. The only difference was that cognitive responses of the subjects to the message were measured. After listening to the messages and filling out the opinion questionnaires, subjects were given three minutes to list the actual thoughts that occurred to them while the message was being presented. They were then asked to place a plus (+) next to each thought that supported the message recommendation, a minus (−) next to each thought that attacked the recommendation, and a zero (0) after each thought that was neutral or irrelevant. Two independent judges then sorted out the statements according to whether they were unfavorable, favorable, or neutral/irrelevant.

As in the first experiment, subjects agreed more with the pro- than with the counterattitudinal message. The inverted U prediction was again supported. Agreement with the message increased ($p < .05$), then decreased marginally ($p < .10$) as exposure frequency increased. The message agreement means for one, three, and five exposures, respectively, were 8.09, 9.77, and 8.86 on an 11-point scale. Subjects recalled more of the arguments when the message was counter- instead of proattitudinal. Recall of message arguments increased as number of exposures increased.

Analysis of cognitive responses indicated that message repetition led to (1) decreasing, then increasing counterargumentation; (2) increasing topic-irrelevant thinking; and (3) increasing, then decreasing favorable thoughts. The number of counterarguments was high with one message exposure, dropped with three exposures, and increased with five exposures. Neutral and irrelevant thoughts started out low with one exposure, increased with three exposures, and was highest with five exposures. The number of favorable thoughts was low with one exposure, increased with three exposures, and then decreased with five exposures.

According to Cacioppo and Petty, analysis of these cognitive responses give us a clearer picture of *why* overexposure often leads to less agreement than moderate exposure. With moderate exposure, subjects are able to study and absorb the contents of the message. However, at higher exposure levels, boredom or defiance (reactance) motivates the receiver to counterargue or to daydream (irrelevant thoughts).

### Message Comprehensibility

Learning theories of persuasion generally assume that the receiver is rational and content oriented and will accept a conclusion on the basis of his or her evaluation of arguments that favor it. If this assumption is correct, then receivers must first be able to understand the message before they can accept its conclusions. Early research, however, has not provided consistent evidence of a positive relationship between retention of message content and attitude change. A common finding is that receivers who do not accept the message's recommendations remember just as much of the message contents as subjects who accept the recommendations.

Eagly points out that there are several reasons why early studies have not found a relationship between comprehension and agreement.[28] First, most of these studies did not manipulate message comprehension directly but measured it as an effect of other communication variables (such as source credibility) that could influence both agreement and comprehension. Second, early studies relied on verbal memory of the message as a measure of comprehension. The typical retention measures combined into single indices material about the position or conclusions advocated by the message and arguments supporting the position. According to Eagly, comprehension is better measured by items that deal only with persuasive arguments, since agreement will be based primarily on these arguments.

Eagly in 1974 conducted a series of three experiments to investigate message comprehension and agreement.[29] She manipulated message comprehensibility directly and operationalized subject comprehension as recall of persuasive arguments.

The first experiment was a $2 \times 3$ factorial design with two levels of comprehensibility and three levels of discrepancy between the message recommendation and subject's initial belief. Eagly expected that agreement would increase with comprehensibility of the message but that comprehension would do little to enhance acceptance of a recommendation highly discrepant from the subject's initial belief.

Subjects were 291 students enrolled in an introductory psychology course. They listened to a message from a highly credible source (a physiological psychologist) who argued that the average person needs only a certain number of hours of sleep a day. Message discrepancy was varied by telling subjects that they needed either six, four, or two hours of sleep per day. Message comprehensibility was manipulated by having the subjects listen to either a good-quality tape (high comprehensibility) or a poor-quality tape (low comprehensibility). Agreement, retention, and evaluations of the source and message were measured after subjects had listened to the tapes.

Results indicate that message comprehensibility had a strong effect on retention of the arguments. Good-comprehensibility subjects (those who listened to the good-quality tape) remembered 3.59 of the six arguments and answered 12.52 of 17 multiple-choice items correctly, while poor-comprehensibility subjects (those who listened to the poor quality tape) recalled 1.76 arguments and answered 7.45 items correctly. Subjects in the poor-comprehensibility conditions rated the source and the message more unfavorably and the listening experience less pleasant than subjects in the good-comprehensibility conditions.

Eagly's main hypothesis was supported by the data. Agreement with the communicator was significantly higher in the good-comprehensibility conditions than in the low-comprehensibility conditions. Message discrepancy did not affect this relationship. Even when the message was highly discrepant, agreement increased as comprehensibility improved.

In the second experiment Eagly added a third level of comprehensibility. The procedures and messages were identical to those in the first experiment, except that a middle level of comprehensibility was introduced and a counterarguing manipulation was employed. The medium-comprehensibility message was a tape with some distortion and background noise.

As in the first experiment, recall of arguments increased as comprehensibility increased. Recall was highest in the high-comprehensibility group, followed respectively by the medium- and low-comprehensibility groups. Ratings of the source, message, and listening experience were more favorable as comprehensibility improved. Again, the main prediction was supported. Agreement with the communicator's recommendation increased as comprehensibility improved. Agreement was highest in the high-comprehensibility group, followed respectively by the medium- and low-comprehensibility groups. Message discrepancy and subject counterarguing did not affect the relationship between message comprehension and agreement.

In the third experiment, Eagly used a 4 × 2 × 2 factorial design with four levels of comprehensibility (good, medium, poor, and irrelevant arguments), two levels of message discrepancy, and two levels of communicator credibility. As in the first two experiments, the message argued that the average person needs only a certain number of hours of sleep a day. However, subjects in this experiment were asked to read the message, which was presented to them in booklet form. Message comprehensibility was manipulated by varying the order of the persuasive arguments. In the good-comprehensibility conditions, the arguments were presented in logical order and were an exact transcription from the taped message used in the first two experiments. The same sentences were presented in the medium-comprehensibility conditions but in random order. In the poor-comprehensibility conditions the sentences were first cut in half. The first and last halves from all the sentences were then randomly joined together and incorporated in the message. Subjects in the irrelevant-argument condition read either a passage on ecology or imprinting. This condition was added as a control.

The high-credibility source was a physiological psychologist on the faculty of the university who was a respected researcher on sleep. The low-credibility source was a freshman psychology student. Message discrepancy was manipulated as in the first two experiments.

Results show that recall of the arguments improved as message comprehensibility increased. Recall was highest in the good-comprehensibility conditions, followed respectively by the medium, poor, and control conditions. The source was rated more favorably and the message more pleasant as comprehensibility increased. The control message (irrelevant arguments) was rated more pleasant than the poor-comprehensibility message. As expected, agreement with the communicator's recommendation and ratings of the convincingness of the arguments increased as comprehensibility improved.

Eagly's three experiments provide strong support for the hypothesis that increased comprehension of a message leads to increased agreement with the message's recommendation. According to Eagly, a person who receives a more comprehensible message is more accepting of its conclusion because of his or her clearer understanding of the arguments and because of lesser annoyance with the experience of listening to or reading the message. We do not learn the arguments from messages that are not comprehensible and often find the experience quite unpleasant. These two mediating processes interfere with acceptance of the message's recommendations.

### Message Characteristics and Source Evaluation

Our evaluations of communication sources are affected not only by what they say but also *how* they say it. In this section we will identify message characteristics that determine whether a source is evaluated favorably or unfavorably.

Carbone in 1975 tested the general hypothesis that a lack of stylistic clarity in the message results in unfavorable evaluations of the source.[30] She studied five stylistic variables that previous research had shown to be related to easy comprehension.[31]

1. *Listenability* (or readability) refers to message comprehensibility. It is usually measured by the average number of words per sentence, the average number of simple sentences, and the number of syllables in words. A message that is highly readable or listenable will have short sentences, short words, and mostly simple sentences.
2. *Human interest* is the extent to which the message relates to the receiver. It is measured by the average number of personal words and the average number of personal sentences.
3. *Vocabulary diversity* is the extent to which the communicator uses different words and avoids repetition of words.
4. *Realism* is the extent to which the communicator avoids abstractions. A message high in realism will have a high number of "empirical sentences." These are sentences that refer to events, conditions, or situations in the real world.
5. *Verifiability* is the extent to which the message contains empirical statements that can be tested objectively in the real world.

Carbone's main hypothesis was that messages from credible sources would be higher in all five stylistic variables than messages from low-credibility sources. She defined credible sources as being expert, trustworthy, and dynamic.[32]

Carbone used a quasiexperimental design and content analysis to test her hypothesis. She presented manuscripts of speeches written by undergraduate students in public speaking to a group of judges, who rated them on credibility. Messages that were rated high and low on credibility were then content analyzed by two independent coders to determine whether they differed in any of the five stylistic characteristics. Results provide strong support for her hypothesis, except for the verifiability measure. Low-credibility sources used longer sentences and words and more complex sentences than high-credibility sources. High-credibility sources included more first-person pronouns (*I, we*) and second-person plural pronouns (*you*) in their messages than low-credibility sources. Highly credible sources contained a greater number of references to specific experts confirming arguments used in the message. They also related the message to specific individuals, while low-crediblity sources generalized their assertions.

High-credibility sources also used a more diverse vocabulary than low-credibility sources. Their messages were less abstract and had more references to real-life experiences. There was a slight tendency for highly credible sources to write messages that were more verifiable.

Although Carbone's study did not manipulate style directly, it provides evidence that messages high in listenability, human interest, vocabulary diversity, and realism are evaluated more favorably than messages low in these style dimensions.

## Message Appeals

What message appeals should we use in persuasion? Should we appeal to our receivers' intellects or to their emotions? How effective are fear appeals? These are some of the questions that research on message appeals has attempted to answer.

### Emotional and Rational Appeals

One of the problems in comparing the effectiveness of emotional and rational appeals has been to distinguish clearly between the two strategies. Emotional appeals are sometimes referred to as "pathos" appeals. These involve creating the appropriate feelings in receivers by appealing to their feelings, values, or emotions or by putting them in a pleasant mood while receiving the message.[33] More recently, emotional appeals have been defined as those arguing for a given belief by pointing out the rewards that would follow from holding the belief. Rational appeals, sometimes referred as "logos" appeals, attempt to convince receivers to adopt a belief by presenting empirical and logical evidence supporting the belief.

McGuire points out that each type of appeal has been shown to be effective.[34] There is evidence, for example, that persuasive impact of a message is enhanced by putting the receiver in a pleasant mood while receiving the message. This can be done by tactics that have nothing to do with the message, such as a humorous introduction,[35] or by feeding receivers a snack while they listen to the message.[36] Additional support for the effectiveness of emotional appeals is provided by research on attitude functions. Attitudes can be changed by manipulating the perceived instrumentality of goals that they help us to obtain, such as social desirability.

Persuasion studies based on learning theory, like those reviewed in the previous section on message comprehension, provide evidence that rational appeals can also be effective. A common finding is that agreement with the message increases as understanding of supportive arguments increases.

According to McGuire, studies directly comparing the effectiveness of emotional and rational appeals have shown that there is no difference or that emotional appeals are more effective.[37] However, he suggests caution in accepting findings that emotional (or rational) appeals are more effective, since it is likely that the two types of appeals are not opposite ends of the same dimension but are two distinct and independent dimensions. This means that emotional messages can also be rational and rational messages can be emotional. It would be difficult, therefore, to isolate independent effects of each type of appeal. For this reason the relative effectiveness of rational and emotional appeals has not received very much research attention in recent years.

### Fear Appeals

Research on fear appeals gives us a complex picture of the relationship between the level of fear arousal in a message recipient and the amount of opinion or behavior change. The first study by Janis and Feshbach more than twenty years ago indicated that low fear appeals in a message were more effective than high-fear appeals in producing attitude change.[38] Since then, however, numerous investigators have found that higher fear appeals lead to more opinion change, or that the relationship between fear appeals and opinion change is mediated by other variables in the communication situation.[39]

In the typical experiment subjects are exposed to messages varying in fear appeals. Fear appeals generally involve a threat to the recipient for noncompliance with the message's recommendations. Most messages have dealt with health topics, such as smoking and lung cancer, dental hygiene, tetanus, seat belts and auto safety, and mumps. Low-fear messages usually incorporate arguments and data backing up the threat; medium fear appeals use arguments and some mildly threatening pictures or sketches; and high fear appeals use the arguments and highly arousing visuals, such as pictures depicting gory operations presented as possible consequences for noncompliance. A number of dependent variables have been measured. These include opinion change regarding the message topic, intention to comply with the recommendations, and actual behavioral compliance. Some studies have measured effects immediately after presentation of the fear appeals, while others have used delayed posttest measures.

Recent research suggests that there are two probable relationships between fear appeals and compliance.[40] The first of these is that the effectiveness of high fear appeals is mediated by other variables in the communication situation. A number of studies, for example, indicate that high levels of fear arousal produce more attitude change as the receiver's chronic anxiety level and perceived vulnerability to the threat decrease. Receivers who are chronically anxious or those who see themselves as highly vulnerable to the threat will tend to avoid high levels of fear. The anxiety aroused by high fear appeals may be too uncomfortable for these receivers, and they are likely to protect themselves from the message by not paying attention or by using other forms of perceptual defenses. Supporting this analysis are the findings by Niles and Leventhal and by Watts that high fear appeals produced more opinion change on the smoking-cancer issue as the receiver's level of perceived invulnerability to cancer increased.[41] Berkowitz and Cottingham also showed that high fear appeals were more effective on the seat-belt issue when the threat was of low relevance to the receivers (when receivers did not drive their automobiles very often).[42]

Another variable affecting the effectiveness of high fear appeals is the message recommendation. There is some evidence that high fear appeals are more effective when the recommendation is specific, clear, and easy to follow.[43]

We can conclude that high fear appeals are effective only under certain conditions. This conclusion is supported by recent theories that question the assumption that people comply with high-fear messages primarily to reduce the emotional arousal (fear) that is elicited by the messages.[44] Instead of focusing on the arousal of fear and the subsequent desire to reduce fear, these theories emphasize the cognitive or thought processes that are activated during exposure to threat or fear information. Rogers' protection motivation theory, for example, says that our cognitive appraisal of the threat in a fear message is more important in explaining how we will react to the message than the emotional arousal elicited by the threat.[45] Cognitive appraisal of the threat includes the following evaluations.

1. Likelihood of being exposed to the threat.
2. Seriousness of the threat.
3. Effectiveness of the recommended actions in preventing or reducing the threat.
4. Personal efficacy, or the perceived ability to perform the recommended action.

Protection motivation theory says that people will accept advice from a high-fear message when they are convinced of: (1) the seriousness of the threat in the message; (2) their susceptibility to the threat; (3) the effectiveness of the recommendations in controlling it; and (4) their ability to perform the recommended action. A number of recent studies and those discussed in this chapter provide support for these predictions from protection motivation theory.[46]

The second probable relationship between fear appeals and compliance is McGuire's nonmonotonic (or curvilinear) hypothesis.[47] According to McGuire, the relationship can best be depicted by an inverted U curve, which shows that medium levels of fear are the most effective. Low fear appeals will not be effective because they are generally less interesting and convincing than high-fear appeals. On the other hand, high fear appeals may lose some of their effectiveness because of defensive avoidance by receivers. Medium-fear appeals can be interesting and convincing and will less likely arouse defensive tendencies in receivers than high fear appeals. Thus, they should be the most effective.

Krisher, Darley, and Darley tested the nonmonotonic theory in 1973.[48] According to them, one reason for the contradictory findings in fear appeals research is that different manipulations of fear appeals are used. The messages used in the low-, medium-, and high-fear conditions may vary not only in fear level aroused in receivers, but in other message factors as well. For example, most high-fear messages are longer than low-fear messages, contain more information, and are accompanied by more pictures or illustrations. These differences may account for the results instead of the amount of fear aroused in receivers. To control for other message characteristics, Krisher, Darley, and Darley used bogus heart rate feedback to induce high fear in their subjects. This technique is based on previous work by Schachter showing that the degree of emotional arousal a person feels depends on his or her physiological arousal and on cues in the situation in which the arousal occurs.[49] The assumption in the Krisher *et al.* study was that bogus heart rate feedback would lead the subjects to believe that they were even more aroused than they really were.

Subjects in the Krisher *et al.* study were sixty male subjects randomly assigned to one of three experimental conditions. The experiment was presented to the subjects as a health research study concerning mumps. Subjects in the low-fear condition were presented with a tape-recorded message about mumps. The facts were presented in a nonthreatening manner. Subjects were informed that mumps was undesirable, that it could cause losses in school and study time, and that a new vaccine could provide protection against the disease. The message was accompanied by slides of simple diagrams of the body showing general areas that might be affected by the disease.

The high-fear message was identical to the low-fear one in the early segments. However, additional information was given about the seriousness of mumps, including the dangerous and painful results of contracting the disease. Slides accompanying the message showed gory operations on the testes and brains of persons supposedly afflicted with mumps.

The high-fear/heart rate message was identical to the high-fear/mumps message. However, subjects in this condition heard what they thought to be their own heartbeats during the message presentation. These heartbeats had been prerecorded and rose and fell according to the fear content in the message from between 70 and 80 beats per minute during calm periods up to 140 beats per minute during high fear segments. The bogus heartbeats were considerably higher than normal and were intended to convince subjects that they were more aroused than they actually were.

After exposure to the message, subjects filled out a questionnaire measuring their opinions about mumps and their intentions to get a vaccination against the disease. Each subject was also given a sheet of instructions on how to get the vaccination. The behavioral measure was whether or not the subject actually got a shot within two weeks after the experiment.

Analysis of subject reactions to the fear manipulations showed that subjects in the low-fear condition expressed the least fear, followed respectively by the high-fear and high-fear/heart rate conditions. These differences indicate that the fear manipulations worked. Subjects who heard the bogus heartbeats showed more fear arousal than subjects in the high-fear condition.

All three messages were equally effective in convincing the subjects of the existence of a mumps vaccine and the viral origin of the disease. Subjects in the high-fear and high-fear/heart rate conditions, but not those in the low-fear condition, were convinced that mumps was a potentially dangerous disease and that mumps, if contracted in adulthood, may cause sterility. There were no differences in agreement with the message between the high-fear and the heart rate groups.

Level of fear in the message did not affect subjects' intent to get vaccinations. On a 7-point scale (with seven indicating strong intention), the means were 5.85 for low fear and 5.90 for both the high fear and heart rate conditions.

Actual shot taking, the behavioral measure, was related to fear appeals. Of the subjects who said they intended to take shots, 43 percent actually did. There was significantly more shot taking in the high-fear than in the high-fear/heart rate condition and in the high-fear than in the low-fear condition. According to Krisher *et al.*, these results provide support for a curvilinear relationship between fear appeals and compliance. Medium levels of fear ("high fear," in their study) were most effective in convincing subjects to comply behaviorally with the message.

## SUMMARY

Research on messages has attempted to identify message structures, stylistic variables, and message appeals that can increase persuasive impact. Many of these studies are based on learning theory principles that predict that compliance with a message's recommendation depends on comprehension of the arguments and on rewards promised by the message. Here are some general findings from research on message characteristics.

1. Messages with explicit conclusions are more effective in changing receiver opinions than messages with implicit conclusions. Very often our receivers will miss the point of the message if we do not draw it for them.

2. More opinion change results when agreeable and pleasant information is discussed first in the message instead of disagreeable or unpleasant information. This strategy improves likability of the communicator and helps comprehension.

3. Material in the beginning of the message is learned best, followed by material at the end. Material at the middle or just after the middle is learned least.

4. The relative effectiveness of one-sided and two-sided messages depends on audience, source, and other message characteristics. One-sided messages (or ignoring the opposition) are more effective when the receivers are initially in favor of the source's conclusion, when the receivers have "low intelligence" or have little formal education, when receivers are not familiar with the issue, when receivers will not likely be exposed to the

other side, and when the topic is not controversial. Two-sided messages (or refuting the opposition) are more effective when receivers have "high intelligence" or have more formal education, when the subjects are initially opposed to the recommendation, when receivers are familiar with the issue, when receivers will likely be exposed to opposition arguments from other communicators, and when the topic is controversial.

5. In general, comparative and noncomparative advertisements are equally effective. However, comparative ads can be more effective when (a) the advertised brand has a small market share or is a newcomer; (b) the advertised brand has a built-in advantage and the claimed superiority is meaningful, demonstrable, and verifiable; (c) the target audience does not have well-established preferences; and (d) the comparative ad is a novelty in its product category. Research also shows that comparative advertising is more effectively used in television than in print or radio.

6. Repeated exposure to a message is sufficient to increase agreement with the message's recommendation. Too much exposure may lower agreement, since continued repetition of the message may lead to boredom and satiation. However, overexposure still can produce more agreement than no exposure. A period of nonexposure can neutralize any boomerang effects resulting from overexposure.

7. Learning increases with message repetition. Message repetition leads to (a) decreasing, then increasing counterargumentation; (b) increasing topic-irrelevant thinking; and (c) increasing, then decreasing favorable thoughts.

8. Increased comprehension of a message leads to increased agreement with the message's recommendations.

9. Communicators are evaluated more favorably to the extent that their messages have the following qualities: listenability (or readability), human interest, vocabulary diversity, and realism.

10. There is generally no difference in persuasive impact of emotional and rational appeals.

11. Medium fear appeals in a message are generally more effective in producing compliance than low or high fear appeals. High fear appeals can be more effective than low or medium fear appeals when (a) the receivers have low chronic anxiety or when they do not perceive themselves to be too vulnerable to the threat; (b) when the recommendations are specific, clear, and easy to follow.

## REVIEW QUESTIONS

1. Look through some of the persuasive messages in the mass media. Pick out one example of each of the following messages: (a) a message with an explicit conclusion; (b) a message with an implicit conclusion; (c) a message

with agreeable or pleasant information at the beginning; (*d*) a one-sided message; (*e*) a two-sided message; (*f*) a message using high fear appeals; (*g*) a message using rational appeals; (*h*) a message using emotional appeals; (*i*) a message that is "easy" to comprehend; (*j*) a message that is "difficult" to comprehend. Evaluate the potential effectiveness of each message for its intended audience.

2. Do you agree with McGuire's assumption that communication audiences are generally "lazy" and that in communication, "it appears it is not sufficient to lead the horse to water; one must push his head underneath to drink?" Support your answer with examples and research evidence.

3. Pick two studies from the research section of this chapter. Evaluate the internal and external validity of each study. Of what value are the results, theoretically and practically?

## ENDNOTES

1. William McGuire, "The Nature of Attitudes and Attitude Change," in G. Lindzey and E. Aronson (eds.), *Handbook of Social Psychology*, 2nd ed., Vol. 3 (Reading, Mass.: Addison-Wesley, 1969), p. 213.
2. Leon Festinger, *A Theory of Cognitive Dissonance* (Stanford, Calif.: Stanford University Press, 1957).
3. McGuire, *op. cit.*
4. J. J. Boddewyn and Katherin Marton, *Comparison Advertising, A Worldwide Study* (New York: Hastings House, 1978).
5. Joseph A. DeVito, "Style and Stylistics: An Attempt at Definition," *Quarterly Journal of Speech, 53,* 1967, p. 249.
6. Alice Eagly, "Comprehensibility of Persuasive Arguments as a Determinant of Opinion Change," *Journal of Personality and Social Psychology, 29,* 1974, pp. 758–773.
7. Tamara Carbone, "Stylistic Variables as Related to Source Credibility: A Content Analysis Approach," *Speech Monographs, 42,* June 1975, pp. 99–106.
8. McGuire, *op. cit.*, pp. 203–205.
9. *Ibid.*, pp. 200–203.
10. C. I. Hovland and W. Mandell, "An Experimental Comparison of Conclusion-Drawing by the Communicator and by the Audience," *Journal of Abnormal and Social Psychology, 47,* 1952, pp. 581–588.
11. McGuire, *op. cit.*, p. 209.
12. W. J. McGuire, "Order of Presentation as a Factor in Conditioning Persuasiveness," in C. I. Hovland (ed.), *Order of Presentation in Persuasion* (New Haven, Conn.: Yale University Press, 1957), pp. 98–114.
13. P. H. Tannenbaum and R. W. Gengel, "Generalization of Attitude Change through Congruity Principle Relationships," *Journal of Personality and Social Psychology, 3,* 1966, pp. 233–238.
14. McGuire, 1957, *op. cit.*
15. C. I. Hovland, A. Lumsdaine, and F. D. Sheffield, *Experiments on Mass Communication* (Princeton, N.J.: Princeton University Press, 1949).

16. McGuire, 1969 *op cit.*, pp. 211.
17. Boddewyn and Merton, *op. cit.*
18. *Ibid.*, pp. 60–64.
19. *Ibid.*, pp. 64–71.
20. *Ibid.*, pp. 96–101.
21. R. B. Zajonc, "The Attitudinal Effects of Mere Exposure," *Journal of Personality and Social Psychology, 8*(2), part 2, 1968 pp. 1–27.
22. Steven Chaffee, "Salience and Pertinence as Sources of Value Change," *Journal of Communication, 17,* 1967, pp. 25–38; Peter C. Gordon and Keith Holyoak, "Implicit Learning and Generalization of the 'Mere Exposure' Effect," *Journal of Personality and Social Psychology, 45*(3), 1983, pp. 492–500.
23. See, for example, R. B. Zajonc, H. Marcus, and W. Wilson, "Exposure Effects and Associative Learning," *Journal of Experimental Social Psychology, 10,* 1974, pp. 248–263; John Cacioppo and Richard Petty, "Effects of Message Repetition and Position on Cognitive Response, Recall and Persuasion," *Journal of Personality and Social Psychology, 37,* 1979, pp. 97–109.
24. L. B. Becker and J. C. Doolittle, "Repetitious Political Advertising and Evaluations of and Information Seeking about Candidates," *Journalism Quarterly, 52,* 1975, pp. 611–617.
25. Allen Greenberg and Charles Suttoni, "Television Commercial Wearout," *Journal of Advertising Research, 13,* 1973, pp. 47–54.
26. Richard Miller, "Mere Exposure, Psychological Reactance and Attitude Change," *Public Opinion Quarterly, 40,* 1976, pp. 229–233.
27. Cacioppo and Petty, *op. cit.*
28. Alice Eagly, "Comprehensibility of Persuasive Arguments as a Determinant of Opinion Change," *Journal of Personality and Social Psychology, 29,* 1974, pp. 758–773.
29. *Ibid.*
30. Carbone, *op. cit.*
31. George Klare, *The Measurement of Readability,* (Ames: Iowa State University Press, 1963).
32. Carbone, *op. cit.*, p. 100.
33. McGuire, 1969, *op. cit.*, pp. 200–203.
34. *Ibid.*
35. R. R. Windes, "A Study of Effective and Ineffective Presidential Campaign Speeches," *Speech Monographs, 28,* 1961, pp. 38–49.
36. I. Janis, D. Kaye, and P. Kirschner, "Facilitating Effects of 'Eating-While-Reading' on Responsiveness to Persuasive Communications," *Journal of Personality and Social Psychology, 1,* 1965, pp. 181–186.
37. McGuire, 1969, *op. cit.*, pp. 200–203.
38. I. Janis and S. Feshback, "Effects of Fear-Arousing Communications," *Journal of Abnormal and Social Psychology, 48,* 1953, pp. 78–92.
39. Howard Levanthal, "Findings and Theory in the Study of Fear Communications," in L. Berkowitz (ed.), *Advances in Experimental Social Psychology,* Vol. 5 (New York: Academic Press, 1970).
40. *Ibid.*
41. See, for example, P. Niles, "The Relationships of Susceptibility and Anxiety to Acceptance of Fear Arousing Communications," Ph.D. dissertation, Yale University, 1964; H. Leventhal and P. Niles, "A Field Experiment on Fear Arousal with

Data on the Validity of Questionnaire Measures," *Journal of Personality, 32,* 1964, pp. 459–479; J. C. Watts, "The Role of Vulnerability in Resistance to Fear-Arousing Communications," Ph.D. dissertation, Bryn Mawr College, 1966.

42. L. Berkowitz and D. R. Cottingham, "The Interest Value and Relevance of Fear-Arousing Communications," *Journal of Abnormal and Social Psychology, 60,* 1960, pp. 37–43.

43. For a review of relevant studies, see Levanthal, 1970, *op. cit.*

44. Kenneth H. Beck and Adrian K. Lund, "The Effects of Health Threat Seriousness and Personal Efficacy Upon Intentions and Behavior," *Journal of Applied Social Psychology, 11*(5), 1981, pp. 401–415.

45. R. W. Rogers, "A Protection Motivation Theory of Fear Appeals and Attitude Change," *Journal of Psychology, 91,* 1975, pp. 93–114.

46. Beck and Lund, *op. cit.;* also, R. W. Rogers and C. R. Mewborn, "Fear Appeals and Attitude Change: Effects of a Threat's Noxiousness, Probability of Occurrence, and the Efficacy of Coping Responses," *Journal of Personality and Social Psychology, 34,* 1976, 54–61.

47. McGuire, 1969, *op. cit.,* pp. 203–206.

48. Howard Krisher III, Susan Darley, and John Darley, "Fear-Provoking Recommendations, Intentions to Take Preventive Actions, and Actual Preventive Actions," *Journal of Personality and Social Psychology, 26,* 1973, pp. 301–308.

49. S. Schachter, "The Interaction of Cognitive and Physiological Determinants of Emotional State," in L. Berkowitz (ed.), *Advances in Experimental Social Psychology,* Vol. 1 (New York: Academic Press, 1964).

# 10 _____

# MEDIA_____

Communication researchers have long been interested in evaluating the relative effectiveness of written, audiotaped, and videotaped messages in persuasion and education. This area of research is sometimes referred to as "communication modality" research. The main question is "Which medium or communication modality is most effective in enhancing attitude change and learning of the message—print (written or visual only), radio (audio or aural only), or television (video or combination of visual and aural)?"

As we have seen in the previous chapter, the learning theory assumption that good reception of the message facilitates attitude change is strongly supported by many studies. This assumption leads us to predict that the medium or communication modality most effective in enhancing learning of the message will also be the medium most effective in changing attitudes. Unfortunately, research on media effectiveness does not support this prediction. A common finding is that live and videotaped presentations are the most effective in changing attitudes, while messages presented in written form are the most easily understood.

## COMMUNICATION MODALITY, COMPREHENSION, AND ATTITUDE CHANGE

Most research indicates that live or videotaped messages are the most effective in changing attitudes, followed respectively by oral (audiotaped) and written messages.[1] An early study by Wilke in 1934 reported that live speeches were more effective than audio or written ones.[2] Reviews of experimental research by Hovland[3] and Klapper[4] concluded that oral presentations (live or audiotaped) are more effective than visual (written) presentations in changing attitudes. Katz and Lazarsfeld reported from field studies of mass media and voting that face-to-face communications were more effective than any of the mass media in influencing voter opinions.[5]

Several explanations have been offered for the superiority of live, videotaped, and audiotaped messages over written ones in changing attitudes. According to Cantril and Allport, orally presented communications permit greater opportunity for "social facilitation," while printed material is more impersonal.[6] Recipients of an orally presented message can identify with the communicator and can therefore engage in a role relationship with him or her. Also, sources of orally presented messages are more personal. It is therefore easier to like them than the impersonal sources of written messages.

Keating suggests that television is more involving for the audience than either radio or print.[7] Also, television can magnify certain characteristics of the communicator. When these characteristics are likely to enhance attitude change (such as trustworthiness, expertise, or attractiveness), the superiority of television over the other media in changing attitudes becomes more apparent.

Carver[8] and Maier and Thurber[9] present evidence that people are more critical of, and perceive as less valid, material that is written as opposed to videotaped and audiotaped material. One possible reason for this, according to Chaiken and Eagly, is that videotaped and live presentations are more distracting to the receiver.[10] Vocal and visual cues in these messages may distract recipients from the contents of the message. Distraction could then lessen their critical attitude toward the message by reducing the ability to counterargue. Chaiken and Eagly also suggest that nonverbal cues in videotaped and audiotaped communications can more easily alter perceptions of the communicator by focusing attention on communicator characteristics that facilitate or inhibit persuasion.

In contrast to findings on attitude change, research on comprehension indicates that written messages are more easily learned and remembered than either audiotaped or videotaped messages.[11] The general conclusion is that we learn more by reading than by hearing or by hearing and seeing.[12] A few studies do show that television results in greater immediate recall of material than either print or radio[13] or that communication modality does not affect comprehension.[14] Most of these studies, however, used simple material or measured recall immediately after presentation of the message. When the message is complex, or when retention is measured some time after presentation of the message, written messages have been found to be superior.

Williams and Derks, for example, presented their subjects with three lists of paired associate trigrams having different levels of pronounceability and association values.[15] As expected, they found that increased pronounceability and association value resulted in greater learning of the words. Also, visual and combined visual and aural presentations were more effective than the aural presentation.

Wilson in 1974 studied the effects of medium on loss of information from news reports.[16] He found that the greatest loss of information was from radio (79.92 percent) and television (79.92 percent), and the least from newspapers (72.83 percent).

Why do we learn more easily from written than from audiotaped or videotaped materials? We seem to be less distracted when reading than when listening to or watching a videotaped message. Thus, we are able to focus attention more completely on the message. Also, researchers studying the central processing of information in people suggest that the information-encoding capacity of the eye is greater than that of the ear.[17]

## RESEARCH

If message comprehension enhances attitude change, why has research shown that oral and videotaped messages are more effective than printed messages in changing attitudes but that printed messages are the most easily understood? This is a question that current researchers are turning their attention to. Current thinking is that oral and videotaped messages are *not* always more effective than print in changing attitudes. Efforts are therefore being directed at identifying those conditions when printed materials may be more effective.

### Chaiken and Eagly's 1976 Study

Chaiken and Eagly tested the hypothesis that written material will be more effective than either videotaped or audiotaped materials in changing attitudes when the message is difficult or complex, while the usual persuasive advantage of audiotaped and videotaped (or live) modalities will be limited to easy material.[18] They based this hypothesis on three assumptions that are supported by previous research.

1. Message recipients more readily yield to or accept information transmitted by videotaped or audiotaped compared with written materials.
2. Message recipients, however, more readily learn written material compared to material presented by videotape or audiotape.
3. Comprehension enhances yielding to the message.

Chaiken and Eagly argue that with difficult messages the yielding advantages of videotaped and audiotaped materials are outweighed by the advantage of written materials in getting the message understood. Therefore, the written mode should be more persuasive with difficult messages.

To test this hypothesis, Chaiken and Eagley exposed their subjects either to an easy or difficult persuasive message through written, audiotaped, or videotaped presentations. The topic of the message was a legal dispute, with the communicator (a law student) arguing for a particular side in the dispute. A control group was not exposed to the message.

The easy and difficult messages were of the same length, argued for the same position, and contained the same number of arguments. The easy version, however, was composed of shorter sentences, had only one or two clauses per sentence, and used simple words. The difficult version was composed of longer sentences, had three or more clauses per sentence, and used more difficult words.

An amateur actor was trained to deliver the message. His delivery was videotaped for the videotape conditions, while the audio portions of the tapes were played in the audiotape conditions. Subjects in the written conditions were presented with the written transcript of the message. The videotape and audiotape messages lasted approximately seven minutes. Subjects in the written conditions were given seven minutes to read through the message.

In addition to message difficulty and communication modality, confidence of the communicator was manipulated in the videotaped and audiotaped conditions. The actor delivered the messages either confidently or nonconfidently by varying tone of voice and body language. Confidence was manipulated to determine whether the videotaped and audiotaped messages would be favored by the expression of high confidence. Eagly and Chaiken reasoned that communicator characteristics are more easily accentuated through videotape and audiotape. The highly confident communicator, therefore, should be even more effective in these conditions than in the written condition compared to the nonconfident communicator.

Subjects in all the treatment conditions showed greater agreement with the message than subjects in the control condition, indicating that, overall, the persuasive message was effective. A communication modality by message difficulty interaction was also observed. As predicted, with easy messages, agreement was greatest in the videotaped, followed respectively by audiotaped and written messages ($p < .05$). Further analysis indicated that only the videotape versus written comparison was actually significant ($p < .01$). When the message was difficult, agreement was greater in the written conditions than in the videotape and audiotape conditions.

Chaiken and Eagly also found that, overall, subjects in written conditions comprehended more of the message than subjects in either videotape or audiotape conditions. Within the difficult message conditions the superior comprehensibility of written over videotaped and audiotaped messages was significant. However, when the message was easy, comprehension did not differ between modes of presentation.

Subjects in the confident conditions perceived the source to be more confident than subjects in the nonconfident conditions. However, confidence did not affect opinions.

In general, subjects receiving easy messages perceived their experiences as more pleasant than subjects receiving difficult messages ($p < .001$). When the message was difficult, subjects in the written conditions rated the experience to be more pleasant than subjects in the audiotape and videotape conditions combined ($p < .05$). However, with easy messages, perceived pleasantness was identical for written, videotaped, and audiotaped messages.

Other findings of Chaiken and Eagley are the following.

1. Subjects receiving easy messages rated both the communicator and his language more appropriate for the communication task than subjects receiving difficult messages.

2. Subjects rated written messages more appropriate for the communication task than videotaped or audiotaped messages ($p < .005$).

3. Subjects receiving the written message reported less distraction than subjects receiving the audiotaped and videotaped versions ($p < .001$).

4. Subjects receiving difficult messages reported greater distraction than subjects receiving easy messages ($p < .001$).

5. Subjects receiving easy messages rated the communicator as more professional and expert ($p < .05$) and more personally attractive and warm ($p < .05$) than did subjects receiving difficult messages.

6. Subjects receiving written messages rated the source as more professional and expert than did subjects receiving audiotape and videotape messages ($p < .001$).

Chaiken and Eagly's study provides support for the hypothesis that with easy messages videotape will be more effective than audiotaped presentations in persuasion and that audiotape will be more effective than written messages. With difficult messages, written messages are superior to both videotape and audiotape presentations. These results are best explained by the interrelationships between communication modality, distraction, and comprehension. We seem to be less distracted with written messages compared to videotape and audiotape presentations. Less distraction leads to greater message comprehension which, in turn, results in more opinion change. The effects of distraction on comprehension, however, are true only when the message is difficult. With easy messages, distraction and communication modality do not affect comprehension very significantly.

Chaiken and Eagly also show that receivers rate written messages more favorably than audiotaped and videotaped messages, particularly when the message is difficult. Easy messages were rated more favorably compared to difficult messages.

## Andreoli and Worchel's 1978 Study

Andreoli and Worchel studied possible interactions between communication medium and trustworthiness of the communicator in producing opinion change.[19] They predicted that television would be more effective than radio or print in changing opinions when the source was trustworthy. However, with sources low in trustworthiness, television would be the least effective of the three media.

Andreoli and Worchel based their hypothesis on the assumption that television is the most involving of the three media and is therefore better able to highlight a communicator's positive or negative characteristics. A trustworthy source, for example, can be more effective with television because his or her trustworthiness is heightened by the medium. On the other hand, with an untrustworthy source, the more involving television presentation can focus increased attention on his or her negative characteristics.

Andreoli and Worchel manipulated three independent variables—com-

municator trustworthiness, message position, and medium. Four communicators were introduced as sources of the message. Pretesting had indicated
that two of these sources were trustworthy (a newscaster and a former state
representative), while two were untrustworthy (a political candidate and a
current state representative). A fictitious name was used for all sources.

The message dealt with the legalization of liquor by the drink in the state.
The source took either a pro- or antiliquor position. The messages were
identical in length and took about three minutes to present orally.

The message was presented over one of three media. Subjects in the television condition watched a videotape of the source delivering the message. The
videotape was presented as a segment from an actual news report (in the
newscaster source condition) or from other television reports (in the former
representative, current representative, and political candidate source conditions). Actually, the source was a graduate assistant who role-played the communicator roles. Subjects in the radio condition heard a tape of the audio
from the video recordings and were told that the tape was from local radio
programs. Subjects in the written condition received the message in the form
of a newspaper clipping. The messages were identical in content and length.

After exposure to the messages, subjects were administered an opinion
questionnaire. Opinions of a control group (which did not receive any message) were used to compute opinion change in the experimental groups.

Manipulation checks indicated that, as expected, the former representative
and newscaster were rated to be more trustworthy than either the candidate
or current representative. Overall, the persuasive messages changed opinions
in the direction advocated. Trustworthy sources were also more effective than
nontrustworthy sources in changing opinions across message positions and
media.

The main hypothesis of the study was supported. A significant source by
medium interaction showed that the trustworthy sources were more effective
in changing opinions when they used television compared to when they used
radio or written presentations ($p < .01$). On the other hand, the untrustworthy source (the candidate) produced more attitude change when he used
radio or a written presentation than when he appeared on television ($p < .05$).

Communicator trustworthiness, message position, and medium used did
not affect recall of information. Subjects did rate the television presentation to
be more involving than the radio presentation ($p < .001$) and the radio presentation to be more involving than the written one ($p < .001$).

Andreoli and Worchel interpret these results as supporting their analysis
of the relationships between medium, communicator trustworthiness, and
opinion change. We can conclude that television, through heightened receiver involvement, focuses attention on communicator characteristics that can
either enhance or inhibit persuasion. When the communicator is trustworthy
or otherwise attractive, TV is the most effective medium compared to print
and radio. However, when the communicator is generally unattractive or low
in trustworthiness, radio and print are more effective than television.

## Chaiken and Eagly's 1983 Study

Chaiken and Eagly further explored the general idea that the persuasive impact of communication modality (or medium) depends on the communicator's personality characteristics or image.[20] They reasoned that nonverbal communicator characteristics such as physical appearance and voice are readily apparent in videotaped and audiotaped messages, while the only information about the communicator that is transmitted to the audience in written messages is the verbal message itself. Audiences of audiotaped and videotaped messages can base their evaluations not only on the verbal message but also on nonverbal communicator characteristics. Thus, communicator characteristics become more important or salient when audiotape or videotape is used and should be more influential in determining audience response than when written messages are used.

Chaiken and Eagly also argued that the increased salience of nonverbal communicator characteristics should enhance the persuasiveness of a communicator who is likable, attractive, or an expert. On the other hand, increased salience of nonverbal communicator characteristics should decrease the persuasiveness of a communicator who is not likable, not attractive, or who is low in expertise. A communicator who is liked by the audience should therefore be more effective when using videotaped and audiotaped messages than when using written messages, since videotaped and audiotaped messages draw attention to nonverbal communicator characteristics (or make them salient). Conversely, a communicator who is *not* liked by the audience should be more persuasive when using a written message (which draws attention to the message and not to nonverbal communicator characteristics).

To test these predictions, Chaiken and Eagly prepared a message arguing that the "University of Toronto should switch to a trimester system of instruction." (The study was done at the University of Toronto.) The message was presented to randomized groups of college students in three forms—videotape (a male communicator delivered the message), audiotape (which included only the audio portion of the videotape), and written (a printed transcript of the message). Half of the subjects in each of the modality conditions received the message from a "likable" communicator; the other half received the message from a "disliked" communicator. Communicator likability was manipulated by providing background information about him. In the likable condition, the communicator praised the University of Toronto, its students, campus, and faculty. In the disliked condition, the communicator insulted the University of Toronto, its students, campus, and faculty. Experimental checks indicated that this manipulation worked—subjects expressed a liking for the communicator who gave praise and disliked the communicator who gave insults. The dependent variables measured were opinion change, comprehension, and cognitive responses of the subjects to the message.

Chaiken and Eagly found support for their predictions. These are some of their results.

1. The likable communicator was more effective when his message was transmitted by videotape or audiotape instead of by written form.
2. The unlikable communicator was more effective when his message was transmitted in written form and not in audiotape and videotape.
3. The likable communicator was more persuasive than his unlikable counterpart only when subjects received the videotaped or audiotaped messages. There was no difference in their relative effectiveness when the written message was used.
4. Subjects in the videotape condition reported more thoughts about the communicator and more distraction from the message contents than subjects in the audiotape and written conditions.
5. Subjects' perceptions of the communicator were the most significant predictors of opinion change in the videotaped and audiotaped conditions, but they did not predict opinion change in the written condition. Evaluations of the message were the most significant predictors of opinion change in the written condition.
6. Delayed opinion change was stronger for subjects originally exposed to written, compared to audiotaped and videotaped, messages.

We can conclude from this study that nonverbal communicator characteristics become more salient or more important determinants of opinion change when videotaped and audiotaped messages are used instead of written messages. Communication receivers focus their attention more on the source than on the message when video and audio media are used. Sources who have attractive characteristics such as "likability" are more effective when using videotaped and audiotaped messages. Sources who have unattractive characteristics (such as those who are disliked by the audience) are more effective when using written messages. Chaiken and Eagly also point out that[21]

. . whereas the immediate impact of a persuasive message can be maximized by utilizing an electronic medium and a communicator with positively valenced personal attributes, a relatively enduring change in opinions may be more likely to occur when the written modality is employed.

## SUMMARY

Media research, sometimes referred to as "communication modality research," has evaluated the relative effectiveness of written, audiotaped, and videotaped messages in persuasion and education. Here are some of the general findings.

1. Live or videotaped messages are generally the most effective in changing attitudes, followed respectively by oral (audiotaped) and written messages. The persuasive advantage of live and videotaped presentations is often

attributed to their ability to focus receiver attention on positive characteristics of the communicator and to distract them from message contents. We are generally more critical of written than videotaped or audiotaped materials.

2. Written messages are more easily learned and remembered than either audiotaped or videotaped messages. This is particularly true when the message is complex and when retention is measured some time after presentation of the message.

3. Communication modality interacts with message complexity in determining attitude change. Written material is more effective than either videotaped or audiotaped materials in changing attitudes when the message is difficult. When the message is easy, videotapes will be more effective than written presentations.

4. Written messages are rated more favorably than either audio or video messages when the message is difficult.

5. Communication modality interacts with communicator trustworthiness in determining attitude change. Trustworthy sources are more effective in changing attitudes when using television instead of print or radio. Untrustworthy sources are most effective when using print or radio.

6. Television is more involving to the receiver than radio, which is more involving than print.

## REVIEW QUESTIONS

1. When are videotaped messages more effective than printed messages in changing attitudes? When is print more effective?

2. What implications does the Andreoli and Worchel study have for political advertising? Based on this study, when should political candidates use TV and when should they use print?

## ENDNOTES

1. Shelly Chaiken and Alice Eagly, "Communication Modality as a Determinant of Message Persuasiveness and Message Comprehensibility," *Journal of Personality and Social Psychology, 34,* 1976, pp. 605–614.

2. W. Wilke, "An Experimental Comparison of the Speech, the Radio and the Printed Page as Propaganda Devices," *Archives of Psychology,* 25(169), 1934.

3. C. Hovland, "The Effects of Mass Media on Communication," in G. Lindzey (ed.), *The Handbook of Social Psychology,* 1st ed., Vol. 2 (Reading, Mass.: Addison-Wesley, 1954).

4. J. T. Klapper, *The Effects of Mass Communication* (Glencoe, Ill.: Free Press, 1961).

5. E. Katz and P. Lazarsfeld, *Personal Influence* (Glencoe, Ill.: Free Press, 1935).

6. H. Cantril and G. Allport, *The Psychology of Radio* (New York: Harper, 1935).
7. J. Keating, "Persuasive Impact, Attitudes, and Image: The Effect of Communication Media and Audience Size on Attitude toward a Source and toward His Position," Ph.D. dissertation, Ohio State University, 1972.
8. M. E. Carver, "Listening Versus Reading," in H. Cantril and G. Allport, *The Psychology of Radio* (New York: Harper and Brothers, 1935).
9. N. R. Maier and J. Thurber, "Accuracy of Judgments of Deception When an Interview Is Watched, Heard and Read," *Personal Psychology, 21,* 1968, pp. 28–30.
10. Chaiken and Eagly, *op. cit.*
11. *Ibid.*
12. *Ibid.*
13. See, for example, L. C. Barrow, Jr., and B. H. Westley, "Comparative Teaching Effectiveness of Radio and Television," *Audio-Visual Communication Review, 7,* 1959, pp. 14–23.
14. W. H. Allen, "Media Stimulus and Types of Learning," *Audio-Visual Instruction, 12,* 1967, pp. 27–31.
15. J. Williams and P. Derks, "Mode of Presentation and the Acquisition of Paired Associates that Differ in Pronunciability and Association Value," *Journal of Verbal Learning and Verbal Behavior, 2,* 1963, pp. 453–456.
16. C. E. Wilson, "The Effect of Medium on Loss of Information," *Journalism Quarterly, 51,* 1974, pp. 111–115.
17. F. Attneave, *Applications of Information Theory to Psychology* (New York: Holt, Rinehart and Winston, 1959).
18. Chaiken and Eagly, *op. cit.*
19. Virginia Andreoli and Stephen Worchel, "Effects of Media, Communicator, and Message Position on Attitude Change," *Public Opinion Quarterly, 42,* 1978, pp. 59–70.
20. Shelly Chaiken and Alice H. Eagly, "Communication Modality as a Determinant of Persuasion: The Role of Communicator Salience," *Journal of Personality and Social Psychology, 45*(2), 1983, pp. 241–256.
21. *Ibid.*

# 11 _____

# AUDIENCES _____

One of the keys to effective communication, we have been told many times, is "to know your audience." Whether writing a feature article, creating an advertisement, or preparing a lecture, our messages should appeal to the interests and needs of our target audiences. To many communication practitioners, audience research means collecting data about audience demographics (age, sex, education, income, ethnic group, and so on), opinion, and behaviors. By knowing these audience characteristics, we are able to infer what their needs and interests are and to create the appropriate messages.

In this chapter we will discuss audiences in a somewhat different way. First, we will take a look at what happens when an audience receives a message—the processes of attention, retention, and perception. This stage in the persuasion process is extremely important because the ultimate effect of our message depends on whether our audience pays attention to it, how well they learn the contents, and whether they perceive the arguments as we would like them to. Second, we will discuss some personality characteristics that can affect how the message is received. Characteristics such as intelligence, anxiety, self-esteem, and open-mindedness affect how the message will be received and are often more important in persuasion than the usual demographic characteristics. Third, following our definition of communication as a transaction between source and receiver, we will discuss ways in which audiences can affect communicators and their messages.

Three theories of persuasion have influenced the development of research on message reception and audience personalities.[1] The first of these, learning theory, assumes that we are basically rational animals who make decisions based on the best information available. The second, consistency theory or, more specifically, dissonance theory, assumes that we are rationalizing and not rational animals and that we react to messages mostly to justify or protect existing opinions, attitudes, and behaviors. The third approach, functional theory, assumes that we adapt new attitudes to fulfill related needs and that we maintain attitudes to the extent that they continue to be useful. These theories do not necessarily contradict each other—in fact, quite often they lead to the same predictions regarding audience reactions to messages. However, they represent three distinct explanations of audience reactions. We will discuss each of them in more detail as relevant research is presented.

## MESSAGE RECEPTION

Mr. Biggott is extremely prejudiced against people from other ethnic backgrounds. Suppose we present him with an antiprejudice message, say, an episode of Norman Lear's "All in the Family" in which Archie Bunker is made to appear especially foolish for his prejudices. (Norman Lear did intend for "All in the Family" to communicate an antiprejudice message.)[2] How would Mr. Biggott react to the show? Traditional theory in message reception predicts that he would avoid the message[3] or, if he is unable to avoid it, interpret is as supporting his prejudices[4] and remember only portions of the episode that are especially supportive of his beliefs. The principles of selective exposure, selective retention, and selective perception are often mentioned in the persuasion literature as defenses that audiences use to protect their existing opinions and behaviors. Given this view of the audience, it would be very difficult to change any opinion or behavior through communication. The main effect of communication becomes reinforcement. Fortunately for communication practitioners, recent research has challenged the traditional assumptions of selective exposure and selective retention. Selective perception, however, is still very much a problem.

### Selective Exposure

The "selective exposure" hypothesis is one of the main derivations from dissonance theory, a rationalizing theory of human behavior. Dissonance theory was formulated by Festinger in 1957.[6] Recent updates on the theory have been presented by Aronson in 1969[7] and Kiesler in 1971[8] The theory attracted considerable attention in the 1960s, drawing both widespread support[9] and criticism.[10] It has been one of the more controversial theories of human behavior, partly because many of its predictions contradict principles of the more established learning theories.

Cognitive dissonance, according to Festinger, is aroused in an individual when two or more relevant cognitions simultaneously held by him or her contradict each other. A cognition is a thought about a behavior, an opinion, an attitude, or a choice. Cognitions contradict each other when logic, personal experience, established knowledge, or other people imply that they are incompatible. An individual is therefore unable to justify the holding of two or more dissonant cognitions at the same time. As an example, suppose you were a heavy smoker. We present you with information that smoking leads to lung cancer, and you accept this information to be true. According to the theory, you will then be in a dissonant state. The knowledge (or thoughts, at any given moment such as when you light up a cigarette) that you are a heavy smoker and that smoking leads to lung cancer are contradictory or incompatible. You will find it difficult (although not impossible) to justify to yourself a behavior (smoking) that can lead to an undesirable consequence (cancer and probable death). Another example is our Mr. Biggott and "All in the Family." If he recognizes the program to be critical of his prejudicial beliefs and if he accepts this criticism as valid, then he would be in a dissonant state. The cognitions that he is prejudiced (if, in fact, he recognizes this) and that prejudice is wrong are incompatible.

According to the theory, dissonance is an uncomfortable drive state that can motivate the individual to action. Thus, a person in a dissonant state is "primed" for action. He or she will be motivated to do something to remove dissonance because it is psychologically uncomfortable. There are many ways in which dissonance can be removed. A person can change a conflicting behavior (stop smoking) or opinion (stop believing that smoking leads to lung cancer). If this is not possible, a person can seek additional justification for the original attitude or behavior (convince himself or herself that the benefits derived from smoking are far more important than potential dangers).

Dissonance theory suggests not only that we will attempt to remove dissonance when it is present, but also that we will actively avoid its arousal. This is where selective exposure to information fits into the theory. Information contradicting existing attitudes, choices, or behaviors can arouse dissonance and should therefore be avoided. On the other hand, information supportive of existing attitudes, behaviors, and choices can reduce dissonance, or maintain the desired consonant state, and should therefore be actively sought. The selective exposure hypothesis has two components: (1) it predicts that we will actively avoid or that we will be less receptive to information contradicting existing attitudes, behaviors and, choices, and (2) it predicts that we will seek out or be more receptive to supportive information. The selective exposure hypothesis has attracted the attention of communication researchers because of its practical implications. If the hypothesis is correct, persuasive messages will reach only those already in agreement with their conclusions, while most of us in the audience will be like ostriches with heads buried in the sand, choosing to ignore any contradictory information. The main effect of persuasion becomes reinforcement.

What does research show about the selective exposure hypothesis? There is evidence that in the real world we do get exposed more to supporting information than to contradictory information, but not necessarily because of a psychological preference for supportive over contradictory information. Researchers call this "de facto" selection."[11] McGuire suggests that we are often surrounded by people and media agreeing with us on important issues.[12] Because of the availability of supportive information, we are more likely to report having been exposed to it than to contradictory information. However, this does not mean that we actively avoid contradictory information. Sears and Freedman[13] and Sears,[14] after extensive reviews of the selective exposure literature, concluded that there is no evidence to support the hypothesis, particularly the avoidance of contradictory information. Other researchers have studied conditions when contradictory information would be preferred over supportive information or when it would not be avoided. Some of these conditions are the following.

1. Perceived interest, salience, and novelty value of the information. Contradictory information that is interesting, entertaining, salient, personally relevant to the audience, or new will not be avoided.[15]
2. Perceived utility of the information. Audiences will be receptive to information that is useful in solving a problem or teaching a skill even if it is contradictory.[16]
3. Confidence in initial position. People who are confident in their initial opinions, choices, or behaviors will not avoid contradictory material because they will expect that they can refute such information.[17]
4. Commitment to behavior, belief, or choice. People are likely to avoid contradictory information only when it deals with behaviors, beliefs, or choices to which they are strongly committed. Decisions that are difficult to reverse are more likely to elicit selective exposure tendencies than reversible decisions.[18]
5. Norm to be open-minded. Most people will not avoid contradictory information if norms of "open-mindedness," fair play, and rationality (implying that all sides to an issue should be considered) are made salient.[19]

We can therefore conclude that many other qualities of messages determine audience attention. These findings are consistent with the learning theory principle that people will attempt to maximize rewards and minimize punishments. If there are rewards in a message that can cancel out possible discomfort from contradictory information, it will not be avoided.

More recently, research on selective exposure has investigated how individuals react to supportive and contradictory messages while they are being exposed to the information. Instead of studying whether persons will expose themselves to the information in the future, researchers are concerned with *selective attention* to the message while it is being received. Studies taking this approach will be discussed in the research section of this chapter.

## Selective Perception

Suppose our Mr. Biggott watches "All in the Family" because he finds it entertaining. Exposure to the program will not guarantee that his prejudicial beliefs will be changed. His *perception* of the program—its characters and their behaviors—is another step in the persuasion process that has to be considered.

Perception refers to the kinds of mental activity involved in recognizing, knowing, and understanding events and objects in our immediate environment.[20] The object or event in the immediate environment—the "stimulus input"—is transformed through perceptual processes into a cognition, which is a bit of knowledge or understanding. The main perceptual process is the assignment of the stimulus to a cognitive category with which we, through previous experience, may already be familiar. By placing the stimulus in a previously defined category, we are assigning it some "meaning." Ideally, this categorization should be based on information about the stimulus' properties and behaviors that we are able to observe upon encountering it. Obviously this does not happen very often. If we stopped to study each stimulus before placing it in a category (or assigning it some meaning), we would get very little accomplished during the course of a day. What often happens is that we act more hastily—by screening out much of the potential information and concentrating only on a few informational cues and by adding predicted information to go beyond what is available in the environment.[21] These two processes enable us to react more quickly to objects and events in our environment. Unfortunately, they are also major sources of error in our perceptions.

Let us illustrate these principles with some examples. Suppose you see a round red object about the size of your fist on a table. A few seconds after seeing it you put it in the category "apple." The object's color, size and shape were obviously the important characteristics or cues that led you to call it an apple. You did not stop to smell it or to take a bite and taste it. From previous experience you "knew" it was an apple. And, by calling the object an apple, you are predicting additional information about it—how it will taste, its nutritional value, and so forth. Most of us would probably not make mistakes in perceiving apples, since we encounter them often enough in our lives and because their characteristics are highly predictable. As some perceptual psychologists would put it, information about the object is "highly redundant."[22]

Let us take another example. Mr. Biggott is walking alone at night. He is stopped by a young black man. He immediately perceives the man to be a mugger, putting him in that category on the basis of his skin color. In this situation Mr. Biggott is reacting prematurely and most probably erroneously, not on the basis of information in the environment but on the basis of his own prejudices.

Although our perceptions of everyday objects and events often turn out to be "correct" (other people around us agree on the categories and meanings we assign these objects), many of our perceptions, especially in the area of intergroup relations, are highly subjective, depending on individual needs, values, and experiences. Krech and Crutchfield, in one of the early articles on perception, discussed several principles that explain how these subjective factors operate in perception.[23] Some of these principles are the following.

1. The perceptual and cognitive field in its natural state is organized and meaningful. Humans are organizing animals. We have the tendency to assign *immediately* meaning to objects and events in our environment. Uncertainty is uncomfortable; therefore, we look for structure and organization. Ideally, we should hold off interpretation or perception until all of the facts are available. Unfortunately, this is not usually the case. As soon as we encounter objects, persons, or events, we organize them into categories that are meaningful. Research on personality impressions, for example, shows that we often base perceptions of other people on only a few cues (or characteristics) and we tend to do this immediately after encountering the person.[24]

2. Perception is functionally selective. As we mentioned earlier, only a few of the characteristics of the stimulus are actually used when we assign

meaning to it. The characteristics we choose to concentrate on and use as the basis for the perception are those that will serve some immediate purpose. The purpose may be to fulfill a pressing need (such as the satisfaction of hunger, the acquisition of rewards, or the avoidance of punishment) or to reinforce mood, mental set, or cultural value (such as reinforceing a belief that the American political system is the "best" in the world).

Let us illustrate with some examples. You are hungry, so you go to the university cafeteria. What do you notice on the menu? Food items or beverages? Levine, Chein, and Murphy have shown that the immediate perception of objects can be shaped by our hunger needs.[25] They presented their subjects with a set of ambiguous line drawings and asked them to describe what they saw. One group of subjects was hungry, while the other group had just had a meal. Subjects in the hungry condition more often perceived food items in the ambiguous drawings than subjects in the other condition.

You are discussing your term paper with your professor. He has just had a fight with his wife. You think you have written a good paper. Your professor does not say anything about the substance of the paper, but he criticizes your margins, the title, a few misplaced commas, and so on. He gives you a D for the paper. Why did he look for everything that might be wrong with your paper and overlook its good points? An early experiment by Leuba and Lucas suggests that our moods can determine selection of informational cues and the meaning we assign to the stimulus.[26] They hypnotized subjects to be in either a happy, critical, or anxious mood and then presented them with a picture of "four college men on a sunny lawn, typing, listening to the radio." Subject descriptions of the picture reflected the mood that they were in. A subject in a happy mood perceived the men as relaxing and as being carefree. When he was in a critical mood, he saw that the men were not too successful in trying to study and that they would ruin their clothes by lying on the lawn. And when he was anxious he described the men as listening to a tight football or baseball game.

What about values and beliefs? There is considerable evidence that a person's attitudes and values affect how that person will interpret and perceive social stimuli. Cooper and Jahoda, for example, studied how prejudiced and unprejudiced people reacted to a series of cartoons critical of prejudice.[27] They found that unprejudiced persons accurately perceived the intent of the cartoons (to make fun of prejudice) and appreciated the humor in them. Prejudiced persons, on the other hand, either missed the message of the cartoons or distorted their meaning to reinforce their prejudices. More recently, studies have shown that perceptions of television characters like Archie Bunker and Fred Sanford are influenced by a person's value structures, such as dogmatism and authoritarianism.[28]

3. The perceptual and cognitive properties of a substructure are determined in large measure by the properties of the structure of which it is a part. This is sometimes called the "whole-part" principle. It explains what happens in the perceptual process when we assign "surplus meaning" to objects not on the basis of information at hand but on the basis of the category in which we place them. Thus, characteristics of the category are immediately ascribed to the object regardless of whether those characteristics were actually observed in the present situation. This principle also explains what happens when we "stereotype" other people. Studies of prejudice, for example, indicate that prejudice is rarely based on first-hand information but usually occurs when objectionable qualities ascribed to a group are assigned to an individual simply because he belongs to that group.[29]

The whole-part principle can also be illustrated by our use of "frames of reference" in perception. We perceive or judge stimuli not in isolation but in relation to other stimuli with which it is organized. McGarvey, for example, found that the rating of any given profession is determined by the entire series of occupations to be judged.[30] Thus, the occupation "journalist" may not rank very high when rated in relation to the professions of law, medicine, and education. However, journalism would probably get higher ratings if ranked in relation to other less prestigious occupations.

4. Objects or events that are close to each other in space or time tend to be apprehended as parts of a common structure. This is often referred to as the "proximity" principle. We tend to perceive objects that are physically close to each other and events that occur simultaneously as belonging to the same structure.

These four principles explain why perception is often subjective. They are important to communication because perception is a necessary step both in the encoding and decoding of messages. Encoding depends on our perception of the message object or topic; decoding of the message depends on how the object *and* the message are perceived. Recent research on perception and communications has studied how perceptions of communicators and messages are affected by values and attitudes of the receiver.

If perception is often subjective, what can communicators do to lead audiences to common perceptions of their messages as they intend the messages to be perceived? Several principles are suggested by research.

1. Although we expect people to differ significantly in their perceptions of various objects, it is also true that within any given culture, there will be broad agreement on the more commonly used categories.[31] Since members of the same culture share enough experiences about common objects in their environment, their perceptions of these objects should be similar. Without such agreement, meaningful communication would be impossible. A communicator should therefore be familiar with categories

common to the audience and use them whenever possible. In advertising, for example, it is important to present themes and situations that are common enough to audiences to elicit the desired interpretations. An ad showing a man preparing dinner in the family kitchen can lead to positive perceptions regarding convenience foods in the United States, where such scenes are not uncommon. However, it is likely to be misperceived in many Asian and Latin American countries, where male and female roles are more traditionally defined and where men are rarely expected to be found in the kitchen.

2. Information received early in the development of a cognitive category or a perception is more influential than later information in shaping that category.[32] The commonsense dictum that "first impressions are lasting" finds support in this principle. Not only are first impressions more influential; much of this early learning is not easily refuted by subsequent experiences. A communicator, therefore, should attempt to establish a positive bond with the audience early in the message and early in the communication interaction. Strategies for gaining early approval from the audience include emphasizing similarities instead of differences; putting the audience in a pleasant mood; and reinforcing the audience for attending to the message. Many of these strategies were discussed in some detail in the chapter on communication sources (Chapter 8).

3. Not all parts of the message are equally important in determining perception of the object of communication. Tannenbaum[33] showed that verbal cues or indexes such as newspaper headlines, newscast leads, certain words, and picture captions can influence how the total message is interpreted. Familiarity with the cues that an audience will readily recognize and evaluate positively can help the communicator gain favorable message perceptions. Many consumers, for example, react favorably to the words "new," "improved," and "save."

## Selective Retention

Learning of the message, like attention and perception, can help reinforce our existing attitudes and behaviors. The instrumental hypothesis of learning predicts that we will learn material that supports our attitudes and behaviors to a greater extent than material that opposes or contradicts them. Supporting material is pleasant and useful in maintaining cognitive consistency, while contradictory material is unpleasant and produces cognitive inconsistency.

The selective learning hypothesis was studied by Levine and Murphy in 1943.[34] They presented pro- and anticommunist subjects with pro- and anticommunist messages. They found that subjects remembered significantly more supportive than contradictory material and that the differences in learning of the material between the pro- and anticommunist groups increased over time. Subsequent research in the 1950s provided additional support for the hypothesis,[35] although one study showed that it was true only under certain conditions. Jones and Kohler, investigating attitudes toward segregation, found that the plausibility of the material was a factor in selective learning.[36] Their subjects learned plausible statements that were supportive of their attitudes and implausible statements that opposed their attitudes significantly better than they did implausible, supportive statements and plausible, contradictory statements.

More recent research has not replicated earlier findings regarding selective learning. These studies have used more rigid controls. They have also investigated alternative explanations to the earlier findings, such as prior familiarity with the material and situational demands of the experiments.

## RESEARCH ON MESSAGE RECEPTION

In this section, we will discuss some recent studies dealing with selective exposure, selective perception, and selective retention. These studies, except those dealing with selective perception, do not support earlier findings. Contradictory findings will be explained and alternative explanations to earlier findings will be offered.

### Selective Attention (Exposure)

Current research in this area has distinguished between selective exposure and selective attention to information. Previous selective exposure studies measured either the receiver's preferences among messages or the amount of time spent reading the messages. Thus, the receiver was given a choice of totally approaching or avoiding future information.

Selective exposure, according to Brock and Balloun, is not a very realistic measure of information preferences.[37] They point out that in the real world we very rarely have the opportunity to evaluate prospective information. What usually happens is that we find ourselves exposed to some message (a television newscast, for example), portions of which may support or contradict an existing attitude, choice, or behavior.

The more appropriate measure of information selectivity, according to Brock and Balloun, is *selective attention,* which is exposure to information with attention only to parts of it. Receivers confronted with contradictory information while attending to a message may tune out this information by *not* paying attention to it or by *not* eliminating sources of noise in the communication situation. Conversely, receivers confronted with ongoing supportive information may tune in this information by paying greater attention to it or by eliminating sources of noise. Using this rationale, Brock and Balloun predicted that receivers would press a static-eliminating button more frequently to eliminate static from ongoing supportive than from ongoing contradictory messages. They did find in an experiment that smokers pressed the button significantly more frequently than nonsmokers to remove static from a message arguing that smoking does *not* cause lung cancer, while nonsmokers pressed a button more frequently than smokers to remove static from a "smoking causes cancer" message.

More recently, Lowin has predicted that the ease or difficulty with which a message can be refuted interacts with selectivity.[38] He suggests that a person can maintain his or her belief system (cognitive consistency) by attending to supportive information that is difficult to refute and to nonsupportive information that is easy to refute. Weak, supportive messages and strong, nonsupportive messages produce discomfort, since they could erode the receiver's confidence in his or her initial position.

Kleinhesselink and Edwards tested the Lowin hypothesis in 1975 using the static-eliminating procedure.[39] They used a 2 × 2 factorial design, varying the subjects' attitude toward the topic (pro or con) and the type of message (easy or difficult to refute). Half of the subjects listened to a taped message consistent with their prior beliefs, while the other half heard a message that was inconsistent with their beliefs. Within each belief condition half the subjects heard a message that was difficult to refute, while the other half heard a message that was easy to refute.

Subjects were college students in an introductory psychology course. The message dealt with the legalization of marijuana sale. Pretesting with a comparable group identified seven easy-to-refute arguments for the legalization of marijuana sale and seven difficult-to-refute arguments for legalization. Subjects were tested individually. They were told that there was quite a bit of static on the tape; they were then shown a button that could be pressed to eliminate the static. To disguise the nature of the experiment, a neutral tape on imprinting in domestic chickens was also played.

Results support the hypothesis. There were no differences between experimental groups on the rate of button pressing for the neutral message (imprinting in chickens). However, there was a significant attitude by type of message interaction for the marijuana messages. Subjects pressed the button to eliminate static more frequently when the message was either supportive and difficult to refute or when the message was nonsupportive but easy to refute. They were significantly less receptive to the supportive, easy-to-refute message and the nonsupportive, difficult-to-refute message. The researchers conclude that in ongoing communication situations the ease or difficulty with which supportive or nonsupportive information can be refuted determines selective attention.

### Selective Perception

Vidmar and Rokeach conducted two surveys in 1974 to determine how a viewer's prejudice or racism would affect perception of the television show "All in the Family."[40] They predicted that nonprejudiced viewers would perceive the show as satire, whereas prejudiced viewers would enjoy the show because it "told it like it is." Also, they predicted that frequent viewers will more likely be persons high in prejudice, identify with Archie over Mike, and approve Archie's language and behavior, particularly his use of racial slurs.

Their samples consisted of 237 adolescents in a senior high school in a small town in the midwestern United States and 130 adults in London, Ontario. Eleven items in the questionnaire dealt with respondent reactions to "All in the Family" and its characters. Prejudice was measured with a set of six questions. There was some slight variation between the United States and Canadian questions on prejudice, to account for cultural differences.

Results indicate that high- and low-prejudiced viewers in both samples (based on a median split of the prejudice scores) did not differ in the extent to which they regarded "All in the Family" as enjoyable or funny. However, they differed in their other reactions to the program. High-prejudiced persons were more likely than low-prejudiced persons to admire Archie over Mike and to perceive Archie as "winning" in the end. High-prejudiced American adolescents were more likely than low-prejudiced adolescents to perceive Archie as making better sense than Mike and to say that their values would be similar to Archie Bunker's twenty years from now. In the Canadian sample, high-prejudiced persons were less likely than those low in prejudice to see the show as poking fun at Archie. In summary, prejudiced persons identified more with Archie, perceived Archie as making better sense than Mike, and perceived Archie as winning. Vidmar and Rokeach interpret this data as supporting the selective perception hypothesis.

Results also indicated that among American adolescents frequent viewers were more likely to be high prejudiced rather than low prejudiced, although overall TV viewing was not affected by prejudice. Frequent American viewers admired Archie more often than Mike, and frequent viewers in both samples were more likely to condone Archie's ethnic slurs than infrequent viewers.

This study provides some evidence that perceptions of "All in the Family" are influenced by an existing attitude or value—prejudice—in viewers. We should remember, however, that the samples were small and may not be representative of most viewers in Canada or the United States.

## Selective Retention

Greenwald and Sakamura in 1967 conducted three experiments to test the selective learning hypothesis.[41] The message dealt with U.S. involvement in the Vietnam war. Subjects were college students in an introductory psychology course. They heard a taped reading of thirty statements—fifteen pro-United States involvement in Vietnam and fifteen anti-United States involvement. The statements were rated by the subjects on prior familiarity and acceptability of content. The main dependent measure was an unexpected recall test of the content of the statements.

Results indicate that subject attitudes on United States involvement in the war did not affect learning of relevant information. Also, prior familiarity with the information was not related to learning. However, statements unsympathetic to U.S. involvement in Vietnam (information that was relatively new to the subjects) were better learned than those supporting involvement. The researchers conclude that learning was not affected by prior attitudes of their subjects. Also, information novelty enhances learning of propagandistic information.

Brigham and Cook in 1969 investigated the selective retention hypothesis, creating conditions that were as similar as possible to those in the earlier Levine and Murphy study (which found evidence of selective retention).[42] In addition, they added the plausibility condition introduced by Jones and Kohler.[43] Their message dealt with racial segregation. Racial attitudes of subjects were measured with the Multifactor Racial Inventory.[44] Subjects were provided with written transcripts that included four statements from each of the following message categories: plausible prointegration, plausible prosegregation, implausible prointegration, and implausible prosegregation. If the earlier studies by Levine and Murphy and by Jones and Kohler are to be supported, then, overall, prointegration subjects should remember more prointegration statements, while prosegregation subjects should remember more prosegregation statements. Furthermore, subjects should learn plausible supportive statements and implausible opposing statements better than implausible supportive statements and plausible opposing statements. Brigham and Cook, however, found no support for either of these hypotheses. Racial attitudes did not affect recall of the material in the direction predicted by previous research. They did find that both pro- and antisegregation groups learned more implausible than plausible material. Their conclusion is that the "attitude-memory relationship, if it exists at all, applies only under certain conditions," and that "the specific nature of these conditions is not as yet understood.".[45]

## PERSUASION AND AUDIENCE PERSONALITY CHARACTERISTICS

In this section our major concern will be the following question: "What personality traits are associated with persuasibility, and under what conditions?" Persuasibility is a person's susceptibility to an influence attempt in which a communicator gives his or her position on an issue and presents arguments to support that position. There are other social influence situations, such as suggestibility (as in hypnosis) and conformity (as in compliance). We are primarily interested in persuasion, since it is an influence situation in which communication plays a major role.

Research concerning the effects of audience personality characteristics on persuasibility has often produced contradictory results. In 1955, for example, Janis[46] found a negative relationship between self-esteem and persuasibility, while McGuire and Ryan[47] found a positive relationship. Cox and Bauer[48] in 1964 reported that *highest* susceptibility to persuasion occurred at intermediate levels of self-esteem; Silverman[49] in the same year found the *least* influencibility to be associated with intermediate levels of self-esteem. Contradictory findings have also been reported for intelligence, anxiety, and other personality variables.

Why the apparent confusion in personality and persuasibility research? McGuire[50] explains these contradictions in terms of interactions, or the effects of other variables in the communication situation on the relationship between persuasibility and a particular personality trait. He argues that there are no general, absolute relationships between personality variables and persuasibility; instead, there are only *interactions,* since the relationships are determined by other variables in the situation.

McGuire's analysis of personality variables and persuasibility is based on the following two assumptions.

1. Persuasion is the end result of a series of steps, beginning with attention to the message, comprehension of the arguments, yielding to the recommendations, retention and, finally, action. The impact of a persuasive message is determined in part by the first two steps—attention and comprehension. Thus, the receiver is a rational, information-processing animal who will change opinions only upon understanding the message.

2. Persuasibility is a general trait. A receiver who is persuasible on one issue will also be persuasible on other issues. Thus, persuasibility is a trait that can be detected in persons across communication situations. Several early studies support this assumption.[51]

Assuming that the receiver is in a rational mode and that persuasibility can be detected across communication situations, McGuire presents six principles underlying personality and persuasibility relationships.

## 1. The Mediational Principle

Persuasion is mediated by two general steps—reception of the message, which includes attention to the message and comprehension of the arguments, and yielding, or acceptance of the message's recommendations. Reception can be measured by recall or recognition tests of the contents of the persuasive message. Yielding is often measured by opinion change scores. Most early persuasion research overemphasized the yielding mediator while overlooking message reception. An overemphasis on yielding may make it difficult to interpret studies on personality and persuasibility, since many personality traits have opposite effects on reception and yielding. Researchers, according to McGuire, should consider the possible effects of a personality variable not only on yielding but also on reception.

To illustrate the mediational principle, let us take two personality variables that have often been studied in persuasion research—intelligence and anxiety. If we were to analyze the effects of intelligence on persuasion using only the yielding mediator, we would predict that the more intelligent the receivers, the less persuasible they would be. We would expect the more intelligent receivers to be more confident in their initial positions, more capable in formulating counterarguments, and more critical in evaluating the persuasive communication. However, according to McGuire's mediational principle, we must also consider the effects of intelligence on the reception mediator. We would then expect the more intelligent receivers to be more receptive to the message. They would be more interested in new information, would have a longer attention span, would be less likely to ignore contradictory information, and would be more likely to comprehend the message. A complete analysis takes into account the tendency of intelligence to facilitate reception but to inhibit yielding. Thus, we might expect intelligence to be positively related to persuasibility when the message is difficult but negatively related to persuasibility when the message is simple. Although most studies have failed to detect either a positive or negative relationship between intelligence and general influencibility, there is some evidence that when the message is difficult the more intelligent receivers will be more persuasible,[52] and when the message is simple (as in suggestion and conformity situations) the less intelligent receivers will be more persuasible.[53]

Anxiety is an even more complex variable than intelligence. We can expect anxiety to facilitate yielding, since an anxious person tends to be insecure and would therefore be more susceptible to social influence. On the other hand, anxious persons are withdrawn and preoccupied with their own problems. They would therefore have more difficulty in attending to and comprehending persuasive messages, particularly when the message is difficult.[54] To add to the confusion, anxiety has drive value.[55] When *some* anxiety is present in a person, he or she will be motivated to action. This leads to the prediction that the inhibiting effect of anxiety on reception will be observed only in the relatively high ranges of anxiety. An intermediate level of anxiety would be optimal for reception and would also facilitate yielding. McGuire points out that much of the research on anxiety and general influencibility has produced contradictory findings. Many of these contradictions can be traced to the failure of the researchers to take into account anxiety level (low, intermediate, or high) and message complexity.

## 2. The Combinatory Principle

Both receptivity to the message and yielding to the recommendations facilitate persuasion. However, most personality traits often have opposite effects on reception and yielding. Intelligence facilitates reception but inhibits yielding. High levels of anxiety inhibit reception but facilitate yielding. When such opposite effects are likely, the net effect of a given personality variable on persuasion is often nonmonotonic, or curvilinear. The most common form of this curvilinear relationship is an inverted U curve, where intermediate levels of the personality variable are associated with the highest levels of persuasibility. Studies of self-esteem, for example, have shown that persons with intermediate levels of self-esteem tend to be the most persuasible, while persons low and high in self-esteem are more difficult to persuade.[56] We can expect self-esteem to have similar effects on reception and yielding as intelligence: persons high in self-esteem will be more receptive to the message but will be more difficult to persuade. The net effect of these opposite tendencies is an inverted U relationship, with intermediate levels of self-esteem being associated with the most persuasibility.

### 3. The Situational-Weighting Principle

As pointed out in our discussion of the mediational principle, total persuasive impact of a communication depends on reception and yielding. The situational-weighting principle says that the relative importance of reception and yielding in determining persuasive impact varies from situation to situation in predictable ways. In some situations reception will be more important than yielding; in others yielding will be more important than reception. Thus, the relationship between a personality trait and persuasibility will vary from situation to situation, depending on the relative importance of reception and yielding.

McGuire suggests, for example, that when the situation results in very little difference among receivers in attention to and comprehension of the message, then the effect of a given personality variable on yielding will determine the relationship between that variable and persuasion. Such a situation might be expected when the message is very simple (when everyone, regardless of personality traits, can understand it) or when the message is very difficult (when everyone might have difficulty understanding it). In these situations total persuasive impact of the message will likely be determined by a given personality variable's relationship to yielding. In simple suggestibility situations (very simple messages), for example, influence is determined by the effect of self-esteem on yielding. As self-esteem increases, influencibility decreases.[57] Likewise, with very subtle, complex messages persuasive impact is determined by the relationship between self-esteem and yielding. As self-esteem increases, persuasibility decreases.

The net effect of a given personality variable on persuasion, according to McGuire, will be nonmonotonic in situations that put an intermediate strain on receptivity. These are situations in which the message is neither too easy nor too difficult. Most mass and interpersonal influence attempts, such as advertising and personal selling, fit this category. In these situations there will be wide differences among individuals in their attention to and comprehension of messages. Therefore, a nonmonotonic relationship, following the combinatory principle, is likely to be observed between a given personality variable and net persuasive impact. Hovland, Lumsdaine, and Sheffield,[58] for example, found that receivers with intermediate levels of self-esteem were the most persuasible when the messages were of intermediate difficulty.

Situations will vary not only in receptivity demands but also in demands on yielding. Some influence situations are such that almost everyone would agree (for example, an expert, trustworthy source arguing for a position on which there is very little prior opinion) or disagree (a source very low in credibility arguing for a position contrary to well-established beliefs). In these situations the effect of a given personality variable on net persuasion is determined by its relationship to reception. In situations that put an intermediate strain on yielding (such as a low-credibility source arguing for a position based on strong evidence) the relationship between the personality variable and net persuasive impact will tend to be nonmonotonic.

## 4. The Confounded-Variable Principle

Many of our personality traits are intercorrelated. Self-esteem, for example, is related to anxiety, intelligence, and depression. When we study only one personality variable and exclude others, the results we get might be spurious. That is, the observed relationship between persuasibility and the given personality variable may, in fact, be determined by other personality traits that the measured variable is intercorrelated with but that we did not measure. McGuire, for example, found that most of the inhibiting effect on persuasibility of depression can be accounted for by the depressive's withdrawal tendencies.[59] Although depressed persons can be expected to be more yielding because of low self-esteem, their withdrawal tendencies will inhibit reception of messages. Thus, withdrawal tendencies interfered with message reception and resulted in little opinion change.

## 5. The Interaction Principle

Personality traits are not the only possible determinants of persuasibility. In any communication situation persuasive impact is also determined by other classes of variables, such as source, channel, and message factors. In a given situation the effects of a personality variable on persuasion might be determined by its interaction with these other variables.

Source factors have been found to interact with various personality traits. Several studies have found that the lower the self-esteem of the receiver, the more he or she would be affected by differences in status of the source.[60] Also, highly authoritarian receivers are highly responsive when the source is positively evaluated but are more resistant when the source is negatively evaluated.[61]

Message factors interact with personality variables. As we have seen in a previous chapter, the effectiveness of fear appeals depends on a number of personality variables, including chronic anxiety level. Persons low in chronic anxiety are more responsive to high-fear appeals, while low-fear appeals are more effective with persons high in chronic anxiety. Intelligence is another personality trait that interacts with message variables. One-sided messages are more effective with less intelligent receivers, while two-sided messages are more effective with more intelligent receivers.

## 6. The Compensation Principle

McGuire uses this last principle as a general explanation of nonmonotonic relationships between personality traits and persuasibility. To adapt to our environment, we must be open, but not too open, to outside influence. If we were completely closed to influence, our sources of information about new ideas would be severely limited. On the other hand, if we were completely open to influence, we would find it difficult to maintain any kind of stability in our thinking and behavior, since any form of social pressure could result in some change. Thus, we adapt to our environment by maintaining our influencibility at an intermediate range. Some of our personality characteristics make us open to social influence, while others help us resist influence. This, according to McGuire, explains why intermediate levels of a personality characteristic are often associated with the highest levels of influencibility.

In summary, McGuire suggests that there are no general principles (or main effects) of personality and persuasibility. The relationship between a given personality trait and persuasibility depends on a number of factors, including other personality variables; source, message, and channel factors in the communication situation; and the tendency of a personality trait to have opposite effects on reception and yielding. Although the field may be totally frustrating to the practitioner (research findings are most easily applied when there are general principles), it challenges the researcher to untangle the many complex interactions between personality and persuasibility.

## RESEARCH ON PERSONALITY AND PERSUASIBILITY

Millman in 1968 tested the hypothesis that intermediate levels of anxiety would lead to the most opinion change.[62] She based this hypothesis on the assumption that anxiety has opposite effects on the reception and yielding mediators of opinion change. High anxiety blocks reception but facilitates yielding. Thus, the net effect on persuasion should be nonmonotonic; receivers with intermediate levels of anxiety should show the most opinion change compared to those with low and high levels of anxiety.

To test her hypothesis Millman first measured chronic anxiety of forty-eight college students, using abbreviated versions of the Taylor Manifest Anxiety Scale. On the basis of a median split she classified subjects as either high or low in chronic anxiety. Acute anxiety of the subjects was then manipulated prior to receiving the message. Subjects in the high-acute-anxiety condition were told that exposure to intense electric shock would be part of their participation in the experiment, while subjects in the low-acute-anxiety condition were told that they would be working in a special "weather room" that would be warm and humid. Subsequent checks on this manipulation indicated that it was effective. Subjects were then exposed to a taped persuasive message. Each subject heard two messages—one on population growth in China and another on mental illness in the United States. There were two versions of each message. One version was designed to provoke additional anxiety (for example, the China message argued that population growth would cause hostility and increased probability of nuclear war), while the other was reassuring (increased population growth would make China more "docile"). All other arguments used in the messages were identical.

Difficulty of the message was also manipulated. Half the subjects heard a clear tape while the other half heard a tape with a lot of background noise.

The dependent variables measured were comprehension of the message and opinion change.

As predicted, opinion change was greatest at an intermediate level of anxiety. Independent of message difficulty and threat in the message, chronic and acute anxiety interacted to produce the predicted nonmonotonic relationship. Greater opinion change occurred when anxiety levels were intermediate—in the high-chronic, low-acute, and low-chronic, high-acute groups. No other interactions were significant, although high-anxiety levels facilitated comprehension. Millman interprets these results as supporting McGuire's receptivity-yielding model of persuasion and personality traits.

## AUDIENCE EFFECTS ON THE COMMUNICATOR

So far our discussion of communication and persuasion has been limited to how communicators affect audiences. In this section we will take the opposite approach. Following our transactional model of communication, we will discuss how audiences can affect communicators.

How does one become a successful communicator? There is, of course, no simple answer, but one of the few general principles to arise out of some of the research we have reviewed is that "liking leads to agreement." Research (and common sense) tells us that we are influenced more by people we like than by people we dislike. And what determines liking? Again, another general principle emerges from the research: "Similarity leads to liking." To be effective in communications, therefore, we must first be liked by our audiences. It is not too surprising that much of the research on audience effects on communicators has focused on what communicators do to enhance social approval from audiences.[63] To gain social approval, communicators attempt to be similar to their audiences, not only in attitudes but also in personality.

## RESEARCH ON AUDIENCE EFFECTS

Newtson and Czerlinsky in 1974 tested the hypothesis that communicators will shift their messages to minimize discrepancies with audiences that are opposed to their views.[64] They conducted a series of four experiments in which subjects were instructed to communicate accurately their opinions to extreme audiences. In the first experiment, twenty-six subjects who had previously been identified to be moderates on the Vietnam War were asked to present their opinions to either a strongly hawkish or strongly dovish audience. As predicted, subjects presented themselves as being more dovish when communicating to a dovish audience and more hawkish when communicating to a hawkish audience. Thus, the extreme audiences induced shifts in communications of attitude in their direction.

Other studies have found similar communicator shifts. Cialdini, Levy, Herman, and Evenbeck in 1973 found that subjects who expected face-to-face interaction with their audiences shifted to a more moderate position regardless of audience position.[65] Manis *et al.* in 1974 had subjects summarize objective speeches to extreme audiences.[66] Their subjects shifted the summaries toward the positions of their audiences even when they were informed of the original communicator's own position.

Hazen and Kiesler studied whether audience positions would affect the contents of a communicator's message.[67] Eighty college and high school students were asked to "develop the most effective speech you can with the information we give you." They were told that the speech was to be between five and ten minutes long on the topic "The Federal Government Should Control Population Growth." They were then given several cards. On each card was printed an argument that might be used in a speech favoring federal involvement in population control. Eight of the statements aroused concern about the *problem* of population growth; fifteen statements provided *solutions* to population growth involving government. The subjects were told that they were writing the speech for one of four audiences: very opposed, moderately opposed, moderately in favor, or no opposition. Each subject was given approximately twenty minutes to prepare the speech.

Hazen and Kiesler found that the greater the opposition of the audience, the fewer solution arguments and the more problem arguments were used. According to the researchers, subjects focused on problems, not solutions, when communicating to extremely opposed audiences because of their desire to "avoid rejection." By avoiding explicit conclusions and focusing on problems, subjects would less likely be rejected by the audience, since their discrepant positions would be less obvious.

In summary, these studies indicate that a communicator's behavior is often affected by the nature of his or her audience. There is some pressure to minimize differences and to emphasize similarities. This strategy helps the communicator to be accepted by the audience and to be more effective in accomplishing the communication task.

## PERSUASION AND COGNITIVE PROCESSING OF INFORMATION

Most persuasion research today considers communication receivers to be actively evaluating and processing information in their environments. This approach is very different from older, more traditional persuasion theories that considered communication receivers to be either passive and easily influenced by external communication stimuli or to be so stubborn and self-defensive that no persuasive message could influence them. The prevailing view today is that audiences are neither easily manipulated nor hopelessly obstinate. Instead, we look at communication audiences as actively evaluating the information available to them. They will follow recommendations of the persuasive message depending on how they evaluate the information. We are therefore interested in identifying and explaining the different strategies of information processing and specifying the conditions that determine what strategies will be used. In Chapter 7, we discussed some models of information processing that explain how information is processed. In this section, we will consider some of the conditions that determine the receiver's choice of information-processing strategy. There are two general types of conditions—situational conditions and dispositional conditions.

## Situational Conditions

Situational conditions exist in the external environment of the receiver and can change from situation to situation. They determine the extent to which individuals will be motivated to think extensively instead of superficially about persuasive information to which they are exposed. Since we are exposed to thousands of persuasive messages a day, we can attend closely to only a few of them. Situational conditions influence which information we will attend to and how the information will be processed. Most situational conditions are determined by the message—how involving it is, the number and strength of arguments, whether the information is consistent or inconsistent with receiver expectations, and the number of competing messages in the environment.

### Issue Involvement and Argument Quality

Issue involvement is the degree to which the communication receivers believe that the message recommendations would affect them personally. High issue-involvement messages are perceived by the receivers to be personally important and to affect them directly. Low issue-involvement messages are perceived by receivers to have few personal ramifications for themselves. For example, a message arguing for a cut in social security benefits would be personally relevant (and therefore would have high issue involvement) for people about to retire, or for younger people with elderly relatives. This message, however, will not be personally relevant (and would have low issue involvement) for younger people who do not have elderly relatives. The general hypothesis is that issue involvement determines the extent to which information will be scrutinized.

Petty and Cacioppo in 1979 exposed their subjects to a persuasive message containing either strong arguments or weak arguments.[68] Strong arguments had elicited primarily favorable thoughts about the message recommendation in a pretest, while weak arguments had elicited primarily unfavorable thoughts about the recommendation. Some subjects were told that the recommendation would affect them personally (high issue involvement), while others were told that the recommendation would *not* affect them personally (low issue involvement). Petty and Cacioppo found that subjects studied the information more carefully (thought more about it) under high than under low issue involvement. Also, argument quality was a more important determinant of attitude change in the high than in the low issue involvement condition. Subjects who believed that the recommendation was personally important were more affected by the strong arguments than subjects who believed the message was unimportant.

Petty, Cacioppo, and Goldman in 1981 exposed subjects to either strong or weak persuasive arguments and attributed them to either a source high or low in expertise.[69] Also, some subjects were made to believe that the recommendations were personally consequential, while others were told that the recommendations would not affect them directly. Petty and his colleagues found that subjects in the high-involvement condition (those who thought the recommendations affected them personally) were more influenced by the quality of arguments in support of the recommendations than by the expertise of the source. On the other hand, subjects in the low-involvement condition (those who thought recommendations would not affect them personally) were influenced more by the expertise of the source than by the quality of arguments.

In a 1983 study, Petty and Cacioppo exposed subjects to a set of either three or nine arguments that were either strong or weak in quality.[70] Half of the subjects believed that the recommendations were personally relevant, while the other half believed that the recommendations were not personally important. Petty and Cacioppo found that subjects in the high-involvement condition (those who thought the recommendations were personally important) were influenced more by the quality of arguments than by the number of arguments, while subjects in the low-involvement conditions were influenced more by the number than by the quality of arguments.

These studies show how issue involvement determines the information-processing strategy that communication receivers use. Information that is highly involving will be studied more carefully. Thus, the quality of arguments is an important influence on persuasion for highly involving messages. For messages that are not personally involving, receivers will use simpler, less cognitively taxing strategies to arrive at a decision. Instead of evaluating the quality of message arguments, for example, they will simply base their decisions on "superficial" communication conditions such as source expertise and the number of arguments supporting the recommendation.

Research on issue involvement has many practical implications. We know that messages that are personally relevant to the receiver will be attended to and studied carefully. Professional communicators should therefore make every effort to make personal connections between their messages and the target audience. Simple strategies such as using personal pronouns (for example, "you"), and showing receivers how the recommendations could affect them personally can increase issue involvement.[71?]

### Distraction

A distraction is any external or internal stimulus that takes away the attention of the communication receiver from the message. A distractive stimulus elicits thoughts from the receiver that are not related to the message that is being attended to. Internal distraction is generated by motivational or emotional states in the receiver. An angry receiver, for example, would find it difficult to concentrate on a message. Similarly, "love-struck" college students could find it difficult to concentrate on a professor's lecture; instead, they might "daydream" about the objects of their affection.

Quite often, distraction is generated by external stimuli—conditions outside of the receiver. Examples are a noisy lecture hall because other students are talking while the professor is lecturing, or family members conversing while you are trying to watch a television program.

What are the effects of distraction on information processing? Of course, we would expect distraction to disrupt message evaluation. We learn less and are not able to evaluate carefully the quality of the arguments supporting a recommendation. Also, we are more likely to use "effortless" communication cues such as source attractiveness in making a decision when distractions are present; this leads to simple, less taxing cognitive strategies for evaluating the message. On the other hand, we pay closer attention to more substantial communication cues such as argument quality when distractions are absent.[71]

### Consistent or Inconsistent Information

Messages that we are exposed to can contain information that is either consistent or inconsistent with our expectations. Consistent information conforms to our expectations based on experience, knowledge, logic, or our biases. Inconsistent information contradicts what experience, knowledge, logic, or our biases would lead us to expect. For example, information telling us that Marco is friendly *and* polite or that Igor is conceited *and* domineering is consistent because we generally assume that these pairs of traits (friendly/polite, conceited/domineering) are likely to be found in the same individuals. On the other hand, information that tells us that Marco is shy *and* sociable or that Igor is irritable *and* tolerant is inconsistent, since we generally assume that these pairs of traits (shy/sociable, irritable/tolerant) would not very likely be found in the same individuals. Very often, messages we get from the mass media and other sources contain information that we might consider to be inconsistent. Of course, there will also be information that we would find to be consistent. How do we process consistent and inconsistent information?

In a 1983 study, Berman, Read, and Kenny exposed their subjects to either consistent or inconsistent trait pairs and associated these trait pairs with male names.[72] The subjects were then asked to recall the traits and the names with which they had been associated. Subjects recalled more of the consistent trait pairs and correctly associated more consistent traits with the corresponding names. This study suggests that we are more likely to recall consistent than inconsistent information. Also, we are more likely to have *accurate* recall of consistent instead of inconsistent information. Consistent information is easier to remember, since it is supported by information that has already been stored by the receiver. This old information is the basis for the expectation in the first place, and any new information that is not consistent with it will be more difficult to integrate and, subsequently, to learn.

### Number of Competing Messages

In everyday life, we are bombarded with many persuasive messages in a short period of time. Take, for example, television. It is not unusual for twenty persuasive messages—advertising commercials—to be shown in one hour of programming. How do we process information in such a "message-dense" communication environment? Baumgardner and his colleagues, in a series of 1983 laboratory experiments, used an *associative* learning model to explain information processing in a message-dense environment.[73]

According to the associative learning model, a persuasive message establishes an association between an opinion object (or stimulus) and an evaluation (response). When we encounter persuasive messages, we learn the new evaluative responses and associate them with the opinion object. If we had encountered messages in the past relating other evaluative responses to the same stimulus, we would also retrieve from memory (remember) those evaluative responses. Persuasion occurs when we learn and accept the new evaluative responses. However, *associative interference* could hinder learning. Associative interference occurs when the communication environment includes many messages that deal with similar opinion objects. For example, during an election campaign, we are exposed to many different persuasive messages dealing with a similar object—political candidates. Or, associative interference could occur when we see many television commercials about brands in the same product category, such as automobiles. Associative interference occurs because of our tendency to generalize responses associated with one opinion object to other similar objects. As a result of this generalization, we might assign an evaluation to an object that had previously been elicited by another, similar object. Associative interference, however, does not always hinder persuasion. If similar opinion objects (for example, automobile brands) have been associated with the same evaluative response (a good buy), then generalization should reinforce persuasive impact. On the other hand, when similar stimuli have been associated with different evaluative responses, then generalization leads to interference, resulting in less persuasive impact.

The associative learning model also makes some predictions about how we cope with information in a message-dense environment. We are limited in the amount of information that we can process in a given amount of time. Information overload occurs when we try to take in too much information. Under conditions of information overload, the receiver often tunes out additional information because continued evaluation becomes uncomfortable and too taxing. To prevent information overload when we are confronted with many messages, we may try to remember only the evaluative implications of each message (that is, an overall summation of the recommendations) instead of the specific bits of information leading to the evaluation. By doing this, we do not try to remember "too many" things and will still be able to act on the recommendations of the message.

Baumgardner and his colleagues tested these predictions from associative learning theory in several studies. Subjects received advertising messages about up to 54 brands from 12 different product categories. Thus, subjects were asked to process information in a message-dense environment. Results generally supported the associative learning predictions. Subjects remembered more of the messages when there were less competing messages. In conditions when many competing messages were available, subjects who received messages advocating *diverse* evaluations of similar products remembered much less of the messages and agreed less with any specific message after a short "forgetting period" compared to subjects who received many messages advocating *similar* evaluations of similar objects. Finally, subjects in the message-dense conditions remembered more message evaluations than specific information. Delayed opinion change in this group was more highly correlated to the number of evaluations remembered than to the number of specific arguments that could be remembered. In general, these results suggest that a message-dense environment interferes with learning any specific message and with persuasive impact of any specific message, particularly when different evaluations are made of similar objects. Also, when confronted with many persuasive messages, people tend to remember summary evaluations of the opinion object instead of specific information supporting those evaluations.

## Dispositional Conditions

Dispositional conditions are found *within* the communication receiver and are quite stable from situation to situation. Personality traits such as self-esteem, intelligence, and chronic anxiety are dispositional conditions that could affect how we process information. More recently, communication researchers have studied the individual's "need for cognition" and level of "information sophistication." We are interested in how these dispositional conditions affect our processing of persuasive information.

### Need for Cognition

The "need for cognition scale," designed by Cacioppo and Petty in 1982, distinguishes between individuals who "dispositionally tend to engage in and enjoy effortful analytic activity and those who do not."[74] Individuals with a high need for cognition compared to those with a low need for cognition will be more likely to approach problems analytically. They are also more likely to gather and analyze all available evidence before making decisions, to abstract ideas from past experiences, and to synthesize ideas. Need for cognition is not related to general intelligence as measured by IQ scores, at least in college student populations.[75] It can therefore be treated as a distinct dispositional factor that could influence information processing.

Cacioppo, Petty, and Morris, in a 1983 study, reported that individuals high in need for cognition differed in their information-processing strategies from individuals low in need for cognition in the following ways.

1. They were more affected by argument quality in making evaluations of the message and the communication source.
2. They reported spending more cognitive effort in evaluating messages with strong *and* weak arguments.
3. They recalled more message arguments, regardless of argument quality.
4. Their attitudes were more affected by argument quality.

These findings, according to Cacioppo, Petty, and Morris, document "a reliable difference among individuals in their tendency to derive information from and elaborate on externally provided message arguments."

## Level of Information Sophistication

People will vary in the amount of previous information they have about a topic discussed in a persuasive message. Some will have a lot of information and experience about the topic. These people have been called "experts" by communication researchers. Others will have very little information, or none at all. These are the "novices." Intuitively, we would guess that experts differ from novices in how they process and respond to new information. The political scientist Phillip Converse, for example, points out that the poorly informed voter confronts a new political announcement "with next to no past information at all, hence (it) is just more political blather: in five minutes, he probably will not remember that he had heard such a statement, much less be able to reconstruct what was said."[76]

Cognitive psychologists have studied differences in how experts and novices organize information. Of course, experts have more knowledge, but their knowledge is also more organized, more cohesive and has more linkages between concepts.[77] Because of better organization of knowledge, experts should be better able to handle new information, even when this information is inconsistent with expectations. Inconsistent information—information that does *not* follow from "consensual knowledge"—requires more elaboration or evaluation to integrate it with existing knowledge. Experts can handle this task. Novices, on the other hand, if they are exposed to both consistent and inconsistent information, will take the easy way out and focus on only a subset of the available information. They will attend to information that is least taxing cognitively, and this would be consistent information.

Fiske, Kinder, and Larter studied these predicted differences between experts and novices in a series of experiments in 1983.[78] They found the following differences in how experts and novices processed consistent and inconsistent information.

1. Novices focused more on consistent than on inconsistent information. Their opinions were more influenced by consistent than by inconsistent information. They were also able to remember more consistent than inconsistent information.

2. Experts focused more on inconsistent than on consistent information. They remembered about an equal number of consistent and inconsistent information. Their opinions were based on consistent and inconsistent information.

Results of this study suggest that the more people know about a topic, the more they will be able to understand and assimilate new information, and the more willing they will be to consider inconsistent information. People who have little information about a topic will not be receptive to new information and will focus primarily on consistent information.

## SUMMARY

In this chapter, we discussed communication audiences from three perspectives. First, we analyzed message reception, which includes attention, perception, and retention. Second, we considered personality variables that affect persuasibility. Third, we discussed how audiences can affect communicators.

Three theories have been influential in audience research. These are learning theory, which assumes that we are basically rational animals who make decisions based on information; dissonance theory, which assumes that we are rationalizing and not rational animals; and functional theory, which assumes that we adopt new attitudes to the extent that they are useful to us.

Research on audiences suggest the following general principles.

1. People do not necessarily avoid information that contradicts their opinions, choices, or behaviors. There are many qualities of messages that are important determinants of audience attention, other than whether they are supportive or not. If there are rewards in a message that can cancel out possible discomfort from contradictory information, it will not be avoided.

2. Perception is often subjective. We have the tendency to organize our environment even when adequate information is not available. We often perceive objects to serve an immediate purpose—to satisfy a need or reinforce a mood, mental set, or cultural value.

3. Accurate and favorable perceptions of the message can be facilitated by (a) (*a*) using objects and categories familiar to the audience; (*b*) establishing a

positive bond with the audience early in the communication interaction; and (c) using message cues that the audience will readily recognize and evaluate favorably.

4. Although early research indicated that we learn information that supports our attitudes and behaviors to a greater extent than material that opposes or contradicts them, recent research has shown no evidence of selective retention. Methodological and theoretical explanations are discussed for this discrepancy in research findings.

5. In an ongoing communication situation receivers will selectively attend to the message. There is some evidence that receivers generally pay more attention to supportive messages than to contradictory messages. Also, messages that are supportive but difficult to refute and messages that are nonsupportive but easy to refute will be given more attention than messages that are supportive but easy to refute or messages that are nonsupportive but difficult to refute.

6. The most common relationship between personality variables and persuasibility is nonmonotonic—an inverted U curve, with intermediate levels of the personality variable being associated with the most persuasibility. Most personality traits have opposite effects on message reception and yielding. The net effect on persuasion, then, is nonmonotonic.

7. Communicators adjust their messages to minimize differences with extreme audiences and to emphasize similarities. These strategies facilitate acceptance by the audience.

## REVIEW QUESTIONS

1. Discuss a communication experience in which you were either source or receiver and that failed because of selective exposure. How could selective exposure have been avoided?

2. Discuss another communication experience in which selective perception was the reason for failure. What perception principles were being used by either source or receiver in this experience?

3. Discuss two stereotypes you believe to be true. Why do you believe them?

4. Discuss two stereotypes you do *not* believe to be true. Why don't you believe them?

5. Evaluate the current state of the "selective retention" hypothesis. What does recent research show about selective retention?

6. Why are there no general principles (or main effects) of personality and persuasibility? Using one or more of McGuire's personality and persuasibility principles, explain how anxiety affects persuasibility.

7. Discuss two ways in which an audience can influence a communicator.

## ENDNOTES

1. William McGuire, "The Nature of Attitudes and Attitude Change," in G. Lindzey and E. Aronson (eds.), *The Handbook of Social Psychology*, 2nd ed., Vol 3 (Reading, Mass.: Addison-Wesley, 1969), pp. 235–272.
2. N. Lear, "As I Read How Laura Saw Archie. . .," *New York Times*, October, 10, 1971.
3. Leon Festinger, *A Theory of Cognitive Dissonance* (Stanford, Calif.: Stanford University Press, 1957).
4. Eunice Cooper and Marie Jahoda, "The Evasion of Propaganda," *Journal of Psychology, 23*, 1947, pp. 15–25.
5. J. M. Levine and G. Murphy, "The Learning and Forgetting of Controversial Statements," *Journal of Abnormal and Social Psychology, 38*, 1943, pp. 507–517.
6. Festinger, *op. cit.*
7. E. Aronson, "Dissonance Theory: Progress and Problems," in R. P. Abelson et al. (eds.) *Theroies of Cognitive Consistency: A Sourcebook* (Chicago: Rand McNally, 1968), pp. 3–27; also E. Aronson, "The Theory of Cognitive Dissonance: A Current Perspective," in L. Berkowitz (ed.), *Advances in Experimental Social Psychology*, Vol. 4 (New York: Academic Press, 1969).
8. C. A. Kiesler, *The Psychology of Commitment* (New York: Academic Press, 1971).
9. Aronson, 1969, *op. cit.*
10. N. P. Chapanis and A. Chapanis, "Cognitive Dissonance: Five Years Later," *Psychological Bulletin, 61*, 1964, pp. 1–22; also D. Bem, "Self-Perception: An Alternative Interpretation of Cognitive Dissonance Phenomena," *Psychological Review, 74*, 1967, pp. 183–200.
11. D. O. Sears, "The Paradox of De Facto Selective Exposure without Preferences for Supportive Information," in R. Abelson et al. (eds.), *Theories of Cognitive Consistency: A Sourcebook* (Chicago: Rand McNally, 1968).
12. W. J. McGuire, "Selective Exposure: A Summing Up," in R. Abelson et al. (eds.), *Theories of Cognitive Consistency: A Sourcebook* (Chicago: Rand McNally, 1968).
13. J. L. Freedman and D. O. Sears, "Selective Exposure," in L. Berkowitz (ed.), *Advances in Experimental Social Psychology*, Vol. 2 (New York: Academic Press, 1965).
14. Sears, *op. cit.*
15. See Freedman and Sears, *op. cit.*, for a review of relevant studies.
16. *Ibid.*
17. *Ibid.*
18. *Ibid.*
19. See McGuire, 1968, *op. cit.*
20. E. E. Jones and H. B. Gerard, *Foundations of Social Psychology* (New York: Wiley, 1967), p. 131.
21. J. S. Bruner, "Social Psychology and Perception," in E. E. Maccoby, T. M. Newcomb, and E. L. Hartley (eds.), *Readings in Social Psychology* (New York: Holt, Rinehart and Winston, 1958), pp. 85–93; also, J. S. Bruner, "On Perceptual Readiness," *Psychological Review, 64*, 1957, pp. 123–152.
22. C. Cherry, *On Human Communication* (New York: MIT and Wiley, 1957).
23. David Krech and Richard Crutchfield, "Perceiving the World," in D. Krech and R. Crutchfield, *Theory and Problems in Social Psychology* (New York: McGraw-Hill, 1958).

24. S. E. Asch, "Forming Impressions of Personality," *Journal of Abnormal and Social Psychology, 41*, 1946, pp. 258–90.

25. R. Levine, I. Chein, and G. Murphy, "The Relation of Intensity of a Need to the Amount of Perceptual Distortion," *Journal of Psychology, 13*, 1942, pp. 283–293.

26. C. Leuba and C. Lucas, "The Effects of Attitudes on Descriptions of Pictures," *Journal of Experimental Psychology, 35*, 1945, pp. 517–524.

27. Cooper and Jahoda, *op. cit.*

28. See, for example, Neil Vidmar and Milton Rokeach, "Archie Bunker's Bigotry: A Study in Selective Perception and Exposure," *Journal of Communication*, Winter 1974, pp. 36–47.

29. Gordon Allport, *The Nature of Prejudice* (Reading, Mass.: Addison-Wesley, 1954).

30. H. R. McGarvey, "Anchoring Effects in the Absolute Judgments of Verbal Materials," *Archives of Psychology*, no. 281, 1943.

31. Jones and Gerard, *op. cit.*, pp. 131–142.

32. *Ibid.*

33. Percy Tannenbaum, "The Indexing Process in Communication," *Public Opinion Quarterly, 19*, 1955.

34. Levine and Murphy, 1943, *op. cit.*

35. See, for example, E. E. Jones and J. Aneshansel, "The Learning and Utilization of Contravaluant Material," *Journal of Abnormal and Social Psychology, 53*, 1956, pp. 27–33.

36. E. E. Jones and R. Kohler, "The Effects of Plausibility on the Learning of Controversial Statements," *Journal of Abnormal and Social Psychology, 57*, 1958, pp. 315–320.

37. T. C. Brock and J. L. Balloun, "Behavioral Receptivity to Dissonant Information," *Journal of Personality and Social Psychology, 6*, 1967, pp. 413–428.

38. A. Lowin, "Further Evidence for an Approach-Avoidance Interpretation of Selective Exposure," *Journal of Expermental Social Psychology, 5*, 1969, pp. 265–271.

39. R. Kleinhesselink and R. Edwards, "Seeking and Avoiding Belief-Discrepant Information as a Function of Its Perceived Refutability," *Journal of Personality and Social Psychology, 31*, 1975, pp. 787–790.

40. Vidmar and Rokeach, *op. cit.*

41. A. Greenwald and J. Sakamura, "Attitude and Selective Learning: Where Are the Phenomena of Yesteryear?" *Journal of Personality and Social Psychology, 7*, 1967, pp. 387–397.

42. J. Brigham and S. Cook, "The Influence of Attitude on the Recall of Controversial Material: A Failure to Confirm," *Journal of Experimental Social Psychology, 5*, 1969, pp. 240–243.

43. Jones and Kohler, *op. cit.*

44. J. J. Woodmansee and S. W. Cook, "Dimensions of Verbal Racial Attitudes: Their Identification and Measurement," *Journal of Personality and Social Psychology, 7*, 1967, pp. 240–250.

45. Brigham and Cook, *op. cit.*

46. I. L. Janis, "Anxiety Indices Related to Susceptibility to Persuasion," *Journal of Abnormal and Social Psychology, 51*, 1955, pp. 663–667.

47. See McGuire, 1969, *op. cit.*, pp. 250–251.

48. D. F. Cox and R. A. Bauer, "Self-Confidence and Persuasibility in Women," *Public Opinion Quarterly, 28*, 1964, pp. 453–466.

49. I. Silverman, "Differential Effects of Ego Threat upon Persuasibility for High and Low Self-Esteem Subjects," *Journal of Abnormal and Social Psychology, 69,* 1964, pp. 567–572.

50. McGuire, 1969, *op. cit.* pp. 243–247.

51. I. L. Janis and P. B. Field, "A Behavioral Assessment of Persuasibility: Consistency of Individual Differences," *Sociometry, 19,* 1956, pp. 241–259.

52. See, for example, C. Hovland, A. Lumsdaine, and F. Sheffield, *Experiments on Mass Communication* (Princeton, N.J.: Princeton University Press, 1949).

53. K. G. Stukat, *Suggestibility: A Factorial and Experimental Study* (Stockholm: Almquist and Wiksell, 1958).

54. See W. J. McGuire, "Personality and Susceptibility to Social Influence," in E. Borgatta and W. Lambert (eds.), *Handbook of Personality Theory and Research* (Chicago: Rand McNally, 1968), pp. 1130–1187.

55. *Ibid.*

56. *Ibid.,* p. 1148.

57. Stukat, *op. cit.*

58. Hovland, Lumsdaine, and Sheffield, *op. cit.*

59. McGuire, 1968, *op. cit.*

60. *Ibid.*

61. *Ibid.*

62. S. Millman "Anxiety, Comprehension, and Susceptibility to Social Influence," *Journal of Personality and Social Psychology, 9,* 1968, pp. 251–256.

63. See, for example, E. Goffman, *The Presentation of Self in Everyday Life* (Garden City, N.Y.: Doubleday, 1959), pp. 1–16; D. Byrne, *The Attraction Paradigm* (New York: Academic Press, 1971).

64. D. Newtson and T. Czerlinsky, "Adjustment of Attitude Communications for Contrasts by Extreme Audiences," *Journal of Personality and Social Psychology, 30,* 1974, pp. 829–837.

65. R. B. Cialdini, *et al.,* "Attitudinal Politics: The Strategy of Moderation," *Journal of Personality and Social Psychology, 25,* 1973, pp. 100–108.

66. M. Manis et al., "The Transmission of Attitude-Relevant Information through a Communication Chain," *Journal of Personality and Social Psychology, 30,* 1974, pp. 81–94.

67. M. Hazen and S. Kiesler, "Communication Strategies Affected by Audience Opposition, Feedback and Persuasibility," *Speech Monographs, 42,* March 1975, pp. 56–68.

68. R. E. Petty and J. T. Cacioppo, "Issue Involvement Can Increase or Decrease Persuasion by Enhancing Message-Relevant Cognitive Responses," *Journal of Personality and Social Psychology, 37,* 1979, pp. 1915–1926.

69. R. E. Petty, J. T. Cacioppo, and R. Goldman, "Personal Involvement as a Determinant of Argument-based Persuasion," *Journal of Personality and Social Psychology, 41,* 1981, pp. 847–855.

70. R. E. Petty and J. T. Cacioppo, "Central and Peripheral Routes to Persuasion: Application to Advertising," in L. Percy and A. Woodside (eds.), *Advertising and Consumer Psychology* (Lexington, Mass.: D. C. Heath, 1983).

71. R. E. Petty, G. L. Wells, and T. C. Broack, "Distraction Can Enhance or Reduce Yielding to Propaganda: Thought Disruption versus Effort Justification," *Journal of Personality and Social Psychology, 34,* 1976, pp. 874–884.

72. Jeffrey Berman, Stephen Read, and David Kenny, "Processing Inconsistent Social Information," *Journal of Personality and Social Psychology, 45,* 1983, pp. 1211–1224.
73. Michael Baumgardner, Michael Leippe, David Ronis, and Anthony Greenwald, "In Search of Reliable Persuasion Effects: II. Associative Interference and Persistence of Persuasion in a Message-Dense Environment," *Journal of Personality and Social Psychology, 45,* 1983, pp. 524–537.
74. J. T. Cacioppo and R. E. Petty, "The Need for Cognition," *Journal of Personality and Social Psychology, 42,* 1982, pp. 116–131.
75. J. T. Cacioppo, R. Petty, and K. Morris, "Effects of Need for Cognition on Message Evaluation, Recall, and Persuasion," *Journal of Personality and Social Psychology, 45,* 1983, pp. 805–818.
76. Phillip Converse, "Public Opinion and Voting Behavior," in F. I. Greenstein and N. W. Polsby (eds.), *Handbook of Political Science,* Vol. 4 (Reading, Mass.: Addison-Wesley, 1975).
77. Susan Fiske, Donald Kinder, and W. Michael Larter, "The Novice and the Expert: Knowledge-Based Strategies in Political Cognition," *Journal of Experimental Social Psychology, 19,* 1983, pp. 381–400.
78. *Ibid.*

# 12 _____

# ATTITUDES AND BEHAVIOR _____

In this chapter we will discuss some methodological and theoretical issues regarding the relationship between attitudes and behavior. Up to this point we have been primarily concerned with attitude formation and change as the major effects of communication. However, many communication researchers are not interested in attitudes per se. We measure attitudes because of the assumption that attitudes lead to behavior. We are primarily interested in predicting behavior—such as voting, aggression, buying, energy consumption, helping others, and social interaction. These are overt behaviors of communication audiences and they are often difficult to observe directly in laboratory or naturalistic settings. Attitudes, on the other hand, are easier to measure. To find out what a person's attitude regarding an object is, we *ask* him or her. We then consider the verbal response to be a measure of that person's attitude.

LaPiere, in 1934, commented on the measurement of attitudes and behavior.

> The questionnaire is cheap, easy and mechanical. The study of human behavior is time consuming, intellectually fatiguing and depends for its success upon the ability of the investigator. The former method gives quantitative results, the latter mainly qualitative. Quantitative measures are quantitatively accurate; qualitative evaluations are always subject to the errors of human judgement.[1]

More recently, Deutscher discussed the importance of predicting behavior from attitudes.

> Our scientific conclusions, for the most part, are based on analyses of verbal responses to questions put by an interviewer. Those responses may be written or oral and the questions may range from forced choice to open ended, but the fact remains that what we obtain from such methods are statements of attitude, opinion, norms, values, anticipation or recall. The policy maker is interested in overt behavior. Although we rarely study such behavior, we do insist that the object of our discipline is to understand and even predict it. Therefore, to oblige the policy maker, as well as ourselves, the assumption must be made that verbal responses reflect behavioral tendencies.[2]

Attitudes are convenient constructs that have helped us quantify our science. We are interested in attitudes because we assume that they lead to related behavior. We are not interested in changing attitudes as a goal in itself; instead, our manipulations are meant to understand and predict behavior. Attitudes are measured as dependent variables mainly because they are more convenient research tools than behavior itself.

However, do attitudes predict related behaviors? This question has been the subject of a continuing controversy in the social sciences for the past 100 years. There are at least four major positions on the attitude-behavior question: (1) attitudes and behaviors are causally unrelated; (2) attitudes cause behaviors; (3) behaviors cause attitudes; and (4) there is reciprocal causation between attitudes and behaviors—attitudes cause behaviors and behaviors cause attitudes.[3] The positions most relevant to communication and persuasion are the first two, and we will limit our discussion to them. The hypothesis that behaviors cause attitudes is discussed by Bem[4] and the reciprocal causation prediction is elaborated on by Kelman.[5]

## FALLACY OF EXPECTED CORRESPONDENCE?

Common sense tells us that people do not always tell the truth or may not even "know" the truth. LaPiere put the issue in clear, simple terms when he said the following.

> Sitting at my desk in California I can predict with a high degree of certainty what an "average" businessman in an average Mid-Western city will reply to the question, "Would you engage in sexual intercourse with a prostitute in a Paris brothel?" Yet no one, least of all the man himself, can predict what he would actually do should he by some misfortune find himself face-to-face with the situation in question.[6]

LaPiere's commonsense analysis appears to be supported by several reviews of attitude-behavior research. Deutscher, after compiling a bibliography of some 200 studies on the general theme of verbal and other overt behavioral responses, noted "the wide variations in the relationships between attitudes and behavior."[7] This view is shared by DeFleur and Westie, who concluded that there is "ample evidence that subjects do not always behave consistently in their verbal and action behavior."[8] This observation led them to refer to the idea that there should be consistency between attitudes and behaviors as "the fallacy of expected correspondence." Wicker concluded that "taken as a whole, these studies suggest that it is considerably more likely that attitudes will be unrelated or only slightly related to overt behaviors than that attitudes will be closely related to actions."[9]

Numerous studies examining racial attitudes and overt behavior have reported inconsistencies between the measure of verbal attitudes and overt behavior.[10] The discrepancy between what people say and what they do is not limited to ethnic relations. Empirical evidence is available that this is also the case among trade union members,[11] that there is no relationship between college students' attitudes toward cheating and their actual cheating behavior,[12] that urban teachers' descriptions of classroom behavior are sometimes unrelated to how they behave in the classrooms,[13] that what rural Missourians say about their health behavior has little connection with their actual health practices,[14] and that the moral and ethical beliefs of students do not conform to their behavior.[15]

According to the proponents of the "fallacy of expected correspondence" position, attitudes do not always predict behaviors because an attitude is only one of the variables that influence behavior. In any given situation calling for overt action, we are also influenced by social norms, habits, and personality characteristics. Thus, whatever effect an attitude may have on behavior can be neutralized by these other factors.

## ATTITUDES CAN PREDICT BEHAVIORS

A more optimistic assessment of attitude and behavior research comes from researchers who argue that attitudes, when properly conceptualized and measured, can predict behaviors.[16] They attribute the lack of correspondence between attitudes and behaviors in many previous studies to either methodological weaknesses in measuring attitudes or a lack of conceptual and theoretical clarity in defining "attitude."

### Methodology

Tittle and Hill[17] suggest that the degree of correspondence between attitudes and behavior depends to some extent on the measurement technique used, the extent to which the behavior is typical or common to the respondent, and the degree to which the behavior has been previously performed by the respondent.

Using these criteria, Tittle and Hill found in a review of pertinent studies and in a laboratory experiment that the degree of correspondence between attitudes and behavior increases when:

1. A particular attitude is measured using a multiitem instrument with high reliability. Comparing Likert, Guttman, Semantic Differential, Thurstone, and a simple self-rating scale to measure attitudes toward individual political activity, Tittle and Hill found that the Likert scale had the highest degree of correspondence between attitudes and behavior and Thurstone, the lowest. Split-half reliability coefficients based on the Spearman-Brown correction formula were highest for Likert and lowest for Thurstone. Thus, the differential predictive power of the various measurement procedures may be partially due to differences in reliability.

2. The behavioral measure or index should consider action taking place under typical social circumstances and should refer to sets of acts indicative of consistent or patterned action. According to Tittle and Hill, the individual encountering a situation that is characterized by unfamiliar contingencies is not likely to have a well-structured attitudinal organization relevant to behavior in that situation. This behavior will therefore more likely be affected by other situational factors. Attitudes can be expected to relate to behavior most when the behavior is repetitious and when it takes place under usual social circumstances. Tittle and Hill found support for this contention in their study.

To increase the predictability of behavior from attitudes, we should also attempt to measure an attitude that is specific for a given individual as he or she relates to that class of behavior.[18] Our attitude measurement should, as much as possible, be unidimensional (measure only *one* attitude), and items should be unambiguous. Content specificity can be increased if the item contains some self-reference, such as the personal pronouns *I* or *me*. The larger the number of self-referent items included in a scale, the more specific the response will be. Using this criterion, Tittle and Hill found that the Likert scale, which had predicted behavior most accurately, ranked first with 87 percent of the items self-referent, and the Thurstone scale, which was the least accurate predictor, ranked last, with only 20 percent of the items including a reference to self.[19]

## Attitude Theory

Another explanation for the lack of consistency between attitudes and behaviors in previous research is failure to take into account the limitations of "attitude" as a research and theoretical construct. These limitations pertain to response threshold of attitudes, respondent interpretations of their attitudes and the researcher's questionnaire (sociolinguistics), and situational constraints on attitudes and behaviors.

### Response Threshold

Campbell, referring to the "pseudo inconsistency in the attitude literature," maintains that verbal reports can be used to diagnose dispositions that are also manifested in overt behavior. However, he admits to the apparent inconsistency in the literature and offers the following explanation.

Inconsistency does, of course, occur, but one can distinguish between consistent mediocrity and inconsistent chatter. For intelligence and honesty, we have achieved dimensionality in our thinking. For more emotion-laden topics, such as standing up for civil rights, we have not. If a university president protects a pacifist professor but fires an atheist, we call him inconsistent. If he protects a pacifist and an atheist, but fires a Communist, we accuse him of backing down under pressure. Conceptually, we have the notion of a total non-defendant of professors' rights and a total defender of professors' rights, and lack any concept of genuine mediocrity which would in consistency produce defense in a situation of low threshold and firing in another situation with a higher threshold value.[20]

According to Campbell, verbal and overt behaviors have different response thresholds. It is sometimes easier, for example, to say yes in response to a question than to actually act out the yes in a behavioral situation. The opposite of this, of course, is also true. Let us take one of the classic examples often used to illustrate the inconsistency between attitudes and behaviors. LaPiere in the early 1930s traveled widely in the United States with a Chinese couple.[21] They stopped at 66 sleeping places and 184 eating places and were refused service only once. Some time later LaPiere mailed the proprietors of the places they had visited a questionnaire asking them whether they would take "members of the Chinese race as guests in your establishment." Of those responding, 93 percent of the restaurants and 92 percent of the hotels said that they would *not* accept Chinese people. LaPiere also sent the questionnaire to a group of restaurants and hotels that they had not visited and got similar results. There was, therefore, quite a bit of inconsistency between the proprietors' verbal reports and their actual behavior. This inconsistency can be explained by Campbell's threshold principle. In a face-to-face situation the proprietors probably found it difficult to refuse service or accommodations to a well-dressed Chinese couple traveling with a European. On the other hand, they found it quite easy to refuse the Chinese as a race in a mailed questionnaire.

Differences in response threshold are often attributed to differences in situational pressures on verbal and overt behavioral responses. These pressures are discussed in a succeeding section.

### Sociolinguistics

An analysis of the meaning of verbal communications can provide a better understanding of the relation between what people say and what they do. For example, one could study the differences in meaning conveyed by different people with the same words. Often, questions and answers in the interview have varying meanings for interviewer and subject and also within groups of subjects.[22] The subject of the interview and the interview itself may be defined in different ways by our respondents. Language, as social and cultural symbols, will vary across cultures and groups of people. When reasonably common meanings of the interview and answers can be achieved, predictability of acts from words can be improved.

### Situational Constraints

A third explanation of the attitude-behavior inconsistency is that the respondent interprets the verbal report situation differently from the overt behavior situation. This may be caused by different meanings that the respondent assigns to the attitude and behavioral objects or by varying normative pressures.

**Symbolic Meanings of Attitude and Behavioral Objects.** According to the symbolic interactionists we act, either verbally or overtly, in response to the symbolic meaning the confronting object has for us in the given situation.[23] The apparent inconsistency between verbal and overt behavior can thus be a result of the actor's perception of the verbalization and the overt behavior as segments of two different acts. Regardless of the investigator's intent, the word and deed may be perceived by the actors as relating to different objects;[24] or, while the investigator or some other observer may think that a particular norm or attitude he or she has measured is pertinent, the actors may not define the situation or action as one in which the norm or attitude applies.[25]

In LaPiere's example, the businessman, when asked how he feels towards a Parisienne prostitute, would be responding to the words and the interviewer; when face to face with a prostitute, he would be responding to a very different set of symbols.

Experimental support for the symbolic-interaction view is provided in a study by Fendrich.[26] Verbal attitudes toward blacks were found to be either consistent or inconsistent with overt behavior, depending on how respondents defined the attitude measurement situation. When subjects were led to define the experimental situation as one approximating what they might expect in real life (through manipulation of commitment), attitudes predicted behavior more accurately than when commitment was not present.

**Normative Pressures.** Situational factors that contribute to a person's definition of a situation calling for overt action include group norms, which are expected patterns of behavior established by groups to which the person belongs or to which he or she would like to belong. These groups are called reference groups. Their norms specify which behaviors are expected and accepted in a given situation.[27] Very often our private attitudes do not always coincide with behaviors prescribed by such social pressures. When this happens, there will be inconsistency between attitudes and behavior.

### Predicting Behavior

Fishbein and Ajzen[28] have presented two models that attempt to improve the prediction of behaviors by taking into account beliefs, attitudes, and normative pressures. The first model, discussed in some detail in Chapter 6, considers the total behavioral pattern of a person toward an object to be determined by his or her beliefs regarding the object, the resulting attitude toward the object, behavioral intentions, and group pressures. The most important of these determinants, according to Fishbein and Ajzen, is behavioral intentions. A specific attitude may give rise to several behavioral intentions. These intentions will have varying strengths, depending on whether the act is perceived to bring rewards or punishments and on normative pressure. Thus, not all of the intentions will actually be carried out, but the total behavior pattern should be consistent with the attitude. If the attitude is positive, then *some* positive behaviors toward the object will be observed.

Ajzen and Fishbein[29] use a similar model to predict specific behaviors. They argue that traditional measures of general attitudes toward objects cannot adequately predict specific behaviors, which are best accounted for by attitudinal variables *specific* to the performance of the behavior. According to this model, behaviors are best predicted by behavioral intentions. A behavioral intention is not the same construct as an attitude. While "attitude" implies general evaluation of an object, a behavioral intention refers to the probability that the person will perform a certain act. Behavioral intentions are determined by the person's attitude toward performing the act and by normative pressures in the situation. Unlike other approaches in attitude and behavior research, Ajzen and Fishbein consider the attitude toward performing the act, instead of the attitude toward the object, as a predictor of the act itself. A person's attitude toward the act will be favorable to the extent that he or she can obtain rewards or avoid punishments by performing it. Also important in predicting behaviors is normative pressure from reference groups. When reference groups are perceived by the person to approve of the act, then it will likely be performed. Ajzen and Fishbein have accurately predicted specific behaviors in a series of studies using behavioral intentions, attitudes toward the act, and normative pressures as predictors.

## SUMMARY

In this chapter we discussed several theoretical and methodological reasons why attitudes and behaviors are not always consistent. Attitude formation and change are often measured as effects of communication because of the assumption that attitudes can predict behavior. We are primarily interested in understanding and predicting overt behavior. However, behaviors are difficult to observe and measure. Attitudes, on the other hand, are easier to measure and can more readily be quantified than behaviors. Thus, attitudes continue to be a major variable in communication research.

Many previous studies have failed to predict behaviors from related attitudes. One view is that we should not expect a correspondence, since there are many other more important variables, such as social norms, habits, and personality factors, that determine behavior. Another view is that there is a correspondence between attitudes and behaviors, but inadequate measurement and conceptualization of attitudes in previous studies have hidden this relationship. Behaviors can best be predicted from attitudes when (1) multi-item instruments with high reliability and specificity are used; (2) the behavioral measure is familiar to the respondent; (3) common understanding of the attitude questionnaire among respondents and between respondent and researcher is achieved; (4) the attitudinal and behavioral objects are defined similarly so as to achieve common interpretations; (5) the attitudinal response and behavioral response are defined similarly to achieve similar response thresholds; and (6) belief intentions and normative pressures are taken into account.

## REVIEW QUESTIONS

1. Discuss an experience in which your attitude about an object, person, or issue was *inconsistent* with your behavior. Why was there inconsistency?
2. When do attitudes predict behavior?

## ENDNOTES

1. R. LaPiere, "Attitudes vs. Actions," *Social Forces, 13,* 1934, pp. 230–237.
2. I. Deutscher, "Words and Needs: Social Science and Social Policy," *Social Problems, 13,* 1966, pp. 235–254.
3. L. Kahle and J. Berman, "Attitudes Cause Behaviors: A Cross-Lagged Panel Analysis," *Journal of Personality and Social Psychology, 37,* 1979, pp. 315–323.
4. D. J. Bem, "Self-Perception Theory," in L. Berkowitz (ed.), *Advances in Experimental Social Psychology,* Vol. 6 (New York: Academic Press, 1972).
5. H. C. Kelman, "Attitudes Are Alive and Well and Gainfully Employed in the Sphere of Action," *American Psychologist, 29,* 1974, pp. 310–324.
6. LaPiere, *op. cit.*
7. Deutscher, *op. cit.*
8. M. DeFleur and F. R. Westie, "Attitudes as a Scientific Concept," *Social Forces, 42,* 1963, pp. 17–31.
9. A. W. Wicker, "Attitudes versus Action: The Relationship of Verbal and Overt Behavioral Responses to Attitude Objects," *Journal of Social Issues, 25,* 1969, pp. 41–78.
10. See, for example, J. Frendrich, "A Study of the Association among Verbal Attitudes, Commitment and Overt Behavior in Different Experimental Situations," *Social Forces, 45,* 1967, pp. 347–355.
11. L. Dean, "Interaction, Reported and Observed: The Case of One Local Union," *Human Organization, 17,* 1958, p. 36.
12. L. Freeman and I. Ataov, "Invalidity of Indirect and Direct Measures Toward Cheating," *Journal of Personality, 28,* 1960.
13. J. Henry, "Spontaneity, Initiative, and Creativity in Suburban Classrooms," *American Journal of Orthopsychiatry, 29,* 1959.
14. E. Hassinger and R. McNamara, "Stated Opinion and Actual Practice in Health Behavior in a Rural Area," *Midwest Sociologist,* May 1957.
15. S. Putney and P. Middleton, "Ethical Relativism and Anomia," *American Journal of Sociology, 67,* 1962, pp. 430–438.
16. See, for example, M. Fishbein and I. Ajzen, "Attitudes toward Objects as Predictors of Single and Multiple Behavioral Criteria," *Psychological Review, 81,* 1974, pp. 59–74.

17. C. R. Tittle and R. Hill, "Attitude Measurement and Prediction of Behavior: An Evaluation of Conditions and Measurement Techniques," *Sociometry, 30,* 1967, pp. 199–213.

18. *Ibid.*

19. Tittle and Hill, *op. cit.*

20. D. T. Campbell, "Social Attitudes and Acquired Behavioral Dispositions," in S. Koch (ed.), *Psychology: A Study of A Science,* Vol. 6 (New York: McGraw-Hill, 1963).

21. LaPiere, *op. cit.*

22. Deutscher, *op. cit.*

23. See, for example, H. Blumer, "Sociological Analysis and the Variable," *American Sociological Review, 21,* 1956.

24. Deutscher, *op. cit.*

25. S. Schwartz, "Words, Deeds, and the Perception of Consequences and Responsibility in Action Situations," *Journal of Psychology, 72,* 1969.

26. Fendrich, *op. cit.*

27. E. Jones and H. Gerard, *Foundations of Social Psychology* (New York: Wiley, 1967), pp. 357–360.

28. Fishbein and Ajzen, *op. cit.;* also, M. Fishbein and I. Ajzen, *Belief, Intention and Behavior* (Reading, Mass.: Addison-Wesley, 1975).

29. *Ibid.*

# PART III_____

# COMMUNICATION, COORIENTATION, AND AUDIENCE NEEDS_____

In this section we will consider two theoretical models that have influenced the work of many communication researchers in the past decade. We have chosen these models from a number of other recent theoretical formulations for two reasons: (1) they have been most influential in charting future directions for communication theory, and (2) they view communication in ways radically different from the traditional, but still influential, persuasion models.

The first of the models to be discussed in this section is Chaffee and McLeod's coorientation model. The basic assumption of the coorientation model is that communication involves at least two people. Thus, analysis of communication should be primarily concerned with interpersonal, not intrapersonal, variables. Interpersonal variables measure relationships between the persons involved in the act, while intrapersonal variables involve the processes that occur within a person before, during, or after the act. Persuasion models are generally interested in the effects of communication on attitudes and opinions that are intrapersonal variables. The coorientation model, on the other hand, considers the relationships between cognitions of the persons involved in the act as possible causes and effects of communication.

The other model discussed in this section is Katz, Blumler, and Gurevitch's uses and gratifications model, which takes as its starting point the audience, not the message or source. The uses and gratifications model considers the audience to be actively using communication to satisfy needs and goals. Thus, the audience is actively involved in communication and influence is two way, not one way.

Let us now discuss these two models in more detail.

# 13

# COORIENTATION

Persuasion is only one of the many goals of communication. As discussed in Chapter 4, we often communicate simply to share information. Sharing information could lead to attitude and behavior change. Very often, however, it simply results in a common understanding of the topic of communication or in a better understanding of how the other person feels. Understanding is often overlooked by persuasion researchers as an effect of communication. In this chapter we will consider the coorientation model of communication, which suggests that understanding is a more common, and perhaps a more important, effect of communication than persuasion.

The coorientation model of communication was developed by Chaffee and McLeod at the University of Wisconsin in the late 1960s.[1] The model defines communication to be an interpersonal act—that is, communication requires the participation of at least two persons. Given this definition, the following assumptions are made.

1. The unit of analysis in communication should be the small social system and not the individual. A social system is made up of the participants in the communication act, including their roles, cognitions, values, and behaviors. A social system can be as small as a dyad, which involves only two persons. Larger systems are groups, organizations, and communities.

2. For communication to occur, the participants should be "simultaneously oriented" to the same object. Communication is possible only if the participants are "talking about the same thing."

3. The main variables of study should be the relationships between the orientations of the participants in the system toward the object of communication, instead of individual (or intrapersonal) variables such as attitudes and opinions. Participant orientations are their evaluations of the object. These evaluations are determined by past experiences with the object and by situational factors such as a particular attribute on which the object is being evaluated at the moment.

4. Our behavior toward an object is based not only on our private cognitions and values but also on our perceptions or estimates of the cognitions and values (or orientations) of others in the system. Thus, behavior is based not only on what we think and feel about the object but also on

our estimates of what others around us think and feel about the object. The influence of "others" in the system is an important variable in the coorientation model.

## ORIGINS OF THE COORIENTATION MODEL

Chaffee and McLeod's coorientation model is an extension of two earlier models of communication—Newcomb's A-B-X or psychological model[2] and Carter's "paradigm of affective relations."[3] Newcomb's model, which we discussed in detail in Chapter 4, analyzes a social system made up of two persons, A and B, who are simultaneously oriented to a common object, X. A and B "know" about X and about each other. The relationship or orientation between A and B, A and X, and B and X can be summarized as positive or negative attitudes. At any given point in time, the orientations in Newcomb's communication system can either be symmetrical or asymmetrical. There is symmetry when A and B have a common understanding of what X is (cognitive orientation) and also when they agree on how they feel about X (affective orientation). A central concept in Newcomb's model is the "strain toward symmetry." We strive for symmetry in our relations with others, since symmetry is reassuring and comfortable. The strength of this strain toward symmetry varies with liking between A and B. The greater the attraction between A and B, the more each person will be motivated to achieve symmetry with regard to X. We generally achieve symmetry by communication.

Carter in 1965 proposed a "paradigm of affective relations in an orientation situation."[4] His model is a detailed analysis of how we assign "value" to an object in our environment. Thus, it can be used to explain how A or B in Newcomb's model assigns value to X, the object of their communication.

Carter's model is shown in Figure 13.1. In this model, I is an individual; $O_1$ and $O_2$ are objects in his or her environment. The value that a person assigns any given object ($O_1$, for example), is based on two concepts—salience and pertinence. Salience, which Carter also calls "psychological closeness," is the result of a person's history of experience with an object. The more positive or reinforcing a person's experience with an object, the more salient that object will be to him or her and, therefore, the greater its value. In Figure 13.1, $S_1$ is the salience of $O_1$ to I, and $S_2$ is the salience of $O_2$ to I.

Another source of value for an object in a given situation, according to Carter, is its pertinence. Our evaluations of objects are not based only on past experience but also on situational variables. In any given situation, we usually evaluate objects in comparison to other objects and on the basis of an attribute shared by the objects and that happens to be important to us at the moment. The pertinence of an object is the degree to which it possesses the shared attribute. In Figure 13.1, $A_1$ is the attribute shared by $O_1$ and $O_2$. $P_1$ is the pertinence of object 1, and $P_2$ is the pertinence of object 2. According to Carter, an object's value is based both on salience and pertinence.

Let us illustrate with an example. Suppose I were evaluating two candidates

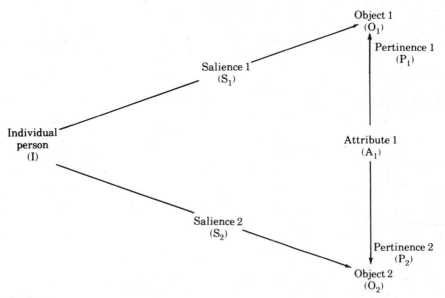

**FIGURE 13.1.** Carter's paradigm of affective relations. Adapted from Carter, 1965.

for political office, $O_1$ and $O_2$. My saliences toward each candidate will be determined by previous responses to the candidates, including party affiliation, peer group alliances, past evaluations of their "images," and stands on issues. At the moment, suppose pollution of the environment is a critical issue to me. Then I would also evaluate the candidates on their positions regarding environment-related issues. This becomes the relevant situational attribute, and their stands on the issue are the bases for my pertinence evaluations. My total evaluation of the candidates will depend both on my previous evaluations (saliences) and on the current, specific evaluation (pertinences).

## THE COORIENTATION MODEL

Chaffee and McLeod's coorientation model extends Newcomb's A-B-X model by elaborating on how A and B assign value to X, the object of communication. They use Carter's model to explain the relationships between A and X and between B and X.

The coorientation model is shown in Figure 13.2.[5] In this model, the participants in the system are persons A and B, who are simultaneously oriented toward an object X. This means that they are both aware that X exists and can therefore communicate about X. When the object X is presented to persons A and B, we can assume that they will be aware of their respective "cognitions" about X. Cognitions here mean their evaluations of X based on both pertinence and salience relationships. We can also assume that person A will have some estimate or perception of B's cognitions and B will have some percep-

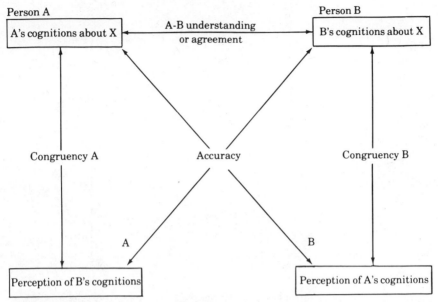

**FIGURE 13.2.** The coorientation model. Adapted from McLeod and Chaffee, 1973.

tion of A's cognitions. The boxes in the model represent A's and B's cognitions of X and their respective estimates of the cognitions of the other person regarding X. The arrows connecting the boxes are the basic variables in the model. They represent three kinds of relationships possible between the boxes. These are congruency, agreement or understanding, and accuracy.

*Congruency* is the degree of similarity between a person's own cognitions and his or her perception of the other person's cognitions. It is the extent to which a person thinks the other person agrees or disagrees with him or her regarding evaluation of the object X. The more agreement there is, the more congruency there is.

*Agreement* is the extent to which A and B have the same salience evaluations of X. It is often referred to in persuasion as "attitude." *Understanding* is the extent to which A and B agree on what attributes to evaluate X on and on their evaluations of the importance of the attributes. Two persons are "cooriented" when there is complete understanding. According to Chaffee and McLeod, understanding is often neglected in communication research and often is taken for granted.

*Accuracy* is the extent to which a person's estimate of the other person's cognition matches what the other person actually thinks. Chaffee and McLeod suggest that accuracy is the ideal criterion for communication effectiveness. The more accuracy there is in the system, the more effective communication has been.

The coorientation model leads us to ask different questions about communication. Traditional persuasion research considers attitudinal and behavioral change to be the major effects of communication. The coorientation model considers accuracy and understanding to be the major communication effects. Accuracy, understanding, and congruency can also cause communication behavior. Let us now review some of the research exploring these relationships.

## RESEARCH

Research on coorientation can be broken down according to the unit of analysis. Some studies investigate coorientation between two individuals (dyads); others look at coorientation in small groups such as the family; still others analyze coorientation between larger groups such as formal organizations and communities.

### Coorientation in Dyads

The major goal of research on coorientation in dyads has been to determine how interpersonal communication affects agreement, congruency, and accuracy. A major finding is that communication more often results in accuracy than in agreement or congruency. Thus, the main function of interpersonal communication is information exchange, not persuasion.

Wackman and Beatty paired two subjects who did not know each other and who disagreed strongly on a topic. Each dyad was allowed one hour to discuss the topic. After discussion, agreement did not increase significantly between the subjects in the dyads; however, there was a significant increase in accuracy.[6]

Chaffee and McLeod allowed seventy married couples to discuss one or two topics for about fifteen minutes.[7] There was no significant trend toward greater agreement or congruency after discussion; however, accuracy was improved.

Chaffee and McLeod induced communication in married couples and pairs of student roommates by either administering a pretest questionnaire or warning them that they were going to be reinterviewed.[8] The assumption was that the pretest and warning would "sensitize" the subjects to the topic and would therefore motivate them to communicate about the topic. They found that the pretest resulted in greater agreement, accuracy, and congruency between pairs when they were reinterviewed two weeks later. However, only accuracy increased after the warning.

### Coorientation in Families

Chaffee and McLeod have used the coorientation model to analyze communication patterns between parents and children.[9] In the family, A can be the parents (or a parent), B is the child, and X is an object in the child's and parent's environments. There are two independent communication patterns that can evolve out of the A-B-X system. When parents stress a child's relationships with others (A-B orientations), there is "socioorientation." A family that is high in socioorientation encourages the child to get along with others, defer to adults, and to avoid conflict. A family that stresses "concepts" (the A-X orientation) more than getting along with others is said to be "concept oriented." Such a family encourages the child to seek new ideas, look at all sides of issues, and to express his or her own opinions. Both communication patterns can be found in varying degrees in one family. Four combinations are possible, resulting in the following family types.

1. *Laissez-faire* families do not emphasize either concept or socioorientations; thus, children are "undirected."
2. Protective families emphasize socio- over concept-orientations; thus, the child is trained to value social harmony and to be "obedient."
3. Pluralistic families stress concept- over socioorientations; the child is rarely constrained in his or her interpersonal relations; open discussion is valued.
4. Consensual parents stress both socio- and concept-orientations. Children are encouraged to discuss ideas, but family debate is avoided.

According to Chaffee and McLeod, these communication patterns are established early in life and can have important consequences for behaviors of children and adults. Their research has shown the following.

1. Children from families that emphasize concept- over sociooriented communication tend to be more competent and active in public affairs and school activities. They are also more likely to be receptive to information contradicting their own opinions and are less persuasible under some conditions.[10]
2. Pluralistic husband-wife pairs increase more in accuracy after discussing a topic; protective couples increase more in congruency; while consensual pairs increase more in agreement.[11]
3. Among junior and senior high school students, family communication patterns predict various political behaviors. Compared to young people from other family types, those from pluralistic families generally use the mass media more for public affairs, know more about public affairs, are more active in political campaigns, are more aware of the political system, and feel more positively toward the political system.[12] Young people from protective families generally score lowest on these indices of political socialization.

   We can conclude from these results that family communication patterns often determine our perceptions of, and responses to, objects around us.

### Coorientation in Larger Groups

Researchers have used the coorientation model to analyze agreement, understanding, congruency, and accuracy on various social issues between large groups of people. Most of this research is descriptive; the main purpose is to measure the degrees to which each of the coorientational variables exist in a given situation.

Grunig measured coorientation between government agencies and interest groups concerned with low-income housing in a wealthy suburban community close to Washington, D.C.[13] He analyzed three groups: personnel of twenty-nine government agencies, low-income residents living close to the suburb, and residents of the suburb. He classified the personnel of the government agencies into two groups according to how they defined the housing problem. The "liberals" were primarily concerned with social equality, while the "economic interest group" was concerned with economic development of the suburb.

Grunig found that the liberals accurately predicted the cognitions of the poor regarding the low-cost housing; thus, accuracy was high. However, congruency and agreement with the poor were low. The "economic interest" personnel, on the other hand, showed low accuracy, low congruency, and low agreement with the poor. Both personnel groups accurately predicted the orientations of the suburbanites regarding low-cost housing. However, both groups showed low congruency and agreement with the suburban orientations.

Stamm and his colleagues examined the "generation gap" between students at a local university and townspeople in Grand Forks, North Dakota.[14] The object of orientation was the Grand Forks police. The researchers found that the two groups' actual evaluations of the police were not significantly different from each other. Thus, agreement was high. There was no objective evidence of a "generation gap." The townspeople, however, perceived their orientation toward the police to be significantly different from the orientations of the students, ascribing a more negative view to the students than their own. Thus, perceived congruency from the viewpoint of the townspeople was low. Townspeople also inaccurately estimated the students to be more negative toward the police than the students actually were. Accuracy was therefore also low.

The students, on the other hand, had higher congruency estimates of the orientations of townspeople. They perceived the townspeople's view of the police to be only slightly more positive than their own.

Stamm *et al.* concluded that the townspeople perceived a generation gap between themselves and the students. This perception was based on inaccurate estimates of how the students actually felt about the police. There was no objective basis for this perceived gap, since orientations of the students and the townspeople toward the police were not significantly different from each other.

Tichenor, Olien, Donohue, and their colleagues at the University of Minnesota have applied the coorientation model to the analysis of consensus (or agreement) in communities.[15] They are interested in determining the communication and social factors that lead to greater or less agreement regarding community issues. One of the communication factors they have isolated is the type of media that is used by the population. Two types are analyzed—metropolitan and local media. Examples of local media are local weekly newspapers. Metropolitan media are "big-city" daily newspapers. In small communities close to large cities, some people use local media, while others depend on the metropolitan media. The researchers assume that a principal function of the metropolitan media is "dissemination of information between interest groups and subsystems so as to provide for conflict management of the larger system."[16] The community medium, on the other hand, is primarily concerned with community cohesion and protecting the small community from perceived external threats. Given this assumption, Tichenor *et al.* predict that persons subscribing to a local weekly will be more supportive of local officials on community issues than subscribers to the metropolitan newspaper. Their research generally supports this hypothesis.

## SUMMARY

The coorientation model considers communication to be an interpersonal act. Thus, the variables of interest are interpersonal relationships such as understanding, accuracy, and congruency, and not the intrapersonal concepts attitudes and opinions. Understanding is the extent to which two persons agree on the object of communication and its attributes. Congruency is the extent to which one person's estimates of the other person's orientations are similar to his or her own orientations. Accuracy is the extent to which a person's estimates of the other person's orientations reflect that person's actual orientations.

Research has indicated that in interpersonal relationships the main effect of communication is accuracy and understanding, not persuasion. The coorientation model has also been used to analyze family communication patterns. "Protective" families emphasize social relations over ideas and concepts. Families that emphasize concepts over social relations are "pluralistic." Families emphasizing neither concepts nor social relations are *laissez faire,* while those emphasizing concepts and social relations are "consensual." These family communication types have predicted a number of responses of children and adolescents, including use of the mass media, political attitudes, and political behaviors.

The coorientation model has been used to analyze how various groups and organizations perceive each other's orientations toward social issues. It has been useful in analyzing consensus in communities, the generation gap between college students and townspeople, and coorientation between government agencies and the various publics they serve.

Although the coorientation model has provided us with new insights into the communication process, much more has to be done if the model is to provide the basis for a theory. We need to know more about the interrelations between the coorientation variables and about their relations to communication. Does congruency, for example, lead to understanding and accuracy and to more frequent communication? Most of the research so far has conceptualized the coorientation variables as "effects" of communication. Can they not "cause" communication as well, and how? Finally, the measures for the three coorientational variables need to be refined, especially when dealing with large groups.

## REVIEW QUESTIONS

1. What new insights into the communication process does the coorientation model provide us that were not provided by the more traditional models of persuasion?
2. Pick two studies discussed in this chapter and evaluate their internal and external validity.
3. Discuss the value of the coorientation model in building communication theory.

## ENDNOTES

1. For a theoretical review of the model, see Jack McLeod and Steven Chaffee, "Interpersonal Approaches to Communication Research," *American Behavioral Scientist, 16,* 1973, pp. 469–499.
2. T. M. Newcomb, "An Approach to the Study of Communicative Acts," *Psychological Review, 60,* 1953, pp. 393–404.
3. R. F. Carter, "Communication and Affective Relations," *Journalism Quarterly, 42,* 1965, pp. 203–212.
4. *Ibid.*
5. Adapted from McLeod and Chaffee, *op. cit.*
6. O. B. Wackman and D. Beatty, "A Comparison of Balance and Consensus Theories for Explaining Changes in ABX Systems," paper presented to the International Communication Association, Phoenix, 1971; also in D. Wackman, "Interpersonal Communication and Coorientation," *American Behavioral Scientist, 16,* 1973, pp. 537–550.
7. In Wackman, 1973, *op. cit.*
8. S. H. Chaffee and J. M. McLeod, "Sensitization in Panel Design: A Coorientational Experiment," *Journalism Quarterly, 45,* 1968, pp. 661–669.
9. S. H. Chaffee and J. M. McLeod, "Coorientation and the Structure of Family Communication," paper presented to the International Communication Association, Minneapolis, 1970; also in G. O'Keefe, Jr., "Coorientation Variables in Family Study," *American Behavioral Scientist, 16,* 1973, pp. 513–535.
10. See O'Keefe, 1973, *op. cit.*
11. Chaffee and McLeod, 1970, *op. cit.*

12. S. Chaffee, "Mass Communication in Political Socialization," in S. Renshon (ed.), *Handbook of Political Socialization* (New York: Free Press, 1977), pp. 223–258.
13. J. Grunig, "Communication in Community Decision on the Problems of the Poor," *Journal of Communication, 22,* 1972, pp. 5–25.
14. K. Stamm and B. Bowes, "Coorientation Variables and Stereotyping: An Analysis of the Generation Gap," paper presented to the Association for Education in Journalism, Carbondale, Illinois, 1972; also see J. Grunig and K. Stamm, "Communication and Coorientation of Collectivities," *American Behavioral Scientist, 16,* 1973, pp. 567–591.
15. See, for example, P. J. Tichenor *et al.,* "Community Issues, Conflict, and Public Affairs Knowledge," in P. Clarke (ed.), *New Models for Mass Communication Research* (Beverly Hills, Calif.: Sage Publications, 1973).
16. P. Tichenor and D. Wackman, "Mass Media and Community Public Opinion," *American Behavioral Scientist, 16,* 1973, pp. 593–606.

# 14

# MASS MEDIA USE AND
# AUDIENCE NEEDS

Why do we use the mass media? What individual needs lead us to use one mass medium more often than others or to choose some types of media contents over others? How successful are the media in fulfilling these needs? These are some of the major questions that media uses and gratifications research attempts to answer.

The mass media uses and gratifications model, like the coorientation model discussed in the previous chapter, is an alternative to persuasion models in communication research. The main question in media uses and gratifications research is not how the media are changing our attitudes and behaviors but how the media are meeting our social and individual needs. Thus, the emphasis is on an active audience, deliberately using the media to achieve specific goals.

The uses and gratifications approach is not new. As early as the 1940s and 1950, researchers were investigating *why* people engaged in various kinds of mass communication behavior, such as listening to radio quiz programs and daytime serials, reading comic books, and reading the newspaper.[1] Berelson in 1954, for example, found that people read the newspaper to participate vicariously in newsworthy happenings, to get useful information, and for companionship.[2] However, it was not until the late 1960s and early 1970s that researchers began systematic research aimed at building a theory of media uses and gratifications. This research has been conducted in a number of countries, including the United States, Israel, Japan, the United Kingdom, Finland, and Sweden.[3] Although there have been some differences in approaches to measuring audience needs and media functions, recent uses and gratifications studies are based on a common set of assumptions.

1. Media use is goal directed. We use the mass media to satisfy specific needs. These needs develop out of our social environment.
2. Receivers select the types of media and media contents to fulfill their needs. Thus, the audience initiates the mass communication process, and we are able to "bend the media" to our needs more readily than the media can overpower us.

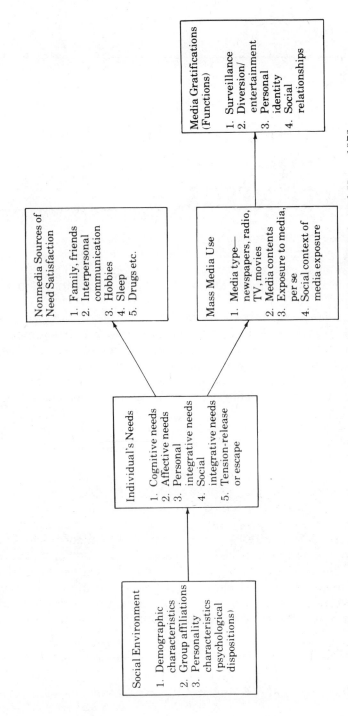

**FIGURE 14.1.** Mass media uses and gratifications model. Adapted from Katz, Gurevich, and Haas, 1973.

3. There are other sources of need satisfaction, and the mass media must compete with them. Some nonmedia sources of need satisfaction are family, friends, interpersonal communication, other leisure activities, sleep, and drugs.

4. The audience is aware of its needs and can report them when asked. They are also aware of their reasons for using the mass media.[4]

The uses and gratifications model is shown in Figure 14.1. The model starts with the social environment, which determines our needs. The social environment includes our demographic characteristics, group affiliations, and personality characteristics. Audience needs can be categorized as cognitive, affective, personal integrative, social integrative, and escapist needs. These needs can be satisfied by nonmedia sources such as family, friends, interpersonal communication, hobbies, sleep, and drugs. The model is mainly concerned with media-related sources of need satisfaction. These include exposure to the media per se, type of media used, contents of the media attended to, and social context of media exposure. The actual needs satisfied by the media are referred to as media gratifications or functions. These include surveillance, diversion or escape, and the development of personal identity and social relationships. Let us now discuss each of these components in more detail.

## AUDIENCE NEEDS

Like most other theories based on human motivations, the uses and gratifications model begins by attempting to classify human needs into distinct and theoretically meaningful categories. The field does not lack for listings of needs.[5] However, it would not be very practical or meaningful to work with specific needs, since the list can be endless.

Katz, Gurevitch, and Haas have suggested a typology of media-related needs that classifies specific needs into the following five categories.

1. *Cognitive Needs.* Needs related to strengthening of information, knowledge, and understanding of our environment. These needs are based on a desire to understand and master the environment. They also satisfy our curiosity and exploratory drives.

2. *Affective Needs.* Needs related to strengthening aesthetic, pleasurable, and emotional experiences. The pursuit of pleasure and entertainment is a common motivation that can be satisfied by the media.

3. *Personal Integrative Needs.* Needs related to strengthening credibility, confidence, stability, and status of the individual. They are derived from the individual's desire for self-esteem.

4. *Social Integrative Needs.* Needs related to strengthening contact with family, friends, and the world. These are based on an individual's desire for affiliation.

*eeds.* Needs related to escape, tension release, and desire for
1.[6]

## AUDIENCE NEEDS AND THE SOCIAL ENVIRONMENT

Katz, Gurevitch, and Haas found in their Israeli sample that media-related
needs are related to education and age.[7] People with higher levels of education reported more needs to be important than people with less education.
Younger people attributed greater importance to needs associated with aesthetic and emotional experience than older people. McQuail, Blumler, and
Brown suggest that the need to escape characterizes individuals with poor
personal adjustment and low self-esteem.[8] These persons come from restrictive and repetitive job and family environments and are alienated from
their peers and from society.

## AUDIENCE NEEDS AND MEDIA FUNCTIONS

Audience needs are served by a set of media functions or gratifications first
discussed by Lasswell in 1948[9] and recently refined by McQuail, Blumler, and
Brown.[10] According to this typology, the mass media perform four functions.
First, the media provide us with information about our environment (surveillance); second, they provide us with escape from the constraints of routine
and from the burdens of problems and are a vehicle for emotional release
(escape/diversion); third, the media are vehicles for personal reference, reality exploration, and value reinforcement (personal identity); and fourth, the
media provide us with substitute companionships and with information that
could be used in our social relationships (social integration).

These functions fulfill specific needs of the audience. Cognitive needs are
served by the surveillance function; affective and escapist needs are served by
the diversion and entertainment function; personal integrative needs are fulfilled by the personal identity function; and social integrative needs are served
by the social relations function.

## MASS MEDIA USE

Katz, Gurevitch, and Haas have listed and defined the mass media use variables that can lead to media gratifications.[11] These characteristics are the
following.

1. Media contents as, for example, news, soap operas, television crime
   drama, and so forth.
2. Media attributes as, for example, print versus broadcasting, and reading
   versus audio or audiovisual modes of reception.

3. Typical exposure situation as, for example, at home versus out of home and alone versus with others.

According to the model, these media variables, or their combinations, can explain how audience needs are fulfilled.

## RESEARCH

To build a theory of media uses and gratifications, we must be able to relate audience needs to media functions or gratifications and explain why these needs were fulfilled by a specific medium or media content and not by others. Unfortunately, media uses and gratifications research has not reached this stage.[12] There has been very little research connecting audience needs to media functions. Most studies have not gone beyond *describing* audience needs and media functions. Few have related the two sets of variables; even fewer have explained why certain media and content characteristics lead to the fulfillment of some needs and not others. A few studies, however, have investigated these theoretical issues.

Katz, Gurevitch, and Haas interviewed 1500 respondents in Israel.[13] Among their major findings were the following.

1. Respondents considered nonmedia sources to be more important than the mass media in satisfying all needs examined by the investigators. Nonmedia sources of need gratification included friends, holidays, lectures, and work.

2. The mass media were more important sources of need gratification to the "alienated," or to those who were more detached from self, family, friends, the state, and society as a whole. However, even for these persons interpersonal communication was an important source of need satisfaction, especially in areas relating to the state.

3. Some needs are better served by the media than others, including the striving for a higher standard of living, satisfying oneself that one's time is well spent, and escapist needs in general. However, self-gratification (affective needs) is generally better served by friends than by the mass media, even the need "to be entertained."

4. Respondents who say that matters of the state and society are important to them consistently rank newspapers as the most important mass medium for information and for other needs connecting themselves to society and the state (social integrative needs). Newspapers are followed by radio, then television. Books and films are rarely mentioned as important in fulfilling informational and social integrative needs.

5. Personal integrative needs and some affective needs having to do with self are associated with different types of media, depending on the specific need. Books best serve the need of "knowing oneself"; films, television, and books best fulfill the need of "enjoying oneself."

6. The need to "kill time" is best served by television but not the need to "escape." Movies and books are more helpful for "escape" than television.

7. Film and television are the most useful for some social integrative needs, such as to maintain friendship and family solidarity. However, the topics of conversation in these social activities are provided by newspapers and books.

8. Television is the least specialized of the mass media. Respondents tend to mention television as satisfying more needs than any other medium. Movies and the newspapers are the most specialized. Movies serve self-gratification (enjoyment) and sociability needs; newspapers fulfill the need to participate in society and the state.

Blumler studied how British voters use the mass media during an election campaign.[14] He suggests that in Britain, reinforcement of political attitudes and choices is best served by newspapers, while vote guidance is best served by television. This is because newspapers editorialize, while television is more "impartial." Also in Britain, Blumler, Brown, and McQuail found that a primary function of a long-running daytime radio serial was reinforcment, or "to uphold traditional family values."[15]

It is obvious that much more has to be done in the area of media uses and gratifications. We need more comparative studies so that we can determine the influence of culture on media uses and gratifications. More attention should be given to relating specific media attributes to audience need satisfaction and to relating media needs to media gratifications. Finally, more work is needed in defining and categorizing media-related needs or drives. This, it seems, is a main shortcoming of media uses and gratifications research as well as of other theories of human behaviors based on motivational forces within the individual. Since this book is heavily influenced by Bandura's social learning theory, we think it is appropriate to end this chapter with a quote from Bandura on the failings of motivational theories of human behavior.

> Theories of this sort were criticized on both conceptual and empirical grounds. The inner determinants often were inferred from the behavior they supposedly caused, resulting in description in the guise of explanation. A hostile impulse, for example, was derived from a person's irascible behavior, which was then attributed to the action of an underlying hostile impulse. Similarly, the existence of achievement motives was deduced from achievement behavior; curiosity motives from inquisitive behavior; power motives from domineering behavior, and so on. There is no limit to the number of motives one can find by inferring them from the kinds of behavior they supposedly produce.[16]

Media uses and gratifications research, to be sure, are an important addition to current theoretical models in mass communication research. However, work in this area, despite the existence of the model for several decades, is still incomplete. As with all the models discussed in this text, only continued, persistent, and dedicated work will push these models into the domain of mass communication theory.

## REVIEW QUESTIONS_____

**1.** What are some audience needs that the mass media can satisfy? Pick examples of messages from the mass media that can satisfy each of these audience needs.

**2.** Evaluate uses and gratifications research. What are some of its weaknesses? Strengths?

## ENDNOTES_____

1. See, for example, H. Cantril, "Professor Quiz; A Gratification Study," in P. Lazarsfeld and F. Stanton (eds.), *Radio Research 1941* (New York: Duell, Sloan and Pearch, 1942); H. Herzog, "Motivations and Gratifications of Daily Serial Listeners," in W. Schramm (ed.), *The Process and Effects of Mass Communication* (Urbana: University of Illinois Press, 1954), pp. 50–55; B. Berelson, "What 'Missing the Newspaper' Means," in P. Lazarsfeld and F. Stanton (eds.) *Communications Research 1948-49* (New York: Harper, 1949).
2. Berelson, *op. cit.*
3. See E. Katz, J. Blumler, and M. Gurevitch, "Uses of Mass Communication by the Individual," in W. Davison and F. T. Yu (eds.), *Mass Communication Research* (New York: Praeger, 1974), pp. 11–35.
4. *Ibid.*
5. See, for example, A. H. Maslow, *Motivation and Personality* (New York: Harper, 1954).
6. E. Katz, M. Gurevitch, and H. Haas, "On the Use of Mass Media for Important Things," *American Sociological Review, 38,* 1973, pp. 164–181.
7. *Ibid.*
8. D. McQuail, J. G. Blumler, and J. Brown, "The Television Audience: A Revised Perspective," in D. McQuail (ed.), *Sociology of Mass Communication* (Harmondsworth, England: Penguin, 1972).
9. H. D. Lasswell, "The Structure and Function of Communications in Society," in L. Bryson (ed.), *The Communication of Ideas* (New York: Harper, 1948.
10. McQuail, Blumler, and Brown, *op. cit.*
11. Katz, Gurevitch, and Haas, *op. cit.*
12. Katz, Blumler, and Gurevitch, *op. cit.*
13. Katz, Gurevitch, and Haas, *op. cit.*
14. J. G. Blumler, "Information and Democracy: The Perspective of the Governed," *Il Politico, 37,* 1972.
15. See Katz, Blumler, and Gurevitch, *op. cit.*
16. A. Bandura, *Social Learning Theory* (Englewood Cliffs, N.J.: Prentice-Hall, 1977), p. 2.

# PART IV

# MASS COMMUNICATION AND SOCIALIZATION

In Part IV we discuss media socialization research. The main questions are *"What* do we learn from the mass media?" and *"How* do we learn from the media?"

The interest in media socialization is a relatively recent development in communication research. Instead of studying attitude and behavior change, many communication scholars today are studying the effects of the media on our acquisition of values, political beliefs, behaviors, and perceptions of social reality.

Chapter 15 discusses Albert Bandura's social learning theory, which explains how we learn from the media. The effects of television violence and media erotica on audiences are analyzed in Chapters 16 and 17. In Chapter 18 we discuss how television can teach children desirable social behaviors and how television can help them in school.

Chapter 19 explains how we depend on the mass media for "reality testing." In Chapter 20 we discuss media influence and political knowledge, feelings, and behaviors.

# 15

# LEARNING FROM THE MASS MEDIA

We are influenced by the mass media in many other ways besides persuasion. As mass communication technology develops and as the mass media become more pervasive in our daily lives, media influence is no longer limited to *changing* or *reinforcing* opinions, attitudes, and behaviors. The mass media have become important socialization agents as well, *creating* and *shaping* many of our shared attitudes, values, behaviors, and perceptions of social reality. The influence of the mass media in the acquisition of these response tendencies is often referred to as "social effects." In this chapter we will discuss a general theoretical framework to help us understand the role of the media in socialization. In the next few chapters we will discuss specific social effects of the media—aggression, prosocial behaviors, stereotypes, and the construction of social realities.

## SOCIAL LEARNING THEORY

We are not born with attitudes, values, perceptions of the world, and repertoires of behavior. These response tendencies (we call them response tendencies because they are reactions to external stimuli) must be learned. Many theories of behavior have attempted to explain how people and animals learn to interact with their environments through the acquisition of response tendencies.

Traditional learning theories assume that learning occurs by actually performing the responses and experiencing their effects. The main determinant of learning is reinforcement, or the extent to which the organism is rewarded (or punished) for performing the response.[1] The response will be repeated (and therefore learned) if the organism is rewarded. The response will not be repeated if the organism is punished or if the response did not lead to some desired goal. Thus, behavior is considered to be externally regulated by the stimulus conditions that elicit it and by the reinforcing conditions that maintain it.

Learning theories are able to explain the acquisition and elimination of wide ranges of behaviors in animals and humans. However, they have recently been criticized for many reasons.[2] Two criticisms relevant to our discussion of mass media and learning follow.

First, in its most radical form (sometimes referred to as "radical behaviorism") learning theory reduces people to robots, totally controlled by the environment. Radical learning theories do not consider the possible influences of motives and cognitions of the organism on learning because these processes cannot be observed directly. Thus learning is a strictly mechanistic process. Responses are learned automatically and unconsciously. This image of people runs counter to the popular notion that humans should have "free will" and that most social behaviors are voluntary. It also conjures up images of Orwell's *1984,* where human behavior is controlled by a few and people *are* robots.

Second, radical behaviorism can explain only a small part of our everyday behavior. Since these theories assume that learning can occur only through trial and error in direct experience, many of our learned behaviors cannot be accounted for. Most of our response tendencies are learned not by first actually experiencing them but by *observing* others and from the instructions of others. A physician, for example, learns surgery first by observation before actually doing it. We are able to acquire behaviors, attitudes, and "pictures" of the world not only through direct experience but also vicariously by observing others casually or purposefully. These observations may be direct, such as when we actually encounter the behavior performed, or indirect, such as when we observe the behaviors performed in the mass media.

Bandura presents a more general theory of human behavior that he calls "social learning theory."[3] It explains how we learn from direct experience as well as from observation or modeling. Thus, it can account for a wider range of behaviors than traditional learning theories.

Social learning theory explains behavior to be the result of environmental and cognitive factors. It considers reinforcing properties of the act and of the stimulus to be important, but it also takes into account the influence on learning of thought processes in the learner. Social learning theory is particularly relevant to mass communication because many of the behaviors we learn through modeling are first observed in the mass media.

Bandura's analysis of social learning is summarized in Figure 15.1. The major elements in his analysis are attentional processes, retention processes, motor reproduction processes, and motivational processes.

## Attentional Processes

The starting point of learning is an event that can be observed, directly or indirectly, by a person. The event may occur during the course of the person's daily activities, or it can be presented indirectly through television, books, movies, and other mass media. The event may involve actual performance of

| | Attentional Processes | Retention Processes | Motor Reproduction Processes | Motivational Processes | |
|---|---|---|---|---|---|
| Modeled Events ⟶ | Modeling stimuli | Symbolic coding | Physical capabilities | External reinforcement | ⟶ Matching Performance |
| | Distinctiveness | Cognitive organization | Availability of component responses | Vicarious reinforcement | |
| | Affective valence | Symbolic rehearsal | Self-observation of reproductions | Self-reinforcement | |
| | Complexity | Motor rehearsal | Accuracy feedback | | |
| | Prevalence | | | | |
| | Functional value ⟶ | | | | |
| | Observer characteristics | | | | |
| | Sensory capacities | | | | |
| | Arousal level | | | | |
| | Perceptual set | | | | |
| | Past reinforcement | | | | |

**FIGURE 15.1.** Bandura's social learning theory. Adapted from Bandura, 1977.

a behavior (such as a novel aggressive act), or it could illustrate patterns of thought (referred to by Bandura as "abstract" modeling). Actual behaviors are learned from observation of those behaviors, while attitudes, values, moral judgments, and social reality perceptions are learned through abstract modeling. Observation of the event may be casual (by chance) or deliberate.

The mass media occupy a central role in social learning theory. Since most of us are limited in what we can directly observe during our daily routines, much of what we learn is observed from the mass media, particularly the visual media. The mass media can significantly enlarge the scope of what we *could* learn by exposing us to modeling events that we would otherwise not have any contact with. Also, the mass media can transmit new behavioral and thought patterns simultaneously to large groups of people. Social learning theory considers the media to be primary socialization agents alongside family, peers, and classroom teachers.

Given an event that can be observed (and therefore modeled), the first step in social learning is attention to that event. Obviously, we cannot learn from an event unless we pay attention to it and accurately perceive its significant features. In any given day we are exposed to hundreds of events that we could model. Which do we pay attention to and why?

According to Bandura, attention to an event is determined by characteristics of the event (or modeling stimuli) and by characteristics of the observer. Events that are distinctive and simple will likely draw attention and therefore are likely to be modeled. Prevalence also determines attention. Opportunities for learning an event are enhanced by repeated observation of that event. A child who rarely watches television, for example, will not likely learn agressive acts shown on TV programs. Last, affective valence of the event should be considered. Events that elicit positive feelings in the observer will be attended to. We feel positively toward events that are salient (related to past, present, or expected experiences) and reinforcing. Events are reinforcing when they fulfill a need—as when they provide solutions to problems or when they provide diversion and entertainment, as the mass media often do.

Certain characteristics of the observer also determine attention. A person's capacity to process information which, up to a certain point is related to age and "intelligence," determines how well he or she can learn from observed experiences. Perceptual set, which is determined by needs, moods, values, and previous experiences, affects what features are learned from the observation. The influence of perceptual set on the interpretation of antiprejudice materials, for example, was illustrated in our discussion of selective perception in Chapter 11. Past reinforcement is another observer experience determining attention. If a person has been previously reinforced or rewarded for attending to an event or class of events, then he or she will likely attend to similar events in the future. This explains why patterns of television viewing, once established, are difficult to change.

A fourth observer characteristic determining attention is arousal level. A person who is emotionally aroused—angry, anxious, afraid—is more likely to be attentive to stimuli that can remove the source of aversive arousal or to stimuli that can reinforce positive arousal. Social learning theory considers arousal to be a facilitator of, instead of a necessary condition for, modeling; learning can occur without arousal.

## Retention Processes

Many of the behaviors that we learn are not or cannot be performed immediately after observation because of lack of opportunity or other practical reasons. Thus, social learning theory is primarily concerned with delayed modeling—that is, performance of the observed event when the model is no longer present.

Delayed modeling cannot occur if we do not remember the observed act. Retention of the act is facilitated by representing the response patterns in symbolic form. The act must be represented in our minds so that we can retrieve the representation when the opportunity to perform the act comes.

According to Bandura, we represent response patterns (the modeled act or event) in two systems—imaginal and verbal. Imaginal representation, sometimes referred to as visual imagery, involves drawing a mental picture of the observed act and storing that picture in our memories. Visual imagery is of course quite a common process. We have "pictures in our heads"[4] of people we know or have known; of experiences, sad and happy; of beautiful vacation scenes; and so on.

Visual images, however, are usually not adequate for modeling. Observational learning is facilitated in humans by our capability to represent symbolically events in verbal form using a common language. We are able to symbolize complex events using verbal codes, thus simplifying the process of information storage and retrieval. It is much easier to memorize abbreviated verbal instructions for a food recipe, for example, than to visualize every step in the process.

The observer must not only represent the event in verbal and visual forms so that it can be stored in memory, he or she must also be able to "mentally rehearse" the act before enacting it overtly. Rehearsal facilitates learning. We are less likely to forget an event if we visualize ourselves performing that event.[5] Research has shown that observational learning is most accurate when we first cognitively organize (using imaginal and verbal symbols) and mentally rehearse the modeled behavior and then enact it overtly.[6]

## Motor Reproduction Processes

Let us suppose that you have observed an act, represented the act with verbal and imaginal symbols, and then stored this representation in your memory. Given an opportunity to actually reproduce the act, how would you go about it?

According to Bandura, behavioral enactment will involve the following successive steps: cognitive organization of the responses, their initiation, monitoring, and refinement on the basis of informative feedback. The first step is remembering the cognitive representation of the act and selecting which responses are to be enacted. In Bandura's model, a person thinks before he or she acts. Thinking here means organizing the responses that have been learned so that the actual behavior can be initiated or performed. Cognitive organization and initiation of the behavior depend on the availability of certain skills in the individual. These include both cognitive and motor skills. Some people, for example, can easily learn how to serve a tennis ball by simple observation; for others, the tennis serve is an impossible task. Those who find it easy to learn probably are able to remember the serving motions more readily and are then able to reproduce these motions because of better muscle coordination.

Very rarely are we able to reproduce accurately behaviors on the first few attempts. Accurate reproduction is usually the product of trial and error. Feedback is therefore important because it allows us to correct for discrepancies between the observed act and our modeling of it. It helps if we are able to observe our attempts at modeling directly (such as by observing ourselves on videotape). However, direct observation is not always possible, and we often rely on information from others (a tennis instructor, for example) as an indication of the accuracy of our modeling.

## Motivational Processes

We do not enact everything that we learn. The probability that a given behavior will be performed does not depend only on opportunity or on motor reproduction processes. Motivation to perform the act is also important. Motivation depends on reinforcement. According to Bandura, there are three types of reinforcement that can motivate us to action: external reinforcement, vicarious reinforcement, and self reinforcement.

External reinforcements are rewards that the actor gets for performing the behavior. These rewards are "external," meaning that they exist outside of the actor. Examples of common external rewards are social approval, money, privileges, and the avoidance of punishment. The probability that an act will be performed is increased to the extent that the actor is rewarded for the performance or to the extent that he or she *expects* to be rewarded. Bandura does not limit reinforcement to actual rewards experienced after enactment of the behavior. We are able to associate certain actions with certain consequences by observing others or from previous experience. Our expectation of consequences for performing an act will therefore be an important influence on future enactments.

Vicarious reinforcement results when we observe others being reinforced for performing certain behaviors. Studies have shown that models who are rewarded are more likely to be imitated than models who are not rewarded.[7] Socially prohibited actions such as violent behavior have been imitated in laboratory studies when these actions were not punished.[8] The amount of modeling generally depends on how much value the observers place on the outcomes and on the type of behavior being modeled.

Finally, self-reinforcement also determines enactment of learned behaviors. We are able to generate reinforcements within ourselves for performing certain behaviors. "Self-satisfaction" and "inner peace" are common self-reinforcers. When a mountain climber is asked why he or she is about to climb a treacherous peak, he or she may answer, "Because it is there." When an author is asked why he or she is writing a book that probably will not sell, the answer may be, "Because I like doing it." Many of our behaviors are performed for these reasons. A modeled act will be repeated to the extent that it is self-reinforcing to the actor.

## SUMMARY

Bandura's social learning theory explains how we learn by observation. Many of our behaviors are learned this way, since opportunities for trial-and-error learning from direct experience are limited. A major source of social learning is the mass media, particularly the visual media.

Observational learning is determined by attentional, retention, motor reproduction, and motivational processes. Events that are distinctive, simple, prevalent, and functional will likely attract the attention of an observer. Sensory capacities, arousal level, perceptual set, and past reinforcement history of the observer also determine attention. After an event is attended to, it is symbolically coded by the observer using verbal and imaginal symbols. These symbols are then stored in memory. The actual enactment of the coded responses depends on the physical and cognitive capabilities of the actor. Self-observation and feedback from others help the actor achieve accurate enactments. Behaviors will be performed to the extent that they have reinforcement value. Reinforcement can take the form of anticipated or actual external rewards, observations that others are rewarded for performing the same acts, and internally generated rewards such as self-satisfaction.

## REVIEW QUESTIONS

**1.** Evaluate the utility of social learning theory in explaining how audiences are affected by the mass media.

**2.** Discuss the role of the mass media in each "step" of social learning.

## ENDNOTES

1. See, for example, Seymour Berger and William Lambert, "Stimulus-Response Theory in Contemporary Social Psychology," in G. Lindzey and E. Aronson (eds.), *The Handbook of Social Psychology*, Vol. 1 (Reading, Mass.: Addison-Wesley, 1969).

2. Albert Bandura, *Social Learning Theory* (Englewood Cliffs, N.J.: Prentice-Hall, 1977), pp. 6–7.
3. *Ibid.*, pp. 2–158.
4. The phrase is borrowed from Walter Lippman, *Public Opinion* (New York: Macmillan, 1936).
5. A. Bandura and R. W. Jeffery, "Role of Symbolic Coding and Rehearsal Processes in Observational Learning," *Journal of Personality and Social Psychology, 26,* 1973, pp. 122–130.
6. R. W. Jeffery, "The Influence of Symbolic and Motor Rehearsal on Observational Learning," *Journal of Research in Personality, 10,* 1976, pp. 116–127.
7. A. Bandura, "Influence of Models' Reinforcement Contingencies on the Acquisition of Imitative Responses," *Journal of Personality and Social Psychology, 1,* 1965, pp. 589–595.
8. R. H. Walters, R. D. Parke, and V. A. Cane, "Timing of Punishment and the Observation of Consequences to Others as Determinants of Response Inhibition," *Journal of Experimental Child Psychology, 2,* 1965, pp. 10–30.

# 16 _____

# TELEVISION VIOLENCE AND AGGRESSION _____

Does exposure to television violence cause aggressive behavior among viewers? This question has been publicly debated for years and has also been the subject of controversy among social scientists. In 1969 the National Institute of Mental Health (NIMH) appropriated $1 million for new research on the effects of TV violence. Three years later the Surgeon General's Scientific Advisory Committee on Television and Social Behavior concluded from the NIMH studies that "there is a convergence of the fairly substantial experimental evidence for shortrun causation of aggression among children by viewing violence on the screen and the much less certain evidence from field studies that extensive violence viewing preceded some long-run manifestations of aggressive behavior. This convergence. . . constitutes some preliminary indication of a causal relationship."[1] The tentative conclusion, then, is that under some conditions viewing TV violence causes aggressive behavior. Although there has been some disagreement,[2] most social scientists who have done research on TV violence seem to agree with this conclusion.[3] In this chapter we will discuss some of the general findings from the perspective of Bandura's social learning theory. We will not attempt to review all of the relevant research, since excellent reviews are available elsewhere.[4] Instead, our purpose is to integrate some of the general findings into the framework of social learning theory. We will also discuss a few recent studies in detail to illustrate methodology in the field.

## TELEVISION VIOLENCE

Public and research attention has focused on the effects of television violence on audiences because (1) television is the most pervasive mass medium in the United States today and (2) television is violent. Surveys by the A. C. Nielsen Company[5] indicate that in the fall of 1976 the average U.S. household with television had the set turned on 6.82 hours every day, an increase of almost 1 hour over the 1963 level. Households where the head had less than one year of college watched more television in 1976 (7 hours per day) than households in which the head had one year or more of college (6.39 hours per day). However, TV viewing in the higher-education households increased significantly from 1970 to 1976 (5.6 to 6.39 hours per day), while the increase over the same time period in lower-education households was minimal (6.80 to 7 hours per day). This trend indicates that TV viewing is increasing in the general population, but more so among people with higher education.

The Nielsen figures for 1976 show that women fifty years or older watch the most television (5 hours per day), followed by men fifty years or older (4.6 hours), women eighteen to forty-nine years (4.5 hours), children two to eleven years (3.9 hours), and men eighteen to forty-nine (3.5 hours). Teenagers (twelve to seventeen years) watch the least television (3.1 hours per day).

Television is the mass medium most trusted by adults and the most used for news and entertainment. In 1974, nationwide surveys by the Roper Organization[6] indicated that 65 percent of adult respondents considered television to be the main source of news, compared to 47 percent saying that their main news source was newspapers. Also, 51 percent said that television was the medium they would be most inclined to believe, while only 20 percent said that newspapers were the most believable. Television viewing is the primary leisure activity of people, to which about 31 percent of free time is devoted.[7]

The evidence indicates that television is an important force in our lives simply because it takes up a good deal of our time. The next question is, how violent are television programs?

Gerbner and Gross have conducted a series of studies to measure violence in television.[8] They define violence as "the overt expression of physical force against self or others, compelling action against one's will on pain of being hurt or killed, or actually hurting or killing." Television programs that tell a story are videotaped for all networks during one autumn week of prime-time and weekend morning broadcasting. News, documentaries, specials, variety programs, and sports are not included in the analysis. Coders then analyze the videotapes, measuring the frequency and nature of violent acts, the perpetrators, victims and the environment in which the acts are performed. Gerbner and Gross have studied TV violence yearly since 1967. Some of their general findings follow.[9]

The percentage of programs containing violence has ranged from 80 to 90 percent; in 1977 it was 75.5 percent. Children's programming during weekend mornings continues to be the most violent.

The rate of violent episodes per hour was highest in 1976 (9.50); in 1977 there were 6.7 violent episodes per hour. The rate of violent episodes per program was 6.2 in 1976 and 5.0 in 1977.

The level of violence during the family viewing hour (8 to 9 P.M. EST) dropped in the 1975-1976 season; however, the level of violence in late evening programming increased significantly during the same period.

From this data we can conclude that there is considerable violence in television, particularly in programs that children are likely to watch. The Gerbner and Gross data are widely accepted.[10] Their measures, however, have been criticized for several reasons.[11] Two common criticisms are that the measures do not take into account the format of the program and that only one episode of a program is coded, which is then taken to be representative of the entire season. The format criticism is that the Gerbner and Gross definition of violence, when strictly used, will code as violent comedy, accidents, and acts of nature, thereby inflating violence estimates per program and per hour. To this criticism Gerbner and Gross reply that violence should be measured wherever it occurs and not on the basis of format.[12] They also say that their definition of violence is clearly not limited to criminal acts or deliberate physical violence among humans. Considering the potential effects on the viewer of observing a violent act, we would have to agree with Gerbner and Gross that their definition is valid. Social learning theory predicts that observers can learn acts of violence regardless of where the act is performed and regardless of format.

Intuitively, we would agree with the critics that Gerbner and Gross should randomly select a number of programs from a series for coding instead of coding only one episode. However, there is evidence that one episode can validly represent an entire series. Clark and Blankenburg,[13] for example, compared ratings based on the Gerbner and Gross violence index with ratings based on synopses from *TV Guide*. They found that there was about 90-percent agreement on which programs were violent and which were not.

Although some of the formulas and weights that Gerbner and Gross have used to analyze violence in TV programs seem to be arbitrary (that is, there seems to be no theoretical justification for combining individual indices), their measures, taken individually, give us a reasonably valid and reliable picture of violence in television.

## EFFECTS OF TELEVISION VIOLENCE

The main prediction of social learning theory is that we can learn new acts of violence by observing the acts performed on television or film. Another prediction is that abstract modeling can disinhibit us from performing violent acts in real life. A third prediction is that desensitization can result from repeated exposure to televised or filmed violence, thus increasing the likelihood that aggressive acts in real life will be tolerated or performed.

We will review the empirical evidence for each of these predictions in the sections that follow.

### Learning New Acts of Violence

Bandura has shown in a series of early experiments that children can learn new and complex aggressive acts simply by observing those acts performed once by a model. In a 1963 study, Bandura, Ross and Ross[14] individually exposed nursery school boys and girls to an adult model who performed a series of novel aggressive actions. The adult model punched a large inflated "Bobo the Clown" doll in the face, kicked the doll, and hit it in the face with a hammer. The model also verbalized the aggressive acts with comments such as "Pow," "Kick him," "Socko," and "Stickit." There were three conditions of exposure: one group saw a live model, another saw a film of the model, and a third group saw a film of the model dressed as a cartoon character. A fourth group did not observe the model.

The children in each of the four groups were then mildly frustrated. They were given attractive toys to play with; then the toys were taken away.

After this mild frustration, the children were allowed to play for twenty minutes in a room containing the plastic doll and other toys. Observers recorded the imitative and nonimitative aggressive acts of the children.

Bandura, Ross, and Ross found that children who had previously observed the model (conditions one, two, and three) performed significantly more aggressive acts toward the doll than children who had not seen the model (the control condition). Most of these acts were directly imitative of the model. The children imitated not only the physical acts but verbalizations of the acts as well. There were no differences between the first three conditions, indicating that method of observation (live, filmed, and filmed cartoon character) did not affect imitation of aggressive acts.

This experiment clearly shows that children can learn and perform new acts of aggression by observing those acts performed once. However, we should be cautious in generalizing these findings, since three very specific conditions existed in the experiment that may not often be found in the real world:[15] (1) the children were *frustrated* just before aggression was observed; (2) the situation in which aggression was observed was very *similar* to the situation in which the model performed; and (3) imitative aggression was made possible for the children *immediately* after the model was observed.

How long will children remember newly learned aggressive acts? Hicks[16] found that these acts can be performed by children up to six months after first observing the model, even when the acts are not shown them again. In the Hicks study children were exposed to films of aggressive models who were shown in a simulated television program. Immediately after observing the models, subjects showed more imitative aggression than subjects who had not seen the models. Subjects were tested again after six months without further exposure to the model. The level of imitative aggression was lower than during the first testing, but subjects who had observed the model still exhibited more aggression than subjects in the control (no observation) conditions.

The results of studies on observational learning of aggressive acts should not be too surprising to us. Most parents know from casual observation that children often imitate others, particularly other children and adults whom they like. What should cause alarm is the indication that children are more likely to imitate aggressive acts than other behaviors. Bandura and Huston[17] have found, for example, that nursery school children were more likely to imitate nonaggressive behavior of a model whom they liked. However, they also found that children imitated aggressive behavior of the model regardless of whether they liked him or not. Considering the number of violent acts that a child can observe in television on any given day, at least some of these acts will be learned. Whether they are performed or not depends on a number of conditions, which we will discuss in the next section.

## The Disinhibition and Facilitation of Aggression

Social learning theory—and common sense—tell us that we do not actually perform everything that we learn from modeling. The performance of the learned behavior depends on many factors—motor skills of the learner, opportunity to perform the act, and motivation. Our main concern in this section is *motivation*. Aggression in real life is not as common as make-believe aggression in television and film because we are normally inhibited from acting aggressively or violently. Social norms, fear of punishment, and anxiety usually associated with violence inhibit us from aggression. Thus, normally, we have little motivation to be violent. When these inhibitions are broken down, the likelihood that learned aggressive acts will be performed is increased. Disinhibition occurs with reinforcement for the violent act. Reinforcement therefore can facilitate aggression. Reinforcement for aggression can occur before the individual observes the model; it can also occur vicariously by observing the televised or filmed aggressive act justified or rewarded; or it can occur after observation of the model and after actual performance of the violent act. Let us consider each of these reinforcement conditions in more detail.

### Preobservation Reinforcement

A general principle of learning theory is that we will most likely perform the acts that have been rewarded in the past, while acts that have been punished will less likely be performed. Accordingly, the Surgeon General's Scientific Advisory Committee on Television and Social Behavior concluded in 1972[18] that the children most likely to behave aggressively after viewing televised or filmed violence are those who are already predisposed to behave more aggressively. Children predisposed to aggression are likely to have been reinforced for such acts in the past or they may come from social environments in which aggression is tolerated. Some factors that affect a child's predisposition to aggression are sex, socioeconomic status, and parental attitudes toward violence. A series of studies by Bandura and his colleagues[19] shows that boys perform more aggression than girls after viewing televised or filmed violence. This is probably due to cultural norms that permit more aggression from males than females. Boys are more likely to have been rewarded in the past for being aggressive, while girls are more likely to have been punished.

Some studies have shown that children from families of lower socioeconomic status are more likely to act aggressively than children from higher-income families, regardless of television viewing.[20] It is not clear, however, whether low-income children will be more affected by televised violence than high-income children, since there is no direct evidence on this question. The important variable, it seems, is how parents regard aggression as a means of attaining goals. Chaffee and McLeod[21] found in several samples that exposure to TV violence and aggressive behavior was weaker in families where the parents punished or disapproved of aggression by their children.

### Vicarious Reinforcement

According to social learning theory, we learn behaviors not only when we are directly reinforced for performing the behaviors but also by observing the consequences when others perform those behaviors. We can therefore predict that, through vicarious reinforcement, viewers will more likely imitate an aggressive model when that model is rewarded for his or her behavior than when the model is punished. Evidence supporting this prediction is provided by Bandura, Ross and Ross in another 1963 study.[22] They showed children a televised model who was either rewarded or punished for his aggression. Two control groups saw either a nonaggressive model or no model at all. Subjects who had seen the rewarded aggressive model subsequently showed significantly more imitative aggression than did the children in the other groups.

In another study Bandura[23] showed that children are less likely to imitate an aggressive model who is punished for his aggression than a model who is rewarded or a model who suffers no consequences for aggression. Subjects were exposed to a rewarded model, a punished model, and a model who was neither rewarded nor punished. Children who had seen the punished model showed less imitation than children who had seen the rewarded or no-consequence models. Also, children who had seen the no-consequence model showed almost as much aggression as children who had seen the rewarded model, suggesting that children may consider "getting away with it" as sufficient justification for an aggressive act.

Berkowitz and his colleagues,[24] in a series of studies, have shown that the extent to which the filmed or televised violent act is justified can determine whether subsequent aggression is elicited in viewers. The general hypothesis is that justified media violence can disinhibit real-life aggressive behavior. Justification can take the general forms of "vengeance" or "self-defense."[25]

Berkowitz in 1965 showed college students a prizefight scene from a boxing film in which one of the boxers receives a bloody beating. The victim was introduced to one group of subjects as a scoundrel who had run off with the other boxer's wife. To another group of subjects, the victim was introduced as an ex-champion who had fallen on bad times and who was trying to make a comeback. After seeing the films, the subjects were mildly angered and then were given the opportunity to deliver electric shocks to another person. Subjects in the justified condition (where the boxer was introduced as a scoundrel) administered significantly more electric shocks than subjects in the nonjustified condition.

In a more recent study, Hoyt[26] varied the nature of justification, portraying it as either vengeance or self-defense. He found that his college student subjects were least aggressive (they delivered the least number of electric shocks) after viewing the no-justification condition. They were also more aggressive in the vengeance condition than in the self-defense condition.

These studies provide support for the vicarious reinforcement hypothesis. Televised or filmed violence that is considered to be "all right" by the viewers is more likely to elicit subsequent aggression than media violence that is punished. Media violence that is rewarded, not punished, or justified as vengeance or self-defense is reinforcing and therefore is likely to elicit subsequent viewer aggression. Unfortunately, much of violence depicted in television is reinforced violence. In a content analysis of popular television programs, Larsen[27] showed that characters most often use violent methods, compared to other possible methods, to achieve desired goals. He also found that socially disapproved methods, including violence, are more frequently portrayed as being successful than are socially approved methods.

### Postobservation Reinforcement

A basic principle of learning theory, as we have seen, is that responses tend to be performed and learned when they are rewarded. The same principle applies to the performance of aggressive responses *after* exposure to aggressive models. Several studies have shown that children are more likely to perform learned aggressive responses when they are promised rewards or when they are actually rewarded for performing the response. Bandura[28] exposed children to aggressive models and recorded their spontaneous imitation of the model's acts. He then promised the children food and trinkets for performing the behaviors they had observed. With this incentive the children performed about twice as many imitative aggressive responses as they had shown in the first testing. Hicks[29] found similar results six months after his subjects had observed an aggressive model. The promise of rewards motivated children to perform more aggressive responses imitative of the model than they had performed spontaneously six months after observing the model. These studies clearly show that incentives facilitate the actual performance of learned aggressive acts.

### Other Factors Facilitating Aggression

There are other factors besides reinforcement that facilitate the performance of aggressive responses learned from a model. Some of these are perceived reality of the observed event, similarity of the postobservational situation to the observed event, aggressive cues in the postobservational situation, and arousal level of the viewer.

A number of recent studies have shown that televised or filmed violence that is perceived to be "real" or true to life is more likely to elicit aggression in viewers than violence that is perceived to be "fantasy." Feshbach[30] showed college students a film of a violent confrontation between students and police. He introduced the film as a news clip to one group and as fictional drama to another group. He found that the news clip group delivered more and higher intensities of noxious noise to their partners than the fictional group. Similarly, Berkowitz and Alioto[31] found that subjects (college students) who were told that the violent film was real were subsequently more aggressive than those who were told that the film was fantasy. According to Bandura's social learning model, reality can increase *involvement* of the viewer with the filmed event. Viewers who are involved with the observed event are more likely to be attentive and therefore will be more likely to learn aggressive behaviors and values by observation.

Perceived similarity between the observed event and the postobservational situation can also facilitate the performance of aggressive responses learned from a model. We are most likely to imitate aggression when we encounter cues in real life that are very similar to the cues in the observed violence.[32] These cues could be elements in the observed scene, such as characters, weapons, or setting, that are also found in the postobservational environment. Meyerson,[33] for example, exposed children to filmed aggressive performances of a model. They were then placed in test situations that had either high, medium, or low similarity to the observed setting. He found that imitative aggression increased as similarity between the film and postfilm settings increased. The perceived similarity factor can also explain why realistic settings are more likely to elicit aggressive responses than fantasy settings.[34] Cues encountered by children in cartoons and other fantasy media contents are not likely to be encountered in real life. Children are therefore more likely to imitate realistic aggression depicted in everyday settings.

Another type of cue in the postobservational situation is what Berkowitz calls "aggression-evoking cues."[35] These are cues that have some association with the filmed or televised aggression, such as weapons, aggressors, and victims. According to Berkowitz, aggressive responses may be aroused by observing televised or filmed violence, but they may not be expressed overtly unless the appropriate cues are present in the environment. Several experiments by Berkowitz and his associates at the University of Wisconsin provide support for this hypothesis. In one study[36] college students were initially insulted or not insulted by a confederate who was introduced as another subject. The confederate was introduced either as a speech major or as a college boxer. Subjects were then shown a film clip of a violent boxing match or a neutral film. After the film, subjects were told they they would be participating in a learning experiment and that they were to give shocks to the confederate every time he made a mistake. The largest number of shocks was given by subjects who had seen the boxing film and to whom the confederate (their "victims") had been introduced as a boxer. According to Berkowitz, subjects associated the "boxer" in the learning experiment with the boxing film. This cue therefore "drew out" the aggressive responses from the angered subjects.

Other research has shown that college students are more likely to administer electric shocks to people when they had been angered by someone having the same *name* as a character in the aggressive film.[37] Also, college students give more shocks when the person to be shocked has the same name as the filmed victim and not the filmed victor.[38]

These studies show that a real-life victim's association with the filmed aggression can produce more intense attacks. This association by itself is not necessary for aggression to be elicited from viewers, but it facilitates the performance of aggressive responses. Although generalizations to real-life situations from these laboratory studies must be done cautiously, there is some social significance in these findings. Goranson, for example, suggests that repeated portrayals of minority groups in television as victims of aggression may increase the likelihood that they will be the victims of violence in real life, since their repeated association with make-believe violence can make them more visible targets in the real world.[39]

Emotional arousal is another factor that can increase the probability that televised or filmed violence will elicit aggression among viewers. Emotional arousal involves two processes: the degree of physiological excitation and cognitive labeling of the physiological excitation.[40] Physiological arousal is manifested in autonomic responses such as heart rate, breathing, sweating, muscular tension, gastrointestinal secretions, vascular reactions, and brain activity levels.[41] Cognitive labeling is the process by which an individual attaches a specific label (for example, anger or frustration) to his or her arousal.

According to Bandura[42] and Berkowitz,[43] a general state of physiological arousal increases the probability of aggression after exposure to filmed or televised violence. More recently, Comstock *et al.*[44] have suggested that general arousal is a *necessary* condition not only for aggression but for any overt behavior.

Most of the early studies showed that emotional arousal from frustration or anger led to greater aggression among viewers after exposure to filmed or televised violence.[45] Typically in these studies, subjects who were angered, insulted, or frustrated aggressed more against a victim after observing filmed violence than subjects who were not so aroused. One theoretical explanation for these findings is that anger or frustration generates an aggressive drive that is heightened by observing filmed violence and that can then be reduced by subsequent aggressive behavior. Recent investigators have shifted their attention from frustration or anger to generalized arousal and the label that individuals attach to the arousal.[46] Studies have shown, for example, that generalized arousal resulting from stimuli such as erotic films and physical exercise can and often does lead to aggression.[47]

These findings seem to support Bandura's social learning interpretation of arousal and aggression. According to this view, arousal increases the probability that an individual will respond to a stimulus. This arousal is not limited to anger or frustration, since different emotions appear to have a similar physiological state[48] and the same physiological state can be experienced or labeled as different emotions.[49] What is important is that there should be some level of physiological arousal in the individual and that he or she is able to label the excitation as *an* emotion. According to Bandura, a general state of emotional arousal can facilitate not only aggression but other behaviors as well, such as seeking help or support, withdrawal and resignation, or self-anesthetization with drugs and alcohol.[50] The response selected by an individual will depend on the modes of response he or she has learned for coping with arousal and their relative effectiveness.

In summary, emotional arousal can facilitate the performance of aggressive responses after exposure to televised or filmed violence. It is not clear, however, whether arousal is *necessary* for aggression to be elicited by observed violence.

### Desensitization to Violence

The research we have reviewed so far provides evidence that exposure to televised or filmed violence affects subsequent aggressive *behaviors* of viewers. Another line of investigation into the effects of televised violence focuses not on behavior but on emotional responses to violence. The main hypothesis is that repeated exposure to filmed or televised violence can make viewers less sensitive to, and less anxious about, real-life violence. As a result of this "desensitization," viewers will be more tolerant of violence and will be more likely to engage in acts of violence.

Research on desensitization to violence assumes, first, that violence normally elicits anxiety in people. Evidence for this assumption is provided by a number of studies. In an early survey of television viewing among children, Himmilweit, Oppenheim, and Vince[51] found that children were upset by watching the killings on television. Several studies by Berger[52] indicate that intense emotional reactions are elicited in persons watching others receiving electric shocks. Lazarus and his colleagues[53] found that subjects reacted emotionally (measured by skin conductance and heart rate) when they were shown scenes from tribal rituals involving painful genital mutilation. In a study by Osborn and Endsley[54] preschoolers reacted more emotionally (measured by skin conductance) to excerpts from aggressive television programs as compared to scenes from nonviolent films. These studies support Maccoby and Levin's contention that members of our culture "do not tolerate aggression comfortably, neither their own nor that displayed by others. It evokes too much anxiety." [55]

If violence normally elicits anxiety in people, will repeated exposure to violence lessen this anxiety? This is a second assumption of research on desensitization to violence. It is derived from the general principle that repeated elicitation of any emotional response will progressively decrease the strength of that response.[56] This phenomenon is often referred to as habituation, adaptation, satiation, or accommodation.

Support for the general principle is provided in a number of desensitization studies by Bandura at Stanford. Desensitization is a process by which habituation of an emotional response (such as anxiety or fear) can be achieved. It involves the progressive introduction of the anxiety-producing stimulus to subjects who are otherwise relaxed and in comfortable, non-threatening environments.[57] For example, suppose I had an unnatural fear of mice. To "cure" me of this unnatural fear, my therapist could place me in a comfortable room, give me a beer, play soft music to relax me, and then expose me to stimuli associated with mice. The therapist could first show me pictures of mice, then rubber mice, then live mice. The trick is to keep me relaxed while the intensity of stimuli associated with mice is increased. After repeated presentations of these stimuli, I could be cured of my fear and might even be able to handle mice without too much anxiety.

Bandura has been able to desensitize children using observational techniques.[58] In one study he selected some children who were abnormally afraid of dogs. One group was repeatedly shown a peer who played with a brown cocker spaniel. Other groups were not shown any model or were only shown the dog. After several sessions, the children who were shown another child playing with a dog showed significantly less avoidance of dogs than children in the other groups. Similar results were observed when the children were shown films of a peer instead of a live model playing with a dog.[59]

Bandura's studies clearly show that repeated observation of anxiety-provoking activities can reduce initial anxiety associated with those activities. However, returning to the original question, will repeated exposure to televised or filmed violence lessen our anxiety about violence? Several recent investigations indicate that the answer is yes. In one study by Cline, Croft, and Courrier[60] children who were either heavy or light television viewers were shown a moderately violent film (clips from *Champion,* a film about boxing). The researchers measured skin conductance and blood volume pulse amplitude (physiological indices of emotional arousal) of the children before and during their exposure to the violent film. Before exposure the children did not differ in these physiological measures. However, while watching the film clips children who were heavy viewers were less aroused than children who were light viewers. Cline *et al.* took this to be evidence of the desensitization effect of television violence. They reasoned that heavy viewers would be more exposed to violence and would therefore be less aroused or less anxious when they encountered violence.

One problem with the Cline *et al.* study is the assumption that heavy television viewing means greater exposure to TV violence. Other researchers have shown that this is not necessarily so.[61] Also, Cline *et al.*'s groups of heavy and light TV viewers differed in socioeconomic backgrounds. This difference might have affected how they reacted to the violent film. A more direct and rigid test of the TV violence desensitization hypothesis is provided by Thomas, Horton, and Lippincott.[62] In two experiments they exposed random groups of subjects to either a film clip from a violent police drama or a clip from an exciting but nonviolent volleyball game. Both groups were then shown a videotaped scene of real aggression. The first experiment used children of both sexes as subjects, ages eight to ten. The real aggression film shown them portrayed preschoolers in a playroom who first exchanged derogatory comments and then hit each other and destroyed toys and furniture. Male and female college students were subjects in the second experiment. The real aggression film for them was an eighteen-minute unedited segment from news coverage of demonstrations during the 1968 Chicago Democratic National Convention. In the film police officers are shown clubbing and dragging injured demonstrators.

In both experiments skin resistance of subjects was measured continually. Results show that, with the exception of adult females, subjects who had previously watched the aggressive clip from the police drama were less aroused by the scenes of real aggression than subjects who were shown the control films. Also, for most subjects, the amount of TV violence viewed at home was negatively related to arousal while viewing aggression in the experimental sessions, a finding similar to that of Cline *et al.* According to the researchers, adult females were probably bored with the control (volleyball) film, and this boredom may have carried over to the riot film. This may explain why adult females in the control condition also showed low arousal when shown the aggression film.

These studies provide strong support that exposure to televised or filmed violence can desensitize viewers to violence. The related assumption that the lowering of anxiety associated with violence will make us more tolerant of violence and will make us more willing to engage in acts of violence has not been tested directly. However, there is indirect evidence supporting this assumption. Desensitized persons who have been "cured" of various phobic anxieties often are able to engage in behaviors that were previously avoided because of the anxiety.[63] Also, conditioned anxiety associated with violence can operate as a restraint against aggressive behavior.[64] It seems reasonable to conclude, then, that desensitization to violence resulting from repeated exposure to media violence can increase the probability of subsequent aggression by viewers.

## Aggression Catharsis

A radically different approach to the investigation of effects of televised violence is research on "symbolic aggression catharsis." Feshbach, the main proponent of this approach, suggests that "fantasy expression of hostility will partially reduce situationally induced aggression."[65] If this is true, then people who are ready to aggress against others because of anger or frustration will be "cleansed" of the aggressive drive by observing filmed or televised violence. The presentation of filmed violence allows viewers to participate vicariously in the violence, which results in a cathartic "draining off" of aggressive energy.

The aggression catharsis hypothesis obviously contradicts most of the work we have reviewed so far. Fortunately for the state of theory in this area, the hypothesis has found little support in research. Only two studies, both by

Feshbach, have shown that angered subjects were less "aggressive" after viewing a violent film as compared to a nonviolent film.[66] However, in both of these studies the measures of aggression were weak (a questionnaire) and the results are more easily explained by alternative interpretations.[67] We must conclude then, considering the weight of evidence in favor of social learning effects of televised violence on aggression, that observed violence does not lead to aggression catharsis.

## Evaluation of Research

Most studies on effects of televised violence have been laboratory experiments where the variables are rigidly controlled by the experimenter in artificial settings. This has the advantage of increasing internal validity—we can be sure that the relationships discovered are "true" within the context of the study. However, there are several weaknesses of laboratory studies on televised violence, most of which pertain to external validity. Some of these are the films used as stimulus materials, the low frequency of exposure to the violent films, the unnatural viewing situation, and the unnatural measures of aggression.[68] Let us briefly consider each of these criticisms.

Many studies use film clips showing extremely violent scenes from a movie or full-length television drama. The researchers assume that the violent film clip will have the same impact on viewers as the entire film. However, as Berkowitz *et al.* point out, this is a questionable assumption, since the type of plot, the events before and after the film clip, and the mood shifts produced by the film may affect subsequent viewer behaviors. Results from laboratory studies could therefore have limited generalizability.

Another problem is frequency of exposure. In the typical laboratory experiment subjects are given a single exposure to televised or filmed violence. In the real world, exposure to media violence is repeated over a long period to time. Of course, we could argue that if a single exposure can cause viewers to be more aggressive we can assume that repeated and prolonged exposure to violence will have an even more pronounced effect. However, this assumption needs to be tested more directly. It is possible that long-term and short-term effects of exposure to televised violence are not identical.

A third problem is that subjects in laboratory studies are usually shown the violent film clip in unnatural environments such as in the classroom or in research laboratories. Most people, of course, watch television at home. Also, most of us watch television in a group, usually with family members or friends. The effects of the viewing environment and other people in the viewing situation need to be clarified.

A fourth criticism is that the measures of aggression typically used in laboratory experiments, such as the delivery of electric shocks or noxious noises to others, and aggression against inanimate objects such as a Bobo doll do not represent the type of aggression we are likely to encounter in real life. This criticism, however, seems to be unwarranted. Several recent studies have shown that children who repeatedly hit a Bobo doll are judged by their peers to be typically aggressive in "real life,"[69] that adolescent boys who deliver electric shocks more frequently and more intensely are judged by counselors to be typically more aggressive,[70] and that children who are rated by their peers to be aggressive are more likely to deliver noxious noises to their peers than those who are rated to be nonaggressive.[71] These validation studies of aggression measures are important because we cannot allow our subjects to aggress "realistically" against each other in the laboratory.


## RESEARCH

Parke, Berkowitz, Leyens, West, and Sebastian[72] recently conducted a series of studies to minimize many of the problems commonly associated with laboratory investigations of televised violence effects. Their studies differed from previous ones in the following ways: (1) subjects were tested in naturalistic settings; (2) subjects were repeatedly exposed to the films; (3) commercially available, unedited films were used as stimulus materials; (4) the measures of aggression were interpersonal behaviors of the subjects as coded by trained observers in the subjects' normal daily environment.

Parke *et al.* conducted their filed experiments in a minimum security penal institution for juvenile offenders in Wisconsin. Subjects were boys in the institution, ages fourteen to eighteen years. The boys had been randomly assigned by the institution to cottages that were self-sufficient and self-contained. Thirty boys lived in each cottage.

The first experiment was conducted over a seven-week period. During the first three weeks, trained observers (college undergraduates at the University of Wisconsin) recorded the behavior of the boys in each of two cottages for about two hours a day on three consecutive days a week. After this initial phase, films were shown to the boys in their cottages every day for five days. Boys in one cottage saw an aggressive movie each evening, while boys in the other cottage watched a neutral, nonaggressive film. The aggressive movies were *The Chase, Death Rides a Horse, The Champion, Corruption,* and *Ride Beyond Vengeance.* The nonaggressive movies were *Buenna Serra Mrs. Campbell, Ride the Wild Surf, Countdown, Beach Blanket Bingo,* and *A Countess from Hong Kong.* An analysis of the films by the researchers indicated that the aggressive films contained more interpersonal, physical, and other forms of aggression, while the nonaggressive films showed more dancing and beach scenes.

On the day after the last film was shown, the boys were given the opportunity to deliver electric shocks to a confederate in the context of a learning experiment under angered or nonangered conditions. Subjects had been angered by a confederate who insulted them; in the nonangered condition the confederate gave the subjects neutral evaluations of a "commonsense" task.

The last phase of the study was a three-week observation period in which trained observers coded interpersonal behaviors of the boys on three consecutive evenings for each of three weeks. The following behaviors were coded: (1) general aggression, which included physical threat, physical attack, verbal aggression, noninterpersonal physical and verbal aggression, and physical and verbal self-aggression; (2) physical aggression; and (3) interpersonal verbal and physical aggression, which included only *interpersonal* physical attack and verbal aggression.

Results indicate that the boys rated the aggressive films as more brutal, violent, aggressive, and cruel than the neutral ones. However, the nonaggressive films were rated as less exciting, less likable, and more boring and silly. The two sets of films, therefore, differed not only in violence contents; the aggressive films were also more interesting than the neutral ones.

Analysis of the first measure of aggression, delivery of electric shocks, showed that the boys who viewed the aggressive movies were more aggressive following an insult than the boys in any of the other conditions. This finding supports previous research showing that increases in aggression are most likely to occur when subjects are both insulted and exposed to aggressive films.[73]

Analysis of interpersonal behaviors of the boys showed that, correcting for initial aggression levels, the boys who saw the aggressive movie were more aggressive than those who saw the neutral movies on all measures. Also, there was no apparent cumulative impact of the movies on aggression. The boys shown the aggressive films were just as aggressive after the first film as they were after the last film.

Parke and his associates conclude that exposure to film violence increases aggressive behavior by viewers. A second experiment using more interesting neutral films basically showed the same results. Since these studies were done in naturalistic settings using "natural" measures of aggression, they have better external validity than most laboratory studies. It is encouraging for the development of theory in this area that results from laboratory and field studies of the effects of televised violence are supportive of each other.

## CURRENT RESEARCH ON TELEVISION AND AGGRESSION

Researchers today are still interested in the effects of television viewing on aggression in viewers. Experimental studies have shown that exposure to television violence can cause short-term arousal and modeling or imitation effects. These experimental results are generally accepted by the research community. However, we are still studying the extent to which experimental results can be projected to the real world.

### Field Surveys

Most current studies use longitudinal field designs in which exposure to television violence, viewer aggression, and control variables are measured over a period of time ranging from one year to ten years.[74] Control variables often measured are aggression level at time 1 (initial aggression level) and family characteristics of the viewer such as self-described values, attitudes toward discipline and child rearing, and belief systems. Many of these studies have found significant and positive correlations between watching televised violence and subsequent aggressive behavior, even when other variables that might cause aggression are controlled for. Singer and Singer, for example, reported in 1983 that heavy viewing of aggressive action, adventure, and cartoon shows predicted later aggression in children, and that neither existing family aggression patterns nor aggression levels in children prior to viewing television violence could explain away these results.[75] A recent evaluation of television violence research offers this conclusion.

> Most television researchers look at the totality of evidence and conclude, as did the Surgeon General's advisory committee, that the convergence of most of the findings about televised violence and later aggressive behavior supports the positive conclusion of a causal relationship.[76]

We should be careful in accepting this conclusion unconditionally. A few recent studies using longitudinal designs offer contradictory evidence. Milavsky, Kessler, Stipp, and Rubens, after a three-year study of the development of aggressive patterns in elementary and high school children, found no significant association between exposure to violence in television and subsequent change in aggression.[77] Milavsky and his colleagues accept the laboratory findings indicating that short-term modeling effects probably exist. However, they believe that "these short-term effects found experimentally do not lead to stable patterns of aggression."

Field studies that show that there is a relationship between televised violence and aggression in viewers usually report small correlations ranging from .15 to .30.[78] Thus, in the typical field study, exposure to televised violence explains only 2.25 to 9 percent of subsequent viewer aggression.

What, then, are we to conclude about television violence and viewer aggression? In a recent article, Tan summarized a position that is gaining acceptance among television researchers.

> . . . the viewing of television violence is only one of the many factors that could lead to aggression in the real world. The relationship between exposure to televised violence and subsequent aggressive behavior is probably causal; however, this relationship cannot be expected to be substantial or to be a major explanation of aggression in the real world. From the viewpoint of social learning theory, to do so would be bad theoretical reasoning . . . .[79]

## Information Processing and Television Violence

Researchers today are adapting information-processing theories to explain how viewers are affected by television programs. They are studying formal structures of the programs as well as program contents. Levin and Anderson, for example, report that attention to segments in children's programs are related to high levels of physical activity, movement, and auditory changes in the programs.[80] In a 1981 study, Huston and her colleagues also found that constant action, change, and noise attracted the attention of children in commerical children's programs.[81]

Some researchers have investigated the extent to which children understand the meaning of television programs and specific acts presented within a narrative. They have found that young viewers (up to age eight years) are unable to infer implications and linkages between scenes in television programs. Collins, for example, reports that young children usually do not understand the context—such as motives and consequences—in which violent acts are presented in television.[82]

The trend in television research is to search for explanations of television effects instead of simply to identify these effects. We are also using cognitive and information-processing theories to explain how people use television.

## SUMMARY

In this chapter we reviewed research on televised violence and aggression from the perspective of social learning theory. Public and research attention has focused on the effects of television violence because TV is the most pervasive mass medium in the United States today. Content analyses of commercial television has shown that TV is violent, particularly those programs that children are likely to watch.

Research on the effects of televised or filmed violence supports the following conclusions.

1. Children can learn new and complex aggressive acts simply by observing those acts performed once by a model.
2. Media violence that is rewarded, not punished, or justified as vengeance or self-defense, is likely to elicit subsequent viewer aggression.
3. Incentives facilitate the actual performance of learned aggressive acts.
4. Viewers are more likely to imitate realistic aggression depicted in everyday settings as compared to fantasy aggression.
5. Aggression is more likely to be elicited by televised violence when aggressive cues are present in the postobservational environment and when this environment is similar to the setting of the observed violence.
6. Emotional arousal such as anger or frustration facilitates the performance of aggressive responses after exposure to televised or filmed violence.
7. Repeated exposure to media violence desensitizes audiences to violence. Desensitization makes people more tolerant of violence and makes them more willing to commit acts of violence.
8. Exposure to televised or filmed violence does not lead to aggression catharsis.

## REVIEW QUESTIONS

1. Discuss the weak and strong points of the definition of TV violence by Gerbner and Gross. Why have some TV networks objected to this definition?
2. When does TV violence lead to greater levels of aggression among viewers? When is there no effect?
3. Discuss how social learning theory can help us understand the relationships between TV violence and aggression among viewers.
4. Pick two studies discussed in this chapter. Evaluate the internal and external validity of these studies.

## ENDNOTES

1. Surgeon General's Scientific Advisory Committee, *Television and Growing Up: The Impact of Televised Violence,* Report to the Surgeon General, U.S. Public Health Service (Washington, D.C.: U.S. Government Printing Office, 1972).
2. See, for example, J. L. Singer, "Influence of Violence Portrayed in Television or Motion Pictures upon Overt Aggressive Behavior," in J. L. Singer (ed.), *The Control of Aggression and Violence: Cognitive and Physiological Factors* (New York: Academic Press, 1971), pp. 19–60.
3. See, for example, G. Comstock, S. Chaffee, W. Katzman, M. McCombs, and D. Roberts, *Television and Human Behavior* (New York: Columbia University Press, 1978).
4. *Ibid.*
5. A. C. Nielsen Company, *National Audience Demographics Report,* 1976.
6. The Roper Organization, *Trends in Public Attitudes toward Television and Other Mass Media, 1959-1974* (New York, 1975).
7. A. Szalai (ed.), *The Use of Time: Daily Activities of Urban and Suburban Populations in Twelve Countries* (The Hague: Mouton and Col, 1972), p. 580.
8. For a recent summary of this work, see G. Gerbner, L. Gross, M. Jackson-Beeck, S. Jeffries-Fox, and N. Signorilli, "Cultural Indicators: Violence Profile No. 9," *Journal of Communication, 28,* 1978, pp. 176–207.
9. *Ibid.*
10. See Comstock *et al., op. cit.,* pp. 64–83.
11. *Ibid.*
12. Gerbner *et al., op. cit.*
13. D. G. Clark and W. B. Blankenburg, "Trends in Violent Content in Selected Mass Media," in G. A. Comstock and E. Rubinstein (ed.), *Television and Social Behavior Vol. 1: Media and Control* (Washington, D.C.: U.S. Government Printing Office, 1972), pp. 188–243.
14. A. Bandura, D. Ross, and S. Ross, "Imitation of Film-Mediated Aggressive Models," *Journal of Abnormal and Social Psychology, 66,* 1963, pp. 3–11.
15. R. E. Goranson, "Media Violence and Aggressive Behavior," in L. Berkowitz (ed.), *Advances in Experimental Social Psychology,* Vol. 5 (New York: Academic Press, 1970), pp. 2–33.

16. D. J. Hicks, "Imitation and Retention of Film-Mediated Aggressive Peer and Adult Models," *Journal of Personality and Social Psychology, 2*, 1975, pp. 97–100.
17. A. Bandura and A. Huston, "Identification as a Process of Incidental Learning," *Journal of Abnormal and Social Psychology, 63*, 1961, pp. 311–318.
18. Surgeon General's Scientific Advisory Committee, *op. cit.*
19. See, for example, Bandura, Ross, and Ross, *op. cit,;* A. Bandura, "Influence of Models' Reinforcement Contingencies on the Acquisition of Imitative Responses," *Journal of Personality and Social Psychology, 1*, 1965, pp. 589–595.
20. See Comstock *et al., op. cit.*, pp. 211–238.
21. S. H. Chaffee and J. M. McLeod, "Adolescent Television Use in the Family Context," in G. A. Comstock and E. A. Rubinstein (eds.), *Television and Social Behavior Vol. 3: Television and Adolescent Aggressiveness* (Washington, D.C.: U.S. Government Printing Office, 1972), pp. 149–172.
22. A. Bandura, D. Ross, and S. Ross, "Vicarious Reinforcement and Imitative Learning," *Journal of Abnormal and Social Psychology, 67*, 1963, pp. 601–607.
23. Bandura, 1965, *op. cit.*
24. See, for example, L. Berkowitz, R. D. Parke, J. Leyens, and S. G. West, "Reactions of Juvenile Delinquents to 'Justified' and 'Less Justified' Movie Violence," *Journal of Research in Crime and Delinquency, 11*, 1974, pp. 16–24.
25. J. L. Hoyt, "Effect of Media Violence 'Justification' on Aggression," *Journal of Broadcasting, 14*, 1970, pp. 455–464.
26. *Ibid.*
27. O. N. Larsen *et al.*, "Goals and Goal-Achievement in Television Content: Models for Anomie?," *Sociological Inquiry, 33*, 1963, pp. 180–196.
28. Bandura, 1965, *op. cit.*
29. Hicks, *op. cit.*
30. S. Feshbach, "Reality and Fantasy in Filmed Violence," in J. P. Murray, E. Rubinstein, and G. A. Comstock (eds.), *Television and Social Behavior, Vol. 2: Television and Social Learning* (Washington, D.C.: U.S. Government Printing Office, 1972), pp. 318–345.
31. L. Berkowitz and J. T. Alioto, "The Meaning of an Observed Event as a Determinant of Its Aggressive Consequences," *Journal of Personality and Social Psychology, 28*, 1973, pp. 206–217.
32. Goranson, *op. cit.*
33. L. Meyerson, "The Effects of Filmed Aggression on the Aggressive Responses of High and Low Aggressive Subjects," Ph.D. dissertation, University of Iowa, 1966.
34. Goranson, *op. cit.*
35. L. Berkowitz and R. G. Geen, "Film Violence and the Cue Properties of Available Targets," *Journal of Personality and Social Psychology, 3*, 1966, pp. 525–530.
36. L. Berkowitz, "Some Aspects of Observed Aggression," *Journal of Personality and Social Psychology, 2*, 1965, pp. 359–369.
37. Berkowitz and Geen, *op. cit.*
38. R. Green and L. Berkowitz, "Name-Mediated Aggressive Cue Properties," *Journal of Personality, 34*, 1966, pp. 456–465.
39. Goranson, *op. cit.*
40. See, for example, A. Bandura, *Social Learning* (Englewood Cliffs, N.J.: Prentice-Hall, 1968); Comstock *et al., op. cit.* pp. 413–421.
41. Bandura, 1978, *op. cit.*
42. *Ibid.*

43. L. Berkowitz, "The Frustration-Aggression Hypothesis Revisited," in L. Berkowitz (ed.), *Roots of Aggression: A Re-Examination of the Frustration-Aggression Hypothesis* (New York: Atherton Press, 1968).
44. Comstock *et al., op. cit.*
45. See, for example, Geen and Berkowitz, *op. cit.*
46. Comstock *et al., op. cit.*
47. See, for example, D. J. Zillman, "Excitation Transfer in Communication-Mediated Aggressive Behavior," *Journal of Experimental Social Psychology, 7,* 1971, pp. 419–434.
48. A. F. Ax, "The Physiological Differentiation between Fear and Anger in Humans," *Psychosomatic Medicine, 15,* 1953, pp. 433–442.
49. J. M. Hunt, M. W. Cole, and E. Reis, "Situational Cues Distinguishing Anger, Fear, and Sorrow," *American Journal of Psychology, 71,* 1958, pp. 136–151.
50. A. Bandura, "Social Learning Theory of Aggression," *Journal of Communication, 28,* 1978, pp. 12–29.
51. H. T. Himmelweit, A. N. Oppenheim, and P. Vince, *Television and the Child* (London: Oxford University Press, 1958).
52. S. Berger, "Conditioning through Vicarious Instigation," *Psychological Review, 69,* 1962, pp. 405–456.
53. See, for example, R. Lazarus and E. Alfert, "The Short-Circuiting of Threat," *Journal of Abnormal and Social Psychology, 69,* 1964, pp. 195–205.
54. D. K. Osborn and R. C. Endsley, "Emotional Reactions of Young Children to TV Violence," *Child Development, 42,* 1971, pp. 321–331.
55. E. E. Maccoby, "Effects of the Mass Media," in M. Hoffman and L. W. Hoffman (eds.), *Review of Child Development Research,* Vol. 1 (New York: Russell Sage Foundation, 1964), pp. 323–348.
56. Goranson, *op. cit.*
57. J. Wolpe, *Psychotherapy by Reciprocal Inhibition* (Stanford, Calif.: Stanford University Press, 1958).
58. See A. Bandura, *Principles of Behavior Modification* (New York: Holt, Rinehart and Winston, 1969); A. Bandura, J. A. Grusec, and F. L. Menlove, "Vicarious Extinction of Avoidance Behavior," *Journal of Personality and Social Psychology, 5,* 1967, pp. 16–23; A. Bandura and F. Menlove, "Factors Determining Vicarious Extinction of Avoidance Behavior through Symbolic Modeling," *Journal of Personality and Social Psychology, 8,* 1968, pp. 99–108.
59. Bandura and Menlove, *op. cit.*
60. V. Cline, R. Croft, and S. Courrier, "Desensitization of Children to Television Violence," *Journal of Personality and Social Psychology, 27,* 1973, pp. 360–365.
61. Comstock *et al., op, cit.*
62. M. Thomas, R. Horton, E. Lippincott, and R. Drabman, "Desensitization to Portrayals of Real-Life Aggression as a Function of Exposure to Television Violence," *Journal of Personality and Social Psychology, 35,* 1977, pp. 450–458.
63. Bandura, 1969, *op. cit.*
64. A. Bandura, *Aggression: A Social Learning Analysis* (Englewood Cliffs, N.J.: Prentice-Hall, 1973).
65. S. Feshbach, "The Drive-Reducing Function of Fantasy Behavior," *Journal of Abnormal and Social Psychology, 50,* 1955, pp. 3–11.
66. *Ibid;* also S. Feshbach, "The Catharsis Effect: Research and Another View," in R. K. Baker and S. Ball (eds.), *Violence and the Media: A Staff Report to the National*

*Commission on the Causes of Prevention of Violence* (Washington, D.C.: U.S. Government Printing Office, 1969), pp. 461–472.

67. Goranson, *op. cit.*, p. 16.
68. These weaknesses are discussed by R. Parke, L. Berkowitz, J. Leyens, S. West, and R. Sebastian, "Some Effects of Violent and Nonviolent Movies on the Behavior of Juvenile Delinquents," in L. Berkowitz (ed.), *Advances in Experimental Social Psychology*, Vol. 10 (New York: Academic Press, 1977), pp. 135–172.
69. Parke *et al.*, *op. cit.* p. 139.
70. *Ibid.*, p. 140.
71. *Ibid.*
72. *Ibid.*, pp. 135–172.
73. *Ibid.*, p. 148.
74. Jerome Singer and Dorothy Singer, "Psychologists Look at Television," *American Psychologist, 38,* July 1983, pp. 826–834.
75. *Ibid.*
76. E. A. Rubinstein, "Television and Behavior: Conclusions of the 1982 NIMH Report and Their Policy Implications," *American Psychologist, 38,* 1983, pp. 820–825.
77. J. R. Milavsky, R. Kessler, H. Stipp, and W. S. Rubens, "Television and Aggression: Results of a Panel Study," in D. Pearl, L. Bouthilet, and J. Lazar (eds.), *Television and Behavior,* Vol. II (Washington, D.C.: U.S. Government Printing Office, 1982).
78. L. R. Huesmann, "Television Violence and Aggressive Behavior," in D. Pearl, L. Bouthilet, and J. Lazar (eds.), *Television and Behavior,* Vol. II (Washington, D.C.: U.S. Government Printing Office, 1982).
79. Alexis Tan, "Social Learning of Aggression," in J. Bryant and D. Zillman (eds.), *Perspectives on Media Effects* (Hillsdale, N.J.: Erlbaum, 1985, forthcoming).
80. S. R. Levin and D. R. Anderson, "The Development of Attention," *Journal of Communication, 26*(2), 1976, pp. 126–135.
81. A. Huston, J. Wright, E. Wartella, M. Rice, B. Watkins, T. Campbell, and R. Potts, "Communicating More Than Content: Formal Features of Children's Television Programs," *Journal of Communication, 3,* Summer 1981, pp. 32–48.
82. A. Andrew Collins, "Cognitive Processing in Television Viewing," in D. Pearl, L. Bouthilet, and J. Lazar (eds.), *Television and Behavior,* Vol. II (Washington, D.C.: U.S. Government Printing Office, 1982).

# 17

# EFFECTS OF MEDIA EROTICA

Erotic material in books, magazines, television, and the movies are often referred to as "obscenity" or "pornography." Most behavioral scientists define erotica as "sexually explicit" materials that can sexually arouse their audiences.[1] Erotica includes pictures or other illustrations of attractive naked young men and women, of attractive couples engaged in various sexual activity (such as intercourse, oral sex, and the like), and explicit verbal or literary descriptions of sexual activity.[2]

Public concern with erotica has focused on its possible harmful effects on audiences. There are widespread public beliefs, for example, that erotica "excites people sexually," "leads to a breakdown of morals," "leads people to commit rape," or "makes people sex crazy."[3] A large majority of the public also believes that erotica has long-term effects on sexual behaviors of people.

How valid are these beliefs? One of the major concerted efforts at empirically investigating the effects of erotica was the series of studies sponsored by the Commission on Obscenity and Pornography, which culminated in publication of *The Report of the Commission on Obscenity and Pornography* in 1971. Some of the major conclusions of these studies were the following.[4]

1. Even brief exposure to erotica sexually arouses most males and females.

2. Exposure to erotica elicits a variety of positive and negative emotional responses and other emotional reactions such as feelings of "impulsiveness," "jumpiness," and "restlessness" among a majority of men and women.

3. Exposure to erotica does not substantially change established patterns of premarital, marital, and extramarital coitus, homosexual activity, and sexual fantasy. These patterns of sexual behavior are generally well-established prior to exposure to erotica.

4. Among the sexually experienced, exposure to erotica leads to temporary (twenty-four to forty-eight hours) and slight increases in the frequencies of previously established patterns of masturbation, coitus, sexual dreams, fantasies, and conversation habits. There are few, if any, changes in overt sexual behaviors among the sexually inexperienced following exposure to erotic materials.

The commission concluded their review of the studies by stating: "Research to date thus provides no substantial basis for the belief that erotic materials constitute a primary or significant cause of the development of character deficits or that they operate as a significant determinative factor in causing crime and delinquency."[5]

In summary, the commission concluded that exposure to erotica results in both sexual and emotional arousal in men and women. Exposure affects sexual behaviors only temporarily, primarily among the sexually experienced, and following established patterns of these behaviors. Finally, there is no evidence that exposure to erotica leads to crime or delinquency.

Although the commission's findings offered little support for many of the public beliefs regarding the harmful effects of erotica, they did not surprise behavioral scientists investigating human sexuality. Previous studies had established that frequencies of coitus, homosexual behavior, masturbation, and other explicitly sexual behaviors are determined by many factors, among them social class, educational level, and religious practices.[6] Thus, it is not surprising that sexual behaviors that are determined primarily by social factors should be only temporarily and minimally affected by sexual and emotional arousal resulting from exposure to erotica.

More recently, research on effects of erotica has moved away from investigation of explicit sexual behaviors and has focused instead on aggression and sexually related but less explicit sexual behaviors as effects of sexual arousal. In this chapter, we will review some recent theories and research regarding the effects of erotica.

## EROTICA AND AGGRESSION

The notion that sexual and aggressive drives are related is not new. Freud suggested that sadism and masochism are frequent components in normal sexual relations and that desires to hurt or be hurt by one's sex partner are pathological only when they dominate normal sexual behaviors.[7] More recently, Berne has suggested that sexual pleasure in both men and women can be increased by the activation of aggressive motives.[8] Also, there is evidence that the arousal of aggressive drives is generally associated with the arousal of sexual drives and vice versa.

These researchers were concerned with the relationship between aggressive and sexual *drives*. Current research has extended the analysis to determine whether there is any relationship between sexual arousal and *overt* aggressive behavior. Some of the major theories in this area are reviewed in the following section.

### General Arousal Model

Bandura's social learning theory of aggression[9] suggests that any source of emotional arousal can facilitate aggression when individuals are "prone to behave aggressively." Sexual arousal resulting from exposure to erotica should therefore facilitate aggression when aggression is a strong or dominant response possibility for the individual after exposure to the sexual materials. For example, a person who is angered and who is then confronted with the source of his or her anger will more likely be aggressive than a person who is not angered. Thus, we can say that aggression will be a dominant response possibility for this angered person. Bandura's theory suggests that for such persons exposure to erotica will increase the probability of subsequent aggression. On the other hand, when aggression is not a dominant response possibility, sexual arousal may lead to nonaggressive responses. Since some of the responses activated by sexual arousal may be incompatible with aggression (such as sexual fantasies and overt lovemaking), sexual arousal in a nonangered person may inhibit subsequent aggressive behavior.

Tannenbaum and Zillmann use a similar analysis to explain the facilitative effects of sexual arousal on aggression.[10] To them, the critical process is "excitation transfer." Take a person who is predisposed to aggression (such as an angered person). Suppose this person is then exposed to erotica and is sexually aroused. According to Tannenbaum and Zillman's excitation-transfer model, this person, if placed in a situation where aggression is a strong, possible response (such as when appropriate targets of aggression are available), will label or interpret sexual arousal as anger and will therefore be more aggressive than if he or she had not been sexually aroused. Aggression is facilitated because the additional arousal resulting from exposure to erotica can "intensify feelings of anger and, ultimately, aggressive reactions."[11]

Support for the general arousal model is provided in research by Zillman and his associates.[12] Their major finding is that exposure to strong erotica, such as films depicting precoital and coital behaviors, can intensify aggressive reactions in angered male adults.

More recently, however, a series of studies by Baron and his associates[13] have shown that exposure to some kinds of erotica can actually *reduce* subsequent aggression. In one study[14] male subjects in two experimental groups were first strongly angered or not angered by a confederate of the experimenter. Subjects who were angered were insulted by the confederate, who also gave them several electric shocks in the context of a learning experiment. In the nonangered conditions subjects were given a very favorable evaluation by the confederate and were given only one electric shock, also in the context of a learning study. After these procedures, subjects were asked to examine and rate some stimuli that the experimenter "was planning to use in another experiment." Half of the subjects in the angered and nonangered conditions were shown pictures of extremely attractive, nude, young women to arouse them sexually. The other half saw pictures of scenery, furniture, and abstract art. After exposure to either the erotic or neutral pictures, subjects were told that they would be teachers in a learning experiment and that the confederate would be the "learner." The subject was then told that he could deliver anywhere from one to ten electric shocks for every error that the confederate made in the learning procedure. The confederate in all conditions had been previously instructed by the experimenter to make twenty errors.

Results indicate that, contrary to expectations, angered subjects exposed to the erotic pictures delivered less intense electric shocks to the confederate than angered subjects who had seen the neutral stimuli. The erotic pictures, however, did not influence aggression in the nonangered group. Baron concluded that exposure to erotic material inhibited subsequent aggression by men who had previously been angered by the victim. Similar conclusions have been reached by Baron and his colleagues from other studies.[15]

At first glance there seems to be a contradiction in results from two groups of studies. Zillmann and others have found that erotica facilitates aggression, while Baron and his colleagues have shown that erotica inhibits aggression. An important difference between the two sets of studies, however, is the type of erotic materials used as stimuli for sexual arousal. Most studies showing a facilitative effect of erotica on aggression use highly erotic films depicting precoital and coital behaviors. Studies showing that erotica can inhibit aggression, on the other hand, use milder forms of erotica, such as pictures of naked, attractive women. We can therefore expect that a higher level of sexual arousal will be elicited by the films as compared to pictures. The difference in degree of arousal and the emotions associated with arousal (whether positive or negative) are the main components of current models attempting to explain why erotica sometimes inhibits and at other times facilitates aggression. We will consider two of these models—an arousal and distraction explanation, and a "hedonic" model.

### Arousal and Distraction Model

Donnerstein, Donnerstein, and Evans[16] have proposed an arousal and distraction model of erotica effects. According to their model, all erotica have two effects. First, erotica can arouse people, and this sexual arousal facilitates aggression when aggression is the dominant possible response, as in angered subjects. This is also the main prediction of the general arousal model that we discussed in the preceding section. Second, erotica can induce "attentional shifts" resulting in distraction from the previous angered condition.[17] (Research on aggression and erotica assume that the effects will be observed only when subjects have been previously angered or have been otherwise predisposed to aggression.) Thus, erotica can also inhibit aggression by shifting or distracting the individual's attention away from previous anger instigation, allowing for the dissipation of anger and therefore of aggressive responses.

According to Donnerstein et al., mildly arousing stimuli such as *Playboy* pictures will result primarily in distraction. *Playboy* nudes have often been used in studies of erotica. However, according to Zuckerman in a review for the Commission on Obscenity and Pornography, "in this era of public nudity, such stimuli [*Playboy* nudes] may have become quite humdrum."[18] Mildly arousing sexual stimuli such as *Playboy* nudes will not elicit enough arousal from male subjects for the arousal to "spill over" and be labeled as anger when an opportunity to aggress against a tormentor comes. The main effect of such erotica will be inhibition of aggression, since the material can shift attention of the subject away from anger.

On the other hand, explicit films depicting intercourse and other sexaul activities will be highly arousing to most viewers. Although highly erotic films will also be distracting, the higher levels of arousal they elicit will not be easily dissipated and can be labeled as anger by previously angered subjects when they are given the opportunity to aggress against the source of anger. Thus, highly erotic stimuli should facilitate instead of inhibit aggression. These predictions hold only when subjects are angered *before* exposure to erotica. Only when they have been previously angered can subjects be distracted by mild erotica from the angered state.

To test these predictions, Donnerstein *et al.* exposed subjects to either neutral, mildly erotic, or highly erotic pictures. Subjects were exposed to one of these stimuli either *before* or *after* they had been *insulted* or *not insulted* by a confederate. The neutral pictures consisted of *Playboy* advertisements for book clubs, cigarettes, soft drinks, and other neutral material. The mildly erotic pictures were *Playboy* nudes and seminudes without complete frontal nudity. The highly erotic pictures were from an "adults only" magazine. These pictures showed complete female and male nudity and implied various sexual activities such as intercourse and oral-genital contact.

After exposure to one of these three stimuli, subjects were allowed to give electric shocks to the confederate in the context of a learning experiment. In support of their general arousal hypothesis, Donnerstein *et al.* found that for subjects who had been insulted (and therefore angered) *after* exposure to erotica the highly erotic pictures elicited more aggression (electric shocks) than either the mildly erotic or neutral pictures. Since subjects who had been angered after exposure to erotica could not be distracted from their angered state, the residual arousal from the highly erotic pictures was labeled as anger and thus instigated more aggression.

For subjects who were insulted *before* they were shown the pictures the mildly erotic pictures resulted in less aggression than either neutral or highly erotic pictures. Thus, mildly arousing sexual materials inhibited subsequent aggression because they were able to distract the subjects from their angered state. Donnerstein *et al.* interpret these results as supporting their arousal and distraction model of erotica effects.

## Hedonic Model

According to the hedonic model, the effects of erotica on aggression are mediated by the affective or emotional responses elicited by the material.[19] Some erotica elicit negative emotions such as disgust, nausea, and guilt. Other erotica result in positive emotions such as arousal labeled as pleasant and entertaining. The hedonic model proposes that exposure to erotic materials that are labeled as unpleasant and disgusting will enhance subsequent aggression among subjects predisposed to aggression (such as angered subjects). On the other hand, exposure to positively evaluated sexual materials will inhibit aggression among the angered subjects. Arousal that is disgusting and unpleasant is more readily labeled by angered subjects as anger, while arousal that is pleasant is less likely labeled as anger. Thus, pleasant sexual arousal will be incompatible with the previous arousal of anger. Anger and subsequent aggression should therefore dissipate, since it would be difficult for subjects to become angry again when confronted with the source of their anger while they are still immersed in pleasant arousal resulting from exposure to erotica.

Indirect evidence is provided for these predictions by Baron, who found that angered females showed increases in aggression after exposure to erotica that had previously inhibited aggression among males.[20] To reconcile these contradictory results for males and females, Baron points out that the erotic materials were labeled by females as disgusting and unpleasant, while males regarded them as positively exciting and pleasant. Thus, females were more likely to interpret their sexual arousal as anger when presented with the source of their anger, while the anger of males may have dissipated because of positive sexual arousal.

A more direct test of the hedonic model was provided by White in 1979.[21] Male college students were first either angered or not angered by the experimenter's confederate. In the angry condition the confederate gave the subject very unfavorable and insulting personality evaluations. In the nonangry condition the ratings given by the confederate were favorable. Subjects were then exposed to one of four sets of erotic stimuli while waiting for the equipment "to be set up for the rest of the experiment." Subjects were shown the stimuli on slides. The four sets of slides were (1) positive response pictures, consisting of mutual genital fondling, sexual intercourse, and mildly explicit fellatio; (2) ambivalent response—moderately explicit mutual oral-genital contact, fellatio, and cunnilingus; (3) negative response—same sex masturbation and highly explicit cunnilingus; (4) neutral response—clothed and partially clothed males and females standing alone or mutually involved in nonsexual activity. A pilot study had indicated that males exposed to the negative stimuli reported much greater disgust, anger, nausea, guilt, and self-disappointment than males shown the other stimuli. In contrast, males exposed to the positive stimuli reported that these pictures were more sexually arousing, more exciting, more entertaining, less boring, and more anxiety provoking than did males shown the other pictures.

After exposure to one set of slides, subjects were given the opportunity to give electric shocks to the confederate in the context of a learning experiment. As the "stimulator," the subject was to shock the confederate (the "responder") to help him memorize a list of words.

Results indicate that *angered* subjects exposed to positive erotic stimuli were less aggressive (delivered less intense shocks) toward the confederate that *angered* subjects exposed to either the neutral or negative stimuli and subjects in a control condition who had not been shown any slides. In contrast, subjects exposed to the negative erotic stimuli were more aggressive than subjects in the control condition. White concludes from these results that aggressive behavior is enhanced by erotic stimuli that is considered to be disgusting and unpleasant. In contrast, erotic stimuli considered to be entertaining and positively exciting reduces aggression among angered individuals even to a level below that of individuals who were never provoked.

## EROTICA AND LESS EXPLICIT SEXUAL BEHAVIORS

Griffitt, May, and Veitch suggest that the primary effect of erotica may be on sex-related behaviors that are "less socially and personally significant and less explicitly sexual than those involving coitus, masturbation, or homosexual activities."[22] Since most explicit sexual behaviors are determined by a number of social factors, erotica generally has been found to affect them only marginally. However, there are several other interpersonal behaviors that can be affected by sexual arousal from erotica. There is previous evidence, for example, that males who are active sexually will more likely rate photographs of women as sexually appealing compared to men who are less sexually active.[23] Also, sexually aroused males, compared to nonaroused males, rate women presented in photographs as more physically attractive.[24]

On the basis of these previous findings Griffitt *et al.* predicted that sexually aroused males and females will evaluate opposite-sex individuals more positively than same-sex individuals and that they will establish closer physical proximity and will visually attend more to opposite- than to same-sex individuals compared to males and females who are not sexually aroused. Thus, they predicted that sexual arousal will make a person more receptive to opposite-sex individuals visually, physically, and affectively.

Griffitt *et al.* tested these hypotheses in two studies.[25] In the first experiment male and female college students were first exposed either to erotic or nonerotic stimuli. The erotic material consisted of short literary passages describing various heterosexual, homosexual, and autosexual acts. The nonerotic materials were nonsexual literary passages. After recording their emotional reactions to these stimuli, subjects were requested to participate in "another" experiment on "interpersonal judgments." They were given an anonymous stranger's responses to a twenty-four item questionnaire and asked to record their evaluations of this stranger on an Interpersonal Judgment Scale. The only information given about the person to be evaluated was his or her sex. Half the subjects in each arousal condition were told that the person was of the same sex, while the other half was told that the person was of the opposite sex.

Results indicate that sexual arousal resulted in more positive evaluations of opposite-sex persons compared to same-sex persons, but only for female subjects. Sexual arousal did not affect evaluations by males. Affective reactions (whether positive or negative) to the erotic stimuli did not influence the evaluations. The researchers conclude that erotica-produced sexual arousal in females produced more favorable evaluations of opposite-sex persons who were not physically present. However, this tendency was not apparent in male subjects, probably because sexual arousal influences male's evaluations of females primarily on perceptual dimensions that are explicitly sexual instead of general.

In their second study Griffitt *et al.* first exposed subjects to either erotic or noncrotic slides. The erotic slides depicted various sexually explicit activities. The noncrotic slides showed various geometric patterns.

After rating their emotional reactions to the slides, subjects were requested to participate in another experiment "to determine how well untrained persons can administer intelligence tests." The subject was to be the tester, and two confederates of the experimenter, a male and female, were to be tested. Before actually testing the two confederates, the subject was asked to wait in a room where the two confederates were also waiting. The seating arrangement around a table was such that the subject had one of two choices: sit closer to the same-sex confederate or sit closer to the opposite-sex confederate. This was the measure of physical receptivity. Eye contact with the confederates while administering the test was the measure of visual receptivity.

Results indicate that sexually aroused subjects of both sexes were more visually receptive to opposite-sex than to same-sex persons. Aroused subjects looked more at opposite-sex persons than did nonaroused subjects. Sexually aroused subjects who responded negatively to the erotic stimuli physically avoided opposite-sex persons by sitting away from them. There were no other differences in choice of seating positions.

These two experiments provide some support for the general prediction that sexual arousal from erotica can affect less explicit sexual behaviors. This seems to be a promising area for future research, since we know little about it. Most studies of erotica effects have concentrated on explicit sexual behaviors and aggression.

We also need to know more about how erotica affects male attitudes toward, and perceptions of, women. As noted by the Presidential Commission on Obscenity and Pornography:

> It is often asserted that a distinguishing characteristic of sexually explicit materials is the degrading and demeaning portrayal of the role and status of the human female. It has been argued that erotic materials describe the female as a mere sexual object to be exploited and manipulated sexually.[26]

Preliminary evidence indicates that exposure by males to erotica does not make them more aggressive toward females than to males.[27] Also, exposure to erotica by males does not lead to an increase in "sex-calloused" attitudes or exploitative sexual behavior toward females or to an increase in aggressive verbal remarks toward females.[28] However, instead of focusing on aggression directed at females or on sexually explicit attitudes, researchers should be investigating the effects of exposure to erotica on male *perceptions* of the role of women in less sexually explicit behaviors.

## EROTICA AND RAPE

Recent research has studied the possible effects of exposure to erotica depicting violence, sadomasochism, bestiality, and rape on the potential for rape among male viewers. The focus of erotica research today is not on "standard erotica" but on violent pornography where participants are also depicted as victims. As Susan Gray pointed out in a 1982 review:[29]

> The key question in research on pornography is whether there is a link between exposure to pornography with sexually violent themes and either sexual violence or greater tolerance by societies of sexual violence.

Early studies did not show a relationship between exposure to violent or nonviolent erotica and the tendency to commit rape. Goldstein and Kant found that rapists and pedophiles (child molesters) admitted to a state hospital in California reported less exposure to erotica than the general male population.[30] They concluded from these results that erotica may perform an educational function for men during their formative years. Rapists and pedophiles seem to be deprived of information about sex; they seem to be less capable of defining what society considers to be "the normal sex act."

Recent laboratory studies provide some support for these early findings. A summary of these studies concluded that:[31]

> Laboratory studies have not demonstrated a strong link between sexual arousal and rape. Current thinking on sexual violence views rape less as a response to sexual arousal and more as an outgrowth of anger.

The evidence tells us that sexual arousal from exposure to erotica by itself does not lead to antisocial acts. The key instigator of sexual violence and nonsexual aggression is anger. Sexual arousal from erotica exposure, however, can increase aggression levels in males who are *already angry*. Aggression is not raised in males who had not been angered. The key question then is, "What causes men to be angry and then to commit violent sex crimes?" Researchers are trying to answer this question by studying instigators of anger in men who have committed violent sex crimes.[32]

Also, we recently have been concerned with how exposure to erotica affects attitudes toward rape and women in general. A recent study by Zillmann and Bryant provides some evidence on this question. Zillmann and Bryant exposed male and female college students to erotica at three levels—massive exposure, intermediate exposure, and no exposure.[33] Subjects in the massive-exposure condition saw six sexually explicit films per session, one session per week, over a six-week period. Subjects in the intermediate-exposure condition saw three erotic films and three nonerotic films per session, one session per week, over six weeks. Subjects in the no-exposure condition saw six nonerotic films per session, also one session per week over six weeks. The erotic films depicted heterosexual activities such as fellatio, cunnilingus, coitus, and anal intercourse. The erotic films did not depict activities that were coerced or that involved the infliction or reception of pain. The nonerotic films were "educational" films that had been judged to be "interesting." They did not depict or mention sex-related behaviors.

To measure their attitudes toward rape, subjects were given a newspaper account of a rape case in which a hitchhiker had been raped. The account reported that the rapist had been convicted, but the sentence was not given. Subjects were asked to recommend a sentence for the offender.

Subjects who had been exposed to massive doses of erotica recommended significantly shorter terms of imprisonment for the rapist than did subjects in the other two conditions. They recommended an average of 49.8 months imprisonment; intermediate-exposure subjects recommended 78.0 months; and no-exposure subjects recommended 94.6 months. There were no differences in the length of imprisonment recommended by males and females.

Zillmann and Bryant also reported these other findings.

1. Subjects in the massive-exposure condition gave higher estimates than subjects in the intermediate- and no-exposure conditions of people in the general population who engaged in various sex acts such as fellatio, cunnilingus, anal intercourse, group sex, sadomasochism, and bestiality.

2. At the end of the experiment, subjects in the massive-exposure condition considered pornography to be less offensive and objectionable than subjects in the intermediate- and no-exposure conditions.

3. Massive exposure to erotica increased male subjects' "callousness" toward women. Callousness was measured by "agree" responses to items such as "Pickups should expect to put out" "A man should find them, fool them, f—— them, and forget them," "A woman doesn't mean no unless she slaps you," and others. Men who were exposed to massive doses of erotica had the highest scores on this scale (23.8), followed by men in the intermediate-exposure condition (15.6), and men in the no-exposure condition (10.5).

Zillmann and Bryant's study looks at erotica effects that have not been thoroughly studied before. Also, it measures effects over a period of time (six weeks). Thus, we are given an indication of possible long-term effects of erotica on our attitudes toward rape, women, and erotica itself. Of course, their study involved only college students, and we should be careful in generalizing results to other populations. We can conclude from their study that massive exposure to erotica can "trivialize" rape, lead to a debasement of women, and lead to more permissive attitudes toward erotica among college students. Also, as the authors of the study put it, "Massive exposure to pornography produced visions of people doing more of anything pertaining to sex."

## SUMMARY

Erotica is defined as sexually explicit materials that can sexually arouse their audiences. Early research indicates that (1) even brief exposure to erotica sexually arouses most males and females; (2) exposure to erotica does not significantly affect established patterns of sexual activity; and (3) exposure to erotica is not a significant cause of crime or delinquency.

More recently, research on effects of erotica has focused on aggression and sexually related but less explicit sexual behaviors. The major theoretical models guiding this research are a general arousal model, an arousal and distraction model, and a hedonic model. Some of the major findings are the following.

1. Angered persons exposed to highly erotic pictures are subsequently more aggressive (deliver more electric shocks) toward the source of anger than persons exposed to neutral stimuli. Aggression is facilitated by highly erotic materials because the additional arousal is often labeled as anger and can therefore intensify feelings of anger and, ultimately, aggressive reactions.
2. Exposure to mildly erotic stimuli can inhibit subsequent aggressive behaviors in angered subjects by distracting them from their angered state.
3. Exposure to erotic materials that are labeled as unpleasant and disgusting facilitates aggression among persons predisposed to aggression (such as angered subjects), while exposure to positively evaluated erotica inhibits aggression. Sexual arousal that is disgusting and unpleasant is more readily labeled as anger. In contrast, pleasant arousal helps the subject to "forget" his or her previous angry state.
4. There is some tentative evidence that sexual arousal makes heterosexual men and women more receptive affectively, visually, and physically to opposite-sex persons.

## REVIEW QUESTIONS

1. What are some common public beliefs about the effects of exposure to "erotica?" Which of these beliefs are supported by research evidence?
2. Using one or more of the models discussed in this chapter (general arousal, arousal and distraction, and hedonic models), explain how exposure to erotica is related to aggression.
3. Take two studies discussed in this chapter. Evaluate the internal and external validity of these studies.

## ENDNOTES

1. See, for example, R. A. Baron, "The Aggression-Inhibiting Influence of Heightened Sexual Arousal," *Journal of Personality and Social Psychology, 30,* 1974, pp. 318–322.

2. See, for example, R. A. Baron and P. Bell, "Sexual Arousal and Aggression by Males: Effects of Type of Erotic Stimuli and Prior Provocation," *Journal of Personality and Social Psychology, 35,* 1977, pp. 79–87.
3. H. Abelson *et al.,* "Public Attitudes Toward and Experience with Erotic Material," *Technical Reports of the Commission on Obscenity and Pornography,* Vol. 6 (Washington, D.C.: U.S. Government Printing Office, 1971).
4. Commission on Obscenity and Pornography, *The Report of the Commission on Obscenity and Pornography* (Washington, D.C.: U.S. Government Printing Office, 1970); D. Byrne and J. Lamberth, "The Effect of Erotic Stimuli on Sex Arousal, Evaluative Responses, and Subsequent Behavior," *Technical Reports of the Commission on Obscenity and Pornography,* Vol. 8 (Washington, D.C.: U.S. Government Printing Office, 1971).
5. Commission on Obscenity and Pornography, 1970, *op cit.,* p. 243.
6. See, for example, A. Kinsey *et al., Sexual Behavior in the Human Female* (Philadelphia: W. B. Saunders, 1953).
7. S. Freud, *New Introductory Lectures on Psycho-Analysis* (New York: Norton, 1933).
8. E. Berne, *Games People Play* (New York: Grove Press, 1964).
9. A. Bandura, *Aggression: A Social Learning Analysis* (Englewood Cliffs, N.J.: Prentice-Hall, 1973).
10. P. H. Tannebaum and D. Zillmann, "Emotional Arousal in the Facilitation of Aggression through Communication," in L. Berkowitz (ed.), *Advances in Experimental Social Psychology,* Vol. 8 (New York: Academic Press, 1975).
11. D. Zillmann, "Excitation Transfer in Communication-Mediated Aggressive Behavior," *Journal of Experimental Social Psychology, 7,* 1971, pp. 419–434.
12. *Ibid.;* also D. Zillmann, J. Hoyt, and K. Day, "Strength and Duration of the Effect of Aggressive, Violent, and Erotic Communications on Subsequent Aggressive Behavior," *Communication Research, 1,* 1979, pp. 286–306; D. Zillmann and B. Sapolsky, "What Mediates the Effect of Mild Erotica on Annoyance and Hostile Behavior in Males?" *Journal of Personality and Social Psychology, 35,* 1977, pp. 587–596.
13. Baron, 1974, *op. cit.;* Baron and Bell, 1977, *op. cit.*
14. Baron, 1974, *op. cit.*
15. See, for example, R. A. Baron and P. A. Bell, "Effects of Heightened Sexual Arousal on Physical Aggression," *Proceedings of the American Psychological Association, 8,* 1973, pp. 171–172.
16. E. Donnerstein, M. Donnerstein, and R. Evans, "Erotic Stimuli and Aggression: Facilitation or Inhibition," *Journal of Personality and Social Psychology, 32,* 1975, pp. 237–244.
17. D. Zillman and R. Johnson, "Motivated Aggressiveness Perpetuated by Exposure to Aggressive Films and Reduced by Exposure to Nonagressive Films," *Journal of Research in Personality, 7,* 1973, pp. 261–276.
18. M. Zuckermann, "Physiological Measures of Sexual Arousal in the Human," in *Technical Reports of the Commission on Obscenity and Pornography,* Vol. 1 (Washington, D.C.: U.S. Government Printing Office, 1971).
19. Leonard White, "Erotica and Aggression: The Influence of Sexual Arousal, Positive Affect, and Negative Affect on Aggressive Behavior," *Journal of Personality and Social Psychology, 37,* 1979, pp. 591–601.
20. Baron and Bell, 1977, *op. cit.;* R. A. Baron, "Heightened Sexual Arousal and

Physical Aggression: An Extension to Females," *Journal of Research in Personality, 13*, 1979, pp. 91–102.

21. White, *op. cit.*
22. W. Griffitt, J. May, and R. Veitch, "Sexual Stimulation and Interpersonal Behavior: Heterosexual Evaluative Responses, Visual Behavior and Physical Proximity," *Journal of Personality and Social Psychology, 30*, 1974, pp. 367–377.
23. S. Epstein and R. Smith, "Thematic Apperception, Rorschach Content, and Ratings of Sexual Attractiveness of Women as Measures of the Sex Drive," *Journal of Consulting Psychology, 21*, 1957, pp. 473–478.
24. W. Stephan, E. Berscheid, and E. Walster, "Sexual Arousal and Heterosexual Perception," *Journal of Personality and Social Psychology, 20*, 1971, pp. 93–101.
25. Griffitt *et al., op. cit.*
26. Commission on Obscenity and Pornography, 1970, *op. cit.* p. 201.
27. Baron and Bell, 1977, *op. cit.*
28. D. L. Mosher, "Psychological Reactions to Pornographic Films," in *Technical Report of the Commission on Obscenity and Pornography*, Vol. 8 (Washington, D.C.: U.S. Government Printing Office, 1971); E. Donnerstein and G. Barrett, "Effects of Erotic Stimuli on Male Aggression toward Females," *Journal of Personality and Social Psychology, 36*, 1978, pp. 180–188.
29. Susan Gray, "Exposure to Pornography and Aggression Toward Women: The Case of the Angry Male," *Social Problems, 29*(4), 1982, pp. 387–396.
30. As reported in Gray, *op. cit.*
31. Gray, *op. cit.*
32. *Ibid.*
33. Dolf Zillmann and Jennings Bryant, "Pornography, Sexual Callousness, and the Trivialization of Rape," *Journal of Communication, 32*, Autumn 1982, pp. 10–21.

# 18

# PROSOCIAL EFFECTS OF TELEVISION

Social learning theory explains not only the acquisition of antisocial behaviors and values such as aggression but also the acquisition of behaviors and values that can have desirable effects on ourselves and those around us. The acquisition of desirable response tendencies is often referred to as "prosocial" learning. Prosocial learning includes two general categories—cognitive effects and behavioral effects. Cognitive prosocial effects include the learning of useful information and the development of cognitive skills such as perceptual discrimination, reasoning, and problem solving.[1] Behavioral prosocial effects include the performance of socially desirable acts such as helping others, altruism, controlling aggressive impulses, delaying gratification, persisting in a task, explaining feelings of self or others, resisting temptation (such as the temptation to cheat), adhering to rules, and expressing sympathy to others.[2]

The principles of prosocial learning are similar to those we used to explain the learning of antisocial responses such as aggression. The general principle, derived from Bandura's social learning theory, is that we can learn prosocial acts and values by simple observation of models. These models may be live or they may be presented on film or television. Learning prosocial responses involves attentional, retention, motor reproduction, and motivational processes. (For a review of these processes, see Chapter 15, "Learning from the Mass Media.")

As in our analysis of aggression, we will concentrate our discussion of prosocial learning on the effects of television, since TV is the most pervasive mass medium in our culture today. Let us now turn our attention to the two major categories of prosocial learning—cognitive effects and behavioral effects.

## PROSOCIAL COGNITIVE EFFECTS

The basic question regarding prosocial cognitive effects is, "Do children learn useful information from television?" There is considerable evidence that children can and do learn from television.[3] Young people's exposure to television newscasts and public affairs programs, for example, causes them to know more about public affairs. Information acquired from these programs covers a wide range of topics, including weather patterns, politics, and the Vietnam War.[4] According to a recent review of television research, "The least contestable generalization about the effects of television on young persons is that they learn from the medium."[5]

A related though more complicated issue is whether television can help children develop cognitive skills necessary to success in formal schooling. Most of the research in this area has focused on "Sesame Street," which was specifically developed to help three- to five-year-old children prepare for school.

"Sesame Street" was first shown in the United States in 1969. Today it is broadcast in its original-language version in more than forty countries and territories outside the United States. Eight foreign-language adaptations are also broadcast in nineteen countries.[6]

The general goal of the series is "school preparation," The specific goals are to aid preschoolers in developing skills with (1) symbolic processes, including the recognition of letters, numbers, geometric forms, and use of symbols; (2) cognitive organization, including perceptual discrimination, understanding relationships among objects and events, classifying, sorting, and ordering; (3) reasoning and problem solving; and (4) relating to the social and physical worlds.[7]

"Sesame Street" is probably the most evaluated television program anywhere in the world. The first large-scale analysis of the effects of the program was conducted by Ball and Bogatz in 1970.[8] This study was commissioned by the Children's Television Workshop, producers of the program. The major objective was to determine whether "Sesame Street" was meeting its stated objectives after one year on the air.

The sample for the Ball and Bogatz 1970 study consisted of 943 children, aged three to five. They came from four "disadvantaged" sites and one "advantaged" site. The disadvantaged children were sampled from the black inner-city sections of Durham and Boston, poor white areas of Boston, Phoenix, and rural Northern California, and a poor Hispanic area of Phoenix. The children were assigned to one of two conditions: a no-treatment control group and an experimental group that was visited weekly by members of the research staff. These weekly visits were designed to encourage viewing of "Sesame Street." During these visits children and parents were given toys, books, and games dealing with the show.

Ball and Bogatz used the "encouragement" method to stimulate viewing because they wanted to test the effects of "Sesame Street" in a naturalistic setting. Thus, most of the children in their sample were encouraged to watch the program at home, although some watched it at kindergarten school.

Ball and Bogatz used a battery of eight specially constructed tests to evaluate the effectiveness of the program. These tests were given to the children just before the first viewing season and again six months later. The test measured knowledge of body parts, letters, numbers, relations, sorting, forms, classification, and parts of whole. These topics were specifically covered in the programs during the six months between pre- and posttesting. Frequency of viewing "Sesame Street" was also measured.

Ball and Bogatz found that encouraged children watched "Sesame Street" more frequently than nonencouraged children, although some of the latter group also watched the program. Controlling for viewing of "Sesame Street" in the control group, they found that there were significant main effects for both encouragement and viewing on seven of the eight tests. This means that children who were encouraged scored higher in these tests than children who were not encouraged; also, children who watched the program more frequently scored higher in the tests than those who watched less frequently. When the children were analyzed by age to control for the possibility that higher viewers had cognitively matured at a faster rate than lower viewers, significant effects for viewing were evident in four of the eight tests—letters, numbers, classifications, and sorting.

Ball and Bogatz conclude from this study that encouragement increased viewing of "Sesame Street," which then increased learning gains of the children. Also, there were no differences between the program's effects on viewers who were boys or girls, blacks or whites, or on viewers at different levels of IQ, age, or socioeconomic status. Thus, "Sesame Street" was an effective teacher for all children.

Bogatz and Ball replicated their first-year study in 1971 with some minor changes.[9] First, only disadvantaged sites were sampled. Second, the Peabody Picture Vocabulary Test and a test of knowledge of social roles were administered before and after the six-month viewing period. The encouragement treatment was similar except that contact was on a monthly instead of weekly basis and was sometimes done by telephone. Nonencouraged children were sampled in sites where "Sesame Street" was available only on cable, thus minimizing viewing by these children.

In this second study encouraged and nonencouraged children did not differ in knowledge before the six-month viewing period. After six months, encouraged children watched "Sesame Street" more frequently than nonencouraged children. Encouraged children also scored higher on the cognitive tests, the Peabody Vocabulary Test, and the social roles test. Summing all of the tests to produce one measure of cognitive development, Bogatz and Ball found that viewing and encouragement independently contributed to learning gains and that the effects of viewing did not depend on encouragement. Children in the nonencouraged group who watched "Sesame Street" also scored higher on the tests than nonencouraged children who did not watch the program.

Diaz-Guerrero and Holtzman[10] evaluated the effects of "Sesame Street" ("Plaza Sésamo") in Mexico. Their subjects were 173 children in four separate day-care centers in Mexico City. The children, aged three to five, were from low-income families. They were randomly assigned to either experimental or control groups. Each of the experimental groups was shown "Plaza Sésamo." Children in the experimental groups were encouraged by a teacher-monitor to pay attention to the program. Children in the control group were not shown the program. They were also kept in the day-care centers two hours longer than the experimental group to minimize home viewing of the program.

Control and experimental groups were given a battery of cognitive tests seven weeks after the beginning of the "Plaza Sésamo" season (pretest) and six months after the first airing (posttest). The Spanish language tests were translated from those used by Ball and Bogatz. In addition, an embedded figures test and a test of oral comprehension were also administered.

Diaz-Guerrero and Holtzman found that the experimental children consistently scored higher on all tests than the control children. These results were observed for boys and girls and for all age groups.

It seems apparent from these studies that "Sesame Street" has facilitated the development of a wide range of cognitive skills among preschoolers. More recently, however, data from these studies have been reanalyzed, leading to somewhat different conclusions.

The main reevaluation of earlier "Sesame Street" studies was done by Cook and his associates.[11] Their major criticism of the Ball and Bogatz studies, as well as of the Diaz-Guerrero and Holtzman experiment, was that the effects of encouragement and viewing were confounded. That is, it was not clear whether increased viewing of "Sesame Street" would lead to learning gains if the children had not been encouraged to view the program. Also, they question the conclusion that "Sesame Street" was particularly more effective in preparing low-income children for school compared to middle- or higher-income children. This is an important issue, since one of the original goals of "Sesame Street" was to "narrow the gap" between low- and high-income children in their preparedness for school. After extensive reanalysis of the earlier data, Cook *et al.* came up with the following conclusions:[12]

1. Interpersonal encouragement combines with increased viewing of "Sesame Street" to facilitate growth among preschoolers in a variety of cognitive areas that are emphasized in the program.
2. The combined effects of encouragement and viewing were stronger and more general than were the effects of viewing without encouragement.
3. Viewing "Sesame Street" without encouragement results in some learning gains. However, these are relatively small compared to viewing with encouragement and are of limited generalizability.
4. "Sesame Street" has not narrowed the gap between advantaged (high- and middle-income) and disadvantaged (low-income) children in their development of cognitive skills.[13] In fact, there is evidence that "Sesame Street" is more helpful to advantaged children.[14]

We can see from this reevaluation that the major conclusions of the earlier studies are still supported, although to a lesser degree. "Sesame Street" has facilitated the development of cognitive skills among both disadvantaged and advantaged children. The gains in learning, however, are not as dramatic as earlier studies suggested and are greatest when the children are also encouraged to watch the program. This should not be surprising, considering our earlier discussions of learning theory. Encouragement, after all, is reinforcement for viewing. It is well known that reinforcement facilitates learning.

## LEARNING PROSOCIAL BEHAVIORS

We have demonstrated that children can and do learn useful cognitive skills from television. Most of these skills involve retention of information and do not require that the child act out what he or she has learned. As we have seen in an earlier chapter on social learning theory, we do not enact everything that we learn. The probability of action depends on motor reproduction skills of the learner, motivation, and opportunity for action. Thus, production of learned behaviors is a much more complicated process than learning of cognitive skills. Very often, however, our main concern is in action. We are interested, for example, in whether television can facilitate prosocial *behaviors,* such as helping or sharing.

Early studies based on social learning theory have clearly established that prosocial behaviors are enacted by children after exposure to a model depicting those behaviors. These studies show that children imitate rule adherence (as well as breaking of rules), altruism, helping, delay of gratification, persistence in task performance, and high performance standards when they are shown live or filmed models exhibiting these behaviors.[15] These studies were, for the most part, laboratory experiments. The modeling behaviors shown were simple and less complex than regular television programs. Also, behaviors measured were often identical with those observed and were measured immediately after exposure to the models.[16] Television programs and the conditions after viewing are obviously more complex than the stimuli and performance conditions in the early laboratory studies. If children are indeed able to learn and perform prosocial behaviors in the real world, we must show that they can learn these behaviors from more complex material in television programs and that they can generalize learning to other situations and over time.

Among the first investigations of prosocial behaviors in naturalistic settings was a series of studies by Friedrich and Stein.[17] They studied the effects of "Mister Roger's Neighborhood" on preschool children in nursery school settings. They compared children who were shown "Mister Roger's" with those shown neutral children's films and those shown aggressive cartoons. The children were observed before the television programs were shown, during a four-week period when the programs were shown three times a week, and for two weeks after the programs had been shown. Results indicate that children who saw the "Mister Rogers" programs persisted more in tasks and demonstrated more self-controlling behavior than children in the other two groups.

Children from low-income families who watched "Mister Rogers" also showed more prosocial interpersonal behavior such as cooperation, nurturance, and verbalization of feelings than low-income children in the other two viewing groups. These effects were not observed in high-income children. The increases in prosocial interpersonal behaviors among low-income children and in self-controlling and achievement behaviors of all children continued to some extent during the two weeks after viewing ended.

More recently, Friedrich and Stein[18] studied the effects of "Mister Rogers' Neighborhood" on learning and helping behaviors of preschoolers. Their subjects were seventy-three kindergarten children who were randomly divided into five groups. Four groups saw prosocial programs from "Mister Rogers' Neighborhood." Each segment lasted about twenty minutes and showed helping and "understanding others" behaviors. Each of these groups was also given a training session after viewing. The researchers reasoned that learning of prosocial behaviors from television could be facilitated by training, and they wanted to find out which training method would work best. The training conditions were verbal labeling, in which the themes were rehearsed using hand puppets; role playing and verbal labeling; and no training, in which children engaged in activity irrelevant to the program. A fifth control group saw the neutral television program and participated in irrelevant activity.

Three measures were taken following exposure to the television programs. Knowledge of the specific contents of the program was measured by a "content test," generalization of the program themes to other situations was measured by a "puppet test" and enactment of the learned behavior was measured by a behavioral index of helping another child.

Children shown the prosocial programs scored higher in the content test than children who watched the neutral film. All groups that received verbal-labeling or role playing training scored higher than the neutral group. Thus, children who saw the prosocial programs learned their content. Learning was also facilitated by verbal labeling and role playing. Girls who were given the verbal-labeling training learned more than girls in the other training conditions, but boys learned equally well from all methods of training.

Analysis of the puppet test showed that children exposed to the prosocial programs learned the specific content of those programs and generalized that learning to the puppet situation. Also, children shown the prosocial programs "helped" a puppet character more than children who watched the neutral program.

The last measure was an actual behavioral index of helping another child in a situation that was very different from the television programs and the training. On this measure exposure to the prosocial program plus role playing led to the most helping for boys and girls. Verbal-labeling training did not result in more helping by boys, but it enhanced helping by girls combined with the role-playing condition.

Friedrich and Stein conclude that children do learn the prosocial content of television programs and can generalize this learning to other situations. Also, both verbal labeling and role playing enhance learning and affect actual helping behavior. Last, but perhaps most important, prosocial programs led to increased helping behavior by boys and girls in situations similar to the program as well as in situations very different from the program.

Similar results are shown in a study by Poulos, Rubinstein, and Liebert.[19] Their subjects were first-grade children, fifteen boys and fifteen girls, from a middle-class, predominantly white public school. The children were randomly divided into three groups. Each group was shown one of the following television films: a prosocial "Lassie" episode in which a boy rescues a puppy from a mining shaft, a neutral "Lassie" episode that depicted the boy's attempts to avoid violin lessons and that had no reference to a human helping a dog; and an episode from "The Brady Bunch," which also did not depict helping behavior.

After viewing the films, the children were given the opportunity to "help" a dog and her puppies by pushing a "help" button. Pushing this button was a sacrifice for the child since it would have meant "less points" for a forthcoming prize. Results clearly show that subjects who saw the prosocial "Lassie" episode helped significantly more than those in the neutral "Lassie" or the "Brady Bunch" conditions. There were no differences in helping behavior of the children between the latter two groups.

Another potential prosocial effect of television is the enhancement of positive attitudes toward people from other groups, particularly other ethnic groups. In a unique study, Gorn, Goldberg, and Kanungo[20] attempted to determine whether educational television can change intergroup attitudes of children. Their subjects were 205 white English-Canadian children from two nursery schools. The boys and girls came from upper-middle-class backgrounds and ranged in age from three and a half to five and a half years. Pretesting indicated that the children strongly preferred playing with white instead of nonwhite children.

The children were shown one of several versions of a segment from "Sesame Street." One group saw the "Sesame Street" segment with inserts showing white and nonwhite (Oriental and Indian) children playing together in familiar settings, while two other groups saw the same segment but with inserts where *only nonwhites* played together in purely ethnic settings. In addition, some of the children saw an insert where the central character, Richard, spoke only French, and therefore was identifiable as a French-Canadian. Other children saw inserts in which Richard could not be identified as French Canadian, since he did not speak at all. A control group saw the same "Sesame Street" segment but without any of the inserts. Frequency of exposure was also varied. Some children saw the two inserts once, while others saw each of the two inserts twice. Thus, total exposure to the inserts was either two or four.

Immediately after viewing the programs, each child was shown two sets of photos taken from the inserts. One set showed white children only; the other set showed Oriental and Indian children. The child was then asked which group of children he or she would like the teacher to bring to the nursery school the next day. The child was also shown a picture of Richard and another child and was asked which of the two boys he or she would like the teacher to bring to the nursery school the next day.

Results indicate that children who saw the inserts with nonwhite children showed a marked preference for playing with the Oriental and Indian children, while children who did not see the inserts preferred to play with the white children. There were no differences in preferences between the group that saw the nonwhite children playing with whites and the group that saw only nonwhite children in purely ethnic settings. Frequency of exposure did not affect children's preferences for playmates.

The inserts showing Richard in a nonspeaking role and those where he spoke French resulted in increased preference for Richard as a playmate. Thus, both inserts of Richard produced more favorable reactions to Richard compared to the control group. There were no differences in preference for Richard between the two Richard inserts.

Gorn *et al.* conclude that even "minimal television exposure produced very clear-cut short-term attitude change toward televised children of other racial and ethnic groups."[21] They interpreted this finding as support for the principle of "mere exposure" leading to liking.[22] Since the television children were presented attractively, mere exposure to them led to liking by the viewers.

These findings are potentially significant, since they suggest that racial prejudice can be neutralized or eliminated by presenting the targets of prejudice attractively in television programs. However, we must be careful in equating children's preference for groups to be brought to their school with "liking" or with any other form of positive effect. It is, of course, possible that the children were expressing their "liking" for Richard and the nonwhite children by asking their teacher to bring them to school. However, it is also possible that they were simply expressing *curiosity* about these children. The effect of the inserts may have been to arouse curiosity of the children instead of to enhance positive attitudes. More direct tests of liking are obviously needed. In spite of this shortcoming, the Gorn *et al.* study provides promising results that warrant further investigation.

## PROSOCIAL ATTITUDES AND BELIEFS

The mass media can teach us to accept attitudes and beliefs that could be beneficial to ourselves and others. Examples are attitudes and beliefs dealing with equality between the sexes and among the races. Sex-role and ethnic stereotypes in the mass media can lead to negative expectations and self-images among the stereotyped groups. This is particularly true in specific belief areas such as career choices. Boys in the early elementary years express interest in three times as many occupations as girls of the same age.[23] Also, blacks have the same aspirations as whites, but they have less knowledge of the "rules" of the social system and of the strategies for extracting rewards from the system.[24] Early stereotyping restricts the career choices of women and members of some ethnic minority groups. There is a need to make children aware of their abilities and career opportunities, regardless of sex or race, so that negative stereotypes can be neutralized.

The National Institute of Education (NIE) in 1975 initiated the production of a television series that it hoped would "expand career awareness of 4th and 6th graders by making ethnicity and sex less significant predictors of pre-occupational (or occupational) knowledge, interests and preferences."[25] The NIE recognized that women and minorities were overrepresented in a narrow range of low-status occupations. It traced this problem partly to a lack of "career awareness" among children. Career awareness includes (1) knowledge of the skills and education required for particular careers; (2) interests and preferences such as liking of activities involved in a particular career; (3) values such as evaluations of attributes of careers; and (4) self-concepts or beliefs about one's ability to perform the activities of a particular career.

The NIE hoped that children who watched their series of television programs—which was called "Freestyle"—would "know more about and prefer or be interested in more non-traditional occupations than they were previously, and would hold less ethnic or stereotyped views of adult and occupational roles."[26]

The "Freestyle" series was produced for NIE by a Los Angeles public television station. "Freestyle" consisted of thirteen thirty-minute television shows that were geared towards breaking down career-role stereotypes based on sex and ethnic background. In addition to the program, printed materials for the children and their teachers were also prepared. These materials reinforced the message of the television programs.

Johnston, Ettema, and Davidson evaluated the effects of "Freestyle" on fourth, fifth, and sixth graders.[27] They tested three conditions: "school full," in which "Freestyle" was shown and the supporting materials were used with teacher involvement; "school view only," in which the programs were shown but supporting materials were not discussed; and "school control," in which neither the program nor supporting materials were made available to the children. Testing was done in Massachusetts, Missouri, Wisconsin, Michigan, and California.

As expected, the most significant effects were found in the "school-full" condition. Changes in this group were observed after a semester of exposure to "Freestyle" in the following beliefs and attitudes of the children.

1. Beliefs about boys in helping roles and girls doing mechanics.

2. Attitudes toward girls as leaders.

3. Beliefs about women in "male jobs" and men in "female jobs."

Johnston, Ettema, and Davidson concluded their evaluation with the following statement.[28]

When implemented under conditions of heavy viewing and extensive classroom discussion, FREESTYLE showed the capability of changing a large number of beliefs and attitudes regarding sex appropriate childhood behavior and adult and family roles. It was less successful in influencing the children's own interests in non-traditional endeavors. With the exception of girls in leadership roles it was noticeably ineffective in changing beliefs and attitudes regarding behavioral skills. Most of these skills are apparently too complex to be dealt with in any single television show and supporting classroom activities.

## SUMMARY

The learning of prosocial behaviors from television can be analyzed using Bandura's social learning theory. Learning prosocial responses involves attentional, retention, motor reproduction, and motivational processes. Some of the major research findings are the following:

1. Children do learn useful information from television. Exposure to television newscasts and public affairs programs increases public affairs knowledge of young people.
2. "Sesame Street" facilitates the development of cognitive skills among disadvantaged and advantaged preschool children. The gains in learning are greatest when children are encouraged by teachers or other adults to watch the program.
3. Children do learn the prosocial content of television programs and can generalize this learning to other situations. Prosocial programs can also increase subsequent prosocial behaviors such as helping and altruism by viewers.
4. Exposure to children of other racial and ethnic groups in television can lead children to express a preference for these groups as playmates.

## REVIEW QUESTIONS

1. According to Cook and his associates, what were the major weaknesses of the Ball and Bogatz "Sesame Street" studies? To what extent were conclusions from the Ball and Bogatz studies supported or changed by Cook's reevaluation?
2. Discuss two prosocial behaviors that children learn from the mass media.
3. Using the Gorn *et al.* study as a framework for analysis, discuss how television can be used in antiprejudice campaigns.
4. Take two studies discussed in this chapter and comment on their internal and external validity.

## ENDNOTES

1. G. S. Lesser, *Children and Television: Lessons from Sesame Street* (New York: Random House, 1974); E. Palmer, M. Chen, and G. Lesser, "Sesame Street: Patterns of International Adaptation," *Journal of Communication, 26,* 1976, pp. 109–123.
2. R. Poulos, E. Rubinstein, and R. Liebert, "Positive Social Learning," *Journal of Communication, 25,* 1975, pp. 90–97.
3. G. Comstock *et al., Television and Human Behavior* (New York: Columbia University Press, 1978), pp. 262–278.
4. *Ibid.*
5. *Ibid.*, p. 261.
6. Palmer *et al., op. cit.*
7. *Ibid.*
8. S. Ball and G. A. Bogatz, *The First Year of Sesame Street: An Evaluation* (Princeton, N. J.: Educational Testing Service, 1970).
9. G. A. Bogatz and S. Ball, *The Second Year of Sesame Street: A Continuing Evaluation* (Princeton, N.J.: Educational Testing Service, 1972).
10. R. Diaz-Guerrero and W. H. Holtzman, "Learning by Televised 'Plaza Sesamo' in Mexico," *Journal of Educational Psychology, 66,* 1974, pp. 632–643.
11. T. D. Cook *et al., Sesame Street Revisited* (New York: Russel Sage Foundation, 1975).
12. *Ibid.*
13. *Ibid.*
14. J. Minton, "The Impact of 'Sesame Street' on Readiness," *Sociology of Education, 48,* 1975, pp. 141–151.
15. See, for example, E. Staub, "The Use of Role Playing and Induction in Children's Learning of Helping and Sharing Behavior," *Child Development, 42,* 1971, pp. 805–816; G. Stein and J. Bryan, "The Effect of a Television Model upon Rule Adoption Behavior of Children," *Child Development, 43,* 1972, pp. 268–273; L. Friedrich and A. Stein, "Prosocial Television and Young Children: The Effects of Verbal Labeling and Role Playing on Learning and Behavior," *Child Development, 46,* 1975, pp. 27–38.
16. Friedrich and Stein, 1975, *op. cit.*
17. L. K. Friedrich and A. H. Stein, "Aggressive and Prosocial Television Programs and the Natural Behavior of Preschool Children," *Monographs of the Society for Research in Child Development, 38* (4, Serial No. 151), 1973.
18. Friedrich and Stein, 1975, *op. cit.*
19. Poulos, Rubinstein, and Liebert, *op cit.*
20. G. Gorn, M. E. Goldberg, and R. Kanungo, "The Role of Educational Television in Changing the Intergroup Attitudes of Children," *Child Development, 47,* 1976, pp. 277–280.
21. *Ibid.*, p. 280.
22. R. B. Zajonc, "Attitudinal Effects of Mere Exposure," *Journal of Personality and Social Psychology, 9* (monograph supplement), 1968, pp. 1–27.
23. D. J. Prediger, J. D. Roth, and R. J. Noeth, "A Nationwide Study of Student Career Development: A Summary of Results" (Iowa City: American College Testing Program, 1973).
24. T. Tomlinson and D. TenHouten, "System Awareness, Explotive Potential and Ascribed Status of Elites," paper presented to the American Psychological Association Annual Meeting, Montreal, 1973.

25. Jerome Johnston, James Ettema, and Terrence Davidson, *An Evaluation of Freestyle, A Television Series to Reduce Sex-Role Stereotypes* (Ann Arbor: Institute for Social Research, University of Michigan, 1980).
26. *Ibid.*
27. *Ibid.*
28. *Ibid.*

# 19

# CONSTRUCTION OF SOCIAL REALITY FROM THE MASS MEDIA

An important function of the mass media is to extend our knowledge of the environment beyond people, places, objects, and events that we can directly experience. As Walter Lippmann saw it in 1921: "The world that we have to deal with politically is out of reach, out of sight, out of mind. It has to be explored, reported, imagined."[1] Lippmann's observation holds true today, not only for the political world, but also for the world that we have to deal with socially. The mass media have made us aware of cultures, social issues, and events that few of us could experience directly. Thus we rely on the pictures presented in the media as guides for the construction of our own social realities.

The emphasis on the construction of social reality as an effect of mass communication is relatively new. This line of inquiry has been referred to as media "cultivation" or "enculturation" research.[2] The crucial question is not so much how the media affect specific attitudes or behaviors but how they affect audience conceptions of social reality. The basic assumption is that the media are able to determine our perceptions about the facts, norms, and values of society through selective presentations and by emphasizing certain themes. And since, for many, the media, particularly television, are the *main source* of information about the social and political environments, this influence can be quite pervasive.

Social learning theory explains not only our acquisition of specific information and response tendencies by observation, but also how such learning can be *generalized* to new situations. When we generalize information we have learned from a specific television program to our own social environment, the program has guided our construction of social reality. Thus, the principles of social learning theory can also be used to explain enculturation effects of the mass media.[3]

The typical research strategy in enculturation studies is first to map out a system or systems of media contents, using content analysis to identify predominant themes, characters, and relationships. The next step is to determine whether exposure to these content systems cultivates in audiences media-emphasized views of social reality. Media content systems that have recently been analyzed, primarily through the Cultural Indicators Project of Gerbner and Gross at the University of Pennsylvania, include the environment of television violence and stereotypical portrayals of women and ethnic minorities in TV news, entertainment, and commercials.[4] Research on the effects of these media content systems on social realities of audiences is in its infancy, and few studies have been published so far.

## TELEVISION VIOLENCE AND VIEWERS' FEAR OF CRIME

In a recent report on their Cultural Indicators Project Gerbner and Gross concluded that violence continues to be an integral part of television drama.[5] They define violence as "the overt expression of physical force, with or without a weapon, against self or others, compelling action against one's will on pain of being hurt or killed, or actually killing or hurting." Using this definition, they have been analyzing samples of prime-time and weekend morning dramatic programs on networks since 1967–1968. They have found that, on the average, eight out of every ten programs and six out of every ten major characters are involved in violence. Also on the average, there have been seven and a half episodes of violence per hour. Weekend daytime children's programs average eighteen violent episodes per hour.

In addition to coding the frequency of violence in television drama, Gerbner and Gross also have analyzed the environment in which violence takes place. They determine, for example, whether certain age, sex, and social groups are more likely to be victims of violence than other groups. Their studies over the past ten years show that certain groups are indeed more likely to be victims of violence than other groups. Likely victims include women of all ages, especially young adult and elderly women; young boys; nonwhites; foreigners; and members of the lower and upper social classes (but not members of middle social classes). The relative risks of female victimization have further increased over the years.

To Gerbner and Gross, the important research question is not whether viewing television violence leads to subsequent overt expressions of aggressive behavior among viewers, but whether television violence affects audience conceptions of social reality. They justify this emphasis with the observation that although TV violence may lead to aggression, imitative aggression among viewers is relatively "low level" and seldon has serious consequences for society. Serious cases of violence that are influenced by television violence, they claim, are rare. On the other hand, television may generate in audiences a fear of being victims of violence in the real world and a fear of the power of the few who are regularly portrayed as aggressors. This, Gerbner and Gross suggest, may be the most significant effect of television violence.

To test the hypothesis that patterns of TV violence affect conceptions of social reality held by viewers, Gerbner and Gross have interviewed adults, adolescents, and children in cities across the United States, dividing their respondents into groups of "heavy" and "light" viewers.[6] Heavy viewers are those whose frequency of viewing is above the median for the entire sample, while light viewers are those who view less than the median. Respondents are then asked questions about their perceptions of social reality, particularly about violence. They are asked, for example, to estimate their chances of involvement in violence, about fear of walking alone at night, perceived activities of the police, and mistrust of other persons. To each question, two sets of answers are offered. One set is based on facts or statistics in the real world; the other set is the television answer, which reflects the "facts" as depicted on television. The main prediction is that heavy viewers will more often give the television answer than light viewers.

In a recent survey Gerbner and Gross interviewed adolescents from New Jersey and New York City. Here are some of their results.[7]

Heavy viewers in both New York and New Jersey were more likely than light viewers to overestimate the number of people involved in violence and the proportion of people who commit serious crimes.

Heavy viewers in New Jersey were more likely than light viewers to feel that it is dangerous to walk alone in a city at night. Among New York respondents, this pattern existed for females, lower socioeconomic status students, low achievers, and those who have not been victims of crime.

Heavy viewers in New Jersey were more likely than light viewers to believe that police must often use force and violence at a scene of violence and that police officers who shoot at running persons actually hit them. Among New York respondents, heavy viewers were more likely than light viewers to overestimate the number of times a day that a police officer pulls out a gun.

Heavy viewers in New Jersey and New York were more likely than light viewers to say that people "are mostly looking out for themselves" instead of trying to be helpful and that one "can't be too careful in dealing with people," instead of saying that they can be trusted.

Gerbner and Gross conclude that heavy viewers do see the world as more violent and express more fear than do light viewers, even when demographic characteristics and use of other mass media are controlled for. Basically the same conclusions have been reached in surveys of adults in Philadelphia, Chicago, Los Angeles, and Dallas.[8]

There seems to be substantial support, then, for the enculturation hypothesis that exposure to TV violence affects our concepts of social reality. This finding has been replicated in various communities, controlling for a wide variety of variables such as age, sex, education, news reading, news magazine reading, prime-time viewing, and viewing of TV news.

Doob and Macdonald have suggested still another variable that should be controlled in studies of the cultivation effects of TV violence—the amount of crime in a viewer's neighborhood.[9] They suggest that the Gerbner and Gross results should be replicated across neighborhoods but that the relationship between TV viewing and fear of violence in the real world should be substantially eliminated or reduced when incidence of crime in the viewer's neighborhood is controlled for. Their reasoning for this prediction is quite simple: "People who watch a lot of television may have a greater fear of being victims of violent crimes because, in fact, they live in more violent neighborhoods."[10]

To test their hypothesis, Doob and Macdonald selected neighborhoods in Toronto, Canada, that were either high- or low-crime areas based on actual police figures. Respondents in these neighborhoods were interviewed door to door and were asked to estimate the likelihood of their being victims of violence as well as about their media use. Media use was broken down into measures of total TV viewing (number of programs watched), TV violence viewing (number of violent TV programs watched), viewing of TV news, listening to radio news, and newspaper reading.

Results indicate that people who lived in the high-crime areas were, in fact, more afraid than people in low-crime areas. Also, people in high-crime areas watched more television and tended to watch more violent television.

Pooling results for all neighborhoods, the findings of Gerbner and Gross were replicated: heavy viewers of television violence were more afraid than light viewers. However, when crime rate and other demographic variables are controlled for, there was no overall relationship between television viewing and fear of being a victim of crime. Doob and Macdonald conclude that television itself may not be a *direct* cause of people's fear of being victims of crime. The most likely cause of such a fear is incidence of crime in a person's neighborhood.

Although there seems to be some contradiction between this study and earlier surveys by Gerbner and Gross, we must point out that Doob and Macdonald did find significant correlations between viewing of TV violence and fear of crime in the high-crime area of Toronto. It is possible, therefore, that the relationship holds only, or primarily, in high-crime areas. One explanation is that television violence in police and other crime shows usually takes place in neighborhoods that are clearly depicted as high-crime areas. Thus, people in low-crime areas may not feel that television violence is relevant to them, while people in high-crime areas may recognize the cues in television violence more readily, since the aggressive cues in television violence and their own communities may be quite similar. As a result, viewers in high-crime areas are more likely to generalize from television violence to their own social realities.

## SEX STEREOTYPES IN TELEVISION

A number of recent studies has evaluated how males and females are portrayed in television entertainment programs. Analysis has included the frequency of female and male portrayals, occupational and social roles, and personal characteristics of male and female characters. Some of the major findings follow.

Males have consistently outnumbered females in television entertainment programs. In recent years males have been given 66 to 75 percent of all scripted parts.[11]

White males are portrayed in a wide variety of occupational roles that are highly professional, prestigious, and powerful, such as physicians, attorneys, detectives, and educators.[12] More often than not they are portrayed as being single.[13] Females, on the other hand, are often portrayed as unemployed, and in marital, romantic, and family roles.[14]

White males are often portrayed as aggressive, powerful, and controlling compared to female characters in prime-time television[15] and in daytime serials.[16] Also, males are depicted as more powerful, smart, rational, stable, and serious than females. In contrast, women are more attractive, sociable, warm, happy, and peaceful.[17] In children's programs males are often depicted as more aggressive, constructive, and succorant, while females are shown as more deferent than males and are often punished for high levels of activity.[18]

In biracial programs where at least one black character regularly appeared in a series, white males were portrayed as more likely than any other group to exert power over others.[19] The general portrait of the white male is powerful, forceful, rule breaking, independent, and rather callous. In these programs, white females were quite similar to black males. White females were not aggressive, often engaged in altruistic acts and in repairing damage caused to others, resisted temptation, and seldom delayed gratification, or persisted in tasks.

These results indicate that women have been stereotyped in television entertainment. It is clear that television women, for the most part, conform to the traditional female role—passive, weak, a sex object, and so on. But how do these portrayals affect audience perceptions of real-life roles?

Some researchers have studied how audience gender affects reactions to the media and how media contents affect sex-role expectations. In one of the early studies Maccoby and Wilson found that seventh graders were more likely to pay attention to and remember actions of same-sex characters.[20] Boys were also more likely to focus on aggressive media contents, while girls were more likely to pay attention to romantic scenes. In another study, Maccoby, Wilson, and Burton found that male viewers spent more time watching the hero and that female viewers paid more attention to the heroine in romantic scenes involving only the male and female leading characters.[21]

Not only do children focus more on same-sex models, they also pay more attention to and therefore learn more from same-sex roles. Hale *et al.,* for example, found that adolescent girls learned more from a film depicting a domestic situation than did adolescent boys.[22]

There is evidence that children use television portrayals of males and females as guides to appropriate sex-role behaviors in real life. Beuf found that over 70 percent of the boys and 73 percent of the girls in her samples chose stereotypical careers for themselves and that this tendency was stronger among heavy than among moderate television viewers.[23] Frueh and McGhee classified their subjects, children in grades two, four, and six, according to whether they were heavy television viewers (twenty-five hours or more per week) or light television viewers (ten hours or less per week).[24] They then administered the IT Scale, which measures the strength of traditional sex-role development, to all the children. High scores on the IT Scale indicate higher identification with traditional sex roles. Among their findings were the following: (1) high TV watchers scored higher on the scale than low TV watchers; (2) boys obtained higher scores than girls; and (3) higher scores were obtained with increasing age.

Television not only shapes stereotypical views of children regarding sex roles, it can also *change* those views. Atkin and Miller showed elementary-age children counter-sex-role models in television commercials.[25] This exposure was effective in altering the children's conceptions of real-life roles for males and females. Boys and girls in a group that saw two girls playing with racing cars, for example, were more likely than children in another group that saw two boys playing with the cars to say that it is appropriate for girls to play with cars.

O'Bryant and Corder-Bolz presented both sex stereotypic and counterstereotypic occupational roles to black children in specially produced TV commercials.[26] Their subjects were boys and girls, six to seven years old, from low-income families. In one set of commercials for "Zing" fruit juice, women were portrayed as having traditional female jobs such as telephone operator, fashion model, file clerk, and manicurist. In the reversed-role commercials, women were depicted in traditionally male jobs such as pharmacist, welder, butcher, and laborer. According to the 1970 U.S. Census, these occupations, which were relatively unfamiliar to the subjects, had at least 90 percent males or females. After the commercials were shown, the children were administered an Occupational Knowledge Test, representing the jobs depicted in the commercials, and an Occupational Preferences Test.

Both the traditional- and reversed-role groups learned about the occupations from the commercials. Their scores on the Occupational Knowledge Test were significantly higher than scores in a pretest administered four weeks before the study. Analysis of scores on the Occupational Preferences Test indicated that girls who saw women in reversed roles registered significantly greater preferences for male jobs after exposure to the television commercials compared to the girls who saw the traditional roles. Boys, however, preferred male jobs in both conditions. These results suggest that counterstereotypic portrayals did increase black girls' preferences for traditionally male jobs. For boys, viewing women working in traditionally male jobs did not affect their own job preferences.

In summary, we can conclude from the studies reviewed here that television has continued to portray females in traditional roles. Children are more likely to identify with, pay attention to, and learn from same-sex roles and models. Children use television as a guide to appropriate sex-role behaviors in real life. Finally, television can effectively change sex-role expectations of children.

## ETHNIC STEREOTYPES IN TELEVISION

The U. S. Commission on Civil Rights began a 1977 report on women and minorities in television with this statement:

> Throughout the early history of television programming, minorities were excluded from the screen except for certain stereotyped roles in programs of a particular type. Blacks appeared most often in comedy and variety shows; Native American roles were limited to the television western; Asian Americans appeared primarily in Fu Manchu and Charlie Chan movies. People of Spanish origin, usually Mexican Americans, appeared primarily as banditis in television westerns or in reruns of movies such as *The Treasure of the Sierra Madre*.[27]

Although there is recent evidence from scientific studies that television today has continued to perpetuate many of these stereotypes, particularly of blacks, early evidence supporting these charges were largely impressionistic. We do not mean to imply that these early charges were groundless; these impressionistic conclusions could have very well been supported by scientific research.

As pointed out in the 1977 report of the Civil Rights Commission, the National Association for the Advancement of Colored People (NAACP) demanded in 1951 that the early television series "Amos 'n Andy" be taken off the air because:

> It tends to strengthen the conclusion among uninformed and prejudiced people that Negroes are inferior, lazy, dumb and dishonest.

> Every character . . . is either a clown or a crook.

> Negro doctors are shown as quacks and thieves.

> Negro lawyers are shown as slippery cowards, ignorant of their profession and without ethics.

> Negro women are shown as cackling, screaming shrews, in big-mouth close-ups, using street slang, just short of vulgarity.

> All Negroes are shown as dodging work of any kind.[28]

In the 1950s and 1960s television was also criticized for its portrayal of Native Americans as "blood-thirsty savages" who are marauders and murderers. The Association on American Indian Affairs (AAIA), for example, criticized a number of television shows for their depiction of the American Indian:

> Indians are shown as drunken, cowardly outlaws. Indians are usually attacking wagon trains. Curiously, the Indians hardly, if ever, score a hit on the white men, whereas they are mowed down with ease. The resultant portrait indicates that the Indians are poor, inept fighters.

> In *Laramie,* Indians were often portrayed holding white girls captive, in addition to other brutal action. In *Overland Trail,* Native Americans were depicted as unbelievably stupid savages, believing in the most ridiculous witchcraft.[29]

The AAIA recommended that Native Americans be portrayed accurately by television.

> Accurate portrayal . . . requires that the American Indian be presented as a brave defender of his homeland and of a way of life as good and free and reverent as the life dreamed of by the immigrants who swarmed to these shores.[30]

The portrayals of Asian Americans in television and the movies also was criticized by some early writers. Paik wrote that "with rare exceptions, Asians are always portrayed as waiters, laundrymen, cooks, villains, warmongers, house servants, gardeners, and karate experts."[31] Asian women, according to Asian Americans for Fair Media, usually are depicted as "docile, submissive, and sexless," or as "exotic, sexy, and diabolical."[32]

More recently, analyses of ethnic minority portrayals in television and other media have used more objective, systematic methods. Many studies have focused on portrayals of blacks in television. For the most part, results have supported conclusions from the earlier impressionistic studies.

In 1970, blacks appeared in 46 percent of all TV programs and 10 percent of the commercials during a one-week period.[33] By 1973 blacks had declined in relative frequency of appearance and all but disappeared from the higher-status occupation and from most of the commonly portrayed occupations.[34] In the middle 1970s, from 6 to 9 percent of all characters in TV shows were black.[35] However, they were generally relegated to minor roles and the less prestigious occupations.[36] In 1977, half of all black characters in TV were concentrated in five situation comedies in which black characters were more stereotyped, lower in social status, and were presented more often in situations involving social and economic problems than blacks in programs with more integrated casts.[37] In comparison to white males, black males are often portrayed as neither forceful nor powerful in traditionally accepted ways in society.[38] The evidence indicates, then, that although there has been some improvement in both frequency and quality of portrayals of blacks in television, considerable stereotyping still occurs, particularly in the environments in which they are portrayed. Blacks, for example, are often depicted in low-income, low-status occupations and problem plagued families. Stereotyping is especially evident in shows where blacks are the major characters. These programs can be expected to attract more black viewers than other shows.

Recent evidence also shows that ethnic minorities are critical of their portrayals in television and newspapers. In one survey, blacks and Mexican-Americans were critical of the frequency, accuracy, and fairness of portrayals of their ethnic groups in television and newspapers.[39] Blacks were more critical than Mexican-Americans, and the more critical persons in both groups tended to have higher education, to be younger, and to have higher self-esteem than those who were not critical.

There is evidence that black children are more likely than white children to say that fictional black characters are like those they know in real life.[40] Also, black children are more likely than white children to identify with black television characters and are more likely to report that they learn from television about occupations, male and female roles, and about how black people dress, behave, and talk.[41]

It is clear then that black children use television to test reality. According to the enculturation hypothesis, their impressions of reality, and of themselves, may be heavily influenced by television.

Tan and Tan tested the hypothesis that negative media stereotyping of blacks in television affects self-concepts of black viewers.[42] There is considerable evidence that self-images are often determined by the expectations of others. Thus, Tan and Tan reasoned that negative black stereotypes in television will lead to negative self-images among blacks who are heavy television viewers. They interviewed 176 black adults and 157 white adults, asking them about their use of television. They also administered a scale to measure self-concept. Controlling for age, education, and other media use variables, heavy viewing of television entertainment programs was related to low self-esteem among blacks but not among whites. They concluded that constant exposure to TV entertainment programs in which blacks are typically absent or relegated to powerless, low-status roles can lead to low self-e' em among black viewers.[43] The correlational nature of their analysis precludes any definitive statement of a causal relationship, so this conclusion should be considered tentative.

In summary, we can conclude that ethnic minorities, particularly blacks, continue to be stereotyped in television. TV is an important source of knowledge about the real world for black children. Negative stereotypes may affect self-concepts of black viewers. There has been very little research to investigate the *effects* of ethnic stereotypes in the media on audiences, and more work needs to be done in this area.

## AFFLUENCE AND BEAUTY IN TELEVISION

Affluence and beauty are common themes in television entertainment and commercials. The affluence portrayed in television has been documented in commercials and programs with contemporary settings.[44] The emphasis on beauty and sex has recently been documented in network television commercials.[45] Let us briefly review the evidence regarding the existence of these themes in television and their effects on audiences.

### Affluence in Television

In 1953, Smythe found that most television programs presented middle-class characters in middle-class settings.[46] Gentile and Miller in 1961 reported that 93 percent of the characters appearing on twenty-six network programs were middle or upper class.[47] DeFleur analyzed the occupations of characters in 250 randomly selected programs with contemporary settings.[48] Most of these occupations were higher-status occupations, resulting in an underrepresentation of lower-status jobs. In 1976, Gerbner and Gross reported that most characters on television were from the middle and upper classes.[40] Fox and Philliber concluded that the middle-class characters who populate the world of television enjoy an affluent standard of living.[50]

Does television affect audience perceptions of affluence in the real world? To answer this question, Fox and Philliber interviewed 595 adults in Ohio in 1975.[51] The respondents were asked their amount of television viewing, the extent to which they perceived television to be accurately portraying the American way of life, and their perceptions of the amount of affluence in the United States. Perceptions of affluence were measured by asking each respondent to estimate the percentage of Americans who "can afford one major trip a year" "own a luxury car," are in the "upper-middle" or "upper" classes, "have homes which cost more than $40,000" "make an annual income over $25,000," "can afford a built-in swimming pool," and "belong to a country club."

Fox and Philliber had three predictions.

1. Affluence perceptions are positively related to amount of TV viewing.
2. Affluence perceptions are positively related to perceived accuracy of television in depicting life in America.
3. Affluence perceptions would relate most strongly to amount of TV viewing among people who perceive TV to be accurate.

None of these hypotheses was supported by the data. Although there were strong positive zero-order correlations between both amount of TV viewing and the perceived accuracy of TV with affluence perceptions, these relationships vanished when controls for socioeconomic status (SES) were introduced. This leads to the conclusion that the relationship between affluence perceptions and TV viewing and perceptions of TV accuracy are accounted for by SES, primarily education.

These results seem to contradict the Gerbner and Gross findings in 1976 that heavy TV viewers are more likely than light viewers to overestimate the proportion of American workers with professional or managerial jobs.[52] However, Fox and Philliber's assumption that total TV watching is a valid measure of exposure to TV affluence is questionable. More refined measures of exposure to television affluence are clearly needed. One approach is to break down viewing of TV programs according to the degree of affluence shown. The enculturation hypothesis regarding perceptions of affluence can be tested more rigidly with TV use measures that can discriminate between varying degrees of affluence in the programs.

## Beauty in Television

In 1977, Tan conducted a content analysis of all TV network advertising during prime time for one sample week to determine the frequency of "beauty" commercials.[53] Beauty ads were defined as those that used as selling points the desirability of sex appeal, youth, or beauty, and/or those in which sex appeal (physical attractiveness) of commercial actors or actresses was a selling point. Thus, a commercial that suggests that using a brand of toothpaste can add "sex appeal" to the user was classified a beauty commercial. So were commercials that used physically attractive models or testimonial givers. Over 31 percent of all commercials were coded as beauty ads. Intercoder reliability coefficients ranged from .70 to .92.

Tan used an experimental design to determine the effects of exposure to TV beauty ads on reality perceptions of viewers. His subjects were fifty-six high school girls ranging in age from sixteen to eighteen. The girls were divided randomly into two groups. One group was shown fifteen network commercials that had been previously determined by objective coders to be "beauty" ads according to the definition used in the content analysis. The other group was shown fifteen network commercials that had been rated to be "neutral" and that did not mention or suggest sex, youth, or beauty. The study was presented to the subjects as a test of advertising effectiveness. After they were shown the commercials, subjects were asked to answer a questionnaire regarding desirable qualities in various real-life roles. This part of the study was introduced as a "forgetting period." After this questionnaire, subjects were given another set of questions to measure ad recall and effectiveness.

Subjects who saw the "beauty" ads were more likely than subjects who saw the neutral commercials to give higher importance ratings to beauty characteristics for the roles "to be popular with men" and "for you, personally." Ratings of beauty characteristics did not differ significantly between the neutral and beauty ad groups for the roles "success in job or career" and "success as wife." These results were interpreted as partial support for the "cultivation" hypothesis. For highly personal roles, exposure to TV beauty ads caused adolescent girls to place more emphasis on beauty characteristics.

## CURRENT RESEARCH ON TELEVISION AND SOCIAL REALITY

Gerbner's early research on television and social reality has been criticized for lack of controls and for using controls only one at a time. Recent studies by

Gerbner and his colleagues have used more rigorous designs and analyses with multiple and simultaneous controls over time. Most of these studies, as summarized and evaluated by Pingree and Hawkins, continue to show a significant, but weak to moderate, relationship between television viewing and social reality.[54] Researchers are giving more attention to how people use television to construct social reality and to the conditions when effects are likely to occur.

## SUMMARY

The emphasis on the construction of social reality as an effect of mass communication is relatively new. The crucial question is not so much how the media affect specific attitudes or behaviors but how they affect audience perceptions of social reality. The basic assumption is that the media can determine our perceptions about the facts, norms, and values of society through selective presentations and by emphasizing certain themes. The principles of social learning theory can be used to explain such enculturation effects, which involve the generalization of information learned from the media to our own social environment. Some of the major research findings are the following.

1. Violence continues to be an integral part of television drama. On the average for the past ten years, eight out of every ten programs and six out of every ten major characters have been involved in violence.
2. The relative risks of female victimization in TV violence have increased over the years. Other commonly victimized groups are nonwhites, foreigners, and members of the lower and upper social classes.
3. Heavy TV viewers see the world as more violent and express more fear than do light viewers. This effect is more evident among viewers living in high-crime areas.
4. Women are generally shown on television in traditional roles—passive, weak, as sex objects, and in traditionally female occupations.
5. Children are more likely to identify with, pay attention to, and learn from same-sex roles and behaviors. Children use television as a guide to appropriate sex-role behaviors in real life. TV can effectively change sex-role expectations of children.
6. Ethnic minorities, particularly blacks, continue to be stereotyped in television. TV is an important source of knowledge about the real world for black children. Negative stereotypes may affect self-concepts of heavy TV viewers among blacks.
7. Affluence and beauty are common themes in television entertainment and commercials. Tentative evidence indicates that heavy TV viewing does not affect viewers' perceptions of affluence in the real world. Exposure to beauty commercials causes adolescent girls to place more importance on beauty-related characteristics in real-life, highly personal roles.

## REVIEW QUESTIONS

1. Using social learning theory as a framework for analysis, discuss how the mass media have affected audience perceptions of the following "social realities": fear of crime, sex stereotypes, ethnic stereotypes, perceptions of affluence in real life, and perceptions of the importance of beauty in role relationships.
2. Evaluate the internal and external validity of two studies discussed in this chapter.
3. Look through messages in the mass media and pick out examples of the following: (*a*) messages in which violence is the main theme; (*b*) messages that stereotype women in "traditional" roles; (*c*) messages that stereotype an ethnic group; (*d*) messages that emphasize the importance of "beauty" and affluence in social relationships.

## ENDNOTES

1. W. Lippmann, "The World Outside and the Pictures in Our Heads," in W. Schramm and D. Roberts (eds.), *The Process and Effects of Mass Communication,* 2nd ed. (Urbana: University of Illinois Press, 1971), p. 284.
2. Among the main proponents of this approach are G. Gerbner *et al.,* "Cultural Indicators: Violence Profile No. 9," *Journal of Communications, 28,* 1978, pp. 176–207.
3. A Bandura, *Social Learning Theory* (Englewood Cliffs, N.J.: Prentice-Hall, 1977).
4. For a recent summary of their work, see Gerbner *et al., op. cit.*
5. *Ibid.*
6. *Ibid.*
7. *Ibid.*
8. *Ibid.*
9. A. Doob and G. Macdonald, "Television Viewing and Fear of Victimization: Is the Relationship Causal?" *Journal of Personality and Social Psychology, 37,* 1979, pp. 170–179.
10. *Ibid,* p. 171.
11. P. Donagher, R. Poulos, R. Liebert, and E. Davidson, "Race, Sex and Social Example: An Analysis of Character Portrayals on Inter-Racial Television Entertainment," *Psychological Reports, 7,* 1975, pp. 1023–1034.
12. *Ibid.*
13. G. Gerbner, "Violence in Television Drama: Trends and Symbolic Functions," in G. A. Comstock and E. A. Rubinstein (eds.), *Television and Social Behavior, Vol. 1: Media Content and Control* (Washington, D.C.: U.S. Government Printing Office, 1972), pp. 28–182.
14. N. S. Tedesco, "Patterns in Prime Time," *Journal of Communication, 24,* 1974, pp. 119–124.
15. Gerbner, 1972, *op. cit.*
16. J. Turrow, "Advising and Ordering: Daytime, Prime Time," *Journal of Communication, 24,* 1974, pp. 138–141.

17. Tedesco, *op. cit.*
18. Donagher *et al., op. cit.*
19. *Ibid.*
20. E. Maccoby and W. C. Wilson, "Identification and Observational Learning from Films," *Journal of Abnormal and Social Psychology, 55,* 1957, pp. 76–87.
21. E. Maccoby, W. C. Wilson, and R. V. Burton, "Differential Movie-Viewing Behavior of Male and Female Viewers," *Journal of Personality, 26,* 1958, pp. 259–267.
22. G. A. Hale, L. K. Miller, and H. W. Stevenson, "Incidental Learning of Film Content: A Developmental Study," *Child Development, 39,* 1968, pp. 69–77.
23. Ann Beuf, "Doctor, Lawyer, Household Drudge," *Journal of Communication, 24,* 1974, pp. 142–145.
24. P. E. McGhee, "Television as a Source of Learning Stereotyped Sex Roles," paper presented at Biennial Meeting of the Society of Research in Child Development, Denver, April 1975; also T. Frueh and P. McGhee, "Traditional Sex Role Development and Amount of Time Spent Watching Television," *Developmental Psychology, 11,* 1975, p. 109.
25. C. Atkin and M. Miller, "The Effects of Television Advertising on Children: Experimental Evidence," paper presented to the International Communication Association, Chicago, April 1975.
26. S. O'Bryant and C. R. Corder-Bolz, "Black Children's Learning of Work Roles from Television Commercials," *Psychological Reports, 42,* 1978, pp. 227–330.
27. U. S. Commission on Civil Rights, *Window Dressing on the Set: Women and Minorities in Television* (Washington D.C.: U.S. Government Printing Office, 1977), p. 4.
28. *Ibid.*
29. *Ibid,* p. 6.
30. *Ibid,* p. 7.
31. *Ibid,* p. 7.
32. *Ibid,* p. 8.
33. C. Roberts, "The Portrayal of Blacks on Network TV," *Journal of Broadcasting, 15,* 1971, pp. 45–54.
34. H. Northcott, J. Seggar, and J. Hinton, "Trends in TV Portrayals of Blacks and Women," *Journalism Quarterly, 55,* 1975, pp. 741–744.
35. C. O'Kelly and L. Bloomquist, "Women and Blacks on TV," *Journal of Communication, 26,* 1976, pp. 179–184.
36. J. Lemon, "Women and Blacks on Prime-Time Television," *Journal of Communication, 27,* 1977, pp. 70–79.
37. C. Banks-McGhee, "A Content Analysis of the Treatment of Black Americans on Television," *Social Education, 41,* 1977, pp. 336–339; also B. S. Greenberg and C. Atkin, "Learning about Minorities from Television," paper presented to the Association for Education in Journalism, Seattle, August 1978.
38. Donagher *et al., op. cit.*
39. A. Tan, "Evaluation of Newspapers and Television by Blacks and Mexican-Americans," *Journalism Quarterly, 55,* 1978, pp. 673–681.
40. B. Greenberg, "Children's Reactions to TV Blacks," *Journalism Quarterly, 49,* 1972, pp. 5–14.
41. *Ibid.*
42. A. Tan and G. Tan, "Television Use and Self-Esteem of Blacks," *Journal of Communication, 29,* 1979, pp. 129–135.
43. *Ibid.*

44. See W. Fox and W. Philliber, "Television Viewing and the Perception of Affluence," *Sociological Quarterly, 19,* 1979, pp. 103–112.
45. A. Tan, "TV Beauty Ads and Role Expectations of Adolescent Female Viewers," *Journalism Quarterly, 56,* 1979, pp. 283–288.
46. D. Smythe, "Reality as Presented on Television," *Public Opinion Quarterly, 18,* 1954, pp. 143–156.
47. F. Gentile and S. M. Miller, "Television and Social Class," *Sociology and Social Research, 45,* 1961, pp. 259–264.
48. M. DeFleur, "Occupational Roles as Portrayed on Television," *Public Opinion Quarterly, 28,* 1964, pp. 57–74.
49. G. Gerbner and L. Gross, "Living with Television: The Violence Profile," *Journal of Communication, 26,* 1976, pp. 172–199.
50. Fox and Philliber, *op. cit.*
51. *Ibid.*
52. Gerbner and Gross, *op cit.*
53. Tan, 1979, *op. cit.*
54. Robert P. Hawkins and Suzanne Pingree, "Television's Influence on Social Reality," in D. Pearl, L. Bouthilet, and J. Lazar (eds.), *Television and Behavior,* Vol. II (Washington, D.C.: U.S. Government Printing Office, 1982).

# 20

# MASS COMMUNICATION AND POLITICAL SOCIALIZATION

How do we learn our political attitudes, values, and behaviors? This is the main question in political socialization research. Political socialization is typically defined either in terms of the outcomes or the process. Definitions stressing the outcomes of socialization identify not only the sources of influence, but also the *nature* of influence, which is often assumed to be in the direction of support for and stabilization of the existing political system. Consider the following representative "outcome" definitions.

> Socialization refers to . . . the process by which a junior member of a group or institution is taught its values, attitudes and other behaviors.[1]

> Political socialization refers to the learning process by which the political norms and behaviors acceptable to an ongoing political system are transmitted from generation to generation.[2]

> The importance of such a formation (of politics as learned behavior) to understanding the stability of political systems is self-evident—humans must learn their political behavior early and well and persist in it. Otherwise there would be no regularity, perhaps even chaos.[3]

We can see from these definitions that the concern is learning of attitudes, values, and behaviors that support the existing system and therefore help perpetuate it. This definition has recently been criticized as being too narrow, since it does not provide for *change* in a system. Easton and Dennis, among others, suggest that a system can change and still persist.[4] Members of a political system need not always share the same political values and behaviors. Take, for example, the disagreement over the Vietnam War in the late 1960s. Disagreement, however, does not necessarily lead to the disintegration of the system. A more realistic definition, according to the proponents of the "process" view, is to consider political socialization as "those developmental processes through which persons acquire political orientations and patterns of behavior."[5] Thus the emphasis is on *how* we acquire political attitudes and behaviors over time, regardless of what those attitudes or behaviors may be.

Recent surveys have indicated that segments of the population differ signifi-cantly on political orientations such as perceived political efficacy, political trust, confidence in political institutions, and strength of party affiliation.[6] Thus, the process definition of political socialization seems to be the most viable and appropriate for modern times. We will use this definition in our discussion of mass communication and political socialization in this chapter.

Political socialization is concerned with how we acquire or learn political cognitions, political affect, and political behaviors. Political cognitions refer to knowledge of the political system—its institutions, authorities, and practices. Included here would be knowledge of campaign issues and candidates during an election and general public affairs. Political affect is how we feel about the system. Some common affect variables are political support and political efficacy. Political support is defined by Easton and Dennis as "feelings of trust, confidence or affection" for the political community, regime or au-thorities.[7] Political efficacy is "the feeling that individual political action does have, or can have, an impact on the political process, i.e., that it is worthwhile to perform one's civic duties. It is the feeling that political and social change is possible, and that the individual citizen can play a part in bringing about the change."[8]

Political behaviors are synonymous with political participation, which is the behavioral component of political efficacy. Examples are voting and active participation in an election campaign. Political participation also includes be-haviors that are not related to elections, such as participation in political demonstrations and rallies, and membership in political organizations.

Traditionally, political socialization research has considered the family, school, and social groups as the primary agents of influence. More recently, the mass media have been studied as sources of political cognitions, affect, and behaviors. We will limit our discussion in this chapter to theoretical for-mulations that can explain the role of mass communication in political so-cialization. We will not attempt to review all, or even most, of the relevant research, since several competent reviews are currently available.[9] Our main objective is to present some of the general findings using an integrated the-oretical framework. We begin by discussing this theoretical framework—so-cial learning theory.

## POLITICAL SOCIALIZATION AS SOCIAL LEARNING

How do we learn political opinions, values, and behaviors? We learn them in the same way that we learn other social behaviors—either by direct experi-ence or by observational learning. Very few of us are exposed early in life to direct experiences with political institutions and authorities. Much of what we learn about political attitudes and behaviors has to be "taught" us by teachers and models, either purposefully or incidentally. This, as we have seen, is a basic assumption of social learning theory.

Although there has been some recent emphasis on psychoanalytic and biological models in political socialization research, social learning theory has provided the field with its dominant models of political learning.[10] Jennings and Niemi, for example, conclude that:

> The older psychological formulation which most reflects our thinking is what Bandura and his associates have come to call observational learning . . . principally modeling, but also matching, imitation, copying, contagion, cue-taking and identification.[11]

According to social learning theory, we learn political attitudes and behaviors from models that are frequently encountered and when we are rewarded, either extrinsically or intrinsically, for imitating the model. Parents and peers, of course, are models that we encounter often, especially early in life. According to Rohter, "the child comes to copy diverse responses performed by his parent because he is consistently and potently reinforced for such behavior."[12] Jennings and Niemi, however, suggest that political socialization in the home is very often "low-keyed and haphazard" and that imitation of political behaviors of parents is only infrequently reinforced.[13] However, infrequent external reinforcements do not prevent the copying of parental political behaviors by their children, since parental imitation in itself may be *intrinsically* rewarding. If the child is extrinsically rewarded for copying nonpolitical behaviors of his or her parents, the positive effect produced by these rewards may be generalized to imitation of behaviors that are not explicitly rewarded. Another important factor in social learning is the homogeneity of behaviors displayed. It is more common for parents to agree on political behaviors than to disagree. Jennings and Niemi have observed that, "almost without exception, the child is more likely to reflect one parent's orientation when the orientation is also shared by the other parent."[14]

Social learning theory can also explain the influence of peers on our political attitudes and behaviors. To Dawson and Prewitt, "the close correspondence in political outlooks among peers and associates seems to indicate that imitation of some sort serves as a means of socialization within relationships."[15] Similarly, Cook and Scioli explain the influence of reference groups in Newcomb's Bennington study in terms of reinforcement: "Conformity to group norms results in group praise (positive reinforcement) and deviation from approved behavior results in group sanctions or the deprivation of group values (negative reinforcement)."[16]

It is clear then that social learning principles can explain the influence of parents and peers in political socialization. Can the same principles be used to explain the influence of the mass media? We now turn to our rationale for ascribing to the mass media a similar influence in political socialization.

## LEARNING POLITICAL ATTITUDES AND BEHAVIORS FROM THE MASS MEDIA

To establish the role of the mass media in political socialization from a social learning perspective, we must show that the media are readily available to and used by prospective learners, that media contents deal directly with political orientations (the responses to be learned), and that learning of these contents will lead to intrinsic or extrinsic rewards in learners. Since a primary concern of socialization research is how political impressions are formed in the *tabula rasa,* much of the discussion that follows concerns the potential influence of the media on children. It is well established that political beliefs and behaviors are learned early in childhood, as early as the second grade.[17] What is the role of the mass media in early learning of political orientations?

## Attention to Political Contents of the Mass Media

Regular, heavy, and purposive television viewing by children starts as early as age three, while general use of newspapers and magazines increases from the middle school years onward.[18] Although regular and purposive use of the mass media specifically for public affairs information does not begin until late adolescence, *any* exposure to the mass media during early childhood results in incidental exposure to public affairs.[19]

Early teen years are often characterized by low levels of attention to news and public affairs contents of television and newspapers.[20] However, teen-agers rate the mass media as the most important sources of political informa-tion and political influence, significantly outranking parents and peers.[21]

Television is the main source of political information for adults. In 1974 television news was cited as the primary source of political information by a national sample of adults.[22] In 1972, 66 percent of the American public said that they learned "most" about national candidates from television; two-thirds said that television was "the best way" to follow candidates for national office; and more than half indicated that they got their clearest understanding of the candidate and issues in national elections from TV.[23] Thus, television is a most ubiquitous source of political information for adults, reaching both those who would ordinarily be receptive to political information in any medi-um and those who would have "virtually no news were it not for television."[24]

Not only is television a pervasive source of political information, it is also readily believed. In 1974, 51 percent of the American people said that televi-sion is the "most believable" of all the mass media as sources of information.[25] Also in 1974, a national sample said that they had greater confidence in television news than in any other American social institution.[26] And Walter Cronkite has been found in several surveys to be America's most credible human.[27]

It is clear that we are exposed to political information in the mass media beginning at an early age. Although this exposure may not be regular and purposive until the late teen years, children and adolescents do consider the mass media to be primary sources of political information and influence. Television is the most pervasive source of political information for adults. It is also considered to be the most credible among major sources of political information. Considering these findings, we conclude that adequate exposure to the political contents of mass media occurs throughout a person's life cycle. There is every opportunity, therefore, for political learning to take place.

## Political Contents of the Mass Media

Political behaviors and orientations can be learned from the mass media if audiences are paying some attention to it. Paul Deutschmann in 1959 and Guido Stempel III in 1962 showed that politics and government was one of the news categories most emphasized by daily newspapers.[28] More recently, Lindeborg and Stone coded the number of front-page stories in six upstate New York newspapers.[29] The news categories appearing most frequently in the front pages were the military (18 percent), politics (14 percent), government (14 percent), and crime (12 percent). Similar results have been found for television. National newscasts usually devote more time to news about government and politics than to any other news category, and about 70 percent of all stories carried by one network during the week are covered by at least one of the other two networks.[30]

We can conclude that political information constitutes a major content item for both newspapers and television. But what about political contents explicitly intended to persuade? A 1972 study by the Newspaper Advertising Bureau indicated that the typical newspaper on the average weekday devotes about 4 percent of its nonadvertising contents to editorial comments and another 12 percent to columns dealing with politics and public affairs.[31] The American Institute for Political Communication in a 1974 study showed that on an average weekday the television networks set aside about 16 percent of their evening news broadcasts for commentary on political and public affairs.[32] Although not as pervasive as straight political information, political editorials and commentaries are available to media audiences.

Audiences report relatively high levels of exposure to the political contents of the mass media. In a recent study 41 percent of a national sample of newspaper readers said that they read editorials and opinion columns "frequently," 38 percent reported reading news items on local politics "frequently" and 37 percent said they read about national politics "frequently."[33] Television newscasts, which report mainly government and political news, are the major source of news of 65 percent of the population.[34] A recent review of research on television and human behavior indicates that a regular audience for network evening news exists, primarily from the elderly, persons with relatively high or low education, males, and college-educated blacks.[35]

## The Nature of Media Political Contents—Motivational Factors

We have so far established two conditions necessary for political learning from the mass media—the availability of political information in the media and audience attention to this material. We now turn to a third condition—motivation.

The role of motivation in political learning is straightforward. According to the principles of social learning theory, motivation to perform a response depends on rewards associated with the performance. These rewards may be extrinsic or intrinsic, immediate, delayed, or expected. For political orientations and behaviors to be imitated from the mass media, we must observe these responses being rewarded in the media or we ourselves must be rewarded for performing them in real life. Let us first consider rewards for performing political responses in real life, since there seems to be less ambiguity regarding motivations for these behaviors than motivations for political behaviors depicted in the media.

## Motivations for Political Responses

We know from research in child development that children copy diverse responses performed by their parents because they are consistently rewarded for such behavior.[36] Although imitation of political behaviors may only be infrequently reinforced, children are able to generalize reinforcement from imitation of other parental behavior to imitation of political responses. Children therefore copy political behaviors of their parents because parental imitation, in general, is rewarding.

Motivation to copy attitudes and behaviors *supportive* of the system are also generally reinforced in the real world. We are reinforced by the system for obeying laws, for showing respect for the symbols and institutions of political authority, for taking the "good-citizen" role. Supportive attitudes and behaviors are reinforced by the system because these responses help perpetuate the system. However, if we were to break down the larger polity into smaller groups of citizens based on geographic locations, age groups, education, and socioeconomic status, then widespread reinforcement for supportive political responses is not always so obvious. For example, community acceptance of an attitude supportive of increased spending for the military may be widespread in a traditionally conservative city such as Dallas, Texas. The same attitude would probably be rejected in a traditionally liberal community like Madison, Wisconsin. Thus, the attitude leads to positive reinforcements in one community and to negative reinforcements in another. As another example, take the assumption that active political participation (such as voting or campaigning for one's candidate) is a vital component of the good-citizen role. Citizens continue to participate actively in the political system as long as they are reinforced for doing so or, as Easton and Dennis put it, as long as they perceive that they are getting what is "justly" theirs from the system.[37] Thus, active political participation is reinforcing to those who "get what they want," while it may be negatively reinforcing to those who are repeatedly frustrated. It is not suprising therefore that low-income groups and some ethnic minorities traditionally indicate lower perceptions of political efficacy. These groups also are less likely to participate actively in the political process (for example, by voting) than middle- and high-income groups. Any analysis of motivations for political attitudes and behaviors should include the primary groups to which the person belongs.

### Motivations and Political Contents of the Mass Media

To what extent are the political contents of the mass media reinforcing to the audience? This question has been a major source of controversy among social scientists and media professionals. On one hand, there are those who claim that most public affairs contents of the media are positively reinforcing to their audiences, assuring them that the system works and that weaknesses in the system can be corrected. The television networks have claimed, for example, that the Watergate hearings increased the levels of political efficacy and trust among viewers.[38]

Another group, made up primarily of social scientists, suggests that the political contents of the mass media, particularly of television, have the opposite effect. The media's emphasis on "bad news," according to this view, has led to political apathy, distrust of the system, lower levels of political efficacy and participation, and a growth of political "malaise" among audiences.[39]

The notion that the political contents of television may be negatively reinforcing to viewers grew out of the observation that the public's increasing dependence on television for news has been accompanied by a decay in political efficacy and trust and a growing concern with law and order. The observation that these two events occur together does not, of course, establish causality. However, many writers have suggested that TV viewing is the cause of political malaise. Wamsley and Pride, for example, observed that TV news denigrated symbols of authority and therefore makes society less legitimate.[40] Weaver argued that the television news format results in "detachment (at best) or cynical rejection (at worst) toward the political institutions of the nation."[41] Shafer and Larson in 1972 suggested that TV news was responsible for creating the "social issue," which has produced political frustrations and discontent among viewers.

> For a long time there were two basic issues in national politics: foreign policy . . . and economics. . . . Now there is a third: Law and Order—shorthand for street crime, race, protest tactics, and revolution. It has been forty years since American politics generated an issue so intense that it could change partisan loyalties for vast numbers of citizens. . . . Where did it come from?
>
> We suggest that the essential midwives in the birth of this issue are Messrs. Cronkite, Brinkley, and their brethren television newsmen.[42]

What is in the political contents of television that leads to political malaise? Robinson in a 1976 paper identified these elements.[43]

1. The practical assumption that each television news item must be of interest to *everyone* who watched.[44] This assumption has led to "thematic" television journalism. The principal need of a television news story, according to Weaver, is a "clear, continuous narrative sustained through-

out the story—something with a beginning, a middle, and an end that will create, maintain, and if possible increase the viewer's interest . . . it needs a theme which can be sustained throughout the story." Epstein cites modern examples in which the need for themes in television reporting has distorted news coverage.[45]

2. Television news tends to emphasize "bad" or negative news—with "what is wrong with our government structure, our leaders, our prisons, schools, roads, automobiles, race relations, pollution laws, every facet of our society."[46] Two studies by Pride and Clarke and by Pride and Richards provide some empirical support for the bad news contention.[47] They found that more negative statements than positive statements were broadcast by the three TV networks in the late 1960s regarding the president, the police, blacks, and students. More recently, Lowry found that a third of all the news items of the three networks in the summer of 1970 fell into the category of "bad news."[48] These categories were armed conflict and war, crime, international tension, social conflict, strikes and riots, and accidents and disasters. There was a tendency also for bad news items to be placed toward the beginning of a newscast and to include pictures in the presentation.

3. Television news emphasizes conflict and violence. A study by Greenwald indicates that television is three times more likely than local newspapers to cover noncriminal violence.[49] Singer compared television news reporting in the United States and Canada.[50] He concluded that American television news was significantly more violent than Canadian TV news. In April and May 1970, for example, CBS devoted 64 percent of its news time to aggressive items, while CBC devoted only 32 percent of its time to aggressive stories. He also found that CBS used more than twice as many "aggressive items" as CBC, even after controlling for news about the war in Vietnam.

4. Television news emphasizes "antiinstitutional" themes. Researchers have not agreed on a common definition of "antiinstitutional." To Efron, it means a bias toward the "Democratic-Liberal-Left axis of opinion."[51] Using this definition, Efron concluded from a content analysis of network TV news that the networks projected this bias. Her coding categories and sampling methods, however, are suspect and have been severely criticized by both the television industry and social scientists.[52] Stevenson et al.[53] and Hofstetter[54] conducted similar studies and found no such bias.

A more rigorous definition of "antiinstitutional" news is news critical of the status quo and news expressing a desire for change. Using this definition, Cutler and Tedesco found that television gives equal attention to figures representing social control (those in power) and social change (those not in power).[55] Network drama portraying social conflict, on the other hand, gives more attention to the forces of social control.

What can we conclude about the nature of television news? Robinson offers this assessment.

Events are frequently conveyed by television news through an inferential structure that often injects a negativistic, contentious, antiinstitutional bias. These biases, frequently dramatized by film portrayals of violence and aggression, evoke images of American politics and social life which are inordinately sinister and despairing. The inadvertent viewer, through television, witnesses these images of the society, regarding them as essentially evil and indicative of sociopolitical decay.[56]

A somewhat different conclusion is reached by Comstock *et al.*

Television as a medium appears to be biased toward events that make for good visual coverage, toward brief, succinct reports that more nearly approximate a newspaper's front page than its full contents, toward emphasis on personalities; and national television is biased toward events of high interest to viewers of all regions.[57]

More work is obviously needed to evaluate the nature of television news. Researchers agree that television news is designed to be of interest to everyone in the audience, that personalities do get more emphasis, and that no systematic political bias is evident. However, they disagree on whether TV news is negativistic and antiinstitutional. Also, we need to know more about attentional patterns of viewers to TV news. What types of news items elicit more attention? Is negative and antiinstitutional news better attended to than other types of news? These are some questions that need to be investigated. Most current research on mass communication and political socialization has been primarily concerned with *effects* of the mass media, neglecting, unfortunately, the nature of the stimuli to which audiences are expected to respond. Let us now review some representative studies and see how they fit into the social learning theory framework.

## RESEARCH

Early studies of mass communication and political socialization investigated the effects of mass media use on change in voter intentions and behaviors during political campaigns. The first of the major election studies was Lazarsfeld, Berelson, and Gaudet's analysis of voters in Erie County in 1940.[58] This was followed by Berelson, Lazarsfeld, and McPhee's survey of voters in Elmira, New York, in 1948.[59] These early studies found that the media had little direct influence on voters, primarily because voting preferences were accounted for by predispositions such as social class, parental party affiliation, group membership, and religion. Also, most voters made up their minds early in the campaign, and the small percentage who did change were more likely to be affected by personal communication sources or "opinion leaders" than by the mass media. These early findings led to the formulation of a "limited effects model," which considers the mass media to be reinforcers of existing political attitudes and behavior and to be relatively ineffective as agents of change.

The limited effects model has recently been criticized for the following reasons: (1) the range of effects considered is too limited; the mass media are more likely to affect the *acquisition* of political cognitions, attitudes, and behavioral intentions instead of *changing* them; (2) the periods studied (election campaigns) were too limited; the mass media are more likely to affect audiences over time, beginning in early childhood and continuing through adolescence and early adulthood; and (3) the measures of mass media use were incomplete or too general.[60]

More recently, political communication researchers, rejecting the limited effects model, have moved away from analysis of change in adult voting behavior and attitudes during political campaigns and have focused instead on the acquisition of political cognitions (knowledge), political affect (political efficacy, trust, and support), and behavior (campaign participation, voting). These models typically predict that the mass media are significant agents in the political socialization process.

## Cognitive Effects

There seems to be little doubt that media use for public affairs information leads to greater knowledge of public affairs, candidates, and issues. Chaffee, Ward, and Tipton showed that media use led to political knowledge gain among Wisconsin junior and senior high school students during the 1968 presidential campaign.[61] Atkin and Gantz provide evidence of a causal relationship among children between attention to television news and gains in knowledge of public figures and current events.[62] In a national survey of high school students and young adults Chaffee found that political knowledge was strongly associated with heavy use of print media.[63]

Another important cognitive effect of the media is "agenda setting." McCombs and Shaw, who were the first to study agenda setting, predicted that "when the media emphasize an event, they influence the audience to see it as important."[64] Studying the 1968 presidential election, they found high correlations between the media's emphasis of issues and how these issues were ranked by voters in Chapel Hill, North Carolina. They concluded that increased salience of a topic or issue in the mass media causes increased salience of that topic or issue among the public. Subsequent studies of the agenda-setting effects of the mass media have supported the original hypothesis in different environments and using different samples. There is evidence that the Watergate hearings led to increased salience of that issue among the public,[65] especially among those who were highly interested in the issue but who were uncertain about their political allegiance.[66] In later studies McCombs and Shaw show that although both newspaper and television news coverage affects the political agendas of the public, newspapers are generally more effective in setting these agendas than television.[67]

We can conclude that the mass media affect political cognitions in two ways: (1) the media effectively inform us about political affairs; and (2) the media influence our perceptions of the importance of political issues.

More recent studies have supported the general conclusion that exposure to the mass media leads to gains in knowledge. Palmgreen, for example, studied the effects of exposure to television and newspapers on knowledge of national and local political topics that were either heavily or lightly covered by the mass media.[68] He found that respondents who used newspapers and television frequently for public affairs information were more knowledgeable about national political issues when the issues were heavily covered in the media, compared to infrequent media users. Heavy media use, however, did not lead to more knowledge about local issues, even when the issues were heavily covered. Instead, media use stimulated interpersonal discussion about local issues, which then led to more knowledge. Palmgreen's study tells us that we do learn about political issues from television and newspapers, particularly when the issues are national in scope and when they are heavily covered by the media. We learn about local issues primarily from interpersonal discussions.

## Emotional Effects

There are two competing hypotheses when considering the effects of the mass media on political affect of the public. We can predict that exposure to positively reinforcing political material will lead to increases in political trust, efficacy, and support. However, we can also predict that exposure to negatively reinforcing material will lead to "political malaise," or to distrust, political cynicism, and erosion of support. The main issue is whether we can adequately define what is positively reinforcing and what is negatively reinforcing in political contents of the mass media. And, as we have seen, there seems to be no agreement on this issue. The same political material—the Watergate hearings, for example—may be positively reinforcing to some members of the public and negatively reinforcing to others. An important determinant of motivational responses to political media contents seems to be primary group memberships of the individual.

Researchers disagree on whether political media contents are positively or negatively reinforcing. However, they agree that the media will have an effect, *somehow*, on the emotional attachments of the individual to the system. Some studies have reported positive associations between mass media use and political affect. McLeod, Brown, and Becker, for example, report that young voters who were relatively frequent users of newspapers and television for public affairs information increased their sense of political efficacy during the Watergate hearings, while sense of political efficacy in other respondents decreased.[69] Chaffee found no significant correlations between media use and either party identification strength or trust in the political system in the total sample.[70] However, increased political efficacy was moderately associated with electronic media use in the high school sample.

Other studies have reported negative associations between media use and political affect. Robinson showed experimentally that exposure to a television political program, "The Selling of the Pentagon," led to negative beliefs and attitudes among viewers about the American military.[71] His subjects were recruited from civic, religious, and labor organizations. Compared to control groups not exposed to the program, subjects who were shown "The Selling of the Pentagon" perceived the military as more likely to lie about the war in Vietnam, more likely to get involved in politics, and more likely to seek political advantage. They also reported lower perceptions of political efficacy. It can, of course, be argued that Robinson used an atypical political program for his stimulus, one that could be expected, by its investigative nature, to lead to negative opinions and attitudes about the military. To validate his experimental findings, Robinson analyzed national samples from the 1960, 1964, and 1968 election studies of the Survey Research Center at the University of Michigan. Some of his major findings follow:

1. Since 1960, heavy reliance on television for political information among voters was accompanied by a decrease in feelings of political efficacy, even when other variables such as education were controlled.
2. Voters who relied on television for political information were less trusting of other people in general than those who relied on other media.
3. Dependence on television journalism was associated with disapproval of the speed of the civil rights movement, even when other variables were controlled.
4. Among Democrats, Republicans, and Independents, dependence on television for political information was positively associated with approval of George Wallace as a third candidate.

Robinson concludes that dependence on television journalism is associated with (1) social distrust, (2) political cynicism, (3) political inefficacy, (4) partisan disloyalty, and (5) third-party viability. He attributes these effects to the negativistic and antiinstitutional nature of political information in television.

In summary, some types of political media contents can lead to increased positive affect toward the political system, while others lead to negative affect. More attention should be given to the nature of the political information and the groups to which the individual belongs if we are to generate plausible hypotheses regarding the relationship between media use and political affect. What is clear from the research so far is that media use does affect our political feelings one way or the other.

### Behavioral Effects

Most studies of mass media effects on political behaviors have focused on election campaigns. This is understandable, since the opportunity for political activity (such as active campaigning and voting) is greatest during an election campaign.

Again, as with political affect, the evidence regarding the effect of mass media use on political behaviors is quite mixed. Some studies report that media use leads to increased political activity,[72] others report that use of a specific medium (television) leads to less activity,[73] while still others report no relationship.[74] The inconclusiveness of these studies can be attributed to the complex nature of political information available in the media—the same information may be positively reinforcing to some members of the public and negatively reinforcing to others.

A promising research strategy that can help clarify the relationship is to analyze smaller groups of citizens by classifying them according to demographic, social, and political characteristics. There is evidence that media use leads to increased political activity, but only for some members of the public. Chaffee found that mass media use encouraged increased political activity among those who would otherwise be disinclined to politics—persons who have low levels of both knowledge and political activity at the beginning of the campaign.[75] Mendelsohn and O'Keefe, in an analysis of voter behavior during the 1972 presidential campaign, found no evidence of important shifts among voters that would be attributed to either television or newspapers.[76] However, they found that mass media reports of various events during the campaign were reported by subsets of voters as influential. Dennis and Chaffee studied the impact of the 1976 Ford-Carter debates on voters.[77] They found that voters who regularly watched the debates changed voting intentions the most during the latter stages of the campaign compared to nonviewers and occasional viewers. Voters in this group also were most affected by differences between the candidates on the issues.

We can conclude from these studies that political information in the mass media can lead to increased political activity among less interested and less knowledgeable voters. However, there is also evidence that, at least for the 1976 presidential campaign, voting intentions of the interested and knowledgeable citizen were affected by the presidential debates.

Research on mass communication and political socialization is still in its infancy. Most of the studies adapting the socialization model have been done in the past ten years. It is not surprising therefore that many of the findings are tentative and inconclusive. What is clear, however, is that the mass media are affecting citizens in ways not considered or measured by the early voting studies. Social learning theory provides an appropriate theoretical framework for analyzing these effects.

There are, to be sure, a number of issues that need further attention. We need to know more about the motivational characteristics of political material in the media and attention by the audience to this material. We also need to investigate possible reciprocal causal relationships between political attitudes and behaviors, and mass media use, particularly in adults. Some recent research, for example, suggests that in adults political attitudes determine media use at the same time that media use determines political attitudes.[78]

## RECENT TRENDS IN MASS COMMUNICATION AND POLITICAL SOCIALIZATION RESEARCH

Political communication researchers have recently been studying how people process political information. We are interested not only in the effects of mass media use on political orientations, but also in understanding how people make political decisions and the role of information in decision making.

### Political Decisions and Information Processing

Political decisions, like other decisions in life, are based primarily on information that is available to us and on how we evaluate this information. The first step in information processing is attention to the message. We are exposed to thousands of messages in a day and can attend to only a few of them. The next step is information evaluation. According to the information-processing models of persuasion that we discussed in Chapter 7, we assign weights to the different pieces of information that we get about an issue. Our decisions are based on an average evaluation of all available information.

#### Selective Exposure

We cannot be influenced by political information that we ignore or that we tune out. Early communication researchers suggested a "selective exposure" hypothesis to explain which information we attend to and which information we ignore. According to this hypothesis, we avoid information that contradicts existing attitudes, beliefs, behaviors, and choices, and we seek out supportive information. As discussed in Chapter 11, experimental studies have not supported the selective exposure hypothesis. We do not ignore messages simply because they contradict us. Other message qualities such as entertainment and functional values determine audience attention.

Chaffee and Miyo studied selective exposure to political information during the 1980 presidential campaign.[79] They interviewed 501 Wisconsin adolescents and one parent of each adolescent in early 1980 and again in October 1980. Some of their results follow:

1. Selective exposure occurred mainly in the adolescent sample, which was less informed and experienced about politics than the adults.
2. Selective exposure was shown by low attention to the opposition candidate and not by increased attention to the respondent's favored candidate.
3. Increased attention to one's candidate led to greater support for the favored candidate as the campaign progressed. Exposure to messages of the opposing candidate also led to some increase in liking for him. Apparently, attention to the opposition candidate's messages retarded a trend toward disliking him as the campaign progressed.

Chaffee and Miyo's study indicates that selective exposure was more a product of their respondent's inexperience and lack of information about politics (characteristics of the adolescent sample) than of prior identification with a political party or candidate. This result is supported by laboratory studies of information processing that we discussed in Chapter 11. Laboratory studies show that "experts" are better able to integrate new information than "novices" and will less likely avoid inconsistent information. Chaffee and Miyo's findings that adolescents (presumably novices in politics) were more likely to show selective exposure tendencies than their parents (who are more likely to be experts in politics) can be explained by the expert-novice information-processing model.

### Media Reliance and Political Information

Most adults in the United States today rely on television instead of newspapers for information about public affairs. Reliance on television news affects how we process information. For one thing, we learn less from television than from newspapers. Television dependence is related to lower levels of knowledge about national affairs, while newspaper reliance is related to higher gains in knowledge, particularly during political campaigns.[80] During noncampaign periods, knowledge about economic affairs is positively related to newspaper reliance and negatively related to television reliance. These results have held even when the researchers controlled for educational level and other socioeconomic characteristics of the respondents.[81]

Experiments on communication modality and learning, which we discussed in Chapter 10, support the results of field surveys indicating that television reliance is related to lower levels of knowledge than newspaper reliance. These experiments show that we learn more from print and less from television when the message is difficult. Most information about politics and economic affairs may indeed be difficult for the average person, since unfamiliar material is being transmitted. Thus, we expect receivers who rely on newspapers instead of television to have more knowledge about these issues. The differences in knowledge levels between newspaper- and television-reliant recipients probably would not be as great if the messages dealt with familiar topics or if only superficial knowledge, such as candidate and issue identification, was measured.

How does media reliance affect information processing? In Chapter 10, we discussed a 1983 experiment by Chaiken and Eagly that indicated that television focuses our attention on communicator characteristics while the print media draws our attention to message arguments. Television magnifies the personal characteristics of communicators who can be seen and heard, thereby drawing attention away from arguments in the message. This distraction does not occur when the print media are used. A recent field survey by McLeod, Glynn, and McDonald[82] supports these experimental findings. McLeod and his colleagues found that television-reliant voters used candidate image characteristics in making their voting choices more often than newspaper-reliant voters did. However, there was no support for their hypothesis that perceptions of the candidates' stands on the issues will be more influential in voting decisions among newspaper-reliant voters.

McLeod, Glynn, and McDonald's study shows that communicator-related information (such as image) was more influential when voters relied on television instead of newspapers. However, message-related information (perceptions of the candidates' stands on the issues) was not more influential when newspapers instead of television were used. Perceptions of the candidates' issue positions do not necessarily correspond to the correct positions of the candidates, since some distortion may occur. The second hypothesis might have been supported if evaluations of the quality of candidate arguments and if knowledge, instead of perceptions, of candidate positions were measured. McLeod and his colleagues did find that television-reliant voters were less accurate in their judgments of the positions of candidates on the issues. This indicates that we do learn *more* from newspapers when the issues are complex and that this knowledge is more accurate.

## SUMMARY

Political socialization is concerned with how we acquire or learn political cognitions, affect, and behaviors. Traditionally, political socialization research has considered the family, schools, and social groups as the primary agents of influence. More recently the mass media have been studied as important socialization agents.

We learn political opinions, values, and behaviors in the same way that we learn other social behaviors—either by direct experience or by observational learning. According to social learning theory, we learn political responses from models that are frequently encountered and when we are rewarded, extrinsically or intrinsically, for imitating the model. Adequate exposure to the political contents of the mass media occurs throughout a person's life. There is every opportunity for political learning to take place.

Some political contents of the media are positively reinforcing; others are negatively reinforcing. Researchers agree that most television news is designed to be of interest to everyone in the audience, that personalities are emphasized more, and that no systematic political bias is evident. However, there is disagreement on whether television news is negativistic and antiinstitutional.

Early studies investigated the effects of mass media use on change in voter intentions and behaviors during political campaigns. These studies led to the formulation of a "limited effects" model, which considers the mass media to be reinforcers of existing political orientations and to be relatively ineffective as agents of change.

More recently, researchers have rejected the limited effects model. They have analyzed the effects of the media on the acquisition of political orientations and have found that we are influenced by the media in many ways other than attitude or behavioral change. Some of the recent findings are the following:

1. The media are effectively informing us about political affairs and are influencing our perceptions of the importance of political issues.
2. Some types of political media contents lead to increases among audiences in political trust, efficacy, support, and political activity, while others lead to distrust, political cynicism, and erosion of support.
3. Two critical factors determining the effects of the mass media on political affect and behaviors are reference groups of the individual and motivations elicited by the political material.

## REVIEW QUESTIONS

1. What is political socialization? What is the role of the mass media in political socialization?
2. Using social learning theory as a framework for analysis, discuss how we learn political attitudes and behaviors from the mass media.
3. Pick out examples from the mass media of messages that can be positively reinforcing to their audiences. Pick out messages that can be negatively reinforcing. What are the differences between the two sets of messages?
4. Compare the early election studies of Lazarsfeld and his colleagues with more recent research on mass media and political socialization. What are some basic differences between these studies?

## ENDNOTES

1. R. D. Hess and J. V. Torney, *The Development of Political Attitudes in Children* (Chicago: Aldine, 1967), p. 7.
2. R. S. Sigel, "Assumptions about the Learning of Political Values," *Annals of the American Academy of Social and Political Science, 361,* 1965, p. 1.
3. H. Hyman, *Political Socialization* (Glencoe, Ill.: Free Press, 1959), p. 17.
4. D. Easton and J. Dennis, *Children in the Political System* (New York: McGraw-Hill, 1969).
5. *Ibid.*
6. M. Robinson, "Public Affairs Television and the Growth of Political Malaise: The Case of 'The Selling of the Pentagon,'" *American Political Science Review, 70,* 1976, pp. 409–432.
7. Easton and Dennis, *op. cit.,* p. 57.
8. D. Easton and J. Dennis, "The Child's Acquisition of Regime Norms: Political Efficacy," *American Political Science Review, 61,* 1967, pp. 25–38.
9. See, for example, S. Chaffee (ed.), *Political Communications: Issues and Strategies for Research* (Beverly Hills, Calif.: Sage Publications, 1975); S. Kraus and D. Davis, *The Effects of Mass Communication on Political Behavior* (University Park: Pennsylvania State University Press, 1976); S. A. Renshon (ed.), *Handbook of Political Socialization* (New York: Free Press, 1977); G. Comstock, S. Chaffee, W. Katzman, M. Mc-

Combs, and D. Roberts, *Television and Human Behavior* (New York: Columbia University Press, 1978).

10. S. A. Renshon, "Assumptive Frameworks in Political Socialization Theory," in Renshon, *op. cit.*, pp. 1–44.

11. M. K. Jennings and R. G. Niemi, *The Political Character of Adolescence: The Influence of Families and Schools* (Princeton University Press, 1974), p. 15.

12. I. S. Rohter, "A Social-Learning Approach to Political Socialization," in D. Schwartz and S. Schwarts (eds.), *New Directions in Political Socialization* (New York: Free Press, 1975), p. 140.

13. Jennings and Niemi, *op. cit.*

14. *Ibid.*

15. R. E. Dawson and K. Prewitt, *Political Socialization* (Boston: Little, Brown, 1969), p. 74.

16. T. J. Cook and F. P. Scioli, "A Critique of the Learning Concept in Political Socialization Research," *Social Science Quarterly, 52*, 1972, p. 956.

17. Hess and Torney, *op. cit.*

18. Comstock *et al.*, *op. cit.*, pp. 173–211.

19. S. Chaffee, "Mass Communication in Political Socialization," in Renshon (ed.), *op. cit.*, pp. 223–258.

20. *Ibid.*

21. *Ibid.*

22. B. Roper, *Trends in Public Attitudes toward Television and Other Mass Media, 1959–1974* (New York: Television Information Office, 1975).

23. *Ibid.*

24. Robinson, *op. cit.*, p. 426.

25. Roper, *op. cit.*

26. L. Harris, *Confidence and Concern: Citizens View American Government* (Washington, D.C.: U.S. Government Printing Office, 1974), p. 33.

27. In M. Barett (ed.), *The Politics of Broadcasting, 1971–1972* (New York: Thomas Crowell, 1973), p. 49.

28. P. Deutschmann, *News-Page Content of Twelve Metropolitan Dailies* (Cincinnati: Scripps-Howard Research, 1959); G. H. Stempel III, "Content Patterns of Small and Metropolitan Dailies," *Journalism Quarterly, 39*, 1962, pp. 88–90.

29. R. Lindeborg and G. Stone, "News Values as Reflected in News Content Found Stable from 1950–1970," *ANPA News Research Bulletin, 7*, 1974.

30. Comstock *et al.*, *op. cit.*, p. 46–63; J. Lemert, "Content Duplication by the Networks in Competing Evening Newscasts," *Journalism Quarterly, 51*, 1974, pp. 238–244.

31. See L. Becker, M. McCombs, and J. McLeod, "The Development of Political Cognitions," in S. Chaffee (ed.), 1975, *op. cit.*, p. 21.

32. *Ibid.*

33. *Ibid.*

34. Roper, *op. cit.*

35. Comstock *et al.*, 1978, *op. cit.*, p. 122.

36. Rohter, *op. cit.*

37. Easton and Dennis, 1969, *op. cit.*

38. Robinson, *op. cit.*, p. 431.

39. *Ibid.*, pp. 409–411.

40. G. Wamsley and R. Pride, "Television Network News: Rethinking the Iceberg Problem," *Western Political Quarterly, 25*, 1972, pp. 434–450.

41. P. Weaver, "Is Television News Biased?" *Public Interest, 26*, 1972, pp. 57–74.

42. B. Shafer and R. Larson, "Did TV Create the Social Issue?" *Columbia Journalism Review, 11,* 1972, p. 10.
43. Robinson, *op. cit.,* pp. 409–432.
44. R. Frank, "An Anatomy of Television News," *Television Quarterly, 9,* 1970, p. 18.
45. E. Epstein, *News from Nowhere* (New York: Random House, 1973).
46. M. Pannitt, "America Out of Focus," *TV Guide,* January 15, 1972, pp. 6–12.
47. R. A. Pride and D. H. Clarke, "Race Relations in Television News: A Content Analysis of the Networks," *Journalism Quarterly, 50,* 1973, pp. 319–328; R. A. Pride and B. Richards, "Denigration of Authority? Television News Coverage of the Student Movement," *Journal of Politics, 15,* 1971, pp. 397–408.
48. D. T. Lowry, "Gresham's Law and Network TV News Selection," *Journal of Broadcasting, 15,* 1971, pp. 397–408.
49. See Robinson, *op. cit.,* p. 428.
50. B. D. Singer, "Violence, Protest and War in Television News: The U.S. and Canada Compared," *Public Opinion Quarterly, 34,* 1970, pp. 611–616.
51. E. Efron, *The News Twisters* (Los Angeles: Nash, 1971).
52. See, for example, C. R. Hofstetter, *Bias in the News* (Columbus: Ohio: State University Press, 1976).
53. R. Stevenson *et al.,* "Untwisting 'The News Twisters': A Replication of Efron's Study," *Journalism Quarterly, 50,* 1973, pp. 211–219.
54. Hofstetter, *op. cit.*
55. W. E. Cutler and A. S. Tedesco, "Differentiation in Television Message Systems: A Comparison of Network Television News and Drama," paper presented to the International Communication Association, New Orleans, April 1974.
56. Robinson, *op. cit.,* p. 430.
57. Comstock *et al., op. cit.,* p. 82.
58. P. Lazarsfeld, B. Berelson, and H. Gaudet, *The People's Choice* (New York: Columbia University Press, 1944).
59. B. Berelson, P. F. Lazarsfeld, and W. McPhee, *Voting* (Chicago: University of Chicago Press, 1954).
60. See, for example, Chaffee, in Renshon (ed.), 1977, *op. cit.;* Robinson, 1976, *op. cit.;* Kraus and Davis, 1976, *op. cit.*
61. S. Chaffee, L. Ward, and L. P. Tipton, "Mass Communication and Political Socialization," *Journalism Quarterly, 47,* 1970, pp. 647–659.
62. C. K. Atkin and W. Gantz, "The Role of Television News in the Political Socialization of Children," paper presented to the International Communication Association, Chicago, April 1975.
63. Chaffee, in Renshon (ed.), 1977, *op. cit.*
64. M. E. McCombs and D. L. Shaw, "The Agenda-Setting Function of Mass Media," *Public Opinion Quarterly, 36,* 1972, pp. 176–187.
65. S. Kraus and S. Chaffee (eds.), "The Ervin Committee Hearings and Communication Research," *Communication Research, 1,* 1974.
66. D. Weaver, M. E. McCombs, and C. Spellman, "Watergate and the Media: A Case Study of Agenda-Setting," *American Politics Quarterly, 3,* 1975, pp. 458–472.
67. M. E. McCombs and D. L. Shaw, "A Progress Report on Agenda-Setting Research," paper presented to the Association for Education in Journalism, San Diego, August 1974.
68. Philip Palmgreen, "Mass Media Use and Political Knowledge," *Journalism Monographs, 61,* May 1979.
69. J. McLeod, J. Brown, and L. B. Becker, "Decline and Fall at the White House: A

Longitudinal Analysis of Communication Effects," paper presented to the Association for Education in Journalsim, Ottawa, 1975.

70. Chaffee, in Renshon (ed.), 1977, *op. cit.*
71. Robinson, *op. cit.*
72. M. Jackson-Beeck and S. H. Chaffee, "Family Communication, Mass Communication, and Differential Political Socialization," paper presented to the International Communication Association, Chicago, April 1975.
73. Robinson, *op. cit.*
74. Chaffee, in Renshon (ed.), 1977, *op. cit.*
75. *Ibid.*
76. H. A. Mendelsohn and G. J. O'Keefe, *The People Choose a President: Influences on Voter Decision Making* (New York: Praeger, 1976).
77. J. Dennis and S. Chaffee, "Impact of the Debates upon Partisan, Image and Issue Voting," in S. Kraus (ed.), *The Great Debates: 1976, Ford vs. Carter* (Bloomington: Indiana University Press, 1977).
78. A. Tan, "Mass Media Use, Issue Knowledge and Political Involvement," *Public Opinion Quarterly, 44,* 1980, pp. 241–248.
79. Steven H. Chaffee and Yuko Miyo, "Selective Exposure and the Reinforcement Hypothesis," *Communication Research, 10,* January 1983, pp. 3–36.
80. Jack M. McLeod, Carroll J. Glynn, and Daniel G. McDonald, "Issues and Images: The Influence of Media Reliance on Voting Decisions," *Communication Research, 10,* January 1983, pp. 37–58.
81. L. B. Becker and D. C. Whitney, "Effects of Media Dependencies on Audience Assessment of Government," *Communication Research, 7,* 1980, pp. 95–120.
82. McLeod *et al., op. cit.*

# PART V

# COMMUNICATORS AND THEIR ENVIRONMENT

Communicators are influenced by many external forces. In this section we will discuss some of these forces and how they influence the communication behaviors of individuals and media organizations. Using principles from structural functional analysis and group dynamics, we will explain how small groups, organizations and the community affect communication behaviors such as news selection, communicator autonomy, media performance, and media organizational structures.

# 21

# COMMUNICATION, MASS COMMUNICATION ORGANIZATIONS, AND SOCIAL INSTITUTIONS

Communicators do not encode their messages in a vacuum. Whether the communicator is a newspaper editor or writer, a scriptwriter for the movies or television, a television news reporter or a radio news commentator, his or her choice of messages and use of symbols is influenced not only by internal forces such as previous experience and personal characteristics, but also by external forces, or conditions that exist outside of the individual. The analysis of internal forces influencing the communicator is often referred to as micro- or intrapersonal analysis. Many of the studies that we discussed in the chapters on communication and persuasion (Part II of this text), analyzed communications at the microlevel. The analysis of external forces influencing the communicator, on the other hand, is often called structural analysis, since many of these external forces are found in the physical or structural properties of the communicator's environment. In this chapter, we will explain how the mass communicator is influenced by both internal and external forces. Mass communicators perform their work within a mass media organization that could be a news organization such as a newspaper or an entertainment organization such as a television network. As we will see, the mass communicator's work is very much influenced by his or her external environment. Very often, these external forces are more powerful than internal dispositions in shaping the form and meaning of the messages that are passed on to the audience.

## EXTERNAL FORCES INFLUENCING THE MASS COMMUNICATOR

Most early studies of mass communicators focused primarily on internal forces. The major premise was that personal characteristics of the communicator such as values, attitudes, professionalization, training, demographic characteristics, and personality attributes determined their selection and encoding of messages.[1] More recently, researchers have realized that often the mass communicator's work—and the ensuing products—are constrained or regulated by forces outside of him or her and over which he or she has very little control. Many of these "regulators" are found within the news and entertainment organizations of the mass media industries. Interest in these external forces has led researchers to study the communication behaviors of professional journalists, television writers, and other producers of mass media messages from within the context of their organizations at both the intrapersonal and structural levels of analysis.

## Understanding Communicators in Organizations: A Structural-Functional Approach

How and why are communicators affected by their organizations? To answer this question, we must first clarify the concept of "organization." There are at least a dozen definitions of organization in the research literature. Farace, Monge, and Russell offer one that I think is the most comprehensive. They define an organization as a *system* consisting of

> ... two or more individuals, who recognize that some of their goals can be more readily achieved through interdependent (cooperative) actions, even though disagreement (conflict) may be present; who take in materials, energy, and information from the environment in which they exist; who develop coordinative and control relationships to capitalize on their interdependence while operating on these inputs; and who return the modified inputs to the environment, in an attempt to accomplish the goals that interdependence was meant to make possible.[2]

Let us look at the elements of this definition more closely. First, an organization is a system. A system is a regularly interacting group of units or individuals who are *interdependent* and who are separated by a boundary from their surrounding environment.[3] The components of a system need not be individuals only; they can be small groups or larger collectivities of individuals. By "boundary" we mean the perimeter or outer limits of the system. Boundaries are usually defined by membership, by the space that the units occupy, or by the time required for the completion of certain tasks. A system should have at least one characteristic that separates it from the rest of its environment.

The five characteristics of an organization in the definition by Farace, Monge, and Russell are size, interdependence, inputs, throughputs, and outputs. The first characteristic is size. It takes at least two persons to make up an organization, since interdependence, another requirement of an organization, cannot occur with only one isolated individual. Organizations can range in size from two individuals to hundreds, thousands, or even millions of members. As size increases, the task of operating the organization to obtain specified goals becomes more difficult. Control and coordination of the members, and the distribution of information, will take more time and effort in larger organizations than in smaller ones.

The second characteristic of an organization is interdependence. In the simplest sense, interdependence means that the individuals making up the organization have to work cooperatively or together to accomplish common goals. Interdependence has other implications besides acting together for a common cause. Participants in an interdependent relationship influence each other, since the behavior of one member is constrained or controlled by the behavior of other members. This "controlling influence" is sometimes reciprocal. It is frequently defined by position within the organizational structure, such as when lines of authority are clearly delineated (for example, between managers and subordinates).

Interdependence is often accepted by members of an organization because they realize that some of their goals can be better obtained if they work together within a given structure of authority instead of working alone as individuals. As Simon points out, organizations can constrain and enhance individual activity.[4] Individual behavior is constrained when a member of an organization is prevented from performing certain activities because these activities do not conform to the organization's operating procedures or goals. On the other hand, individual activity may be enhanced when, through a division of labor, coordination of effort, and guidance, individual abilities are effectively directed toward the attainment of the organization's goals.

The third characteristic of an organization are the inputs into the organization. These inputs could take many forms: materials such as the raw materials that go into a manufacturing plant; energy, such as electricity into a power utility company; or information, such as the news reports that go into a newspaper organization.

The fourth component of an organization is "throughput" activity. Farace, Monge, and Russell define "throughput activities" as ". . . the passage of materials, energy, and information from point to point within the organization, up to exit."[5]

In the process of throughput, the inputs are manipulated by the organization's members so that some final "payoff" to them can be realized. This payoff could be in the form of salaries, satisfaction, or recognition. Control and coordination processes within the organization determine whether these final payoffs to the organizational members will be realized from the manipulation of inputs. Control processes regulate how and when throughput activities are performed and include processes such as assigning work, implementing quality standards, and detecting and correcting errors. Coordination is achieved by making each member of the organization perform their specified tasks in harmony with others.

The last component of an organization is the output. Outputs are inputs modified by "throughput" processes that are returned to the environment. In mass media organizations the outputs are the messages that are sent to the mass audience—the newspaper, a television newscast, or an advertisement.

As we can see from this definition, organizations are systems that are best understood when all of its five components are considered in the analysis. One analytical model that can help us understand how organizations function and how the individual member is affected by his or her organization is called *structural-functional analysis*. Structural-functional analysis looks at organizations as systems with identifiable structures that perform specific functions for the entire system. We have already introduced you to the concept of system. Let us now consider structures within the system and their functions.

According to structural-functional analysis, a structure within a system is a pattern of activity that occurs with predictable regularity and that restrains or controls throughput activities and the resulting output.[6] Structures are determined by the physical properties of the system. Size of the organization, for example, determines the communication structures (or communication rules) of the system. In a very large organization, communication activities are rigidly structured. The channels of communication that are open to an individual member are determined by the hierarchy in the organization. In a very small organization, communication is less structured. Face-to-face encounters between members will be more frequent than in larger organizations, and there will be fewer rules regulating the flow of information. System structures are also determined by the roles and norms (accepted behaviors) within the organization (such as the relationship between managers and subordinates); the inputs into the system (such as the flow of news reports into a newsroom); outputs from the system (such as how news is defined by a news medium); and environmental forces impinging on a system (such as public opinion on issues that are important to the system).

Organizational structures or regular patterns of activity control individual behaviors within the organization and, consequently, the outputs of the system. Taking the structural-functionalist view, the question to ask in mass communicator analysis is: "How are the behaviors of individual mass communicators regulated, constrained, or otherwise affected by the structures of the organization to which he or she belongs?"

Another important concept in structural-functional analysis is function. A function is utility in achieving specified goals and objectives. Structures are maintained in organizations because they are functional—because they perform useful purposes for the organization. In structural-functional analysis, we ask: "What does this structure do for the organization?"

Farace, Monge, and Russell provide us with a useful list of functions that structures, including communication structures, perform in organizations.[7] These are production, innovation, and maintenance. Production functions refer to the achievement of the organization's output goals. These goals may be specified for individual members of the organization (such as the completion of a news story by a specified deadline) and for the organization (such as a specified profit level). Innovation functions refer to the "generation of new ideas and behaviors for improving the organization."[8] The creation of new program ideas within a television network is an innovation function. Maintenance functions are the functions that preserve the desirable structures of the system. Berlo breaks up maintenance functions into the following categories: (1) the maintenance of the individual member's self-concept, including his or her satisfaction in being a member of the organization; (2) the maintenance of interpersonal relationships within the organization; and (3) the maintenance of the production and innovation functions. These functions are important in structural-functional analysis because they determine whether structures are kept or discarded within the system. Structures that are functional—those that contribute to the attainment of important goals—will be kept, while structures that are dysfunctional (those that interfere with goal attainment) will be discarded.

Now that you are familiar with the important concepts in structural-functional analysis—system, organization, structure, and function—we can discuss the steps in this type of analysis and see how it can help us understand the behavior of communicators in mass media organizations.

Structural-functional analysis includes the following steps:[9]

1. Identify the organization, its components or parts and their interrelationships, and its structures and the functions of these structures. In analyzing mass communicators, we should first look at their media organization, identify the components of the organization, the structures or regular patterns of activity within the organization, and the purposes or functions of these structures.

2. Identify the conditions in the organization's external environment that affect or could affect its performance. We should consider not only the mass media organization, but also the social, political, and economic environments within which that organization operates. We should therefore consider the prevalent social norms and values in the mass medium's community and the prevailing political and economic structures within which the mass medium operates.

3. Identify the traits that are essential to the organization's survival. Essential traits are characteristics of the system that are required for its continued existence. Examples are profit, return on investments, and quality, timeliness,and completeness of information. The absence of an essential trait could lead to the collapse of performance by individual members and, consequently, of the organization itself.

4. Determine the range of desired and acceptable values for the essential traits. We must know the range of values that the traits may take within the system and the range these traits must assume so that the organization can continue to operate effectively. For example, if "timeliness" of information is an essential trait in a news organization, the question we would ask is: "What do we mean by timeliness—an event that happened a few hours ago, yesterday, last week?" We would also ask: "How timely should a news event be (what value should it take) before we consider it to be news?"

5. Identify the mechanisms that determine the values of these traits, potential problems, and means for correcting these problems. If we take total profit to be a trait, we should then determine what activities within the organization ("throughputs") lead to profit, what could reduce profits, and how these potential obstacles to profit could be corrected.

From a structural-functional view, mass communicators are not totally free to choose and encode their messages. Their behaviors are constrained or controlled by forces external to the individual—structures within their organizations, conditions in the social, political, and economic environment, activities within the media organization designed to retain essential "traits," and the functions of the media organization itself. Any analysis of mass communicators should take into account these external forces and how they affect the behaviors of the individual communicator.

## Understanding Communicators in Organizations: A Group Dynamics Approach

Mass communicators perform their work as members of groups, ranging from large groups such as the media organizations that employ them to smaller, informal groups within the media organizations. Membership in these groups has important consequences for individual communicators, since their behavior is often influenced by other group members. Consequently, an individual's behavior is shaped and restricted by the groups to which he or she belongs. In this section, we will use group dynamics principles to explain how group membership affects the individual. Group dynamics is the study of how groups function and change—how they complete tasks, work out conflicts, influence members, and make decisions.[10]

### What Is a Group?

There are many kinds of groups, but the one that concerns us most in our analysis of mass communicators is the psychological group. A psychological group is a collection of persons who have common goals and common norms and whose members are interdependent. Members of a psychological group share a sense of "belonging." They identify with the group because other members of the group are important to them.[11] Two types of psychological groups are membership groups and reference groups. A membership group is a group to which a person belongs because he or she shares at least one important characteristic with other members of the group. Membership groups can be based on religion, nationality, occupation, and social class. A small-town newspaper journalist might be perceived by an observer to belong to the group "print journalists," simply because he or she shares the same occupation as other print journalists. A reference group is made up of individuals whose standards of behavior, values, and goals are desirable to the individual. We therefore compare ourselves to our reference groups and try to be like their members. The major difference between a membership group and a reference group is the degree of psychological attachment of an individual member. This attachment is much stronger in reference groups. Of course, some membership groups are also reference groups. For example, a journalist may belong to the membership group "journalists" and could also be strongly attached to the group. When this attachment is strong enough so that standards of behavior of the group are perceived by the member to be desirable, the membership group also functions as a reference group. You should convince yourself, however, that not all membership groups are reference groups.

Two important characteristics of psychological groups are goals and norms. Psychological groups exist mainly because individuals perceive that membership in the group will help them achieve goals that are important to them. These goals can take many forms. Sometimes they are very specific and agreed on by all members, such as the goal of a group of journalists from several Western countries, as pronounced in the Declaration of Talloires, to "preserve world press freedom."[12] At other times group goals may simply be the goals of individual members, and there may be little agreement on common goals for everybody. An example would be the different reasons that individual members may have for belonging to a professional association. Some may belong to advance his or her career; others may be members to uphold professional standards and values in their field. Research has shown that the more explicit the goals are and the more agreement there is about them, the more psychological attachment members will have toward the group.[13]

Another important characteristic of psychological groups is the acceptance of norms by group members. A norm is a shared expectation or beliefs about how people in a group should act and think.[14] Groups have norms about behavior, self-presentation (such as dress), values, and attitudes. Members of a psychological group accept the group's norms because they care about the group and the other members of the group. Conforming to norms shows that we like the group, thus helping us to get accepted by other members of the group.

### The Influence of Groups on Individual Members

A group's influence on its members depends on the group's cohesiveness. Cohesiveness is the "sum of all of the forces that hold people together as members of a group."[15] A group's cohesiveness is determined by external and internal factors. External factors include all of the conditions outside of the group that keep people in a group. For example, people in a prison camp, members of a family, and members of a profession are members of their respective groups because of external, usually involuntary, conditions. Internal factors determining group cohesiveness are conditions that are found within the group. An example would be the commitment that the members feel toward the group. Commitment is the degree to which a person is psychologically bound to group membership.[16] If a person feels very strongly that he or she should be a member of a group, then commitment is high. The stronger the commitment of the members, the more cohesive the group will be.

Groups that are highly cohesive will be more effective in influencing individual members than groups that are not cohesive. The process by which group members follow group norms is called conformity. Two forms of conformity are compliance and internalization. Compliance is public acceptance of a group norm without private acceptance; internalization is private acceptance of a norm.

In general, compliance is more likely to occur than internalization when group cohesiveness is based on external factors.[17] Compliance occurs whenever we do something publicly (such as wearing a coat and tie to work each day) that we do not believe in privately. There are a number of reasons why group members comply with group norms. One is a member's need for social support or to be accepted by others. People who are insecure socially—those who need emotional support or who fear isolation—are more likely to comply to group norms than people who are secure in their acceptance by others.[18] Also, the group members who are most likely to conform are those who are the marginal members of the group (those who are least accepted) and those who are in leadership positions. The marginal members comply because in doing so, they are trying to increase their acceptance by the group. On the other hand, leaders comply because they are expected to do so. They are responsible for leading the group in achieving its goals. Since norms are held to achieve group goals, compliance with the norms will facilitate attainment of the goals. Also, compliance by group leaders maintains their power within the group.

Internalization in groups occurs because groups are often the major sources of information, emotional support, and self-identification of the members.[19] As members become more dependent on the group, group goals become individual objectives, and group norms become individual beliefs.[20] Members often have to justify to themselves (and to others) continued membership in groups. While they may not be willing to admit dependence, they can justify membership by professing group goals to be their own individual goals and by convincing themselves that group norms are their own attitudes, values, and behaviors.

## Group Dynamics and Mass Communicator Behaviors

To analyze how the behaviors of mass communicators are influenced by their psychological groups, we should first identify these groups, their norms, and goals. We should then attempt to measure the degree of cohesiveness in the groups, taking into account external factors and the commitment of members to group membership. Finally, we should identify the conditions under which compliance and identification take place.

## A MULTILEVEL MODEL FOR ANALYZING MASS COMMUNICATION

As we have seen in the preceding discussion, mass communication and the behavior of individual mass communicators are best analyzed if we take into account the influence of their external environment. Dimmick and Coit have formulated an analytical model that identifies these external forces. This "multilevel" model is shown in Figure 21.1.

At the very core of the model is the individual communicator. Analysis of communication behaviors here is at the *intrapersonal level*. The major question is, "How do individual orientations affect job performance of the mass communicator?" Some of the individual orientations that have been studied are professional orientation, political ideology, and demographic characterist-

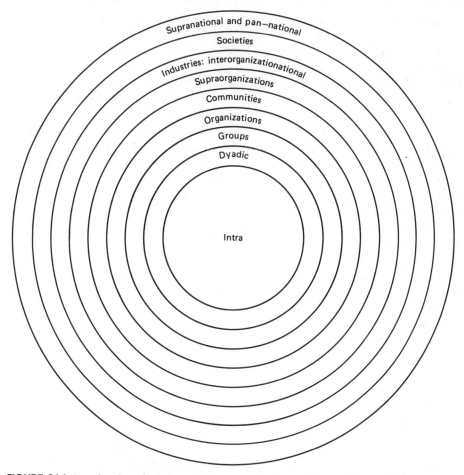

**FIGURE 21.1.** Levels of analysis in mass communication. Adapted from Dimmick and Coit, 1982.

ics.[21] Job performance variables have included definitions of news, news selection, and perceptions of autonomy.[22]

As we move outward from the core, each concentric circle represents a larger level of analysis, beginning with *dyadic* influences on the communicator. Dyadic influences are the interpersonal relationships of the communicator. Interpersonal relationships often occur in face-to-face contact between a few individuals. Examples are the interactions between reporters and their news sources and between interviewers and their guests in television entertainment and news programs. The question here is how individual behaviors of the communicators, such as selection of news events to report, are affected by face-to-face contact with another person.

At a slightly larger level of analysis are the formal and informal groups to which the mass communicator belongs. Examples of formal groups are the editorial staffs of newspapers or other news organizations that meet regularly and that are charged with specific responsibilities. Informal groups are those collections of individuals with whom a communicator comes into contact but that have no formal structure or goals. Examples are other reporters who cover the same beat. The principles of group dynamics discussed in the preceding section can be used to analyze how an individual communicator's behaviors—such as news judgment—are influenced by other members of the group.

Mass communicators are employed by media organizations, which is the next level of analysis. The media organization is a system. It is also a formal group with a formal structure, delineation of roles among its members, specific objectives (such as to make a profit), and interdependence among its members. The major question at this level of analysis is how organizational structures and their functions affect the individual communicator. Group dynamics utilizing the concepts of norms. cohesiveness, goals, and structure can be used to analyze how the organization functions.

Community influences on the individual communicator and the media organization should also be taken into account. These variables include community size, composition, competition from other media, availability of leisure services, and economic indicators such as national and metropolitan dominance.[23]

The next level of analysis, the *supraorganizational* level, consists of the larger organizations to which a mass medium may belong, such as media conglomerates, broadcast chains, and newspaper groups. Our concern at this level of analysis is how these supraorganizations influence the contents, organizational structure, and organizational policies of the individual mass medium.

The mass media can be classified according to the *industry* that they belong to. For example, we have the television, print, and radio mass media industries. At this level of analysis, we are concerned with the differences in performance and structure of individual mass media organizations that could be traced to their industry and the relationships between competing firms within the industry. We could analyze, for example, the effects of monopolies and oligopolies on the diversity in media content.

The *societal* level of analysis includes all the influences on the mass media that originate from the political and economic institutions of the country in which the media operate. The functions, structure, and "rights" of the mass media depend largely on their legal definitions within their societies. Press freedom and the functions of the mass media, for example, are defined differently in socialist, communist, and democratic political systems. Even within one political system, the rights assigned the different media may differ. In the United States, newspapers as an industry are protected by the First Amendment and are relatively insulated from direct government control. The broadcast industry (radio and television), on the other hand, is more vulnerable to government influence because stations are licensed by the Federal Communications Commission.

The largest level of analysis is at the *supranational* and *pan-national* levels. Supranational influences are exerted formally by international organizations to influence the media systems within nation-states. The United Nations Economic, Social and Cultural Organization (UNESCO), for example, in its Mac-Bride Report, outlined several policy guidelines regarding the distribution of news between developed and developing countries.[24] At the pan-national level, we are interested in how one nation can influence the media structure, contents, and policies in another country. The "media imperialism" issue, for example, can be analyzed at this level. Media imperialism is the situation in which one nation, usually more economically developed, influences the media system and audiences in another country by exporting technology, information, and actual media contents such as television programs and news copy.

## RESEARCH

There has been a recent resurgence of interest among researchers in the analysis of external forces influencing the individual mass communicator.[25] Many of these studies have been done by sociologists, using observational and qualitative methods.[26] The important theoretical influence has been structural functionalism, although a few have used group dynamics theories to explain organizational influence on communicators. In this section, we will review some studies that have used empirical methods to analyze communicator behaviors within organizations. Studies will be grouped according to the behaviors that the investigators were attempting to explain. In some cases, these were behaviors of the individual communicator such as news selection. In other cases, media "behaviors" were studied, such as quality of the product, circulation, and audience size.

### News Selection

The problem of news selection and news definition, is a constant one for journalists. Given the infinite number of events occurring each day in countless places, news reporters, copy editors and wire service editors, and others in the communication chain must select events that they consider to be "news-worthy." The major research question then, is "What influences the individual communicator's selection and definition of news?"

Over thirty years ago, White analyzed the selection process of one wire service editor, whom he called "Mr. Gates," referring to that person's role as a "gatekeeper." The gatekeeping concept was borrowed by White from the sociologist Lewin. White saw the wire service editor as a gatekeeper who got more stories from the wire service than he could print in his paper. Mr. Gates had to select a few stories that would "pass through the gate" and get published. After this case study, White concluded:

> Through studying his overt reasons for rejecting news stories from the press associations, we see how highly subjective, how based on the gatekeeper's own set of experiences, attitudes and expectations the communication of "news" really is.[27]

White concluded that *intrapersonal* forces—the gatekeeper's personal orientations—were responsible for news selection.

Other researchers have recently reanalyzed White's data and have come up with a different conclusion. McCombs and Shaw, and Hirsch suggest that the important influence on Mr. Gate's news selection is not his personal subjectivity, but simply the amount of news available, which is a structural variable.[28] Their analysis of White's data shows that the more news available in a content category from which the editor could make a selection, the more likely a story from that category would be selected.

Other writers have focused on organizational variables in their analysis of how communicators define news. DuBick, for example, puts it simply: "News is where you look for it."[29] He argues that the division of labor that defines a newspaper's editorial structure and that provides a focus for news gathering determines how the newspaper will define news. As DuBick sees it:

> The sources of news which journalists routinely seek are located in organizational centers of a society or a community (Lippmann, 1922). Organizational elites are cited frequently by news reporters as authoritative sources (Sigal, 1974), especially leaders of prominent government and private agencies. If organizational elites, themselves, are not direct news sources, press agents or public relations personnel are the contacts used by reporters (Nimmo, 1964; Sigal, 1974; Roschco, 1975). Even when covering unforeseen personal tragedies such as accidents and fires, reporters depend on police or fire officials for "accurate" information (Tuchman, 1973). Although this reliance on organizational sources routinizes newsgathering somewhat, it is never completely clear which organizations will generate significant news on a given day. Thus, metropolitan newspapers try to cover as many government, business, charitable, and voluntary organizations in their communities as they can.[30]

DuBick's point is that organizational structure (such as the beats assigned to reporters in a newspaper) routinizes the coverage of news and therefore defines what news is.

Although many studies of news selection have been guided by structural-functionalist principles and have therefore looked at external influences on the individual communicator, others have focused on intrapersonal variables. A study in 1967 by Johnstone, Slawski, and Bowman of 1300 working journalists in the United States indicated that journalists could be placed on a continuum anchored by two opposing views about the profession and practice of journalism.[31] At one end of the continuum were the "neutrals," or traditionals. These were the journalists who considered news to emerge naturally from events. They strongly believed that journalism should adhere to standards of objectivity and factual accuracy and objected to biased, sensational, or excessive coverage. At the other end, of the continuum were the "participant" journalists, who saw the reporters as actively involved in defining the "truth." Participant journalists believed that reporters must report the news in context and should sift through available information to find implications, causes, and meaning. They object strongly to news suppression and to irrelevance and superficiality in news reporting. Like the neutrals, however, they strongly believed in the concept of fairness in journalism.

Johnstone also found that traditional and activist journalists differed from each other in some personal attributes. Activist or participant journalists, compared to the neutrals, had higher levels of formal schooling, were more likely to have attended "quality" universities, were younger, had higher incomes, were more likely to be working in large cities and in large and prestigious news organizations, and were more likely to socialize with their professional colleagues.

Building on the work of Johnstone, Culbertson studied the news orientation of 258 reporters and editors on 17 U.S. newspapers.[32] He identified three clusters of journalists based on their news orientations—traditional, interpretative, and activist journalists. Traditional journalists endorse conventional decision rules in journalism such as timeliness, consequence and human interest in news, formal layout, the inverted pyramid, and the summary lead. Interpretative journalists believed that is it important to process large amounts of information before making news judgment decisions. Consequently, they believed that the journalist should define implications and causes and not simply report the facts. The activist journalists believed in interpretation of news events. They were also concerned about space, time, and organizational constraints that could limit the treatment of controversy and were more inclined than the other two groups to take sides in a controversy. Culbertson then studied how a journalist's news judgment was influenced by his or her news orientation and other intrapersonal and organization variables. News judgment was measured by asking the journalist to evaluate the importance of emphasizing different types of news such as investigative, spot, international, national, and local news. Among the explanatory variables studied were news orientation of the journalist (activist, traditional, or interpretative), years of media experience, and circulation of the respondent's paper. Culbertson found that activists emphasize investigative news and deemphasize spot news.

Traditionals emphasize spot news and local news and deemphasize investigative, international, and national news. Interpretatives favored a national emphasis in news. Other results indicated that the more years of media experience a journalist had, the more likely it was that he or she would favor an international news emphasis and the less likely it was that an investigative emphasis would be desired. Respondents from larger papers were more likely to favor international and national news compared to journalists from smaller papers.

## Communicator Autonomy

Communicator autonomy is the amount of freedom that an individual communicator has in encoding messages. Since actual autonomy is difficult to measure, the variable often studied is *perceived* autonomy. Perceived autonomy is measured by asking a communicator how much freedom he or she has in selecting and encoding messages. Most of the studies of communicator autonomy have focused on journalists.

Johnstone reported that perceived autonomy of journalists varied inversely with organizational size.[33] Journalists from smaller news organizations perceived that they had more autonomy than journalists from larger organizations. Becker reanalyzed Johnstone's data and concluded that differences in organizational type (newspapers, broadcast media, or wire service) were a more important determinant of perceived autonomy than size.[34]

Dimmick and Coit studied communicator autonomy in more detail, also using Johnstone's data and including structural, organizational, and intraindividual variables in their analysis.[35] Two measures of reporter's perceived autonomy were used—story selection autonomy and content autonomy. Story selection autonomy was measured on a four-point scale by asking the respondents how much freedom they had in selecting their stories. Possible answers were "almost complete freedom," "a great deal," "some," and "none at all." Content autonomy was measured on a three-point scale by asking respondents how much freedom they had in deciding which aspects of a story should be emphasized. Possible answers were "almost complete freedom," "a great deal," and "not too much." These two measures constituted the "reportorial autonomy" variable, which was the intraindividual behavior that Dimmick and Coit wanted to explain. The explanatory or predictor variables were the following.

1. Whether the reporter's firm was a member of a chain (a larger organization) or not. This was a supraorganization variable.
2. The size of the chain or number of news organizations owned by the parent company (size of the supraorganization).
3. The size of the market served by the reporter's organization (market size, a community variable).
4. The size of the editorial staff (organization size, an intraorganization variable).

5. The reporter's professional experience (years experience, an individual-level variable).
6. Respondent's political orientation, from extreme left to extreme right, with "middle of the road" as the midpoint.

Dimmick and Coit found that the significant predictors of selection autonomy were, in order of importance, years of experience, industry, political lean, and market size. Reporters who had more years of experience perceived greater selection autonomy than reporters who had fewer years of experience. Reporters in the newspaper industry perceived less selection autonomy than reporters in the broadcast industry. Left-leaning reporters perceived *less* selection autonomy than right-leaning reporters. Reporters in larger markets perceived *less* autonomy than reporters in smaller markets. Organization size, supraorganization size, and chain or nonchain variables were not related to perceived selection autonomy. The model (all variables used as predictors, taken together) explained only 9.6 percent of the variance in perceived selection autonomy. This indicates that the significant relationships uncovered by the analysis are *weak*, although we can be quite certain that they occur in the population represented by the sample of journalists that was studied.

Story content autonomy was significantly predicted by only two variables—years of experience and industry. Again, reporters with more years on the job perceived greater story content autonomy. Also, reporters in the broadcast media perceived greater autonomy than reporters in the print media. All the variables in the model explained only 7.2 percent of the variance in story content autonomy. Years on the job was the most important predictor of selection and story content autonomy. Two explanations are suggested by Dimmick and Coit for the importance of years on the job as a predictor of autonomy. First, as Breed's analysis of social control in the newsroom suggests, experienced reporters are left alone because they have absorbed news policy and can be trusted to conform to its requirements.[36] Second, the strong craft norms in journalism value on-the-job experience highly.[37] As a result, the work of the newcomer is closely watched, while the more experienced journalists are monitored less.

Dimmick and Coit's analysis also showed that more control was exercised over selection autonomy than story content autonomy. This indicates that control is exercised more often over the reporters' freedom to select stories and less often of their writing and structuring of facts. Dimmick and Coit suggest that, from the viewpoint of organizational management, this is an effective control strategy. Since reporters place a high value on autonomy,[38] indirect control at the early stages of news gathering (such as in the selection of news stories) is less likely to produce conflict between editors and reporters than more direct control measures such as killing or editing stories that do not conform to the organization's policy.

Another interesting result of the Dimmick and Coit study is the influence of the industry-level variable on autonomy. Dimmick and Coit found that broadcast journalists perceived greater autonomy than newspaper journalists. However, they also found that left-leaning reporters were more likely to perceive *less* autonomy when they were members of the broadcast industry than when they were newspaper reporters. There are several explanations for this finding. The broadcast industry is more vulnerable to government control than the print industry, since individual broadcast stations are licensed by the Federal Communications Commission. Given the conservative political climate at the time the study was conducted in 1971, two years after attacks on the press by the Nixon administration, the broadcast industry may have been more likely to constrain left-leaning reporters in response to the Nixon administration's criticisms of the press.

Another explanation may be found in inherent differences between print and broadcast journalists. Still another reanalysis of the Johnstone data by Becker showed that broadcast journalists in general were more likely to reject the neutral role of the press and more likely to analyze and interpret the news than print journalists.[39] They also reported higher levels of autonomy in selecting news stories, less editing of their copy, and more extensive feedback from superiors, colleagues, and their audience. It seems then that a "ceiling effect" could explain why left-leaning broadcast journalists perceive less autonomy than left-leaning print journalists. Autonomy is already given *all* broadcast journalists, and more autonomy is not possible for the left-leaning journalists, since additional autonomy could mean total loss of control by management over their reporters.

## Media Performance

How does one measure media performance? The structural-functionalist model we discussed earlier in this chapter suggests that we look at the goals or objectives of the organizational system for answers to this question. Given the "social-responsibility" view of the press in American society, we would have to say that a major goal of the press (or the mass media) is to serve the informational and decision-making needs of the community. We could then study the audience of a particular mass medium and see if these "effects" are forthcoming from media use. Another strategy is to analyze the *products* of the mass media—the contents of newspapers and broadcast programming. We can make certain assumptions about what types of contents and message formats could lead to an informed audience and then see whether these attributes are found in the products of mass communication. The former approach, known generally as "effects analysis," is treated extensively in Part IV of this text, which includes chapters on mass communication and socialization. In this chapter, we will examine the content and format attributes of the mass media as indicators of media performance. We will also identify the organizational and structural determinants of media contents and formats.

There is another important measure of media performance, given the capitalist system of the U.S. economy. The mass media in the United States are operated—many say primarily—as businesses. A major goal, then, is to make money. Profitability is often (but not always) associated with audience numbers. Thus, from a structural-functionalist view, another question that has to be asked is, "What conditions or variables determine audience size, circulation and profitability?"

### Format and Content Measures of Media Performance

Most empirical studies of the formats and contents of the mass media have been of newspapers. Newspapers are often judged on the basis of their contents and formats, and lists of good and poor newspapers are available periodically.[40] Generally, the following qualities are ascribed to "good" newspapers.[41]

1. *News Existence:* Extent of local, regional, national, and international coverage; amount of investigative and background pieces; stories about minority groups and special-interest groups in the community.
2. *News Evaluation:* The thoroughness and balance of the stories mentioned under "news existence."
3. *Editorial Page:* Comment on local, state, and national issues; endorsements for local, state, and national government offices; balance of editorial columnists; quality of arguments.
4. *News Presentation:* Quality of writing, editing, typography and layout, photography, picture use, headlines, and selection and play of stories.

Using these criteria, Becker, Beam, and Russial rated 109 newspapers in New England. The ratings were based on essays about the papers that had been written by thirteen journalists and ex-journalists about each paper in that region.[42] Each newspaper was assigned a score that indicated the "quality" of its performance. Becker and his colleagues then correlated eight community variables and twenty one organizational variables with the newspaper ratings to find out which variables would be significant predictors of press performance. The community measures were community size, community growth, market growth, retail sales, median school years of the adult population, family income in the community, religious diversity, and newspaper competition. The organizational measures were number of full-time news editorial staff, number of part-time news editorial staff, number of total news editorial staff hours, number of women on the news editorial staff, number of women on the women's page editorial staff, number of blacks and Hispanic reporters on the news editorial staff, starting salary for reporters with no experience, top salary, years to top salary, staff turnover, education and experience of recent employees, whether the staff was unionized, participation of staff in professional organizations, percent of expenditures for news editorial, average size of news hole, type of ownership (whether the paper was a single corporation, a member of a small chain, or a member of a large chain), whether an audience survey was done in the last five years, publisher's profitability estimate, advertising revenues, daily circulation, and whether a Sunday edition was published.

Becker, Beam, and Russial found that organizational variables were correlated more frequently with newspaper performance than community variables. The following variables were significantly and *positively* related to performance (meaning that an increase in each variable was accompanied by an increase in performance): number of full-time staff ($r = 0.25$); number of women on the news editorial staff ($r = 0.29$); number of women on non-women's page news editorial staff ($r = 0.28$); starting salary, no experience ($r = 0.27$); education and experience of recent employees ($r = 0.41$); participation of staff in professional organizations ($r = 0.25$); whether an audience survey had been done in the last five years ($r = 0.23$); average size of the news hole ($r = 0.19$); type of ownership ($r = 0.34$); daily circulation ($r = 0.24$); and whether a Sunday edition was published ($r = 0.25$).

Only two community variables were significantly related to newspaper performance. These were median school years ($r = 0.18$) and religious diversity ($r = 0.21$).

According to Becker *et al.*, these results show that organizational variables are more important correlates of newspaper performance than community variables. "Good" newspapers had the following characteristics: more full-time news editorial staffers, more women on the news editorial staff, higher salaries for starting staffers with no experience, more educated and experienced recent staffers; staff members who participated in professional seminars and workshops; larger circulations; larger news holes; and those belonging to large media corporations.

This study is important, since it is among the first to analyze relationships between structural-organizational variables and media performance. However, we should remember that the correlations reported do not "prove" causality. We cannot tell from the analysis, for example, whether a newspaper is good because it has a large circulation or whether it has a large circulation because it is good. Also, the analysis was done for papers in only one region of the country (New England.)

It is interesting that Becker *et al.*, found a *positive* correlation between media performance and chain ownership. Most earlier studies have shown that intermedia monopolies such as chains were not related to the quality and diversity of the daily newspaper.[43] Cross-media ownership—a monopoly where the newspaper owners also own the broadcast media in a community or vice-versa—is another matter. Stempel in 1973 compared mass communication behaviors in a town where a cross-media monopoly existed with mass communication behaviors in two comparable towns where the newspapers and broadcast media were owned by different firms.[44] He found that:

1. Residents in the monopoly town knew less about current events than residents in comparable cities with media competition.
2. Residents in the monopoly town got less news than residents in the other towns.

Stempel concluded that overall, the cross-media monopoly did not serve the residents of that town well; they used the media less, were less informed, and less news was available to them.

### Audience Size

Audience size is often considered to be an important indicator of a mass medium's performance; the greater the audience size, the better the medium is performing in the marketplace, and the more profitable it should be. This principle is more readily apparent in the broadcast industry, where Nielsen and ARB ratings—measures of audience size—determine how much the broadcaster can charge for advertising time. In the newspaper industry, circulation and readership are sometimes related to profitability; at other times, they are not. Blankenburg has shown how a large newspaper chain can control circulation to increase profits.[45] Most studies of media performance, however, have looked at audience size as a measure of "successful" performance. Many of these studies have dealt with newspapers.

Blankenburg classifies the factors that could affect newspaper consumption into two categories: structural factors and discretionary factors.[46] Structural factors are those that the publisher cannot control because they are found in the newspaper's external environment. Examples are demographics and economic conditions in the community in which the newspaper is distributed and competition. Discretionary factors can be controlled by the publisher; they are often found within the newspaper's environment and include content, design, and marketing strategies.

Blankenburg points out that there is a common assumption among publishers and some mass communication researchers that discretionary or quality factors are important determinants of circulation. He questions this assumption and suggests that structural factors are more important. Blankenburg analyzed newspapers in forty-six Standard Metropolitan Statistical Areas (SMSA) and compared the relative effectiveness of quality and structural variables in predicting newspaper circulation. The quality variable was whether a newspaper had been classified as a "bad" or "good" paper by a journalism review. The structural variable studied was number of households in the SMSA area. Blankenburg's results follow.

1. The total circulation of all newspapers in a market is not related to the number of dailies published in that market. This indicates that demand for newspapers is "inelastic"—more newspapers do not mean that more people will be reading newspapers. As more newspapers are published in an area, those newspapers will simply have to share the same "pie," and each paper will get a smaller share of the pie. This finding is also reported by McCombs in his test of "relative constancy" in the newspaper marketplace.[47]
2. The quality of an individual newspaper is not related to its circulation. A similar result is reported by Weaver and Mullins in their comparison of

the content and format characteristics of "leading" (those with higher circulations) and "trailing" newspapers in the same market.[48]

3. The single best predictor of newspaper circulation in the study was number of households in the SMSAs: the more households, the greater a newspaper's circulation.

Blankenburg's study provides evidence that a newspaper's circulation is determined primarily by its environment. In particular, circulation depends on the number of households in its market. Discretionary variables such as the quality of the paper had little effect on circulation.

## The Organizational Structure of Newspapers

In this section, we will take a slightly different approach and consider how an organizational variable—the structure of a newspaper—is affected by its environment. We have so far looked at how behaviors of the individual communicator and performance of the mass media are affected by structural variables. Now we will take the media organization's structure as the dependent variable and analyze how community structures affect it.

A newspaper's organizational structure, according to DuBick, is determined to a large extent by characteristics of the community.[49] DuBick defines newspaper structure in two ways: the number of distinct departments in the organization, and the evenness of distribution of personnel among the different departments. A newspaper with many departments and with just about equal numbers of personnel in each department is a highly differentiated organization.

The organizational structure of newspaper is susceptible to influence from the community because the newspaper depends on the community for both its organizational inputs and outputs. The inputs are the information supplied to it by the community, which it then processes into news; outputs are the revenues of the paper from advertising and subscriptions. The organizational structure of the newspaper should be able to maximize both the flow of inputs (information) into the organization and the resulting outputs (revenue).

The characteristics of the community studied by DuBick follow.

1. National and metropolitan dominance, an indicator of the strength of the communities' retail economies and measured by the following indices: number of scientific journals published, number of airline flights from the city, number of voluntary organization headquarters, number of multinational corporation headquarters, number of foreign trade offices, number of celebrities born in the city, number of U.S. district court judges, percent of SMSA labor force in the city, percent of SMSA retail sales in the city, retail sales per capita, and total newspaper circulation per capita.

2. Leisure services, which included the number and diversity of available

leisure activities such as restaurants, nightclubs, and movie theaters.

3. Heterogeneity of the population, measured by racial and occupational differentiation.

4. Social class, indicated by the proportion of "middle-class" residents.

5. Competition, measured by the proportion of newspaper circulation accounted for by the two largest newspapers in a metropolitan community (the larger this proportion, the less competition there was).

DuBick tested six hypotheses regarding the relationship of these community variables to the organizational structure of newspapers.

**Hypothesis 1.** Greater differentiation in newspaper structure occurs in newspapers located in nationally dominant cities.

DuBick argues that an important goal of a newspaper is to obtain as much advertising revenue as it can. This requires a complex organization, or one that is highly differentiated. Therefore, when a community has a strong retail economy, the newspaper would need a more differentiated staff to tap the advertising revenue potential in that community.

**Hypothesis 2.** Greater differentiation occurs in newspapers published in metropolitan-dominant cities.

Cities that dominate their immediate surroundings (a metropolitan-dominant city) act as retail trade centers. Therefore, more advertising revenue is potentially available.

**Hypothesis 3.** Greater differentiation occurs in newspapers when metropolitan leisure services are more abundant.

Since an increasing proportion of urban personal income is spent on leisure and since businesses providing these leisure activities are potential sources of advertising revenue, a more differentiated organization will be needed to tap these sources of revenue.

**Hypothesis 4.** Greater differentiation occurs in newspapers when the metropolitan population is largely middle and upper middle class. The potential audience for newspapers is made up of middle- and upper-middle-class people. The larger this group of people in a community, the more likely it is that they will have diverse interests and news preferences. Therefore, in that situation, a newspaper would have to be more differentiated in structure to satisfy the variety of news preferences.

**Hypothesis 5.** Greater differentiation occurs in newspapers when the metropolitan population is more racially and occupationally diverse (same rationale as Hypothesis 4).

**Hypothesis 6.** Greater differentiation occurs in newspapers when metropolitan competition is higher. In such a situation, there will be a need to penetrate new markets (such as suburban markets) to increase or maintain circulation. Broader and more varied news coverage must be provided as well as better distribution and subscription efforts. Consequently, a more complex or differentiated organizational structure is needed.

To test these hypotheses, DuBick studied the newspaper structures and community variables in seventy-two newspapers from sixty-seven metropolitan centers. He found that national dominance and the volume of leisure services were the most important predictors of evenness of distribution of personnel in a newspaper among departments (D). This supported Hypotheses 1 and 3. Also, occupational and racial heterogeneity were related to D (support for Hypothesis 5). The other community variables did not predict D.

When number of departments in the newspaper organizational structure (Nd) is used as the dependent variable, six of the seven community variables were found to be significant predictors. Social class was the strongest predictor of Nd, followed by leisure services and national dominance. The only variable not related to Nd was occupational differentiation.

These findings suggest that functional divisions within newspapers, as indicated by the number of departments, increase when the newspaper's metropolitan environment provides greater uncertainties about resources (advertising), audiences (social class and racial differentiation), and competition (market concentration). To deal with these uncertainties, the newspaper would have to be highly organized with highly segmented structures.

On the other hand, the distribution of staff across departments (the D measure) depends primarily on the complexity of news channels leading into the newspaper. Metropolitan communities with many and diverse government, corporate, and voluntary organizations generate more news; therefore, a newspaper would have to distribute its staff more evenly to cover these different sources of news.

DuBick provides convincing evidence that a newspaper's environment determines to a significant degree how it will be organizationally structured.

## SUMMARY

Communication is best understood if we take into account the environment of communicators—their organizations, communities, and other social institutions to which they belong. Communicators in organizations can be analyzed using the structural-functional and group dynamics theoretical models.

Communication behaviors such as news selection, perceptions of autonomy, and media performance can be explained by organizational and other structural variables. The organizational structure of communication organizations can be explained by the structure of the communities in which the newspapers operate.

## REVIEW QUESTION

**1.** Discuss some examples of how organizations and social institutions have affected the behaviors of individual communicators.

## ENDNOTES

1. For example, D. M. White, "The Gate-keeper: A Case Study in The Selection of News," *Journalism Quarterly, 27,* 1950, pp. 383–396.
2. Richard Farace, Peter Monge, and Hamish Russell, *Communicating and Organizing* (Reading, Mass: Addison-Wesley, 1977).
3. F. K. Berrien, *General and Social Systems* (New Brunswick, N.J.: Rutgers University Press, 1968).
4. Herbert A. Simon, *Administrative Behavior,* 2nd ed. (New York: MacMillan, 1957).
5. Farace, Monge, and Russell, *op. cit.*
6. *Ibid.*
7. *Ibid.*
8. *Ibid.*
9. *Ibid.*
10. Drury Sherrod, *Social Psychology* (New York: Random House, i982).
11. *Ibid.*
12. Kusum Singh and Bertram Gross, "MacBride: The Report and the Response," *Journal of Communication, 31,* 1981, pp. 104–117.
13. Sherrod, *op. cit.*
14. *Ibid.*
15. D. Cartwright and A. Zander (eds.), *Group Dynamics: Research and Theory* (New York: Harper & Row, 1968).
16. C. A. Kiesler, *The Psychology of Commitment: Experiments Linking Behavior to Belief* (New York: Academic Press, 1971).
17. Sherrod, *op. cit.*
18. *op. cit.*
19. J. Cooper and B. L. Duncan, "Cognitive Dissonance as a Function of Self-Esteem and Logical Inconsistency," *Journal of Personality, 39,* 1971, pp. 289–302.
20. Sherrod, *op. cit.*
21. John Johnstone, Edward J. Slawski, and William W. Bowman, *The News People* (Urbana: University of Illinois Press, 1976).
22. For example, John Dimmick and Philip Coit, "Levels of Analysis in Mass Media Decision Making," *Communication Research, 9,* 1982, pp. 3–32.
23. Michael DuBick, "The Organizational Structure of Newspapers in Relation to Their Metropolitan Environments," *Administrative Science Quarterly, 23,* 1978, pp. 418–433.
24. Singh and Gross, *op. cit.*
25. James Ettema and D. Charles Whitney, *Individuals in Mass Media Organizations* (Beverly Hills, Calif.: Sage Publications, 1982).
26. For example, G. Tuchman, "Making News By Doing Work: Routinizing the Unexpected," *American Journal of Sociology, 79,* 1973, pp. 110–131.
27. White, *op. cit.*
28. M. McCombs and D. L. Shaw, "Structuring the 'Unseen Environment,'" *Journal of*

*Communication, 26,* 1977, pp. 18–22. Also P. M. Hirsch, "Occupational Organizational and Institutional Models in Mass Media Research," in F. G. Kline (ed.), *Strategies for Communication Research* (Beverly Hills, Calif.: Sage Publications, 1977).

29. DuBick, *op. cit.*
30. *Ibid.*
31. Johnstone, Slawski, and Bowman, *op. cit.*
32. Hugh M. Culbertson, "Three Perspectives on American Journalism," *Journalism Monographs, 83,* 1983.
33. Johnstone, Slawski, and Bowman, *op. cit.*
34. L. B. Becker, "Organizational Variables and the Study of Newsroom Behavior: A Review and Discussion of U.S. Research," paper presented at the 11th Annual Conference of the International Association for Mass Communication Research, Warsaw, Poland, 1978.
35. Dimmick and Coit, *op. cit.*
36. W. Breed, "Social Control in the Newsroom: A Functional Analysis," *Social Forces, 32,* 1955, pp. 326–335.
37. D. E. Garvey, "Social Control in the Television Newsroom," Ph.D. dissertation, Stanford University, 1971.
38. Johnstone, Slawski, and Bowman, *op. cit.*
39. Becker, *op. cit.*
40. For example, William B. Blankenburg, "Structural Determination of Circulation," *Journalism Quarterly, 58,* 1981, pp. 543–551.
41. L. B. Becker, R. Beam, and J. Russial, "Correlates of Daily Newspaper Performance in New England," *Journalism Quarterly, 55,* 1978, pp. 100–108.
42. *Ibid.*
43. *Ibid.*
44. Guido H. Stempel, III, "Effects on Performance of a Cross-Media Monopoly," *Journalism Monographs, 29,* 1973.
45. William Blankenburg, "Newspaper Ownership and Control of Circulation to Increase Profits," *Journalism Quarterly, 59,* Autumn 1982, pp. 390–398.
46. Blankenburg, *op. cit.,* 1981.
47. Maxwell McCombs, "Mass Media in the Marketplace," *Journalism Monographs, 24,* August 1972.
48. David H. Weaver, L. E. Mullins, and Maxwell McCombs, "Competing Daily Newspapers: A Comparison of Content and Format," *News Research For Better Newspapers, 7,* July 1975, pp. 45–55.
49. DuBick, *op. cit.*

# PART VI_____

# MASS COMMUNICATION AND SOCIETY_____

The mass media can influence not only individuals, but social
institutions and communities as well. In this section we use principles from the social change theories of functionalism, Marxism, and
neo-Marxism to explain the role of mass communication in the
diffusion of information, opinions, behaviors, and culture. Analysis
is at the macro or societal level and the emphasis is on how social
stability *and* change can be facilitated by mass communication.

# 22 _____

# MASS COMMUNICATION
# AND SOCIAL CHANGE _____

In this chapter we will consider the role of mass communication in social change. We will define social change and discuss two sociological theories that explain how social change occurs. Then we will look at the role of mass communication in three specific areas of change: the diffusion of information, the diffusion of innovations, and the diffusion of culture. Finally, we will discuss how the introduction of new technology in mass communications has affected various social systems.

## SOCIAL CHANGE

What changes in "social change?" Who changes? What do we mean by change? These are some of the questions that we will have to answer in defining social change.

### What Changes?

According to the sociologist Emile Durkheim, "social facts" are the variables that change in the analysis of social change. Social facts are aggregations of individual actions in a social system that

> . . . yield new phenomena, differing from those which take place in individual consciousness. These facts reside exclusively in the very society itself which produces them, and not in its parts, i.e., its members. They are, then, in this sense external to individual consciousness. . . . Here, then are ways of acting, thinking, and feeling that present the noteworthy property of existing outside the individual consciousness. These types of conduct or thought are not only external to the individual, but are, moreover, endowed with coercive power, by virtue of which they impose themselves upon him, independent of his individual will.[1]

Let us take a closer look at Durkheim's definition of social facts. First, social facts exist "outside of the individual." They are aggregates or collections of individual actions, thoughts, and decisions. They are properties of a group or social system and not of the individual members, although they do originate in individual action. Second, social facts can influence or exercise "external constraints" on the actions and thoughts of individuals who belong to the group or social system. Social facts can influence individuals because they are a source of rewards and punishments and are sometimes used by individuals as a measure of what the rest of the group or social system is doing.

Social facts can be subdivided into two sets: the institutional or structural set and the aggregative or distributive outcomes set.[2] The institutional or structural set consists of the physical properties of a social system such as the social stratification system (distribution of social classes), legal rules, transportation system, postal system, and so on. A nation's communication system— the number and location of its newspapers, television and radio stations, and other mass media—belongs to the structural or institutional set of social facts. The aggregative or distributive outcomes set consists of collections or summaries of individual actions such as marriage rates, rates of television viewing, newspaper reading and radio listening, and rates of diffusion of information, new ideas (innovations), and life-styles. Both the structural and aggregative sets originate in individual actions and choices and represent collections of these actions and choices. The major difference is that the structural set consists of tangible or substantially material variables, while the aggregative set is intangible. For example, I can "see" a community's mass media system, but I cannot see a community's divorce rate or the rate at which information about a public event spreads.

Social facts exist outside of the individual members of a social structure. You cannot analyze the legal structure *in* individuals, since our courts and laws exist outside of individuals. Similarly, aggregates of individual actions such as divorce and suicide rates are properties of the group being analyzed and not of its individual members.

How do social facts influence individuals? Our discussion of the micro- and macrolevels of analysis in Chapter 5 can help us understand how social facts influence individual behaviors. Social facts are macrovariables while individual actions, thoughts, and choices are microvariables. Individual behaviors are limited by macrovariables in many ways. First, macrovariables can impose physical limitations on individual action. We are limited in what we can know of international affairs, for example, by the availability of news media in our communities and by the availability of international news in the media. Second, macrovariables or social facts can determine how rewards and punishments are distributed in a social system. Laws punish certain behaviors. A person's position in the social structure determines the availability of economic and other resources such as information and credit facilities. Finally, macrovariables or social facts guide individual behaviors in less coercive ways by providing the individual with an assessment of how others in the social system are behaving. Information about the divorce rate in the community, for example, can influence an individual's decision to get married or not get married.

Although we are mainly concerned in this chapter with how social facts change and how they influence individual behaviors, we should remember, as we had emphasized in Chapter 5, that social facts are best understood by first understanding individual behavior. Social facts constrain or influence individual actions. They are also determined by individual actions. The relationship between individual and collective behaviors or social facts is reciprocal, not one way.

## Who Changes?

In analyzing social change, the unit of analysis is a group of individuals, not the individuals themselves. There are many definitions of "group," but the one we will use is the definition given in Chapter 21 of a membership group. A membership group is a collection of individuals who have at least one important characteristic in common, who have common goals, common norms, and who are dependent on each other for obtaining the group's goals. To Durkheim, a group can be a small unit of co-workers, a social class, or a nation-state.[3] A group exercises some control over its members. Because its members are interdependent, a group is a social system.

When we study social change, we consider how groups of individuals change. Groups can be small units such as the workers in a factory or the reporters in a newspaper office. Groups can also be large units such as members of a socioeconomic class in a country (for example, tenant farmers in a developing nation) or all of the population in a nation. The important characteristic of these groups is that they are able to influence behaviors of individual members—directly, through rules, or indirectly, such as by showing social approval for following group norms.

## What Is Change?

In analyzing social change, we have said that social facts change and that the unit of analysis is the membership group. But what do we mean by "change?" Appelbaum, a sociologist, gives a useful guide for defining change. He says that change has the following characteristics.[4]

1. *Magnitude.* The magnitude of change refers to the proportion of the social system or group that is affected, the centrality to the system of the affected individual units, and the degree of difference between the new state or condition of the system brought about by the change and the old state. Using these criteria, change can either be "large scale" or "small scale." Most studies of social change are interested in large-scale change, where a large proportion of the social system is affected, the affected members are important or central to the system, and the new state of the system brought about by the change is different in many ways from the old state.

2. *Time Span.* Change can occur quickly, in weeks, or slowly, in generations of group members. Also, change can be temporary or permanent. These distinctions refer to the time span of change. Change that takes a long time or that is permanent is long-term change. Change that takes less time or that is relatively temporary is short-term change.

3. *Effect on Changing Unit.* Change in a social system is generally brought about by two types of variables: endogenous and exogenous variables. Endogenous variables originate within the system. An example is an increase in profits of an automobile manufacturer. Exogenous variables originate outside the system. Examples for the automobile manufacturer are government regulations regarding pollution or a shortage of oil. In either case, these variables are potential sources of change in the system.

The analysis of social change does not require that potential sources of change—endogenous or exogenous variables—actually bring about a change in the system. We are interested in the effects of these variables on the system. These effects could either be what Parsons calls "equilibrium," or "structural change."[5] Equilibrium, sometimes called homeostasis, is "no change." Analysis of equilibrium focuses on the processes that serve to maintain the system without any important changes in its structure, even when potential sources of change are introduced. In our example of the automobile manufacturer, if an oil shortage does not cause any changes in the assembly plants, hiring policies, or in output (automobiles manufactured), then we would analyze why no change occurred. Structural change, on the other hand, is characterized by a change in the social system. This change could be in its organization, policies, or outputs. More realistically, we would expect an oil shortage to change policies and outputs of the automobile manufacturer. Smaller, gas-efficient automobiles would probably have to be built; workers would have to be laid off if the public does not buy as many automobiles as are being produced. The analysis of social change is just as concerned with the processes leading to equilibrium as it is with processes leading to structural change.

## What Causes Change?

What causes a social system to change? This question is a controversial one in sociology. The answer depends on which theory of social change you accept. (Two of these theories are discussed in the next section of this chapter.) Social change theories have identified the following variables as potential causes of change in a social system.

1. *Group and Class Conflicts.* This is often referred to as the "materialistic" view of society and social change and was first suggested by Karl Marx.[6] According to the materialistic view, social conflict in a system brings about a change in the ownership and control of the means of production (of economic goods). Consequently, the major cause of any change in the social system is *conflict*.

*Media responsible for* [handwritten marginal note]

2. *Ideas and Values.* According to some social change theorists, social change is preceded by a change in ideas or values held by individual members. Max Weber, for example, suggested that a change in values—from whatever was existing to an acceptance of the "Protestant ethic"—is necessary for the economic development of a system.[7] The Protestant ethic, as defined by Weber, places importance on achievement, self-denial, self-reliance, and the saving and investing of wealth. Weber believed that the Protestant ethic is a requirement for the development of a capitalist economic system that then leads to economic prosperity.

To Daniel Lerner, the "development" of a social system from a "traditional" to "modern" society requires that members of the system first develop an "empathic" personality.[8] Empathy, as defined by Lerner, is the ability to place or imagine oneself in new situations. This ability, Lerner believes, allows a traditional person such as a peasant in a village to imagine what it would be like to live under better economic conditions. Empathy motivates the individual to work harder and to achieve the imagined "good life."

Although Weber and Lerner had many supporters, their hypotheses regarding the importance of values in social change have not been unequivocally supported by empirical studies. There have been too many contradictory results for us to accept the assumptions that the Protestant ethic or the empathic personality are necessary for economic or national development.

3. *Technological Change.* For some scholars, technological change or the introduction of innovations is the main cause of social change. Thus, new technology such as direct satellite television or a new corn hybrid could cause changes in a social system. This is the area of study favored by diffusion researchers such as Everett Rogers.[9]

## THEORIES OF SOCIAL CHANGE

Many theories of social change have guided the analysis of national development, population mobilization, cultural change, and economic change. Two theories, in particular, have been influential throughout the years. These are functionalism and Marxism.[10]

### Functionalism

Functionalism has been one of the dominant theories in American sociology during the past thirty years. Applied to the study of social change, functionalism is best exemplified by the "grand" theories of Parsons.[11]

Functionalism is an equilibrium-type theory of social change. It focuses on how social systems remain stable in the presence of forces that might lead to change. This is how Parsons defines stability.

A system then is stable or (relatively) in equilibrium when the relation between its structure and the processes which go on within it and between its environment are such as to maintain those properties and relations, which for the purposes in hand have been called its structure, relatively unchanged. Very generally, always in "dynamic" systems, this maintenance is dependent on continuously varying processes, which "neutralize" either endogenous or exogenous sources of variability which, if they went far enough, would change structure.[12]

Functionalists study how and why social systems *do not* change. They are interested in four processes within social systems that neutralize forces that could lead to change. These processes, which Parsons calls "functional prerequisites for existence," are adaptation, goal attainment, integration, and latent pattern maintenance. Adaptation is the system's ability to exist in its physical or organic environment (which might harbor forces for change) with a minimum of change in its structure. Goal attainment is the ability of the system to direct the activities of its individual members in a concerted effort to achieve the system's goals. Integration refers to how well the different individual units of the social system work together. Latent pattern maintenance refers to how well the system can maintain its cultural patterns or values. The main focus of functionalism is the stability of the system, including the variables and processes that maintain stability.

Most functionalists believe that a change in cultural patterns or values in a system is a prerequisite for structural change. However, they also believe that changes in cultural patterns occur only with great difficulty and over long periods of time. The result is that social systems, although capable of changing, rarely change.

Although functionalism has been an influential theory of social change, it has been criticized on many points. Guessous, for example, point out that:

An equilibrium theory like that of Parsons can neither explain the occurrence of radical changes in society nor account for the phenomena which accompany them; it says next to nothing about what happens when a social system is in disequilibrium, and only tells us what that system will be like if and when it has reached a new position of rest. It is tied to the image of society whose historical development holds no surprises. Nothing new and unique, no important transformations ever happen in the normal world of equilibrium theory.[13]

It is clear then that functionalism explains stability in social systems. Like other equilibrium theories, it conceives of society as a fairly stable organism with parts that go together in a system of functional interdependence. Although change is possible, change seldom alters the fundamental structure of society. Functionalism helps us understand why some social systems (such as the United States in the modern age) have not changed significantly. However, it cannot explain why other systems—many of them existing today—have changed drastically.

## Marxism

Another class of social change theories, in contrast to equilibrium theories, considers change as inherent in all social systems. These theories are generally known as "conflict theories." They focus on the study of change itself instead of on stability. Like equilibrium theories, conflict theories consider social systems to be made up of mutually interdependent structures. However, they "see structural change everywhere," while equilibrium theories "see stability everywhere."[14] Most modern conflict theories have been heavily influenced by Karl Marx, so we will discuss him first.

We cannot, of course, discuss Marx (or Parsons) fully in an introductory text such as this. His writings deal not only with social change, but also with various philosophical or metaphysical propositions such as the ideal of the "classless society." What we present here is a summary of his ideas about social change.

According to Marx, progress in society is achieved primarily through conflict. Dahrendorf, an influential neo-Marxist (modern-day Marxist), interprets Marx's analysis of the role of conflict in social change in this way.

> For Marx, society is not primarily a smoothly functioning order of the form of a social organism, a social system, or a static social fabric. Its dominant characteristic is, rather, the continuous change of not only its elements, but its very structured form. This change in turn bears witness to the presence of conflicts as an essential feature of every society. Conflicts are not random; they are a systematic product of the structure of society itself. According to this image, there is no order except in the regularity of change.[15]

Marx is interested in the changing "structural form" of society. This structural form, as seen by Marx, is represented by the forces of production in a social system. Stinchcombe explains Marx's concept of production forces as social structure in this way.

> The relative power of social classes is determined by the mode of production, by the authority system required by a given technology, and by who owns the productive property. The mode of production changes over time with advancing technology, extensions of the market, larger units of production, and the like. Hence the distribution of power among classes changes systematically over historical time.[16]

The social structure in Marxist theory consists of the mode of production (for example, cottage industries or large factories), ownership of productive property (by large corporations or the workers themselves), and the distribution of economic power among the classes (the economic gap between workers and owners). These are the elements of the social structure that change. Change occurs because of conflict between the workers who perform the productive function and the owners of the means of production.

Let us take a closer look at the Marxist analysis of class conflict as a cause of social change, because it is in these metaphysical arguments (postulates that cannot be tested empirically) that most neo-Marxists have disagreed with Marx. According to Marx, social change in a capitalist society occurs in these sequential steps.[17]

1. In a capitalist society, the classes tend to polarize increasingly. Society breaks up into two opposing classes—the bourgeoisie and the proletariat. The bourgeoisie own the means of production; they are the factory owners and the landowners. The proletariat are the workers in factories and farms.

2. The classes become increasingly different from each other as they polarize. The proletariat, or sections of it, become increasingly poorer while the bourgeoisie accumulates more wealth. Wealth is increasingly concentrated in a fewer members of society—members of the bourgeoisie class.

3. As the classes polarize, members of each class become more homogeneous. Other groups in society are absorbed by either the proletariat or bourgeoisie classes.

4. Extreme polarization, as indicated by increased domination of the proletariat by the bourgeoisie, brings about violent revolution. Social change is completed when the formerly oppressed class (the proletariat) gains power.

To Marx, social change is accomplished by a proletarian revolution. The result of this revolution is a "classless" society, where all private property is abolished. This, of course, is the Marxist vision of the ideal communist society.

The Marxist theory of social change can be criticized on many grounds. Appelbaum, for example, points out that history has not supported many of the Marxist predictions.[18] Capitalist societies have not always polarized into two opposing classes (the proletariat and the bourgeoisie). These classes have become, in some cases, heterogenous instead of homogenous, with many different subgroups within each major grouping. Also, social mobility, as indicated by the growth of the middle class, has been and can be observed in many modern nations.

Dahrendorf criticizes Marx for focusing on violent revolution as the only means of social change or as the only way of resolving class conflicts.[19] He also finds fault in the philosophical elements of Marxist theory. Philosophical elements, according to Dahrendorf, are "not subject to empirical proof or refutation."[20] For example, the propositions that capitalist society is the last class society of history and that communist society leads to complete human freedom can be accepted or denied, but they "cannot be refuted with the tools of science."[21] American and English social change theorists lost interest in Marxist theory in the twentieth century. However, there has been a recent revival of interest in Marxist principles of social change in many of the social sciences (including mass communication), mainly as an alternative to structural-functional theories of society.

## Modern Conflict Theory

Conflict theory today is being revived not only in sociology and political science but also in mass communication. Many modern conflict theorists have used the Marxist concept of conflict between social classes to explain social change. However, most of them have rejected Marxist "metaphysics" (the philosophical elements of Marxism). They see conflict theory as a realistic alternative to structural-functional theories. They consider social change, not stability, to be more likely in the modern world. Dahrendorf presents a useful comparison of the assumptions underlying structural-functional and conflict theories of social change in Figure 22.1.[22]

We can see from this comparison that structural-functional theories focus on stability of a social system and on how the elements in the system work together to bring about this stability. Conflict theory considers social systems to be unstable. Its emphasis is on how internal and external forces lead to change and on how the elements of a social structure constrain or control other elements. The major research questions in conflict theory, according to Dahrendorf, are the following:

1. How do conflicting groups arise from the structure of society?
2. What forms can the struggles among such groups assume?
3. How does conflict among such groups effect a change in social structures?

Modern conflict theories, as represented by Dahrendorf, differ from traditional Marxist theory in many ways. First is the rejection of the metaphysical concepts from Marx, such as the concept of freedom in a classless society. Second is the role of violent revolution in social change. To Marx, social change could result only from violent upheavals. To Dahrendorf and other

| *Underlying Assumptions* | |
|---|---|
| *Structural-Functional Theory* | *Conflict Theory* |
| 1. Every society is a relatively persisting configuration of elements | 1. Every society is subjected at every moment to change; social change is ubiquitous |
| 2. Every society is a well-integrated configuration of elements | 2. Every society experiences at every moment social conflict; social conflict is ubiquitous |
| 3. Every element in a society contributes to its functioning | 3. Every element in a society contributes to its change |
| 4. Every society rests on the consensus of its members | 4. Every society rests on constraint of some of its members by others |

**FIGURE 22.1.** A comparison of structural-functional and conflict theories of social change. Adapted from Dahrendorf, 1964.

modern conflict theorists, social change can be brought about by violent revolution *and* other ways, such as legitimate change in political authority through elections. Finally, Marx defined social class only in terms of property relations; the proletariat was made up of workers and the bourgeoisie owned the means of production. Dahrendorf and other neo-Marxists define social class in terms of authority relations or dominance, which do not necessarily originate in ownership of the means of production. This definition of social class broadens the analysis of social change by focusing not only on conflict between antagonistic interest groups. The underlying assumption, as in Marxist theory, is that conflict within social structures is inevitable and that conflict leads to structural change.

## EVALUATING SOCIAL CHANGE THEORIES

If social change theories are correct, regardless of whether they follow the structural functional or Marxist model, then change or stability in social systems should be predictable with some degree of certainty. The evidence from three decades of scientific research, however, is not very promising. Lipset, for example, has compiled a number of cases where predictions from theories of social change failed.[23] Caplow summarizes one of these "failed" social change studies in this way.

> We did not discover consistent trends of equalization, secularization, bureaucratization, increased mobility, and depersonalization as various theories of social change led us to expect. . . . The reality of social change in a community is much less manageable intellectually than the myths we make about it when our imaginations are not fettered by hard data.[24]

Why are predictions from social change theories often *not* supported in studies of communities and other social systems? Boudon attributes this failure to the basic assumptions that social change theories (including structural functional and Marxist theories) make about social structures and change processes. These assumptions, according to Boudon, do not have any basis in the real world. They are the following.[25]

1. The assumption that because of their "coherence," the two typical reactions of social structures to forces of change are either no change or complete change. If social structures are coherent—that is, if they are made up of interdependent and complementary parts—then either change should not occur because a change in any of the elements implies a change in others, or change should be complete because when a change is introduced, it will generate a chain reaction and affect all the elements in the system. This assumption is wrong, according to Boudon, because the interdependence of the parts of a social system does not mean that all elements must be affected in the same direction by forces of change. For example, change may occur in the economic structure of a system while no change might be simultaneously ob-

served in the cultural structures. Or, put another way, the members of a community might accumulate wealth, but their cultural values may remain the same. Boudon also says that change in a social structure does not always have to go in the same direction. A new irrigation project in a village, for example, could strengthen some traditional values while eroding others. The irrigation project could influence the peasants to plant another, more economically rewarding crop that could lead to more income and an exchange economy instead of a subsistence one. Some sociologists might consider this as change toward modernization. At the same time, the new irrigation project could increase disparities between various groups of farmers, thereby reinforcing the traditional structure of the village. Landowners, for example, could gain more from the irrigation project than their tenants. If this happened, change would be observed in two opposite directions—one toward modernization and another toward the maintenance of a traditional feature of the system. According to Boudon, the more common occurrence is bi- or multidirectional change instead of unidirectional change. Elements in a society more often change in many different ways, not always "coherently." Social change theories fail because they do not account for this possibility.

2. The assumption that there are general laws of social change that can be detected empirically and that have universal validity. The physical sciences routinely make the assumption that there are general and universal laws that explain the physical environment. When applied to the study of social change, this assumption breaks down because most social change principles are highly specific to individual situations and general principles are rarely observed. Boudon gives the following example to illustrate this point.

A classical analysis "shows" that the nuclear family is more easily compatible with an industrialized society than the extended family. This theory leads to the corollary that industrialization should be accompanied by a nuclearization effect on family structures. Contrary to this conclusion, however, many studies have shown that industrialization can reinforce rather than weaken the extended family. E. Vogel has drawn attention to this point in the case of Japan: in that country, businessmen used to negotiate the hiring of a new worker with his family; if the worker was fired for reasons which the family considered illegitimate, the family would mobilize its solidarity resources, use them for the purposes of retortion, and make the hiring of new workers difficult for the businessman. As the industrialization process provided the extended family with the opportunity to use its solidarity as a resource, the value of family solidarity tended to increase, and solidarity was reinforced.[26]

The point that Boudon makes is that exceptions to general principles of social change can always be found, and these exceptions make it very difficult to predict the direction or directions of social change in any given social structure.

3. The assumption that the main determinants of social change can be detected in social structures and that these determinants are always responsible for change or should always be observed whenever change occurs. Social

change theories have identified the major determinants of social change to be either value change, conflict, or technological change. This assumption is faulty, according to Boudon, because, if we conceive of change as "the product of the aggregation of individual actions," then the great number of variables that can affect individual actions makes it impossible to determine which are the main *causal* variables responsible for change. The more common situation, according to Boudon, is one in which many variables cause change and in which some of the variables may be reciprocally related—that is, variables may be caused and influenced by other variables. Boudon gives this example to illustrate a reciprocal relationship between variables of change:

> A government makes a decision which provokes a reaction that in turn generates a modification of that decision. In this case, neither the initial decision nor the reaction nor the reaction to the reaction can be considered as the main variable responsible for the final form of the decision. Rather, all the variables are responsible for that final form.[27]

To summarize, current criticisms of social change theories fault these theories for their narrow approach to the study of social change. Instead of looking for "coherent" changes in social structures, we should consider how the different elements of a social structure can change in different ways. Instead of looking for general principles of social change, we should consider principles that may be specific to only a few situations. And instead of looking for a few "main" determinants of social change, we should look at many possible causes of change and analyze reciprocal influences between these causes. Many of these criticisms also apply to theories of mass communication and social change.

## MASS COMMUNICATION AND SOCIAL CHANGE

The role of the mass media in social change is not explicitly explained by most sociological theories of social change. These theories, as we have seen, attribute change in social structures primarily to change in values, technology or social conflict. Mass communication, however, clearly has a central role in social change theories. Social change involves influencing large numbers of people (members of the social unit) so that their "social facts" are altered. The mass media, because they are able to reach large audiences simultaneously, can be effective tools of influence. Thus, mass communication logically and naturally should take a central role in the study of social change. Before existing values can be changed, the new values should be made clear to members of the social unit; the mass media could be the vehicles by which these new values are introduced. Before technological change can be accepted, members of the community must be informed about the new technology and its advantages. Even Marxist theory has a role for mass communication. Marx considered the press to represent "the speaking bonds between the individual, the state and the whole world."[28] Although Marxist theory sees social change as coming only through violent revolution, it assigns the mass media the important function of consolidating support for the revolution among members of the working class. Structural functionalists, on the other hand, would consider how the media can be used to preserve the existing order. Either way, the media are agents of influence that could be used to support change or stability. Whether the media are actually agents of change or reinforcers of existing social conditions is an empirical question that should be considered for specific social structures. There can be no general answers. Obviously, there are times when the media bring about change and other times when they resist change. The task of the researcher is to identify the conditions when each possibility occurs.

In the remainder of this chapter, we will consider four important functions of mass communication in social change: the diffusion of information, the diffusion of new opinions and behaviors, the role of the mass media in national development, and the diffusion of culture. In discussing these various roles of mass communication, we will look at the media as endogenous and exogenous agents of social change and as reinforcers of existing social structures.

## Mass Communication and the Diffusion of Information

How does information diffuse or spread within a community? Early studies indicated that the mass media are primary carriers of information into communities. The rate of information diffusion depends on several conditions— the importance to the community of the information, the extent of mass media coverage, educational and interest levels of members of the community, and the type of information that is covered by the media.

Events that are significant to the community because almost everbody is affected will generally receive full and concentrated mass media coverage. Under these conditions, diffusion of the information is rapid and complete. News of the assassination of John F. Kennedy and the Wallace shooting, for example, reached almost all members of various communities studied within the first day that the news events were reported.[29] The rate of information diffusion of news events that are less significant and that receive less media coverage is, as we would expect, slower. Only about 49 percent of respondents in various communities had heard of the launching of Explorer I, and only about 26 percent of respondents had heard of Alaskan statehood within the first day of news coverage. News diffusion studies also show that the mass media and interpersonal communication (other people) are important first sources of information for significant events, while only the mass media are mentioned as first sources of information for less significant events. People who say they had heard of the event from another person also say that they turned immediately to the mass media for verification. We can conclude that the media are primary sources of information about news events, especially for "less significant" events. Even when the media are secondary sources, they still perform the important function of providing verification and more information about events first learned about from other members of the community.

## The Knowledge Gap Hypothesis

Early studies showed that knowledge levels and the rate of information diffusion about news events are not the same for all segments of the community. Usually, we find that people with higher levels of formal education are more likely to be informed about an event and to have more detailed knowledge about it. Some researchers have referred to those members of the community who have low levels of knowledge about local, national, and international affairs as "chronic know-nothings."[31] Poorly informed community members have been characterized as blue collar, low income, older, and with low levels of formal schooling.[32]

Early findings that some segments of a community are poorly informed about public issues led three researchers from the University of Minnesota to propose a "knowledge gap" hypothesis. Tichenor, Olien, and Donohue first proposed their knowledge gap hypothesis in 1970:

> As the infusion of mass media information into a social system increases, segments of the population with higher socioeconomic status tend to acquire this information at a faster rate than the lower status segments, so that the gap in knowledge between these segments tends to increase rather than decrease.[33]

The knowledge gap hypothesis has generated a considerable amount of research in the past ten years,[34] perhaps because it has important implications for our ideas about the functions of the press in a democratic society. If we accept the proposition that information is a source of power (those members of a community with information are more likely to participate actively in and run its affairs), and if the knowledge gap hypothesis is true, then the lower socioeconomic segment of our communities will continually lose power as new communication technology infuses more information into the community. Class polarization—a potential source of conflict in the social structure—could result. This, of course, is not the intent of a democratic press protected by the First Amendment.

Research on the knowledge gap hypothesis can be grouped into two types. First, we have studies that measure the relationship between educational level of the respondent and public affairs knowledge at one point in time. Second, we have studies that measure the relationship between education and public affairs knowledge at more than one point in time. The second group of studies allows for a direct test of the knowledge gap hypothesis, since it permits the researcher to determine whether the knowledge gap between low- and high-education respondents increased or decreased over time.

Studies of the knowledge gap hypothesis at one point in time generally show that segments of the community who have higher levels of formal education also have higher levels of public affairs knowledge compared to those segments with less education. However, two conditions determine the size of this knowledge differential.[35]

1. *Topic*. Knowledge gaps are likely to be found with national and international news and are less likely to be found with local topics. Also, knowledge differentials are often found when knowledge is conceptualized as detailed information about a topic instead of as awareness or familiarity and as "textbook" knowledge or information that one is likely to acquire in a civics class.

2. *Extent of Media Coverage*. Some studies show that the knowledge differential decreases when topics are covered heavily by the mass media, particularly by newspapers.

Studies of the knowledge gap hypothesis *over time* generally indicate that the knowledge differential between segments of the community with high and low education decreases instead of increases as more information becomes available to the community through the mass media. This decrease in the knowledge gap over time is facilitated by the following conditions:[36]

1. High levels of conflict associated with the issues, which make the issues interesting or personally relevant to all segments of tbe community regardless of socioeconomic status.

2. High levels of newspaper coverage, which make detailed information about the issue available to all segments in the community.

3. Homogenous, as opposed to heterogenous structure of the community. Homogenous communities are smaller, and class distinctions based on occupation, education, and income are less apparent than in heterogenous communities. Members of a homogenous community are likely to have the same basic concerns. Issues that are interesting to one segment will also be interesting to other segments. Also, homogeneity allows for more interpersonal discussion of the issues. All these conditions lead to "knowledge leveling" in the community, meaning that all segments are equally informed about public issues.

More recently, some researchers have suggested that the critical variable in studying knowledge gaps should be interest in the issue and not education.[37] They have criticized the focus on the education variable as "elitist" because it implies that segments of the community with lower levels of education are somehow inferior in their information-processing capabilities than segments with more education. Issue interest, on the other hand, cuts across socioeconomic groups. An issue could be interesting to community members regardless of education, income, or occupational class. Interest can motivate the individual to seek out information about the issue, which would then lead to higher knowledge levels.

Genova and Greenberg compared education and interest as predictors of knowledge in fifteen Michigan communities.[38] They broke down interest into two components: self-interest and social interest. Self-interest is perceived usefulness of the news information for oneself. Social interest is perceived usefulness of the news information in one's social groups (for example, as a topic of conversation). Genova and Greenberg also had two measures of knowledge. Factual knowledge was a person's information about specific news items, dates, names, places, facts, and figures. Structural knowledge was a person's understanding of the why's and how's of an event that represented a deeper understanding of the event. The two events that Genova and Greenberg studied were the National Football League strike and developments in the impeachment of Richard Nixon. Measures of knowledge were taken at two points in time, ten days apart. They found that overall, interest (combined self-interest and social interest scores) were more powerful predictors of overall knowledge (combined structural and factual knowledge) than was education. Also, the greater power of interest (over education) to predict knowledge was more evident for structural than factual knowledge. Apparently, interest is even more of a factor in predicting knowledge than education when the knowledge requires an understanding of the event (structural knowledge). Genova and Greenberg also found that social interest was a more powerful predictor of knowledge than self-interest, and that the knowledge gap based on interest decreased instead of increased over time. All in all, this is convincing evidence that interest in an issue, particularly social interest, is a better predictor of knowledge than education.

In another recent study that compared education and issue interest as predictors or knowledge, Ettema and his colleagues evaluated the impact on a community in Minnesota of a mass media campaign to increase cardiovascular health knowledge.[39] They found that before the campaign began, education was a significant predictor of knowledge. However, education was no longer a significant predictor of knowledge at the conclusion of the campaign, indicating that a knowledge gap based on education had decreased. The researchers found that two variables that were related to interest in cardiovascular health information (age and perceived threat of a heart attack) were *not* significant predictors of knowledge before the campaign began but were significant predictors at the end of the campaign. Thus, a knowledge gap based on interest, not education, was observed.

These results suggest that the mass media can close as well as open knowledge gaps in a community and that knowledge gaps are more likely to be caused by differences in issue interest than by education. If one of the functions of the mass media is to inform all segments of a community so that power can be equally distributed (at least, the power to make informed decisions), then these results are encouraging. It is much easier to perform this function by increasing issue interest in the community through heavy media coverage than by increasing educational levels of large segments of the community.

## Mass Communication and the Diffusion of Opinions and Behaviors

We have seen in the last section that the mass media can inform diverse segments of the community about important public issues. Theoretically, opinions and attitudes are based on information, and overt behaviors are based, in turn, on opinions and attitudes. This leads us to the next question regarding the role of the mass media in social change: "Can the mass media affect public opinion and behaviors?"

### Public Opinion

Public opinion is commonly defined today as verbal or expressed choices or preferences in matters of public issues or policies.[40] Usually, public opinion is measured by stating the issue to the respondents and then asking them to give their position in an agree-disagree or other appropriate scale. In studying social change, we are interested in the opinions of the community or segments of it and whether this collective opinion changes over time or remains stable.

There are two major theoretical positions today regarding public opinion change in communities. One position says that opinions are highly volatile or subject to change, especially opinions concerning foreign policy.[41] This view holds that the average person is "uninterested in politics, unaware of what is going on, and subject to influence by a host of arbitrary forces."[42] The other view of public opinion is that although individual opinions may be volatile, "the aggregate distribution of preferences are generally quite stable and change slowly."[43] In either case, we are interested in the role of the mass media as agents of public opinion change or as reinforcers of existing opinions.

There are several ways in which the mass media could either change or stabilize public opinion. One is simply by providing information about the issues, which individuals could then use to form their opinions. The opinion formed will depend on the amount and nature of information that the individual acquires, and processes of selective exposure and selective perception could lead to stabilization instead of change. Second, the media could influence the public's perceptions of which issues are important and which issues they should hold opinions about. This effect of the media, as discussed in Chapter 20, is called "agenda setting." Another way in which the media could affect public opinion is by directly proposing choices on public issues. Under some conditions, the media can influence the public by *changing* their opinions on the issues. According to Noelle-Neumann, two of these conditions are "media consonance" and the individual's perception of what others in the same public are thinking.[44] Consonance is media agreement on the issues—"a majority agreement of argumentation and representation in the media." Consonance and the individual's estimate of what others in the community are thinking are the bases of a public opinion process that Noelle-Neumann calls the "spiral of silence."

The process of an interaction between individual and environment, where dominant opinion is defended and new opinion is established, was termed "spiral of silence." People, so the thesis claimed, by nature social beings, live in perpetual fear of isolating themselves and carefully observe their environment to see which opinions increase and which ones decrease. If they find that their views predominate or increase, then they express themselves freely in public; if they find that their views are losing supporters, then they become fearful, conceal their convictions in public, and fall silent. Because the one group express themselves with self-confidence whereas the others remain silent, the former appear to be strong in public, the latter weaker than their numbers suggest. This encourages others to express themselves or to fall silent, and a spiral process comes into play.[45]

The spiral-of-silence hypothesis predicts that the majority opinion, or the opinion of the perceived majority, tends to seem stronger than it really is, primarily because those who do not agree are reluctant to express themselves in public for fear of isolating themselves. Public opinion change is possible only when the proponents of the change are perceived to be the majority and are able to get this point across in the media.

Noelle-Neumann has shown in a series of studies in West Germany that changes in political opinions, self-concepts, and moral convictions of West Germans have been accompanied by media contents supporting the changes.[46] For example, a collective decline in self-evaluations by West Germans was observed in the years when "negative stereotypes of the German character permeated the entire media system." Of course, the analysis is correlational and does not show causality. However, this is interesting evidence that at the very least, social change is accompanied by supporting changes in media contents.

Studies of public opinion change and mass communication in the United States have produced mixed results. The dominant thought today seems to be that public opinion in the United States is relatively stable and that when it does change, the change can be attributed to changes in the public's social and economic environments instead of to media intervention.[47] Of course, we should consider how the individual members of the public are informed about environmental changes. A logical source is the mass media. We can therefore attribute at least an indirect role to the media in public opinion formation and change.

### Changing Behaviors

Behaviors are not easily changed. At the individual level, behaviors are notoriously resistant to change, primarily because they are based on so many conditions—the individual's perception of rewards and punishments for performing the act, effort required, and social norms. However, the mass media can and do change behaviors at even the collective level in many ways, through advertising, propaganda, and public communication campaigns. Rice and Paisley have collected an impressive number of case studies in which public communication campaigns effectively changed the collective behaviors of different publics on a wide variety of issues, including health campaigns, family planning, and the prevention of wildfires in national forests.[48] In this section, we will focus on public communication campaigns and how they can change collective behaviors of the public.

Paisley defines a public communication campaign as "someone's intention to influence someone else's beliefs or behavior, using communicated appeals."[49] Public communication campaigns have a component of *social control,* since most of them are carried out by organized groups or institutions in a community. A public communication campaign, therefore, is often one group's attempt to control the beliefs and behaviors of another group. The underlying objective of the campaign is often "benign," that is, the target group is perceived to benefit from the change.

An example of a public communication campaign that was successful in changing community behaviors is The Stanford Heart Disease Prevention Program (SHDPP) Three Community Study.[50] The objective of the SHDPP was to determine whether community education could effectively reduce the risk of cardiovascular disease in a community. To accomplish this, the community members would have to adapt new behaviors such as engaging in more physical exercise and changing their diets. The SHDPP used the mass media as the primary carriers of information.

The study was done in three Northern California towns. Extensive mass media campaigns were implemented in two of the communities in both English and Spanish over a two-year period. In one of these communities, the mass media were supported by intensive face-to-face instruction for a small group of high-risk individuals. The third community did not receive any messages and served as the control. Members of each community were surveyed before the campaign and one and two years after the campaign started. Measures included knowledge and behavior related to cardiovascular risk such as blood pressure, relative weight, and plasma cholesterol. Results indicated that the initial decrease in cardiovascular risk was greater in the mass media and intensive-instruction community than in the other two communities. By the end of the second year, however, the decrease in cardiovascular risk in the mass media only community had equaled the decrease in the media-intensive-instruction community. Risk in the control community *increased* over the two-year test period. These results strongly suggest that the mass media, when used in a "saturation" campaign, can change behaviors of large segments of the community, at least those behaviors related to reducing the risk of heart attack and stroke. Contributing to the success of the campaign was the use of *all* mass media and the personal significance of the topic to the audience.

## Mass Communication and National Development

The role of mass communication in bringing about national development— which is social change at the largest and most significant level—has been studied by scholars from many disciplines for the last three decades. At first, there were great expectations regarding what the mass media could do to speed up national development. These expectations have not been met. Today, we assign mass communication a more modest role in the development process.

### Older Models of Mass Communication and Development

The older or traditional school of mass communication and national development is represented by Schramm, Lerner, and Pye.[51] These scholars in their early writings attributed a central and causal role to the mass media in national development. They defined development purely in economic terms. Development to them required an increase in economic productivity as indexed by gross national product (GNP), per capita income, and industrialization. They saw the mass media as causing a change in the values and ways of thinking of people in "underdeveloped" or poor countries. Development required this change, which the media could bring about. An important component of their theories was the assumption that "development" required new values and skills, such as the ability to imagine oneself in different situations (empathy), a desire to achieve (achievement motivation), and open-mindedness so that change could be readily accepted. People with these characteristics, according to the traditional model, are more receptive to new ideas and practices, work harder for economic prosperity and, therefore, could lead the community to economic development. The media could facilitate the development of these characteristics in the members of the community by teaching and demonstrating the skills and personal qualities needed for development as well as by showing the end results of development (economic prosperity). Thus, the media were seen as "mobility multipliers," raising levels of aspiration and providing incentives for action.

The traditional models of mass communication and national development have many shortcomings. Unfortunately, these models were adapted by many poor countries who attempted to develop massive and complicated media systems in their quest for economic prosperity. Most of these "mass communication projects" have ended in failure. The infusion of modern mass media in traditional societies has not resulted in increased economic development.[52] The failure of the traditional models to predict social change can be traced to two faulty assumptions. First is the assumption that members of "underdeveloped" societies do not possess the values and skills needed for development. Second is the assumption that structural factors in the community are not important.

The first assumption has been contradicted by many recent studies of people in developing countries.[53] These studies show that peasants and other economically deprived members of developing communities carefully evaluate suggestions for change (for example, new crop varieties) and are willing to adapt these changes when structural support is available (for example, irrigation facilities, credit for more fertilizer, and other inputs needed for the new crop variety) and when they are convinced that rewards important to them (which are not always economic) will be forthcoming.

The second assumption of the traditional models—that structural factors are not important—clearly contradicts the experience in many modern development efforts. Many case studies have shown that economic and political structures have to be changed before development can take place. As Brown and Kearl, agricultural communication scholars from Wisconsin, explain it:

> Skillful communication can change a peasant's perceptions of his situation, but it cannot, acting alone, change the situation very much. It can help a backward farmer to see opportunities he ignores, but if few opportunities exist, information will not create them.[54]

## New Models of Mass Communication and Development

In recent years, new models of mass communication and development have been proposed. These models differ from the older ones in many ways.

1. *Definitions of National Development.* National development is no longer defined only in economic terms. An important concern in modern conceptions of national development is how economic resources, information, and power are allocated within the community. A good example is the definition proposed by Rogers.

   > Development . . . is a widely participatory process of social change in a society intended to bring about both social and material advancement (including greater equality, freedom, and other valued qualities) for the majority of the people through their gaining greater control over their environment.[55]

   Roger's definition is still filled with concepts that are difficult to measure objectively—"advancement," "greater equality," and "freedom." However, it is an improvement over the traditional definition that measured development only in economic terms.

2. *Role of the Mass Media in the Development Process.* The mass media are no longer seen as "mobility multipliers," but simply as carriers of information and as tools for education. Instead of changing underlying value systems, the media are to be used to relay new information that could help members of the community increase production and attain goals that they set for themselves. "Big" media such as newspapers and television are still important; however, equal attention is now directed to the development of "little" media such as radio and traditional folk media.

3. *Role of Economic and Political Structures in the Development Process.* Older models ignored these structures. Modern models consider them to be important constraints on the behaviors of individuals.

Using new models of development, researchers have recently been able to isolate media effects in developing countries.[56] These effects, while not on the scale expected by the traditional theories, have been found in the fields of education (for example, television in China and India), family planning (television, radio, and print media in India), and agriculture (radio in the Philippines). These studies have shown that the mass media can be effective carriers of information and educational material. There is, therefore, an important role for the mass media in national development programs.

## Mass Communication and the Diffusion of Culture

Culture represents the behaviors, values, and perceptions of the world that are shared by members of a community. In this section, we will discuss how the mass media affect the culture of communities. Two situations will be considered: the effects of indigenous media (media originating from within the community) and the effects of exogenous media (media originating from outside the community).

### Indigenous Media

A popular theoretical assumption in the analysis of indigenous media effects on culture is that the media will homogenize or standardize culture.[57] Homogenization of culture is often studied as an effect of television, and most studies have been done in the United States. We will discuss one of these studies—the cultural indicators project of Gerbner and his colleagues. We discussed some aspects of this research program in Chapter 19. In this section, our concern will be on television and the homogenization of culture, or "mainstreaming," as Gerbner calls it.

Gerbner and his colleagues have focused on television as carriers of culture because:

> Television is a centralized system of storytelling. Its drama, commercials, news, and other programs bring a relatively coherent world of images and messages into every viewing home. People are now born into the symbolic environment of television and live with its repetitive lessons throughout life. Television cultivates from the outset the very predispositions that affect future cultural selections and uses. Transcending historic barriers of literacy and mobility, television has become the primary source of everyday culture of an otherwise heterogenous population.[58]

Since television emphasizes the same cultural elements over and over, viewers will accept these representations as "true" and adapt them as their own. The result is a standardization of culture. There will be little variation in values, beliefs, behaviors, and perceptions of reality and cultural patterns will be stable and resistant to change. Gerbner describes this process as "mainstreaming."

> The "mainstream" can be thought of as a relative commonality of outlooks and values that exposure to features and dynamics of the television world tends to cultivate. By "mainstreaming," we mean the expression of that commonality by heavy viewers in those demographic groups whose light viewers hold divergent

views. In other words, differences found in the responses of different groups of viewers, differences that can be associated with other cultural, social, and political characteristics of these groups, may be diminished or even absent from the responses of heavy viewers in the same groups.[59]

Mainstreaming is the cultivation of similar world views among heavy viewers from the different segments in the television audience. We can expect different audience groups (such as those with high and low levels of education) to have different opinions, values, and perceptions of society. The effect of heavy television viewing, according to Gerbner and his colleagues, is to "homogenize" these groups. That is, their outlooks and values become similar because of heavy exposure to television. Television appeals to the common denominator in audiences, so it can attract the largest audience possible. Thus, it caters to the "average" viewer, depicting themes and values that are likely to offend the least number of audience members. The result of these "average" presentations, according to Gerbner, is mainstreaming.

Gerbner analyzed over 6000 respondents from national samples and divided them into light television viewers (24.6 percent of the sample), who said they watch TV less than two hours a day, medium viewers (45.3 percent), who said they watch two or three hours a day) and heavy viewers (30.1 percent), who said they watch four hours or more a day). He then further subdivided his sample according to demographic characteristics (sex, education, income, political ideology) and asked them to indicate their "world views" about a number of issues. He found the following "mainstreaming effects" of heavy television viewing.[60]

1. *Perceptions of Economic Class.* Low socioeconomic status (SES) respondents were most likely to call themselves "working class," but only when they were light TV viewers. Heavy TV viewers of the same low SES group were less likely than light viewers to say that they were working class and were more likely to say they were "middle class." On the other hand, more high SES heavy viewers consider themselves to be "working class" than do high SES light viewers. These results, according to Gerbner, suggest that TV viewing "blurs" class distinctions. It makes more affluent heavy viewers think of themselves as working people with average income. It also makes less affluent heavy viewers think of themselves as middle class.

2. *Political Ideology.* Significantly more heavy than light television viewers in all demographic subgroups called themselves "moderates" and significantly fewer called themselves "conservatives." Gerbner calls this the "centering" effect of television. People are more likely to call themselves political moderates when they are heavy television viewers.

3. *Opinions on Specific Social Issues.* Light-viewing liberals and light-viewing conservatives disagreed strongly in their opinions about a number of issues, including abortion, homosexuality, and marijuana. However, the

attitudes of heavy-viewing liberals and heavy-viewing conservatives were much closer to each other.

4. *Opinions about Economic Issues.* On questions about national spending for health, the environment, cities, education, foreign aid, and welfare, heavy-viewing conservatives and heavy-viewing moderates converged on the liberal position (for example, more spending). This indicates that heavy TV viewing cultivates a more "populist streak" among political conservatives and moderates.

Gerbner and his colleagues have presented us with an interesting and innovative analysis of television's possible influence on the homogenization of culture, or mainstreaming. Their early results are promising. However, we should remember that their analyses are derived from cross-sectional samples, and data are taken only at one point in time. We cannot be certain that television viewing *causes* mainstreaming. Perhaps it is the other way around: people already in the mainstream are attracted to television. Also, more attention should be given to the contents of television. We need more information on what themes and depictions in television programs lead to mainstreaming. More research is needed before we can accept the mainstreaming hypothesis.

### Exogenous Media

We are interested in exogenous media—media that originate from outside a community or social structure—primarily because recent developments in information technology have made it possible to introduce mass communications even to the remotest village. We are concerned that the nations controlling the flow of information and information technology will also be able to control the social, political, economic, and cultural strucutres in the importing nations or communities. Very often, the importers of information and information technology are economically disadvantaged nations, and many of them are in the Third World—countries that are officially unaligned.

There are many ways in which an exporter of information or information technology can influence or control the importing nation.[61] One is by directly requiring political concessions for providing the "goods." Another is indirectly, by introducing new ways of managing the new technology. A third is by controlling the amount and type of information (as in the flow of news) between the exporting and importing nations. And a fourth is by introducing, through the mass media, new values, life-styles, and world perceptions. We are particularly interested in this last possibility of control. It is often referred to as "cultural imperialism."

Cultural imperialism is the imposition by an exogenous source of new values, ways of thinking, life-styles, behavior patterns, and world perceptions on members of a social structure with an existing culture of their own. The new culture often will clash with the older or traditional culture, particularly in communities that have been isolated from the outside world. When the new and old cultures clash, the social system is destabilized. Conflict arises among its members, and normal functioning is disrupted. There are many ways in which new cultures can be introduced. Colonization or actual occupation by the dominant culture is one. Another way is by sending messages through the mass media. We are concerned here with how the mass media, particularly television, can subjugate existing cultures and replace them with new ones.

Although a great deal has been said about the cultural imperialism hypothesis in the last few years,[62] very little empirical research has been done to test the hypothesis that imported mass media such as television can disrupt existing cultures. One study was recently completed in central Canada by Granzberg.[63] Using survey and qualitative observational methods, Granzberg studied the effects of the introduction of television on the culture and life-styles of the Algonkian Indians.

Television was brought to the Algonkian Indians by the Canadian government. The programs, commercials, and experience of viewing television were new and alien experiences for most Algonkians. Many of the programs were imported from the United States. Using before and after measures and a control group of Algonkians who had not been exposed to television, Granzberg observed the following changes after television had been introduced.

1. *Outgroup Identity*. Outgroup identity is a person's tendency to model behaviors after groups to which he or she does not belong. Granzberg found that Algonkian children who were exposed to television were more likely to say that they would model various behaviors after the behaviors of Euro-Canadians instead of after other Algonkians, compared to children who were not exposed to television.

2. *Purchasing Behavior*. After television was introduced, there was a general increase in purchases of "outgroup material products" such as frozen foods, presweetened children's cereals, cake mixes, popcorn, potato chips, toiletries, beauty aids, and other household products.

3. *Aggressive Behavior*. After television was introduced, children fought more, used dangerous weapons, and did more damage to each other. Specific behaviors shown in television were "faddishly" adapted, such as karate actions, athletic activity, and the favorite actions and phrases of television heroes (such as Fonzie's "Sit on it" and "Whoa" and J.J.'s "Dyn-o-mite").

4. *Language and Aspirations*. Among adults and children, the percentage of respondents in the experimental community (where TV had been introduced) speaking Cree at home and having traditional job and educational aspirations *declined* over time as they were exposed to television.

5. *Perceptions of Television*. Most Algonkians took television too seriously. They became infatuated with TV characters and looked at them for behavior guides.

The general picture seems to be negative. Television disrupted traditional culture and introduced alien and possibly dysfunctional behaviors among the Algonkians. However, Granzberg reports that there were also some positive effects, at least in small segments of the community. Some adults developed "critical viewing skills." They started analyzing the behaviors and values shown in television and began teaching their children how to watch TV critically. Also, some adults developed very negative views of the programs and warned others not to watch them.

We obviously have much to learn if we are to understand the effects of introducing alien cultures to traditional communities through television or other mass media. It is difficult to study the cultural imperialism hypothesis, since the manifestations of culture—values, behavioral patterns, and lifestyles—are not easily measured. Also, other variables affecting culture such as structural changes in the community should be accounted for. We are currently engaged in several ongoing studies of the cultural imperialism hypothesis—in the Philippines, Greece, Thailand, Hong Kong, and some Latin American countries. Hopefully, these studies will give us a clearer understanding of the role of the mass media in the diffusion of culture.

## SUMMARY

Social change occurs when social facts change over a period of time. Social facts are aggregations of individual actions. Two theories of social change that are currently popular are functionalism and neo-Marxism. Functionalism emphasizes the conditions leading to the stability of social systems; neo-Marxism focuses on conditions leading to change.

Mass communication is an important agent of social change (or stability) in the diffusion of information, the diffusion of opinions and behaviors, national development, and the diffusion of culture.

## REVIEW QUESTIONS

1. Discuss the weaknesses of the Marxist and functional theories as explanations of social change (or stability).
2. Give examples of how mass communication has led to either social change or system stability.

## ENDNOTES

1. Emile Durkheim, *The Rules of Sociological Method* (New York: Free Press, 1964).
2. Gudmund Hernes, "Structural Change in Social Processes," *American Journal of Sociology, 82,* 1976, pp. 513–547.

3. Durkheim, *op. cit.*

4. Richard Appelbaum, *Theories of Social Change* (Chicago: Markham Publishing Co., 1970).

5. Talcott Parsons, *The Social System* (New York: Free Press, 1951).

6. Karl Marx, *Capital, Vol. I, The Process of Capitalist Production* (New York: International Publishers, 1967).

7. Max Weber, *The Theory of Social and Economic Organization* (New York: Free Press, 1964).

8. Daniel Lerner, *The Passing of Traditional Society* (Glencoe, Ill.: Free Press, 1958).

9. E. M. Rogers, *Diffusion of Innovations* (New York: Free Press, 1962).

10. Raymond Boudon, "Why Theories of Social Change Fail: Some Methodological Thoughts," *Public Opinion Quarterly, 47,* Summer 1983, pp. 143–160.

11. Parsons, *op. cit.*

12. Talcott Parsons, "A Functional Theory of Change," in Amitai Etzioni and Eva Etzioni (eds.), *Social Change* (New York: Basic Books, 1964).

13. Mohammed Guessous, "A General Critique of Equilibrium Theory," in W. E. Moore and R. M. Cook (eds.), *Readings on Social Change* (Englewood Cliffs,N.J.: Prentice-Hall, 1967).

14. Appelbaum, *op. cit.*

15. Ralf Dahrendorf, *Class and Class Conflict in Industrial Society* (Stanford, Calif.: Stanford University Press, 1959).

16. Arthur Stinchcombe, *Constructing Social Theories* (New York: Harcourt, Brace & World, 1968).

17. Appelbaum, *op. cit.*

18. *Ibid.*

19. Dahrendorf, *op. cit.*

20. *Ibid.*

21. *Ibid.*

22. *Ibid.*

23. S. M. Lipset, "The Limits of Social Science," *Public Opinion,* October – November 1981, pp. 2–9.

24. As quoted in Boudon, *op. cit.*

25. Boudon, *op. cit.*

26. *Ibid.*

27. *Ibid.*

28. Marx, *op. cit.*

29. See Cecilie Gaziano, "The Knowledge Gap: An Analytical Review of Media Effects," *Communication Research, 10,* October 1983, pp. 447–486.

30. *Ibid.*

31. H. H. Hyman and P. B. Sheatsley, "Some Reasons Why Information Campaigns Fail," *Public Opinion Quarterly, 11,* 1947, pp. 412–423.

32. S. P. Spitzer and N. K. Denzin, "Levels of Knowledge in an Emergent Crisis," *Social Forces, 44,* 1965, pp. 234–237.

33. P. J. Tichenor, G. A. Donohue, and C. N. Olien, "Mass Media Flow and Differential Growth in Knowledge," *Public Opinion Quarterly, 34,* 1970, pp. 159–170.

34. Gaziano, *op. cit.*

35. *Ibid.*

36. P. J. Tichenor, G. A. Donohue, and C. N. Olien, "Conflict and the Knowledge

Gap," in *Community Conflict and the Press* (Beverly Hills, Calif.: Sage Publications, 1980).

37. For example, J. S. Ettema, and F. G. Kline, "Deficits, Differences and Ceilings: Contingent Conditions for Understanding the Knowledge Gap," *Communication Research, 4,* 1977, pp. 179–202.

38. B. K. L. Genova and Bradley S. Greenberg, "Interests in News and the Knowledge Gap," *Public Opinion Quarterly, 43,* Spring 1979, pp. 79–91.

39. James S. Ettema, James W. Brown, and Russell V. Luepker, "Knowledge Gap Effects in a Health Information Campaign," *Public Opinion Quarterly, 47,* Winter 1983, pp. 516–527.

40. Benjamin Page and Robert Shapiro, "Changes in Americans' Policy Preferences 1935–1979," *Public Opinion Quarterly, 46,* Spring 1982, pp. 24–42.

41. For example, William Caspary, "The Mood Theory: A Study of Public Opinion and Foreign Policy," *American Political Science Review, 64,* 1970, pp. 536–47.

42. Page and Shapiro, *op. cit.*

43. *Ibid.*

44. Elisabeth Noelle-Neumann, "Mass Media and Social Change," in E. Katz and T. Szecsko (eds.), *Mass Media and Social Change* (Beverly Hills, Calif.: Sage Publications, 1981).

45. *Ibid.*

46. *Ibid.*

47. Page and Shapiro, *op. cit.*

48. Ronald Rice and William J. Paisley (eds.), *Public Communication Campaigns* (Beverly Hills, Calif.: Sage Publications, 1981).

49. *Ibid.*

50. Douglas S. Solomon, "Health Campaigns on Television," in D. Pearl, L. Bouthilet, and J. Lazar (eds.), *Television and Behavior,* Vol. II (Rockville, Md.: National Institute of Mental Health, 1982).

51. Lerner, *op. cit.*; W. Schramm, "Communication and Change," in D. Lerner and W. Schramm (eds.), *Communication and Change in the Developing Countries* (Honolulu: University Press of Hawaii, 1967).

52. Goran Hedebro, *Communication and Social Change in Developing Nations* (Ames: The Iowa State University Press, 1982).

53. *Ibid.* Also Emile G. McAnany (ed.), *Communications in the Rural Third World* (New York: Praeger, 1980).

54. M. R. Brown and B. E. Kearl, "Mass Communication and Development: The Problem of Local and Functional Relevance," University of Wisconsin, Land Tenure Center Paper No. 38, 1967.

55. Everett Rogers, "The Rise and Fall of the Dominant Paradigm," *Journal of Communication, 28,* Winter 1978.

56. For example, McAnany, *op. cit.*; Also Alexis Tan, *Mass Communications in the Third World* (Norwood, N.J.: Ablex, 1985, forthcoming.)

57. George Gerbner, Larry Gross, Michael Morgan, and Nancy Signorielli, "Charting the Mainstream: Television's Contributions to Political Orientations," *Journal of Communication, 32,* Spring 1982, pp. 100–127.

58. *Ibid.*

59. *Ibid.*

60. *Ibid.*

61. For example, Marc U. Porat, "Global Implications of the Information Society," *Journal of Communication, 28,* Winter 1978.
62. For example, H. I. Schiller, *Communication and Cultural Domination* (New York: International Arts and Sciences Press, 1976).
63. Gary Granzberg, "Television as Storyteller: The Algonkian Indians of Central Canada," *Journal of Communication, 32,* Winter 1982, pp. 43–52.

# Author Index _____

# SUBJECT INDEX